EARLY CHILDHOOD STUDIES

A STUDENT'S GUIDE

EDITED BY
DAMIEN FITZGERALD &
HELOISE MACONOCHIE

Los Angeles | London | New Delhi
Singapore | Washington DC | Melbourne

Los Angeles | London | New Delhi
Singapore | Washington DC | Melbourne

SAGE Publications Ltd
1 Oliver's Yard
55 City Road
London EC1Y 1SP

SAGE Publications Inc.
2455 Teller Road
Thousand Oaks, California 91320

SAGE Publications India Pvt Ltd
B 1/I 1 Mohan Cooperative Industrial Area
Mathura Road
New Delhi 110 044

SAGE Publications Asia-Pacific Pte Ltd
3 Church Street
#10-04 Samsung Hub
Singapore 049483

Publisher: Jude Bowen
Development editor: Christofere Fila and
Laura Walmsley
Assistant editor: Catriona McMullen
Senior assistant editor, digital: Chloe Statham
Production editor: Victoria Nicholas
Copyeditor: Sharon Cawood
Proofreader: Elaine Leek
Indexer: David Rudeforth
Marketing manager: Lorna Patkai
Cover design: Wendy Scott
Typeset by C&M Digitals (P) Ltd, Chennai, India
Printed in the UK

Editorial Arrangement and Introduction © Damien Fitzgerald &
Heloise Maconochie, 2019
Chapter 1 © Rita Winstone, 2019
Chapter 2 © Heloise Maconochie, 2019
Chapter 3 © Fufy Demissie, 2019
Chapter 4 © Karen Daniels & Roberta Taylor, 2019
Chapter 5 © Sarah Rawding, 2019
Chapter 6 © Tanya Richardson, 2019
Chapter 7 © Caron Carter, 2019
Chapter 8 © Eunice Lumsden, 2019
Chapter 9 © Philippa Thompson, 2019
Chapter 10 © Penny Borkett, 2019
Chapter 11 © Pamela Dewis, 2019
Chapter 12 © Marie Lavelle, 2019
Chapter 13 © Ginny Boyd, 2019
Chapter 14 © Sigrid Brogaard-Clausen, Sofia Guimaraes,
Michelle Cottle & Sally Howe, 2019
Chapter 15 © Ester Ehiyazaryan-White, 2019
Chapter 16 © Alison Glentworth, 2019
Chapter 17 © Heloise Maconochie & Jill Branch, 2019
Chapter 18 © Monica Edwards, 2019
Chapter 19 © Jenny Robson, 2019
Chapter 20 © Damien Fitzgerald, 2019
Chapter 21 © Adam Holden, 2019
Chapter 22 © Jane Murray, 2019
Chapter 23 © Amanda Hatton, 2019
Chapter 24 © Karen Barr, 2019
Chapter 25 © Caroline Leeson, 2019
Chapter 26 © Mary E. Whalley, 2019

First published 2019

Library of Congress Control Number: 2018940218

British Library Cataloguing in Publication data

A catalogue record for this book is available from the British Library

ISBN 978-1-4739-9794-3
ISBN 978-1-4739-9795-0 (pbk)

EARLY CHILDHOOD STUDIES

Early childhood is now widely recognised by many countries as significant and there is a move towards a graduate professional workforce. The reasons for this vary: from a recognition of early childhood in its own right as a distinct phase in life; through consideration of parenting in early childhood and evidence of the significance of what happens in the earliest years to brain development; on to evidence that early childhood experiences have lifelong consequences, opportunities and costs; and a neoliberal concern with children as future economic and societal capital. Underpinned by ecological theories of development concerned with children, families and communities, the book also provides the reader with philosophical, economic and socio-logical insights and with the latest thinking emerging from post-humanism. In so doing, it provides tools that enable students to research childhood, to understand the complexities of often seemingly simple matters and to navigate critically ever-changing policy and practice in early childhood. Its breadth, depth and currency cannot fail to impress.

Ian Barron
Professor of Early Childhood Studies
Manchester Metropolitan University

CONTENTS

GUIDE TO YOUR BOOK

A range of features in the book and resources online have been designed to help you succeed in your early childhood journey:

https://study.sagepub.com/fitzgeraldandmaconochie

Here's how this book helps you:

GET TO GRIPS WITH THE BASICS

Spotlights on people, policy and practice introduce you to the influences on early childhood education. These snapshots on principle theorists, concepts, policy and practice act as launch pads for your learning.

The **Glossary** at the start of the book and the **online flashcards,** available on the website, help you get to grips with key terminology, build your knowledge and act as handy revision tools.

LEARN FROM OTHERS

Videos, available on the website, provide insights from academics and practitioners on relevant chapter topics.

Hear fellow students' perspectives on their own experiences and what they found most useful about the book with the start of chapter **student voice** feature.

PREPARE FOR ASSIGNMENTS

Build your bibliography with the **further reading** resources. These save you time searching for the materials you need, give you a deeper understanding of topics and help build your bibliography! Each chapter includes:

- **Further reading suggestions** with short summaries.
- Free access to **journal articles** available on the website.
- **Weblinks** to relevant websites and documentation.

Spotlights on research introduce you to relevant academic research from the field so that you can demonstrate a deeper and more critical understanding in your assignments.

Become a critical thinker and achieve higher marks with the **reflection points**.

RELATE TO PRACTICE

Case studies from real-life settings prepare you for practice. By helping you visualise interactions, scenarios and possible outcomes, they show how key ideas apply to everyday practice and get you reflecting on your own actions.

Action point activities get you critically considering chapter concepts and relating theory to practice. Providing useful suggestions for working with children, they give you steps to improve your own practice.

DON'T FORGET....

When you see this icon then visit **https://study.sagepub.com/fitzger aldandmaconochie** to access the online resources.

ABOUT THE EDITORS AND CONTRIBUTORS

EDITORS

Damien Fitzgerald PhD is Head of Area for Early Childhood and Childhood at the Sheffield Institute of Education, Sheffield Hallam University. His research interests include gender and childhood, heteronormativity in family contexts and same-sex parenting, and this informs his undergraduate and post-graduate teaching. Prior to working at Sheffield Hallam, he worked as an advisory teacher in early years special needs and in other teaching roles in schools. He is also qualified as a nurse, working mainly in emergency care.

Heloise Maconochie PhD is Visiting Scholar of Early Childhood Education at Purdue University Fort Wayne, USA. Her research interests include children's experiences and perspectives of early childhood services, curriculum in the early years, disabled children's childhoods, early intervention, children's rights and participatory methodologies. She has worked in the UK as a Senior Lecturer in Early Childhood Studies and Teacher Education, and as an early years coordinator and primary school teacher. She is a Court Appointed Special Advocate for abused and neglected children in Allen County, Indiana.

CONTRIBUTORS

Karen Barr is Senior Lecturer at the Sheffield Institute of Education, Sheffield Hallam University, where she teaches on Early Childhood Studies and Early Years courses. She is currently studying for a PhD, with the aim of exploring how affect, materiality and space shape students' experiences in early childhood studies placement assemblages.

Penny Borkett is Senior Lecturer in Early Childhood Studies at the Sheffield Institute of Education, Sheffield Hallam University. She began her early years career as a playgroup leader and then became a teaching assistant where her interest in inclusion began.

Ginny Boyd is Senior Lecturer at the Sheffield Institute of Education, Sheffield Hallam University teaching on the BA (Hons) Early Childhood Studies and BA (Hons) Childhood degree. Ginny is a qualified social worker and her teaching and research interests involve working with families, children's rights, multi-agency working and mental health.

Jill Branch is Lecturer in Early Childhood Studies and Childhood Studies at the Sheffield Institute of Education, Sheffield Hallam University. She studied for a Masters in Health Care

Education and was a health visitor practice teacher, teaching clinical practice in the health visiting field. Her interest lies in working with preschool children and families.

Sigrid Brogaard Clausen is Senior Lecturer and Researcher in Early Childhood Studies at the University of Roehampton. Her research interests arise from her experience of the Danish and English early years, and range from the policy conditions for children's wellbeing, learning and democratic participation to the development of professional identity in early years.

Caron Carter is Senior Lecturer in Early Childhood Education at the Sheffield Institute of Education, Sheffield Hallam University. She has worked in early years as a teacher, deputy headteacher and acting headteacher in primary and infant schools. Her PhD focused on children's friendships.

Michelle Cottle is Senior Lecturer in Early Childhood Studies at the University of Roehampton. Her research interests include policy enactment within early years settings and primary schools, creativity in relation to learning and teaching, teacher and practitioner perspectives on their work with children and families, children's learning experiences and children's participation in research.

Karen Daniels is Senior Lecturer in Primary English at the Sheffield Institute of Education, Sheffield Hallam University. She leads the development of provision for English in teacher education courses and her recent research focuses on the material-discursive and affective dimensions of young children's literacy practices.

Fufy Demissie works in Initial Teacher Education at the Sheffield Institute of Education, Sheffield Hallam University and is a passionate advocate of Philosophy for Children. Her research interests are in developing student teachers' and educators' reflection through enabling pedagogies. She is a SAPERE accredited Level 1 trainer (in Philosophy for Children) and has also recently become a Senior Fellow of the Higher Education Academy

Pam Dewis is Principal Lecturer and a Senior Fellow at the Sheffield Institute of Education, Sheffield Hallam University. She has taught on the BA (Hons) Early Childhood Studies degree at Hallam since 2005. A nurse, midwife and health visitor by professional background, her specialist teaching areas are children's public health and medical conditions.

Monica Edwards is Senior Lecturer in the Faculty of Education at Manchester Metropolitan University. She is interested in postcolonial and feminist perspectives on childhoods and families, and enjoys working with undergraduate students to think about young children's learning and development from a sociocultural point of view.

Ester Ehiyazaryan-White is Lecturer in Children and Childhood at the Sheffield Institute of Education, Sheffield Hallam University. Her interest in children learning English as an additional language started in response to her own experiences of being ethnically Armenian, born in Bulgaria and migrating to the UK.

Alison Glentworth is Senior Lecturer in Early Years in Primary Teacher Education at the Sheffield Institute of Education, Sheffield Hallam University. Areas of professional interest and expertise in the field of Higher Education include development of student teachers' professional practice using active learning approaches.

Sofia Guimaraes is Senior Lecturer in Early Childhood Studies at the University of Roehampton, having previously worked as an early years teacher, a researcher and senior lecturer in both Early Childhood Studies and Psychology. Her research interests include children's literacy acquisition and bilingualism/multilingualism with attention to equality of opportunities.

Amanda Hatton is Senior Lecturer in Childhood Studies at the Sheffield Institute of Education, Sheffield Hallam University. Research for her doctoral thesis was based on the participation of children and young people, using creative arts and methods, from which she developed a model of participative practice.

Adam Holden is Executive Head of the Albert Einstein Institute in Panama City, Panama. His research interests include digital technologies and blended learning, on which he has written multiple publications. He serves on the editorial boards of the *Journal of Online Learning Research* and *Contemporary Issues in Technology and Teacher Education*, and has been a contributor to ASCD's SmartBlog on Education.

Sally Howe is Lecturer in Early Childhood Studies at the University of Roehampton. Her research interests include children's identity development in relation to educational contexts, and how wellbeing and learning relate, the assessment of children in early years, with specific attention to transition into school.

Marie Lavelle is Lecturer and Joint Programme Lead for the BA Early Childhood Studies at the Plymouth Institute of Education, Plymouth University. Her research interests reflect her professional heritage as a midwife and her academic background as a sociologist.

Caroline Leeson is Senior Lecturer in Early Childhood Studies at York St John University. Her research interests are in social justice; children with a parent in prison; children who go missing and/or are vulnerable to sexual exploitation; as well as the involvement of children in decision-making processes.

Eunice Lumsden is Head of Early Years at the University of Northampton, Fellow of the Royal Society of Arts, Senior Fellow of the Higher Education Academy and a registered social worker. Her research interests include the professionalisation of the ECEC workforce, child maltreatment, poverty and adoption.

Jane Murray works at the Centre for Education and Research at the University of Northampton where she researches and teaches in the field of education, specialising in early childhood education, social justice and participatory research. Before working in higher education, Jane was a teacher for 20 years in early childhood and primary school settings in the UK.

Sarah Rawding is Senior Lecturer in Early Years at the Sheffield Institute of Education, Sheffield Hallam University. Her teaching interests focus around the role of the adult in enhancing early years practice through play-based pedagogy, reflective practice and teamwork and leadership within the early years.

Tanya Richardson is Senior Lecturer in Early Years at Northampton University. She has previously managed and led her own 'outstanding' day nursery and out of school club. She is currently undertaking a PhD, researching the impact that different learning and play environments have on young children's speech and language development.

Jenny Robson is Senior Lecturer in Early Childhood in the Cass School of Education and Communities at the University of East London. Her research interests explore the ways in which early childhood education and care practitioners understand and navigate issues of justice, equality and children's rights in their practice.

Roberta Taylor is a Senior Lecturer in English and Education at the Institute of Education, Sheffield Hallam University and a Senior Fellow of the Higher Education Academy. She researches collaborative classroom learning from a multimodal perspective in primary, secondary and higher education settings.

Philippa Thompson is Senior Lecturer in Early Childhood Studies at the Sheffield Institute of Education, Sheffield Hallam University. Her research interests in early childhood include play; participation; risk and adventure; and the wellbeing of young children, families, practitioners and undergraduates.

Mary E. Whalley is an independent early childhood consultant. Her doctoral study focused on pedagogical leadership with infants and toddlers (birth to 30 months) and she continues to research in this area.

Rita Winstone is Senior Lecturer at Teesside University and the Programme Leader for the BA (Hons) Early Childhood Studies. Her initial background is teaching in schools in both the primary and secondary sector. Her interests in the higher educational field are in inclusion and diversity and in special educational needs.

ACKNOWLEDGEMENTS

PUBLISHER'S ACKNOWLEDGEMENTS

The author and the publisher are grateful for permission to reproduce the following material in this book:

Figure 3.1, 'The 4 Cs' from *Dialogic Education*, Phillipson, N. & Wegerif, R., © 2016, Routledge, reproduced by permission of Taylor & Francis Books UK.

Chapter 8, extract from *Family Support as Reflective Practice*, Dolan, P. et al., © 2006 Jessica Kingsley Publishers. Foreword © 2006 Neil Thompson. Reproduced with permission of the Licensor through PLS Clear.

Figure 10.1 from Shier, H. (2001) 'Pathways to Participation: Openings, Opportunities and Obligations – A new model for enhancing children's participation in decision-making', *Children and Society*, 15(2). Reproduced with permission from Harry Shier.

Figure 15.1 is reproduced with permission Dr Janice Bland and Emma McGilp.

Figure 15.2 is reproduced with permission of Sarah Coles, on behalf of EMTAS.

Figure 15. 3 is reproduced with permission of Les Petits Poissons.

The publisher and the editors and contributors wish to thank all the students who contributed to the development of the text.

EDITORS' ACKNOWLEDGEMENTS

Early Childhood Studies has developed substantially as an academic discipline over recent years with input from many individuals. We are grateful to each author for their contribution to make this accessible to readers of this book. The collection of chapters introduces varied disciplines and practice areas to help readers develop their knowledge and awareness of the valuable role they can play in young children's lives. We are also immensely grateful for the students who have made a contribution to this text. Your chapter commentaries provide a clear insight into the relevance of each chapter in introducing new concepts and, perhaps most importantly, provoking thought and questioning. Each contributor has enabled us to produce a text that goes beyond each chapter in engaging readers in the many academic debates that are important in the discipline of early childhood. Our thanks also go to Jude Bowen, Christofere Fila and the wonderful team at SAGE who have worked so hard to produce this book. We hope in making the discipline accessible to readers we convey the difference knowledgeable, analytical and reflective practitioners can make to children, families and colleagues in early childhood education and care.

GLOSSARY

Accommodation: the process of modifying or creating new schemas to integrate new experience/information.

Act of Parliament: the name given to either the creation of a new law or to changes to an existing law. This is achieved by the process of a bill receiving approval from both the House of Commons and the House of Lords and then given Royal Assent by the monarch.

Agency: an individual having the power to act upon the world, by shaping their own lives and society around them; or an organisation responsible for providing a service.

Agentic: how far children (and adults) exercise **agency**, or are able to construct their own social worlds and lives.

Animated object: an object brought to life through children's imagination.

Anticipatory socialisation: anticipating the social behaviours and patterns for a group in readiness for the transition to the group; a preparation for a future role.

Apgar score: a scoring system ranging from 0–10 to assess the health of a baby. It is assessed immediately after birth and may be used again to assess any change in condition. It is based on five factors, with each scoring between 0 and 2. The higher the score, the better. A healthy newborn infant would expect to receive a score of 7–10.

Assemblage(s): this term can be used to describe a collection of affective materials within a given situation. Materials in an assemblage include interconnected elements in particular circumstances that interact with and affect other elements.

Assent: affirmative agreement given by children to participate in an activity or a research study, especially for younger children where parents or adult gatekeepers may have given consent.

Assessment: early childhood practitioners' explanations of data that they have captured about young children's behaviours, used to enhance young children's development and learning.

Assimilation: the process of integrating new experience/information to existing schema.

Asylum seeker: a person seeking sanctuary in another nation, who is applying for asylum and the right to recognition as a refugee and thus to receive legal protection and assistance.

Attainment level: the level a child is working at in a subject area.

Authoritative (parenting): a child-centred approach to parenting with close interaction between parent and child. Parent has high behaviour expectations, sets clear limits and is consistent and fair.

Authoritarian (parenting): a strict approach to parenting with little discussion or explanation from the parent for decisions. The response from the parent to child is limited and expectations for achievement and behaviour are set high.

Beings or becomings: these descriptions are often used in the discourse of children's rights. When children are considered as active contributors in society and valued in their own right as humans, they are termed 'beings'. Once they are seen as 'mini' adults being prepared for adult targets in life that they have not yet attained, then they are perceived as 'becomings'. This discourse of childhood has an impact on the design of curricula in Western society.

Bi-directional relationship: this can be seen as a form of knowledge exchange between (in this instance) play and the curriculum. It considers that the two can learn from each other to benefit the child whilst supporting research and policy.

Brainstem: the section of the brain that is responsible for basic vital life functions such as breathing, heartbeat, blood pressure and swallowing. It is situated beneath the limbic system and connected to the spinal cord.

Brain development: cellular and physiological processes by which the nervous system, which includes the brain, develops from conception throughout life. The complex interaction of nature (genetic inheritance) and nurture (environmental experiences) determines how the brain will develop.

Brain-imaging technology: non-invasive techniques used to research the living brain. Current techniques include Electroencephalography (EEG), Event-Related Potential (ERP), Positron Emission Tomography (PET), Magnetic Resonance Imaging (MRI) and Functional Magnetic Resonance Imaging (fMRI).

Carnegie Task Force: part of the Carnegie Corporation which exists to develop and diffuse knowledge and understanding with the aim of influencing policy makers. The corporation's main areas of focus are international peace, the advancement of education and knowledge and democracy.

Cerebellum: an area of the brain that is made up of two hemispheres and is associated with regulation of movement, posture and balance.

Cerebral cortex: the outer layer of grey matter in the cerebrum, associated with higher brain functions such as learning, memory and reasoning.

Characteristics of effective learning (CEL): a framework built on the work by Ferre Laevers' 'Leuven Scale for Involvement for Young Children', and also forms part of the Early Years Foundation Stage guidance and assessment framework. The DfE proposed that the CEL be *playing and exploring* – children investigate and experience things, and 'have a go'; *active learning* – children concentrate and keep on trying if they encounter difficulties, and enjoy achievements; and *creating and thinking critically* – children have and develop their own ideas, make links between ideas and develop strategies for doing things.

Child protection: the process of protecting individual children who have been identified as either suffering, or being at risk of suffering, significant harm as a result of abuse or neglect.

Child public health (CPH): a rapidly developing field and subspecialty of Public Health and Paediatrics, CPH is concerned with the distribution of health and illness (focusing mainly on the latter) across entire childhood populations. CPH is also concerned with factors influencing the health of childhood populations, both positively and negatively, and ways in which children's health can be improved through effective health promotion.

Childline: a counselling and information service for children under the age of 19 years in the UK. Counsellors are available around the clock, and contactable either by phone or email. The service is free and confidential.

Children Act 1989: ascribes duties to local authorities, courts, parents and other agencies in the UK to ensure children are safeguarded and their welfare is promoted. The central premise is based on the idea that children are best cared for within their own families; however, it also makes provision in circumstances where this is not possible.

Children in need: defined under Section 17 of the Children Act 1989. A child will be considered in need if:

- they are unlikely to achieve or maintain or to have the opportunity to achieve or maintain a reasonable standard of health or development without provision of services from the Local Authority
- their health or development is likely to be significantly impaired, or further impaired, without the provision of services from the Local Authority
- they have a disability.

Children's centres: provide a range of education and support services to young children and families.

Children's voice: children being able to and given the opportunity to express their views, often associated with the notion of children's **participation**.

Chromosome: thread-like bodies containing chromatin, which determine the characteristics of an organism. In humans there are 23 pairs and one pair, the X and Y chromosome, determine biological sex.

Circle of friends: a group created to support the creation and maintenance of friendships.

Co-constructor: this phrase is used in the discourse of rights and education and suggests that children and adults working together 'construct' knowledge and identity.

Cognitive: a psychological process that relates to perception, thinking and analysis.

Cognitive development: development that relates to perception, thinking and learning.

Cognitive dissonance: people like to have a set of consistent beliefs, opinions, values and behaviours. People also have a tendency to assume that others see the world the way they do, especially those they are close to or look up to. When different perspectives are presented, this creates an uncomfortable situation known as dissonance and action needs to be taken to diminish the discomfort, either through changing attitudes or seeking further information to make a more informed choice. People might also diminish the importance of the dissonance if it contradicts their opinions.

Common Assessment Framework (CAF): a shared assessment tool used to help practitioners with the early identification of children's additional needs and strengths, and to provide them with a co-ordinated multi-agency support plan to meet those needs.

Complementary school: an extra-curricular school which supports children with learning their home language. These are usually run by volunteers on weekends. Some have links with mainstream schools.

Conduct disorder: refers to a wide range of acting out persistent and pervasive behaviours.

Consent: agreement to participate and take part in the research process, usually confirmed by signature on a written consent form. Informed consent is where the participant has been given verbal and written information about the research and is fully aware of the implications of being involved.

Constructs of childhood: the idea that 'childhood' is a **social construction**. Constructs of childhood differ widely over time and context: from the idea that children are 'weak' and 'vulnerable' to an image of children as 'rich' and 'competent'.

Consultation: finding out people's views, usually to inform decision making.

Consumerist: the idea that early childhood institutions can be seen as places that provide a commodity to the consumers – parents and children. Some scholars and practitioners argue that this causes issues in terms of the development of sound pedagogical practice.

Contextual literacy: the idea that a person or leader is able to 'read' the situation and make leadership decisions that take full account of the type of setting, children and families and the community served. The leader understands that early childhood settings are dynamic and not static organisations. He/she allows for fluctuations in staffing and can adapt and adjust to new thinking and ideas.

Continuous provision: an environment that is set up with resources and experiences that are constantly available for children to explore. Continuous provision allows children the freedom to make choices.

Cortisol: a stress hormone produced by the adrenal gland.

Creativity: a disposition whereby individuals take on different approaches to solve a problem in an original way.

Cultural competence: delivering services in a way that is respectful of the cultural values and traditions that families bring with them.

Cultural symbols: artefacts or items that relate to a specific culture.

Curiosity: being inquisitive and showing an interest in learning and finding out more about something.

Curriculum Guidance for the Foundation Stage: statutory guidance for early years practitioners in the Foundation Stage (aged 3–5 years). The Guidance was replaced by the Statutory Framework for the Early Years Foundation Stage (0–5 years) in 2008, updated in 2014 and in 2017.

Data: information about young children's behaviours and related events, captured by early childhood practitioners' systematic observations and notes that record those observations.

Datafication: a suggestion that pedagogy in early childhood education and care has been reduced to the production of accessible data and measurable outcomes. This is often used alongside discussions of school readiness.

Democracy: the system of governance in which people can exercise the right to choose how they are governed and by whom, enabling the election of individuals who represent the people in an elected house such as parliament. A way for the voice of the people to (in theory) be heard through the ability to vote for government which will represent your views. However, the extent to which a democracy does this is debatable. Democracy also requires that citizens participate in public life.

Deprived background: refers to a deprived childhood featuring lack of money to purchase often basic necessities. It also refers to poor living conditions such as damp housing, lack of accessible amenities and leisure facilities, and to not being able to enjoy the pleasures in life often taken for granted by others.

Development: the physical and psychological changes that an individual undergoes in a lifetime.

Developmental phases: distinct stages of child development.

Diabetes: a medical condition characterised by high blood sugar brought about by lack of insulin and insulin resistance.

Digital citizenship: the accepted norms or standards of appropriate and responsible behaviour regarding the use of technology.

Digital competence: the set of skills, knowledge and attitudes that enable creative and critical use of technologies.

Digital device: any single piece of equipment that contains a computer or electronic controlling system.

Digital identity: online or networked information representing a person, organisation, application or thing.

Digital literacy: the ability to successfully use digital technologies to communicate, locate, evaluate, use and create information.

Digital native: a person who has been exposed to digital technologies from a young age.

Digital technology: electronic tools, systems, devices or resources, that generate, store or process data and information.

Digital texts: electronic versions of fiction and non-fiction texts available on a variety of digital devices.

Disability: a dynamic interaction between individual impairment and the social effects of impairment as a consequence of environmental, social and attitudinal barriers that prevent people with impairments from maximum participation in society.

Disabled child: a child who is treated differently because of an individual impairment.

Discipline: an area of study, e.g. psychology, sociology, anthropology.

Discourse(s): written or spoken communication that is coherent and organised and imbued with meaning. In linguistics, discourses construct versions of events, objects, situations and people in different ways. Language, and therefore discourse, is not neutral; it carries powerful messages, values and beliefs, often hidden and implicit. Discourses are often used by qualitative researchers to make sense of culture and social phenomena (e.g. masculinity).

Discursive practice: a term used by the French philosopher and theorist Foucault. Discursive practice is about the social realities and actions that construct identities. The power of discourse (language) is often evident in practices (e.g. boys don't cry; girls don't play roughly). This subtle power is often evident in day-to-day interactions and can have an empowering or disempowering impact on different groups (e.g. men/boys; women/girls).

Disposition: internal characteristics, such as a tendency, habit or approach to learn in a particular way, that explain an individual's behaviour or outlook; attributed to personality rather than environment or culture.

Distal and proximal factors: used in Bronfenbrenner's ecological model of human development to describe the relative position of an outcome to its cause, distal being distant from the cause and proximal being close.

Diversity: difference, e.g. in race, social class, ethnicity, religion, ability and other social characteristics.

Dyad: a pair or duo (used in friendship literature).

Early childhood education and care setting: a generic term applied in policy and research to describe and name any setting in which there is the provision of early education and care outside the child's home and family.

Early help (intervention) approach: refers to the theory and process whereby support is provided by practitioners to potentially vulnerable children, young people and their families as soon as problems start to emerge.

Early years professional (EYP): in England, the title given to the graduate leader role awarded by meeting a set of prescribed standards for leading practice across the Early Years Foundation Stage, from 2006 to 2013.

Early years teacher (EYT): from 2013, the early years teacher role replaced early years professional (EYP) as the graduate leader role. New standards for the award replaced those for the EYP.

Ecology: a term that explores relationships between organisms and their environment. It can be used across many subject disciplines. In this context it is about the relationship between people (e.g. children, parents) and their immediate and broader communities. Bronfenbrenner's theory is based on ecological systems.

Ecological theory (later named **ecological systems theory (EST)**): Bronfenbrenner recognised the importance of studying children in the context of their environment and that this had an impact on the child's development. He called the environment level systems as follows: the **microsystem, mesosystem, exosystem, macrosystem**, and **chronosystem**.

Education, health and care plan (EHC): a legal document that describes a child/young person's special educational, health and social care needs. The plan details the extra support (beyond that normally provided in a mainstream education setting) that will be given to meet those needs.

Educational standards: educational goals that children should have attained at certain points in their education.

Education Reform Act 1988: the act made profound changes to the way schools were managed and the relationship with local authorities. It also introduced the National Curriculum and key stages.

Effective Provision of Preschool Education (EPPE): beginning in 1997, the study followed a cohort of children from age 3 onwards. The findings documented the gains to children's development that early childhood education could provide and influenced government policy during the early part of the 2000s.

Egocentric speech: can be described as when children talk for themselves, without interaction with another person. It is also seen to be the internalised 'inner speech' related closely to thinking.

Egocentricity: behaviour/attitude that denotes an inability to see/consider events outside one's own perspective or position.

Emancipatory: loosening, the act of people being set free.

Enact(ed): put into action – with regard to policy, how policy comes into practice, is made real.

Environment: the physical and social surroundings in which an individual operates.

Epidemiology: a branch of medicine that studies the incidence and causes of disease.

Equality of opportunity (or equal opportunities): the right to be treated without discrimination.

Equilibrium: a stable cognitive state where existing schemas/concepts explain individuals' perceptions of the world.

Essentialist: individuals have a set of characteristics that make them what they are. An essentialist view of gender would ascribe that men and woman are fundamentally different biologically, irrespective of social and cultural factors.

Ethnographic approach/Ethnography: a branch of social research that involves the researcher's close engagement with participants in the research setting. Often ethnography involves a longitudinal study where the researcher aims becomes part of the social culture, usually over a prolonged duration and to gain insider perspectives by living or working in the research setting.

Ethnographically contextualised multimodal discourse analysis: a researcher using this approach examines interaction with some insider perspective of the participants' experience. This enables the researcher to analyse and understand the participants' interaction more deeply.

Eudaimonic: a state of wellbeing that arises from finding meaning and purpose in life.

Every Child Matters (ECM): a UK government initiative for England and Wales launched in 2003 at least partly in response to the death of Victoria Climbié. The ECM Green Paper identified the five outcomes most important to children and young people: Be healthy; Stay safe; Enjoy and achieve; Make a positive contribution; Achieve economic wellbeing.

Evidence: data about young children's behaviours that have been captured, organised and explained by early childhood practitioners to inform decisions about provision for young children's development and learning.

Executive function: skills that develop over childhood and into early adulthood that are largely associated with the prefrontal cortex. They enable us to plan, organise, make decisions and resist impulses. Lack of sensitive caregiving, conflict and stress can impair executive skill function.

Exosystem: refers to one or more settings (that do not directly involve the child) but in which changes may happen that would impact on the child (e.g. media reports, local government, housing association, police).

Experience: the interaction an individual has with their environment.

Experience-dependent: interactions that depend on experiences that are unique to individuals, e.g. learning to read or ride a bicycle.

Experience-expectant: types of sensory stimulation that the brain expects as a result of experiences in the environment that are (or should be) common to all members of the human species, e.g. patterned light, sound, language, opportunities to move.

Expressive language: a way of communicating wants and needs.

Facilitate: to support, help and direct.

Facilitator: an individual who guides and supports others to achieve specific aims.

Family: a basic social unit usually consisting of at least one adult together with the child(ren) under their care. The definition of 'family' varies across cultures and according to social norms.

Family practices: the idea that 'family' is actively created by its members, therefore family is something that people 'do' rather than something that people 'are'.

Funds of knowledge: the knowledge and understanding that children gain from their family, home environment and community, including abilities and skills, the way things work, how to learn and their wellbeing. This is deeper than simply recognising children's interests. Rather, this notion encourages professionals to have a deeper engagement with what children 'bring' to play in the early childhood setting. The family and community are seen as an important source of cultural learning for the child.

Gender typing: the process of an individual becoming aware of their gender. Acquiring this awareness involves incorporating values, motivations and behaviours considered appropriate to the male-female binary. Gender typing is informed by gender stereotypes. Gender typing can be disempowering to individuals if it restricts or problematises behaviour.

Genes: the basic physical unit of inheritance. Genes are transferred from parents to offspring and contain the information to specify different traits.

Genetic determinism: the theory that human development is shaped by the genes that comprise the individual's genotype rather than by culture. In other words, how the brain develops depends on the genes you were born with.

Glia: the cells of the brain that provide structural support and protection for neurons, coat axons in myelin, and form the blood–brain barrier.

Global south: nations located in the Southern hemisphere with lower economic wealth.

Globalisation: the ways systems such as trade, travel and communication interconnect the world.

Gross domestic product (GDP): the total value of everything produced by a country in a year; is a way of measuring the size of the economic activity of a country. Comparisons are often made on a quarterly basis. For each quarter of the year, a figure is calculated to show how much GDP has increased or reduced. If GDP falls (a negative figure) for two successive quarters, this is usually seen as indicating that the country is in recession.

Head Start: the US government-funded project which began in the 1960s to help some of America's poorest families.

Health and wellbeing boards: the Health and Social Care Act 2012 establishes health and wellbeing boards as a forum where key leaders from the health and care system work together to improve the health and wellbeing of their local population and reduce health inequalities.

Health and wellbeing strategy: a written strategy that sets out how the health and wellbeing needs, identified by a preceding joint strategic needs assessment, of a locality are to be addressed and includes recommendations for joined-up working on the part of commissioners and services.

Health determinants: factors that affect health, either negatively or positively.

Health indicator: in public health, health indicators are characteristics of a population frequently measured to denote the health status of a given population. Most commonly used are categories of mortality and morbidity.

Health inequalities: refers to differences in the health status of individuals or groups brought about by social, geographical and biological factors, where the worst off in society experience poorer health and shorter lives.

Health promotion: the World Health Organisation (WHO) defines health promotion as the process of enabling people to increase control over, and to improve, their health. It moves beyond a focus on individual behaviour towards a wide range of social and environmental interventions.

Hedonic: a state of wellbeing that arises from the presence of positive feelings and the absence of negative ones.

Hegemonic: about control and dominance. When used in relation to gender it often relates to idealised notions of masculinity and the belief that men need to be strong, controlling and dominant. This disempowers women/girls and any man (or boy) who does not meet these expectations.

Heritage culture: a bilingual child or an EAL learner draws on two cultures – that of the country they are growing up in and that of their ancestors and family, which can be described as heritage culture.

Heterogeneity: describes the diversity or non-uniformity of something – for example, if the experiences of a group of people are heterogenous, it means that everyone's experiences are different.

Heteronormative: a world view that promotes heterosexuality as the only sexuality and as normal. A heteronormative view sees heterosexuality as applying to all and consequently can lead to exclusion and homophobia.

Hippocampus: a region of the limbic system that plays a part in converting short-term episodic memories into long-term ones.

Home language: the child's mother tongue; often the language which is spoken at home.

Home learning environment: activities and interactions that happen in the home between parents/carers and children to support children's learning, such as reading together and playing letters and numbers games.

Home-schooled: if a child is taught at home either full or part time, this is called home-schooling or home-schooled. The term 'flexi-home schooling' is also referred to in this book with reference to part-time home-schooling.

Homogenous: alike or equivalent in composition and characteristics.

Horizontal friendships: friendships at the same level or equal in nature, e.g. children in their peer group.

Human capital: a term originally associated with economics, it has frequently been used in education to describe the intellectual and cultural resources which parents pass on to their children. Seen as the monetarisation of human worth, it includes acquired and accumulated knowledge, skills, social attributes, dispositions and personal behaviours which enable the individual to make an economic contribution. The theory is attributed to economist Gary Becker.

Hyperkinetic disorders: a term used interchangeably with attention deficit disorder and attention deficit hyperactivity disorder to describe problems of poor attention, hyperactivity and impulsivity manifesting in early childhood.

Ideology: a set of beliefs and ideals held by a society or group, particularly where the shared views influence practices or policy systems.

Imaginary object friend: an object that children personify and perceive to be their friend.

Immigrant: a person who leaves their country of origin to live in a new country.

Impairment: the functional limitations of a person's body; impairments can be physical, sensory, cognitive/communicative, adaptive or socio-emotional.

Inclusion: enabling all people in society to fully participate in all areas of life. In the context of education, inclusion refers to providing support so that all children can learn together in mainstream schools and early childhood settings, regardless of dis/ability, race, language spoken, gender, poverty or any other social difference.

Inclusive development: development that challenges inequalities in wealth and opportunities that occur through globalisation.

Individualism: a focus on a single person.

Infant mortality: the death of infants under 1 year old per thousand live births.

Inference: the ability to draw conclusions from facts and evidence.

Information and communication technologies (ICT): technologies that provide access to communication through telecommunications.

Interactive technology: all forms of digital technology that emphasise human/user-centred approaches or audience engagement.

International development: support between nations aimed at improving various aspects of people's lives.

International organisations (IOs): organisations recognised by member nations and established by formal legal agreements.

Interpretive reproduction: the process where children take adult conventions and adapt them to make their own specific peer culture.

Interprofessional practice: the ability to work with other professionals both across settings within the care and education sector and in other closely related sectors, especially health and social services.

Intertextuality: in the context of social semiotics considers how meanings can be shared as they make links with meanings made in other contexts.

Invisible companion: a friend a child creates that is invisible.

Joint strategic needs assessment (JSNA): co-ordinated by health and wellbeing boards, JSNAs are joint assessments of the current and future health and care needs of a locality and are used to inform planning and commissioning (buying) of appropriate health and care services.

Language acquisition device (LAD): part of Noam Chomsky's nativist language theory, proposing that children have an innate ability to develop language. The LAD functions to help the child pick up regularities in sound, language, grammar and internalise these, making them an active part of their own speech.

Lead professional: a professional who is appointed as part of the delivery of integrated support to children with additional or complex needs. The role involves coordinating the delivery of the actions agreed by the professionals working with the child and family.

Leadership: has many definitions but, in this book, is defined as the capacity to set direction and encourage and enable others in building effective practice and bringing about positive change.

Leadership within: a new conceptualisation of leadership from McDowall, Clark and Murray which defines three core components: *catalytic agency*, where the leader intentionally brings about changes to practice; this is based on *reflective integrity*, where the leader is able to challenge and question practice in order to bring about improvements; and *relational interdependence*, where everyone in the team is viewed as contributing to the overall leadership.

Learning difficulty: an impairment that affects a child's ability to learn.

Learning power: dispositions, values and attitudes which create a capacity to learn.

Lifelong learning: the ability to learn and develop beyond the formal schooling years.

Limbic system: a system of structures in the brain that play a role in emotion, motivation and memory.

Macro-politics: these relate to the big structural factors in society, including issues of social inequality and social justice, health, housing, etc.

Macrosystem: a term used by Bronfenbrenner to describe the culture in which children live; describes the beliefs, ideologies and public policies that influence all the systems.

Mainstream school: any school which is not identified as a specialist school and/or education provision.

Majority world: used in preference to 'third world' or 'developing countries', it identifies nations as lacking in resources and covers those nations where most of the global population live.

Management: different from leadership in that it involves the functions of policy making, organisational considerations – such as staffing, resources and budgets – and ensuring the organisation runs efficiently.

Maturation: a theory first proposed by Gessell that developmental changes in a child's body or behaviour are simply a result of maturing, or growing older.

Media: the collective communication tools or outlets that store, share or deliver information.

Mesosystem: the pattern of relationships and activities experienced by two or more settings (e.g. home, school, neighbourhood).

Metacognitive awareness: an awareness of one's thoughts and processes and the ability to influence them.

Metalinguistic abilities: knowledge of how language works and the ability to analyse language, gained through studying the rules of language.

Microsystem: a pattern of relationships and activities experienced by the child in their immediate setting (e.g. parent/carers, wider family, faith centre, ECEC setting).

Midbrain: the middle of the three primary divisions of the brainstem.

Migrant: a person living temporarily or permanently in a country s/he was not born in but has significant social ties to.

Migration: the movement of people from one place to another. This may be within a nation – internal migration or between nations – international migration.

Minority world: preferable to 'first world' or 'developed countries', it is a term used to refer to countries traditionally viewed as 'developed'. It clarifies how a small number of nations, where the minority of the global population live and hold disproportional amounts of power and wealth.

Modalities: the sensory channels or pathways through which individuals give, receive and store information.

Mode: a mode in social semiotics is a resource for communicating meaning, and can be visual, verbal, written or gestural.

Morbidity: disease/illness.

More knowledgeable other (MKO): a term related to Vygotsky's theory of the zone of proximal development. The more knowledgeable other is a person (usually an adult) who facilitates or scaffolds the child's learning interactions in a way which is appropriate for the child's level of development.

Mosaic Approach: developed by Clark and Moss, the Mosaic Approach is a way of engaging children in active participation in research, through the use of multiple and child-friendly methods. These methods could include drawing, photography, guided tours, etc.

Multi-agency: co-operation between services, such as professionals from health, education and social care working together in partnership with the child and their family, to produce an integrated delivery to meet their needs.

Multimodal: communication that involves multiple modes simultaneously.

Myelination: the formation of myelin, a fatty, insulating sheath around axons which allows faster communication between neurons.

Nature–nurture debate: an ongoing debate centring on the balance and importance of the impact of innate characteristics (genes) on development and the impact of social and environmental factors.

Neglectful (parenting): little or no response from parent to child leading to emotional distance. A lack of interaction and guidance often leaves children to make decisions with little or no check from parents.

Neoliberalism: a form of liberalism which extends economisation into all facets of Western life. It is a model of policy and political ideology which promotes free-market principles, competition and rational self-interest, and positions citizens as consumers in a market-driven economy. It assumes that democracy is achieved in a society by means of citizens making choices about buying or accessing services and products, thus forcing competition between service providers to offer goods or services that consumers will choose. A reduction in the role and size of the state in the lives of individuals and society is key here.

Neonatal period: the period from birth to one month of age.

Neuron: a nerve cell located in the brain.

Neuroscience: the scientific study of the nervous system. It comprises a number of fields that deal with the structure and function of the brain, its development, genetics, biochemistry, physiology, pharmacology and pathology.

Neurotransmitter: a chemical that transmits messages between nerve cells; dopamine and serotonin are among the many neurotransmitters.

Non-governmental organisations (NGOs): not for profit, national or international groups generally run by people with a common interest.

Object friend: a small object that children view as a friend.

Ofsted: the Office for Standards in Education, Children's Services and Skills. Ofsted inspects and regulates services that care for children and young people, and services providing education and skills for learners of all ages.

Online safety: safeguarding against risks to private information and property associated with the Internet.

Organisation for Economic Co-operation and Development Countries (OECD): an intergovernmental economic organisation comprising 35 high-income member states whose mission is to develop economic progress and world trade. It began in 1961 following the establishment of the new OECD Convention on 14 December 1960. The latter built on the former 'Organisation for European Economic Co-operation' (OEEC) established in 1948 in which individual governments were encouraged to recognise the interdependence of their economies. Today there are 35 OECD member countries worldwide who, together, identify, discuss and analyse problems.

Overweight and obesity: in childhood, overweight is defined as a Body Mass Index at or above the 85th percentile and below the 95th percentile for children of the same age and sex. Childhood obesity, on the other hand, is defined as a Body Mass Index at or above the 95th percentile for children of the same age and sex.

Paediatrics: a field of medicine focusing on managing medical conditions affecting babies, children and young people.

Parental responsibility: defined in the Children Act 1989 as the legal rights and responsibilities all mothers and most fathers have regarding their children. It states that the most important roles are to provide a home for the child and to protect and maintain the child; in addition, it states responsibility for disciplining the child, choosing and providing for the child's education, agreeing to the child's medical treatment, naming the child and agreeing to any change of name, and looking after the child's property.

Participation: in political terms, participation involves people in expressing their views, making decisions about matters that affect their lives and helping to bring about change.

Participatory research: provides opportunities to develop research processes with people and emphasises co-construction of meaning and knowledge. It focuses on people's lived experiences, creating a space where everyone involved has a role to play. A key element is the collaboration between researchers and participants in all aspects of the research process, including planning and design, implementation and dissemination.

Partnership: a collaborative relationship between two or more parties based on trust, equality and mutual understanding for the achievement of a specified goal.

Pedagogy/pedagogical leadership: the approach educators take to achieve a particular educational aim. Early childhood pedagogy encompasses everything that supports children's learning and development. Pedagogical leadership requires early childhood professionals who understand children's needs, are highly knowledgeable about early development and understand different theories and approaches to learning.

Peer culture: social interaction involving specific routines, practices, rules and artefacts.

Permissive (parenting): low parental expectations towards children and a high level of response. Parents are often loving but provide limited guidelines and expectations to children. Rules are rarely enforced and this can lead children to lack self-regulation.

Personified friend/object : a friend or object that children create and bring to life using their imagination.

Phenotype: overt characteristics of an individual brought about by the interaction between the individual's genetic make-up (genotype) and the environment.

Plasticity: the capacity of the brain to change its structure and function in response to experience.

Playful pedagogies: an approach to teaching that welcomes and encourages the uncertainty and risk of child-initiated play and is open to following children's lead in their play.

Playground friend: a child who volunteers to support other children in the playground to enter play and initiate and maintain friendships.

Policy as espoused: a course of action outlining the intentions of government or of an institution/agency.

Political ideologies: conscious and unconscious beliefs, ideas and ideals shared by a group of individuals associated with a particular political stance.

Popular: a term used in the field of psychology to describe children who have lots of peers that would like to play and be friends with them.

Positionality: a way of exploring your bias and subjectivity, and you can therefore be more impartial and aware of how your own beliefs and values may impact on the research process.

Prefrontal cortex: situated behind the forehead in the frontal lobe of the brain, it is responsible for many higher-order thinking skills such as decision making and plays a role in the regulation of complex cognitive, emotional and behavioural functioning.

Professionalisation: the process by which the status of a work role is transformed into that of a 'professional'. This typically equates to the recognition of qualifications and the perceived value of the role.

Programme for International Student Assessment (PISA): a triennial international survey. The aim is to evaluate education systems worldwide by testing the skills and knowledge of 15-year-old students. Over half a million students, representing 28 million 15-year-olds in 72 countries and economies, took the internationally agreed two-hour test in 2015. Science, mathematics, reading, collaborative problem solving and financial literacy were assessed.

Psychology: a field of study focusing on the mind and behaviour.

Qualitative: research methods and data that are usually descriptive, offering people's views, feelings and opinions; may include interviews, questionnaires, photographs, videos, visual images and artefacts.

Quantitative: research methods and data that provide statistical information that may be measured or provide percentages, often in numerical form in surveys and questionnaires.

Reciprocal relationship: a term used to describe friendships that are mutual and where both parties would like to be friends with each other.

Reciprocity: behaviours in which two people or groups help and support each other.

Reflective practice: the practice of looking at an ongoing situation in practice to discuss if something different can be done to change that situation.

Reformation (1517–1648): a schism from the Roman Catholic church which saw several Protestant churches established. It began in Germany with Martin Luther but different factions spread independently throughout Europe. The emergence of the printing press during the mid-fifteenth century enabled the spread of ideas and information more readily.

Refugee: a person forced to flee their country because of war, persecution or violence and who has been granted protection.

Rejected: a term used in the field of psychology to describe children who are rejected by their peers; their peers do not want to play with them or make friends with them.

Renaissance (fourteenth to seventeenth centuries): generally denotes the period between the Middle Ages and the modern era. The period was a cultural movement focusing on humanities and saw the revival of art, literature and learning.

Resilience: a disposition characterised by the ability to be persistent and recover from setbacks.

Resourcefulness: the ability to find quick and novel ways to overcome difficulties.

Safeguarding: the action that is taken to promote the welfare of all children and protect them from harm.

Scaffolding: Bruner's notion of scaffolding extends Vygotsky's zone of proximal development (ZPD). Here the adult extends a child's learning by reducing its freedom and focusing on the skill to be acquired. In this way, the child is supported, becomes increasingly independent and progresses to the next stage of mastery.

Schema (plural schemas or schemata): a cognitive (mental) framework, made up of concepts and groupings, developed by an individual from experience and used to organise knowledge and understanding. Schemas are used to maintain information to make sense of social situations or phenomena. In young children, this is often evident in strongly held ideas about gender.

Schoolification: a term used to describe how compulsory school education has begun to 'take over' the discourse of early childhood education. Terms such as **school readiness** also form part of this discourse.

School readiness: the point where a child has the confidence, independence and skills to actively and fully engage in their allocated/selected school or setting.

Section 47 (of the Children Act 1989): outlines the statutory responsibility of the local authority to investigate the safety and welfare of a child if they have information that the child may be at risk of or suffering significant harm.

Self-esteem: confidence in one's own worth and competence.

Self-surveillance: Foucault described the way individuals police themselves through what he called the 'conduct of conduct'. Self-surveillance is one way power operates in society. Instead of a higher authority operating on individuals, individuals monitor and adjust their own behaviour *as if* they are being watched.

Semiotic resources: the resources that a person can use to make meaning. Very often this involves 'ensembles' or collections of modes used together to communicate meaning. For example, a child may speak, point and use facial expression to communicate ideas, as they draw on all available semiotic resources.

Serious case review (SCR): the name given to an in-depth multi-agency review which is convened where a child has been abused or neglected, resulting in serious harm or death, and there is cause for concern as to the way in which agencies have worked together to safeguard the child.

Silent period: emerging from Patton Tabors' writing on children in the early years developing ability in a second language. Tabors describes that often children may go through a silent period when realising that their home language does not 'work' in a new setting.

Social cognition: refers to a child's understanding of social conventions and practices.

Social construction: the process of assigning meanings based on a society's values and priorities. Childhood is seen as a social construction, usually by adults, which is both historically and culturally determined.

Social constructivism: the concept that human development is socially situated. Developed by Vygotsky, he theorised that knowledge and learning could not be separated from the social context.

Social investment: this is the economic value given to the rationale for economic intervention or action in the social aspects of life.

Social rehearsal: the opportunity to practise social episodes with others, e.g. siblings, before re-enacting with peers.

Social semiotic perspective: one based on studying how people make and share meanings together through drawing upon multiple modes of communication.

Socio-economic group: differences between groups of people on the basis of social and economic factors.

Sociology: a field of study focusing on societies and how groups of people interact with one another.

Socio-metric testing: testing used in the field of psychology where children select the peers they like to play with (research prior to the twenty-first century involved children also being asked to select children they did not like to play with).

Special educational needs and disabilities: a label or category given to children whose development and learning are considered to be atypical compared to their peers.

Special Educational Needs and Disability Code of Practice (0–25 years): this statutory code details the legal requirements and explains the duties of local authorities, health bodies, schools and colleges to provide for those with special educational needs under part 3 of the Children and Families Act 2014.

Special Educational Needs Co-ordinator (SENCO): the person who provides strategic oversight for working with families and children identified as needing SEN support within an educational establishment.

Special school: a school that is specially organised to provide an education for children with special educational needs. Children will usually need a statement of special educational needs or an Education, Health and Care Plan to access a placement at a special school.

Standards-driven education: a model of education in which pupil attainment is measured against a set of agreed educational standards, and schools are held accountable for pupil attainment against these standards. There can be consequences for schools whose pupils fail to attain specific levels of performance.

Statement of educational need: a document written by the family and professionals associated with a child with special needs. The statement gave access to funding and a process by which the child should be educated. This has now been replaced by the Education, Health and Care Plan.

Statutory guidance: outlines what agencies and practitioners must do to comply with the law.

Stress: a psychological and physiological response to actual or potential threats to a person's wellbeing. Stress results when demands exceed the immediately available resources.

Subjectification: the way power operates to construct, shape and mould the individual subject; who we are and who we think we are. The term was first used by Foucault.

Sure Start: a UK government area-based initiative announced in 1998. It applied primarily in England with slightly different versions in Wales, Scotland and Northern Ireland. The aim of the programme was to improve the health and wellbeing of families and children from pre-birth to age 4. The majority of the 524 programmes in neighbourhoods where a high proportion of children lived in poverty became children's centres, originally providing early education and full day care. Provision included identification of and support for children with special educational needs and disabilities, health services, parental outreach and family support. More limited services are now provided by many centres.

Synaesthetic activities: in this book it relates to the way children are drawn to synaesthetic activities, which draw on all their senses and use visual, kinaesthetic and gestural modes.

Synapse: a junction between two nerve cells consisting of a microscopic gap across which electro-chemical impulses pass by means of a chemical neurotransmitter.

Synaptic pruning: the process that eliminates unused synaptic connections.

Syntactic development: the process of learning how to organise words into meaningful sentences. Knowing where to place a word and how to make small changes, i.e. adding an s to indicate plural, to make sense.

tabula rasa: a blank slate. John Locke considered that children's minds were a blank slate – something to be written upon by experience creating knowledge.

Transitions: changes within our circumstances that we need to respond and adapt to in order to manage them. Often, transitions tend to be conceptualised as single events, such as starting school or university, or a new job, but transitioning can also be thought of as experiencing ongoing processes without a clear start and finish.

Treasure basket: a box filled with everyday items often made up from natural materials, such as keys, feathers, fir cones, metal spoons.

Typology: refers to a system or set of descriptions of types, for example, of behaviours or attitudes.

United Nations: an international organisation formed in 1945 that aims to increase political and economic co-operation among member countries and works on economic and social development programmes to improve human rights and reduce global conflicts.

United Nations Convention on the Rights of the Child (UNCRC): a globally recognised human rights treaty for children. It guarantees three types of right for children: provision, protection and participation. Among the articles specifiying provision, it acknowledges the importance of play in children's lives and the right to education from birth.

Vertical friendships: relationships with a hierarchy or imbalance of power, e.g. parents, older siblings.

Working theories: a term used to describe the ideas and theories that are created by children as they play.

World schooling: the term 'world schooling' can be broadly defined as the use of the world around you as your classroom to facilitate learning. Sometimes described as 'edventures', longer-term trips are taken by families where children learn during their extended trip. It is important to note that the definition and approach to 'world schooling' varies depending on the parent or family. In the context of this book, World School refers to a short-term stay with a home-school family in Spain during which they were immersed in the culture and language in the local environment.

Zone of proximal development (ZPD): a concept devised by Vygotsky to express the difference between what a learner can do with and without help, and between their actual and potential development. There is a point at which (the zone) if an adult, or more competent peer, 'scaffolds' a child's thinking or learning, this could support the child to move on to the next 'level' of their thinking/learning. Cognitive development is founded upon dialogue with a teacher, adult or peer (a knowledgeable other) and this supports a child's learning. The adult use of questions and rephrasing can aid this development.

Zygote: a sex cell formed from the fertilisation of an ovum and sperm cell.

INTRODUCTION

BY DAMIEN FITZGERALD
AND HELOISE MACONOCHIE

If you ask a range of people to describe a child, there are likely to be several commonalities in their responses. If the same group were then asked to describe what influences the way children develop, there may be a broader range of answers. This is likely to reflect, at least to some degree, broader historical, cultural and social influences. Traditionally, some of these influences were studied as part of the discipline of psychology. However, during the twentieth century it was increasingly realised that whilst psychology offered a valuable insight into young children, a broader perspective and understanding were needed.

Early Childhood Studies (ECS), as an academic interdisciplinary subject, emerged in response to this. This raises two key questions: what is the discipline of Early Childhood Studies and what does it offer in addition to other disciplines that explore the development and lives of young children? ECS positions children as complete, having agency, and sees the early years as an important stage of lifelong development. Early childhood focuses on children from conception up to middle childhood. The precise age may differ; however, early childhood generally includes children up to age 8. Early Childhood Studies is about the ecology of childhood, recognising the range of relationships and contexts children experience from birth onwards. A key aspect of Early Childhood Studies is recognising the rights of children as active participants in their world.

A key theorist who acknowledged this was Bronfenbrenner in his ecological theory. The theory positions children with a level of independence and autonomy from birth, but emphasises the relationships that children form, initially with immediate carers, then other family members, and later more broadly through their interactions with others in the wider social environment. This is reflected throughout the five parts of the book. Starting with the individual child, the chapters explore the context of childhood and children's early development neurologically, cognitively and creatively. This is followed by an exploration of children's interactions with carers, family, peers and friends. To enable children to reach their potential, they need to be included and able to participate. This involves children interacting with an increasingly wide group of people, including multidisciplinary professions. This is explored in the third part of the book. The social environment impacts increasingly on babies and young children but what is meant by this varies according to context and culture. As a concept, 'childhood' is not static but continues to evolve and can mean different things to different people at different times. The fourth part explores and includes discussion of technology and the global context on the lives of children. The final part of the book focuses on your developing identity as a specialist in early childhood.

The book includes a number of learning features that will enable you to:

- **get to grips with the basics** through the glossary and online flashcards for key terminology and the spotlight boxes on people, policy and practice introducing you to influences in early childhood
- **learn from others** through free academic and practitioner videos on the website, and student features at the start of each chapter giving you an insight into their own experiences and how each chapter can direct your learning
- **prepare for assignments** with the further reading resources, reflection points and spotlights on research
- **relate to practice** using the case studies and action point activities to think critically about how theory applies to your practice in real life settings.

Being an effective practitioner requires individuals to question practice, learn from others, observe and think critically and, in time, develop the ability to manage and lead others. To support readers, each chapter is written to help promote this critical thought. All chapters introduce readers to key theories and discussions of the subject and then build on this by presenting more challenging concepts, ideas and practice examples to promote discussion, debate and learning. No book can cover every aspect of a subject and this text is no different. However, it introduces readers to both well-known and topical areas of study. In doing so, the overall aim is to assist readers to reflect on how they work with children and others to help each child to achieve their potential, whatever that may be.

PART 1
THE INDIVIDUAL CHILD

GO TO **https://study.sagepub.com/fitzgeraldandmaconochie** *for free access to SAGE videos on topics covered in this book*

THE EMERGENCE OF EARLY CHILDHOOD STUDIES: AN HISTORIC OVERVIEW

BY RITA WINSTONE

This chapter is an extremely interesting read. It will help you improve your knowledge and understanding of the history and philosophy of early childhood with helpful examples throughout.

The section on key theorists has improved my knowledge and I am now able to identify the impact and influence that each key theorist has had on early childhood. The chapter also includes the impact of the United Nations Convention on the Rights of the Child (UNCRC). I haven't found many other books during my studies that cover this. It has also made me reflect on my own experiences when it comes to implementing policy and where I have seen it be a success but also when I have seen it fail.

FRANCESSCA JENNINGS
BA (HONS) EARLY CHILDHOOD STUDIES
TEESSIDE UNIVERSITY

learning outcomes

By actively reading this chapter and engaging with the reading material, you will be able to:

- discuss the concept of childhoods and how this has been a fluid concept throughout history
- consider the impact and influence of Urie Bronfenbrenner and his ecological theory
- evaluate the current understanding of childhoods considering the impact of the United Nations Convention on the Rights of the Child and how this has influenced policy
- question the current philosophy, political and social stance on children and early childhoods in society today.

INTRODUCTION

This chapter positions childhood in a broad context – historically, socially and culturally – and explores the fluidity of the concept mainly within a Western European context. The aim is to help readers understand that childhood is a socially constructed concept and to appreciate that different families, groups and cultures will have different views on childhood. The chapter will explore how childhood is linked to where and how children are situated in their family context and the broader social environment. This draws on **Bronfenbrenner's ecological theory** which facilitates an understanding of the dynamics of the influences on children within families and society and the impact this has on their development and experiences. Children and childhood are considered as a holistic whole.

The chapter will also explore the emergence of the field of Early Childhood Studies, which is presented as an alternative to the dominant paradigm of developmental psychology and theories of socialisation. It considers the importance of Early Childhood Studies being a multi-disciplinary field in that it is not just educationally focused but also embraces other academic disciplines such as sociology, psychology, history, social care, health, children's geographies and social policy. This multi-disciplinary approach reflects the ecology of young children's lives in their different contexts. Within the chapter, some of the key theorists relating to our understanding of children and early childhood will be explored, including Ariès and the social construction of childhood. In addition, the chapter will critically consider the work of Bronfenbrenner and explore the impact of his work on our current understanding of children and early childhood (Bronfenbrenner, 1979).

THE PERCEPTION OF CHILDHOOD IN HISTORY AND THE FLUIDITY OF THE CONCEPT

This section presents an overview of the perception of childhood in history which demonstrates the fluidity of the notion of childhood and the movement towards the multi-disciplinary approach and the emergence of the focus on the agency of the individual child.

PLATO (428–327 BC)

Children and childhood have been viewed differently by society throughout the ages. In the time of Plato, the child was considered the responsibility of the whole community (Giardiello, 2014). Childhood was simply considered as the forerunner to engaging in full society. Children would be encouraged to play but it was perceived as functional. In this context, **anticipatory socialisation** was based on an assumption of trade. For instance, the children were encouraged to practise sword fighting if their trade was anticipated as being a soldier, and to play with clay-making bricks and moulds if they were destined to be a mason. Free play was considered unwelcome. This was not based on the fear of children learning to fight but rather on the basis that play often involves rules and, more importantly, making rules to fit the game. Again, with anticipatory socialisation in mind, this could well have led to changing society's rules – a situation not to be encouraged. There was an understanding implicit in this that society and the social bearings were a key factor in a child's development and learning. Play and work were inextricably linked. Play was purposeful and the child's future role the responsibility of the state, with childhood considered by society as the path to citizenship and support of the state (Giardiello, 2014). Since the education of children was key to citizenship, Plato advocated a control of the curriculum within education.

ARISTOTLE (384–322 BC)

Aristotle was a student of Plato, incorporating some of his ideas. However, Aristotle also advocated stages of learning, each of seven years, as he determined that education should be lifelong learning. The first stage embraced early childhood, and the responsibility for the child and their learning and development remained with the family. There was no formal education until age 7 and play was encouraged. Aristotle recognised the importance of early childhood in learning and development, and that the child's experiences during that period were key. He also identified that it was most successful when it harnessed the child's interests and talents.

QUINTILIAN (35–100 AD)

Over 200 years after Plato, Quintilian drew on the central philosophy inherent in Plato's work but extended this to his own ideas about the purpose and value of education – children need a strong foundation of education and should enjoy learning. Quintilian also had some strikingly familiar rhetoric – arguments we still hear today. He considered that observations were important as they provided an insight into the child's abilities and that teachers needed to be well-educated. However, Quintilian also cited poor parenting as an issue. Uneducated and disengaged parents could have a detrimental effect on the child (Giardiello, 2014). Importantly, this in itself suggests that the influences and responsibility for the child were shared between society and parents. The positioning of childhood was still strongly linked to education.

Throughout the early AD centuries, the dominating influences were Greek and Roman and their views on children and childhood were those of preparation for good citizenship – an expansion on the basic concept of anticipatory socialisation. Europe also emphasised the need for education, including supporting poorer children, though again this was more to do with society and advancement than a recognition of childhood. Interest re-emerged in the work of

Quintilian in the fourteenth century and other influences at that time included Martin Luther (1483–1546) and Comenius (1592–1670) who emphasised the importance of play and considered the mother as the important educator in the child's first six years.

REFORMATION AND RENAISSANCE

During the **Reformation** and **Renaissance** periods, the understanding of the nature of childhood and children took a dramatic shift in that the upbringing and education of the child became more concerned with the moral compass rather than citizenship. Children were viewed in many societies across Europe as inherently wicked. Children had to be corrected and brought to salvation. Martin Luther considered a good education to be a divine requirement. Children were entitled to an education and society should be supporting that aim. That was the duty of parents and society. However, there were significant changes to both the spiritual and cultural aspects of society. The emergence of the printing press and other industrialisation had an impact on attitudes to the understanding of children and childhood. Children were needed to be literate in order to make a contribution to society. The idea of children as adults-in-waiting prevailed. Societal needs impacted on the understanding of children's learning and development. Play was still considered vital to learning and development. Childhood was, however, simply the phase before adulthood, a precursor to adulthood rather than a separate stage.

JOHN LOCKE (1632–1704)

In the late seventeenth and early eighteenth centuries, there were changes to the way society in Europe began to consider philosophies and the way the world was viewed. This became known as the Age of Reason and this impacted on the way childhood was considered in the light of these philosophies.

John Locke believed that a child's mind was a **tabula rasa – a blank slate –** and, as such, it was important to fill children's minds with knowledge and learning. He still maintained a philosophy of play and, indeed, thought children should divert themselves and engage in their own learning provided it was not detrimental to their health and wellbeing. He prescribed a mixture of kindness and good sense in bringing up children (Ingleby et al., 2015). He argued that their experiences informed them and children needed to have a reasoned approach so that they could grow freely yet develop respect. The idea of a blank slate was passive – the child waiting to be filled up with knowledge (Waller and Swann, 2009).

JEAN-JACQUES ROUSSEAU (1712–1788)

In contrast to this view, Rousseau espoused that children would flourish given the right conditions. He argued that, given the right environment, children would learn and develop through discovery and exploration and in using their own imagination. This partly forms the basis of the **nature–nurture debate**. The debate centres upon whether children learn because of their genetic make-up or because of their environment, or indeed a combination of the two. However, for their learning and development to be simply a product of their environment, as envisaged when children were considered to be blank slates, is no longer considered credible as it poses the question of how children make sense of the world around them in order to process these environmental experiences and benefit from the learning (Ingleby et al., 2015).

There are three key ideas central to Rousseau's view of children and development. First, Rousseau believed in the primacy of feeling and the centrality of matters of the heart. In the Age of Reason in which Rousseau lived, where science and technology were key, this was a radical concept. Second, he proclaimed the basic goodness of human nature. Again, this was radical as the prevailing doctrine at that time was one of original sin. People, and therefore children, were perceived as being born wicked and needing to attain redemption. Third, he did not consider children to be imperfect adults but saw childhood as a distinct and precious period of life with its own developmental stages. These ideas have significantly influenced contemporary approaches to children and their development. Within this reasoning came the recognition of the importance of including children within the fabric of the social world (Ingleby et al., 2015).

SOME OF THE KEY FIGURES IN PIONEERING UNDERSTANDING OF CHILDREN AND EARLY CHILDHOOD

During the next century, there were many influential individuals who pioneered the understanding of children and childhood and in many cases linked these to practice. These include Friedrich Froebel (1782–1852) who considered the outdoors as a learning platform; the McMillan sisters, Rachel (1859–1917) and Margaret (1860–1931), who were social reformers; Susan Isaacs (1885–1948) (see Chapter 22) who focused on the importance of social development and the centrality of the child; and Maria Montessori (1870–1952) who developed a child-centred educational approach.

Maria Montessori was a medical doctor who worked with children in the deprived areas of Rome (Nutbrown et al., 2008). She developed her philosophy and principles for childcare based on observations of children within their own environments, and her ideas impacted on our understanding of childhood and how children learn. From her observations, she devised her 'Montessori method' which considered children by ability rather than chronological age. She was a pioneer in the field of childcare and had a huge impact on children's education. She developed an innovative approach to children's education and development in that she believed that children responded to their environment and society. The Montessori method was based on the concept that all children have potential and they should be given the freedom to explore this, which could mean learning within mixed-age groups and allowing children opportunity for independent exploration and discovery. Adults are observers whilst the child is the protagonist (Neaum, 2016).

 reflection point 1.1

Reflect on the Ideas and Philosophies of the Early Pioneers of Children and Childhood

Already, it can be seen that the concept of childhood is not a universal given. Each society and its dominant thoughts and ideas inform its approach to how children and childhood are constructed. In addition, whilst this is only a brief overview, it demonstrates that children and childhood reflect the culture of the society as well.

Reflect on some of the ideas inherent in the philosophies of the early pioneers of children and childhood. Read further on those mentioned above. Consider:

- Does society still view education as a tool for a role in adult life?

With this brief overview of historical understandings of children and childhood, it is clear that much of it was linked to education and often specifically to education in preparation for an adult role in society. It was generally viewed as a precursor to being an adult and not considered as a stage of development in its own right. The eighteenth century witnessed huge change across Europe. Advances in science brought about a belief that scientific study could be applied to further understanding and this included the study of children and childhood. This was the beginning of perceiving childhood as a distinct phase. Much of this was initially rooted in physicality and psychology. However, what was also emerging was the social construction of childhood.

The evolution of the understanding of children and childhoods also emphasises that the concept of children and childhood is not a fixed perception (Walkerdine, 2017) and varies across continents, and yet we often try to discuss this as a single concept; one where we make assumptions that we all consider children and childhood in the same light. Children experience many different understandings of childhood (Waller, 2009). The focus on childhood up to this point was also closely linked with their education – training for a place in society, rather than the more holistic approach that is evident today.

THE EMERGENCE AND DRIVING FACTORS OF THE CONCEPTS OF CHILDREN AND EARLY CHILDHOOD IN WESTERN EUROPEAN SOCIETY

PHILIPPE ARIÈS (1914–1984)

Ariès was a historian who challenged the current thinking on the concept of childhood and viewed it as a social construct. In doing so, he also challenged the idea of childhood as a universal concept (James and Prout, 1997). His book *Centuries of Childhood* (published in French in 1960 and translated into English in 1962) marked the beginning of the systematic study of the history of childhood (Lowe, 2004) and still influences historic studies of childhood today. Within the text, he contested that in medieval times the idea of childhood did not exist (Ariès, 1996). Ariès suggested that childhood, as a concept and distinct period of development, only came to be recognised in the sixteenth and seventeenth centuries. He argued that this lay in early infant mortality, where parents kept an emotional distance, and in the need for children to enter the labour market so that parents viewed them as a small adult. As the need for the child to enter the labour market so quickly receded with increasing affluence and improvements in health, the idea of childhood emerged (Lowe, 2004). Though some of Ariès' suppositions were persuasive (Lowe, 2004), they have since been contested as being based on narrow parameters

(Parker-Rees, 2015) and on the basis that evidence is weak that children were in fact treated as mini adults (Parker-Rees, 2015). In addition, Wyness (2014) notes that although the work of Ariès provides an understanding of the modern childhood, the child's voice is missing. Yet, nevertheless, his work marked the shift to a study of the historic consideration of childhood and provided a means to explore the concept of childhood as a social construct (Wyness, 2014).

By the end of the twentieth century, there was concern about the way in which children's psychology did not include a greater awareness of the impact of the social context in which a child functions. The need to consider the influences and impact of the wider social structures was acknowledged. Critique of developmental psychology led to the emergence of the social model of childhood and Bronfenbrenner's theories, as well as Vygotsky's understanding of the importance of the social impact on children's development. It also reflected the nature–nurture debate which centres on how far behaviours are learnt and how far they are a combination of genes and experience. Over time, it was acknowledged that an either/or position was too simplistic as development occurs as a combination of both (Ingleby et al., 2015). This debate links to the philosophies of John Locke who considered the mind a *tabula rasa* – a blank slate. Later theorists, including Bronfenbrenner and Vygotsky, recognised the importance and impact of children's earliest experiences. The current understanding of childhood continues to acknowledge that both nature and nurture are significant in children's growth and development. Maynard and Thomas (2004) hold that arguments around whether the biological factors or the social and cultural environmental factors are the most important, actually deflect recognition of the importance of the tension and relationship between the two influences. Indeed, it is a complex amalgamation of the two aspects that reflects the historical understandings and current perceptions of children and early childhood (Neaum, 2016).

LEV VYGOTSKY (1896–1924)

Lev Vygotsky also emphasised the importance of the social world in relation to children's learning and development. He recognised relationships with others around the child as having a direct impact on the child's learning and development. His theory of **social constructivism** was based on the concepts of a **more knowledgeable other** (MKO) and a **zone of proximal development (ZPD)**. His assertion was that a group working together could construct their knowledge to a higher degree than individuals working alone. This was, of course, dependent on the levels of interaction between members of the group. A more knowledgeable other might share their experiences and expectancies which would, in turn, promote the growth of knowledge and understanding (Waller and Swann, 2009).

THE INFLUENCE OF BRONFENBRENNER (1917–2005) AND ECOLOGICAL THEORY

Bronfenbrenner's ecological model (later named **ecological systems theory** – **EST**; see Figure 1.1) considered the impact of the environment. He developed a system based on the principle that the child was at the centre of a number of settings that influenced development. He developed terminology to define these influential layers:

- The **microsystem** is the layer of influence closest to the child. This would be the immediate environment in which the child lives, the family and the home, and care or school environment.
- The **mesosystem** considers the connections between the structures of the child's microsystem. The exosystem becomes more important as the child grows older (Gillibrand et al., 2016).
- The **exosystem** encompasses the larger social systems that would have an impact such as the neighbourhood, the extended family and the workplace of the family members.
- The **macrosystem** is embedded in the cultural values and would include the impact of government policies.
- Bronfenbrenner later added a further layer to the system: the **chronosystem,** which recognised the impact of patterns or time events in a child's life. (Christensen, 2016; Neaum, 2016)

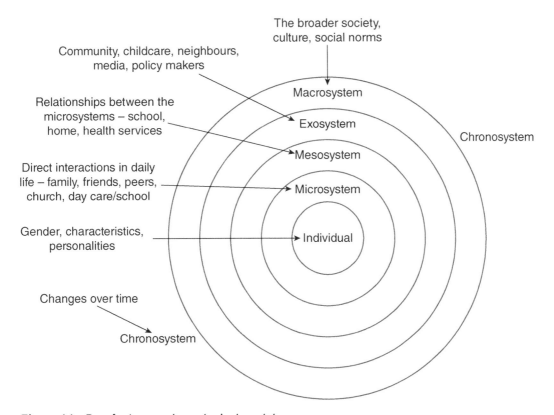

Figure 1.1 Bronfenbrenner's ecological model

Source: Diagram based on Bronfenbrenner (1979)

The impact of Bronfenbrenner's work was to reframe the understanding of children, to recognise that biological factors were subject to other influences and that social experiences were equally important (Neaum, 2016). Whilst the layers are complex, they are also bi-directional and reinforce the concept of the unique child (Ingleby et al., 2015). Bronfenbrenner also achieved a shift in the way children and childhood were studied, moving towards a more natural approach where children are studied in their own environment within natural conditions (Brendtro, 2006).

 spotlight on people 1.1

Urie Bronfenbrenner (1917–2005)

Urie Bronfenbrenner was born in Moscow, though moved to the United States as a young boy and spent his working life in America. He became a psychologist and as an academic became one of the leading scholars in developmental psychology.

Against the predominant view of child development as simply biological, Bronfenbrenner argued that the environment and experience all contributed to the development of the individual. He criticised the research of that period as being artificial and sought to promote practical studies of children in their own environment (Brendtro, 2006). He devised his theory on developmental psychology – ecological systems theory – which was first proposed in the 1970s. The principles of the ecological model were based on the child being at the centre of the model. The model acknowledges that the child affects and is affected by the settings they find themselves in. The most important setting for the child is the family. The principles recognise that the child's development is determined by their experiences in such settings. Bronfenbrenner argued that the quality of those experiences and interactions had important implications for development.

Following America's commitment to tackle poverty in the country, Bronfenbrenner was invited to discuss his theories and argued that it would be more productive to focus on the family and the environment, than poverty, as the impact would be more positive. As a result, the Head Start programme set up in the USA to try to combat the issues of poverty included a focus on outreach efforts and working within the community. As a point of comparison, a similar programme in the UK would be the Sure Start initiative.

The impact of Bronfenbrenner's work was significant. It reframed the prevailing understanding of children away from the idea that children and childhood are universal constants that could be defined and observed as if a scientific model. Instead, there was an acceptance of the more complex view of children and childhood. There was also an appreciation of the assertion that childhood was experienced in different ways by different children in different societies (Neaum, 2016).

This meant that whilst many biological factors remained similar across different societies, differences in children and childhood were linked to their social experience.

Critiques of ecological systems theory (EST)

There are, however, critiques of EST that focus on it not embracing the full extent of interaction and influence. Whilst acknowledging the benefits of the theory in providing an insight into factors that impact on growth and development, Christensen (2016) notes that it is difficult to define your own values as they are an integral part of yourself and, as such, perception of this is selective. It is hard to be yourself and see yourself.

Christensen (2016) also raises the issue of resilience, arguing that it is key to understanding an individual and their capacity to cope. The term resilience was less prevalent when EST was first postulated, but, overall, much of Bronfenbrenner's work was focused on what may now be thought of as social resilience. This is particularly interesting in light of the notion of the 'diminished child', where Ecclestone and Hayes (2009) argue that the child is being diminished by repeated concern with emotions within learning. The resilience is apparent in a sense of purpose, goals and aspirations and an aim in life that is believed to be achievable (Benard, 2004).

Benard argued that these qualities further the adaptation process and are a means to effect change. In addition, Benard (1995) considered that we are all born with an inborn capacity for resilience; that it is part of our genetic base. This means that all children can achieve and the impact of support and society is very relevant. Resilience is the tool we use to develop competence and our problem-solving thinking skills. Importantly, this suggests that interventions can be successful and that there is a need to move away from the narrow paradigm of the social world having the sole impact on learning and development (Benard, 1995).

Neal and Neal (2013) considered that nested systems do not fully reflect the complexity of the way in which the systems interact and impact on each other, and that a networked configuration or intersecting circles would more properly reflect the complexity of the interrelationships of the levels. Furthermore, Penn (2014) argued that Bronfenbrenner's ecology system was too orderly and did not reflect real life and the chaotic complexity of these interactions and impacts, and highlighted Rogoff's preposition that humans do not function in isolation; that thinking is a culturally informed activity by which we make sense of life. Therefore, experiences are determined by our cultural surroundings and this is a dynamic process (Penn, 2014).

Finally, there is also a difficulty expressed in the lack of understanding within the model of international influence, particularly in the current culture of globalisation and the impact of internationalism on society (Christensen, 2016).

 action point 1.1

Reflect on how you think your upbringing has influenced your life and your pedagogy.

Bronfenbrenner's ecological model recognises the influence and impact of the social and physical environment on the individual. Consider each of the systems outlined in the model. How do you think you have been influenced by these factors? It might be as simple as the fact you always had a story read to you at bedtime. Who read it? Did it form a bond between reader and listener? Has it influenced you in wanting to do that for others? What feelings do you attach to that experience?

Did you have an experience at school that would impact on the way you would relate to children yourself?

Try discussing some of these memories with others. Are their experiences similar? Should they be? Why might they differ? What other social influences might be impacting on the variations?

THE EMERGENCE OF A BROADER UNDERSTANDING OF CHILDHOODS

The idea that childhood is an identifiable concept is in itself problematic. At what age does childhood end? Is it a physical stage? An economic stage? A stage of innocence? It is also dependent on cultural and societal understandings (Thurtle, 2005). However, in recognising the fluidity of the concept there has been a growing emergence of a broader understanding of childhoods, and studies focus on the uniqueness of the child whilst embracing the transient understanding of childhoods. James and Prout (1997) move the discourse towards an understanding of diverse childhoods and challenge the concept of a child as waiting to be developed, rather seeing the child as an active agent in their own development.

UNITED NATIONS CONVENTION ON THE RIGHTS OF THE CHILD (UNCRC)

A significant change to the way childhood was considered came in the form of the United Nations Convention on the Rights of the Child (UNCRC) (UN, 1989), a human rights treatise for children. In the following years, 192 countries have signed up to this legal and international agreement, though this did not include the USA. The UNCRC set out 54 articles which were binding in law, for political, civil, economic and social rights for every child. They included articles that established the child's right to choose, to health and wellbeing, to be safe and to play. The UNCRC articles fall into three broad categories: rights of provision, protection and participation. The right to have a say in all matters that affect the child (one of the participation articles) was a significant step forward in recognising the child's voice. The UK signed the document in 1990 and it came into law by 1992. There was also a recognition that there are different childhoods, but children's rights remained essentially the same.

A study of childhood now recognises the voice of the child and the strength of this is cited in the Convention (Friedman, 2007). However, giving the child a participatory, active role in Childhood Studies is not going unchallenged. Hammersley (2017) contends that the idea is fraught with inconsistencies. The voice of the child could be construed as more a reflection of adult views and, in addition, giving the child a positive role should also lead to a designated responsibility. In addition, the rights of the child might well conflict with the parental right to make a decision in the best interests of the child. It is therefore important to recognise the problematic nature of the social construction of early childhood (Hammersley, 2017).

In England, the emergence of Every Child Matters (HM Treasury, 2003) at least in part reflected some of the priorities set out in the UNCRC (e.g. being healthy, safe and making a positive contribution). Importantly, part of the Every Child Matters agenda was the realisation of a degree-led workforce. It became possible to engage in Childhood Studies which, in turn, considered the focus as wider than just education, psychology or physical attainment. It merged all these disciplines and considered the social construction of childhood in a holistic embrace. The focus was the child and childhoods. Policy does not always support this emphasis, with a focus on enabling parents to enter the workforce and a vision, at times, of children as the future workforce and education not as enrichment but a narrow approach with a curriculum-driven focus on what is needed for future employment.

reflection point 1.2

Based on your reading, consider your responses to the following:

How have ideas about children and childhood evolved and changed over time?

How do the approaches discussed underpin wider societal and political constructs of childhood?

Can you identify in what ways policies take account of our knowledge of childhood (e.g. socially, emotionally and cognitively)? And those that do not?

SUMMARY

- There are multiple and diverse childhoods and no single perspective can embrace the full understanding.
- There is also the intricacy of cultural impacts and the socialisation of the child. It is difficult therefore to attain a fixed understanding of childhood.
- History has embraced many approaches and the current realisation is one that is dynamic and responsive to the social, cultural and physical environment. The work of Bronfenbrenner was seminal in emphasising the reciprocal impact of the child and their environment.
- A defining feature of the current Eurocentric philosophy of Early Childhood Studies is its multi-disciplinary approach.

 online resources

Make sure to visit https://study.sagepub.com/fitzgeraldandmaconochie for selected SAGE videos (with questions), SAGE journal articles, links to external sources and flashcards.

FURTHER READING

Christensen, J. (2016). A Critical Reflection of Bronfenbrenner's Development Ecology Model. *Problems of Education in the 21st Century*, 69(3): 22–8.

The article utilises EST to reflect on current aspects of approaches to education.

Neal, J. and Neal, Z. (2013). Nested or Networked? Future Directions for Ecological Systems Theory. *Social Development*, 22(4): 722–37.

All theories need to be considered in the context of current understanding. This article applies the work of Bronfenbrenner alongside more recent developments to think about ecological contexts.

REFERENCES

Ariès, P. (1962/1996). *Centuries of Childhood*. London: Pimlico.

Benard, B. (1995). *Fostering Resilience in Children*. ERIC Digest. [online] Available at: https://files.eric.ed.gov/fulltext/ED386327.pdf [Accessed 2 July 2018].

Benard, B. (2004). *Resiliency: What We Have Learned*. San Francisco, CA: WestEd Regional Educational Laboratory.

Brendtro, L. (2006). Voices of Pioneers: The Vision of Urie Bronfenbrenner. *Reclaiming Children and Youth*, *15*(3): 162–6.

Bronfenbrenner, U. (1979). *The Ecology of Human Development*. London: Harvard University Press.

Christensen, J. (2016). A Critical Reflection of Bronfenbrenner's Development Ecology Model. *Problems of Education in the 21st Century*, *69*(3): 22–8.

Ecclestone, K. and Hayes, D. (2009). *The Dangerous Rise of Therapeutic Education*. London: Routledge.

Friedman, R. (2007). Listening to Children in the Early Years. In: M. Wild and H. Mitchell (eds), *Early Childhood Studies*. Exeter: Learning Matters, pp. 81–94.

Giardiello, P. (2014) *Pioneers in Early Childhood Education*. London: Routledge.

Gillibrand, R., Lam, V. and O'Donnell, V. (2016). *Developmental Psychology*, 2nd edn. Harlow: Pearson Education.

Hammersley, M. (2017). Childhood Studies: A Sustainable Paradigm? *Childhood*, *24*(1): 113–27.

HM Treasury (2003). *Every Child Matters*. [online] Available at: http://webarchive.national archives.gov.uk/20130401151715/http://www.education.gov.uk/publications/eOrdering-Download/DfES10812004.pdf [Accessed 20 March 2017].

Ingleby, E., Oliver, G. and Winstone, R. (2015) *Early Childhood Studies: Enhancing Employability and Professional Practice*. London: Bloomsbury.

James, A. and Prout, A. (1997) A New Paradigm for the Sociology of Childhood? Provenance, Promise and Problems. In: A. James and A. Prout, *Constructing and Reconstructing Childhood: Contemporary Issues in the Sociological Studies of Childhood*. London: RoutledgeFalmer, pp. 7–33.

Lowe, R. (2004) Childhood through the Ages. In: T. Maynard and N. Thomas (eds), *An Introduction to Early Childhood Studies*. London: Sage, pp. 65–74.

Maynard, T. and Thomas, N. (2004) Introduction. In: T. Maynard and N. Thomas (eds), *An Introduction to Early Childhood Studies*. London: Sage, pp. 1–6.

Neal, J. and Neal, Z. (2013). Nested or Networked? Future Directions for Ecological Systems Theory. *Social Development*, *22*(4): 722–37.

Neaum, S. (2016) *Child Development for Early Childhood Students and Practitioners*, 3rd edn. Exeter: Learning Matters.

Nutbrown, C., Clough, P. and Selbie, P. (2008). *Early Childhood Education: History, Philosophy and Experience*. London: Sage.

Parker-Rees, R. (2015) Concepts of Childhood: Meeting with Difference. In R. Parker-Rees and C. Leeson (eds), *Early Childhood Studies*, 4th edn. London: Sage, pp. 191–203.

Penn, H. (2014). *Understanding Early Childhood Issues and Controversies*, 3rd edn. Maidenhead: Open University Press.

Thurtle, V. (2005). The Child in Society. In: J. Taylor and M. Woods (eds), *Early Childhood Studies: An Holistic Introduction*, 2nd edn. London: Hodder Arnold, pp. 163–84.

United Nations (UN) (1989) *United Nations Convention on the Rights of the Child (UNCRC)*. New York: UN.

Walkerdine, V. (2017). Development Psychology and the Child-centered Pedagogy. In: M. Kehily (ed.), *An Introduction to Early Childhood Studies*. Maidenhead: Open University Press.

Waller, T. (2009). Modern Childhood: Contemporary Theories and Children's Lives. In: T. Waller (ed.), *An Introduction to Early Childhood*, 3rd edn. London: Sage, pp. 2–15.

Waller, T. and Swann, R. (2009). Children's Learning. In: T. Waller (ed.), *An Introduction to Early Childhood*, 3rd edn. London: Sage: 31–46.

Wyness, M. (2014). A History of Childhood: Adult Constructs and Children's Agency. In: T. Waller and G. Davis (eds), *An Introduction to Early Childhood*, 3rd edn. London: Sage, pp. 11–26.

CHAPTER 2

THE BRAIN AND CHILDREN'S EARLY DEVELOPMENT

BY HELOISE MACONOCHIE

Being someone who is not overly informed about the different concepts of neuroscience, I appreciated that the explanation of these areas, and some of the more 'nitty-gritty' subjects, were kept simple and concise. The use of examples also help you to contextualise this complicated phenomenon so you don't feel overwhelmed and confused.

I like the chapter's holistic approach and links to children's development. It is clearly explained that neuroscience is very much an influencer that should be acknowledged alongside other developmental aspects and environmental, rather than as a separate domain. The chapter appreciates the balance of nature vs nurture and does not let one outweigh the other. However, I like how each section seems to bring focus back to the underlying role of the environment and importance of personal experience.

ELEANOR HEDLEY-DENT
BA (HONS) CHILDHOOD STUDIES
SHEFFIELD HALLAM UNIVERSITY

learning outcomes

By actively reading this chapter and engaging with the material, you will be able to:

- explain the main processes that characterise early brain development
- identify environmental factors that impact on young children's neurodevelopment
- apply neuroscience evidence to promoting children's healthy development
- discriminate between different types of plasticity
- critically evaluate the co-option of neuroscience into early childhood policy.

INTRODUCTION

This chapter outlines how the process of young children's **development**, including the developing architecture and function of the brain, is much more than a process of **maturation**. Today, researchers suggest development occurs as a complex interaction between genetic factors and the **environment** a child experiences, starting in utero and continuing throughout the lifespan (Simpkins, 2013). The brain develops faster in early childhood than at any other time (Center on the Developing Child, 2016). Advances in **neuroscience** have enabled researchers to examine how the environment and children's early experiences affect **brain development**. In spite of these advances, the integration of neuroscience into child-related disciplines such as Early Childhood Studies is only just beginning (Twardosz and Bell, 2012). Responsive caregiving coupled with a stimulating environment helps the brain to develop well, whereas adverse experiences early in life, such as chronic **stress**, can have harmful consequences for brain development, leading to potential difficulties in learning, health and behaviour. The chapter discusses the brain's 'plasticity' or ability to develop and change in response to environmental influences. Key issues such as 'experience-expectant' and 'experience-dependent' plasticity and 'critical' and 'sensitive' periods of development are considered, as well as some common 'neuromyths'. Finally, the chapter considers the co-option of neuroscience into social policy related to early childhood, early intervention and parenting, and critically examines its effects: both beneficial and misleading.

THE ROLE OF NEUROSCIENCE IN UNDERSTANDING CHILDREN'S DEVELOPMENT

Children's bodies and brains are interdependent. Decades of research and theory in the developmental sciences, and more recently in the neurosciences, have produced a wealth of knowledge about human development. Studying how children grow and develop is an important part of Early Childhood Studies, and often involves considering development from four different but interrelated domains: physical (perceptual, motor, physical wellbeing and health); cognitive (thinking, memory, language and problem solving); social and emotional (temperament, emotional regulation, attachment and peer relationships) and brain development (cellular and physiological processes coupled with environmental influences by which the brain develops). Thompson (2001) argues that scholars know considerably more about these first three domains of development than they know about brain development. This is unsurprising considering that the integration of neuroscience into the child-related disciplines such as psychology, sociology, health, education and early childhood, has only occurred since the 1990s as a result of advances in neuroimaging technologies (Twardosz and Bell, 2012). Given that **brain-imaging technology** is relatively new, our understanding of human brain development is limited. Therefore, as with all research findings, it is important that early childhood professionals treat neuroscientific assertions as provisional and open to interpretation. Nevertheless, it is also vital that we recognise the contribution of neuroscience in helping us to understand optimal environments for promoting children's healthy development.

HOW DO YOUNG CHILDREN'S BRAINS DEVELOP?

Development occurs as a complex interaction between genetic factors and the environment a child experiences, starting in-utero and continuing throughout the lifespan. The debate on whether development is the product of nature or nurture is becoming obsolete as researchers acknowledge that human development, including neurodevelopment, is shaped by both nature (**genes**) and nurture (**experience**) (Moore, 2015). The brain begins to develop soon after conception and is the only organ in the body incomplete at birth. It develops faster in early childhood than at any other time and then slows around a child's seventh birthday. During adolescence, the brain undergoes a restructuring, and then continues to develop until reaching maturity around the third decade of life. From then, the mature brain still has the capacity to adapt and change in response to experience, albeit with less flexibility than in the early years of childhood (Nagel, 2012). Since the development of children's brains and bodies is not simply a naturally unfolding process of maturation or **genetic determinism**, but is also powerfully influenced by environmental factors, it is essential that professionals and carers have some basic understanding of how early experiences affect children's developing brains. Research by neuroscientists suggests that the experiences and relationships that fill a child's first days and years, notably the first 1001 days (see Chapter 8 for discussion), have a profound impact on the developing architecture and function of the brain that can last a lifetime (Shonkoff, 2010). Genes provide a basic blueprint for how children develop, but it is these early experiences that can either enhance or diminish innate potential, laying a strong or weak foundation for learning and behaviour, as well as physical and mental health in later life (Center on the Developing Child, 2016). Children's early experiences vary. Some children receive loving, responsive care whilst others suffer abuse or neglect; some enjoy economic prosperity whilst others experience poverty. Therefore, since every child's socio-cultural context is different, it follows that although children's development may share similarities, their brains will grow differently in each of these environments.

The first environment a baby experiences is the uterus. During the in-utero period the neural tube forms, leading to the production of millions of **neurons**, which, with the aid of **glia**, then migrate to different regions of the nervous system. At this time, the brain is particularly vulnerable to the effects of alcohol, drugs, chemical toxins, malnutrition and infection (Wills et al., 2008). For example, exposure to alcohol in-utero can lead to babies being born with Foetal Alcohol Spectrum Disorders; nutritional deficiencies during pregnancy can result in neural tube defects, such as spina bifida; and babies born to women infected with the Zika virus can have severe neurological complications.

Once migrated, neurons differentiate and become specialised to assume different functions, for example vision, hearing and touch. With the assistance of **neurotransmitters**, neurons transmit information to one another through electrochemical signals across microscopic gaps called **synapses**. At birth, very few synapses have formed. However, synaptic connections occur at an astounding rate during the first three years of life in response to the young child's experiences. These connections form circuits that become the foundation of brain architecture. Consequently, the brain changes with environmental stimulation, as new synaptic connections are made and reinforced through repeated use and practice. Meanwhile, connections that are used less disappear, through a normal process of **synaptic pruning**, so that circuits become more efficient. Synpatic pruning occurs during early childhood, and then continues through adolescence and the 20s in parts of the cortex involved in higher cognitive functions. This process of creating, strengthening and discarding connections among the neurons is considered to be the foundation of learning, and is the means by which we learn, remember and adapt to new circumstances (Nagel, 2012). Neural connectivity helps to explain why, for example, sensory stimulation and physical touch are so important for babies. As Nagel (2012) argues, whenever a newborn hears, sees, touches, smells or tastes something, the brain sets about building neural connections of that experience. Repeated experiences hardwire particular neural connections. Conversely, a lack of stimuli has the potential for lifelong difficulties.

Myelination is another important process that takes place in the brain. Myelin is a fatty substance that insulates neurons and acts as a conduit for transmitting information between one neuron and another. The thicker the myelin, the greater the speed of transmission. Young children tend to process information slowly because they lack the myelin necessary for neural information to be passed quickly. Myelination begins in the sensory and motor areas of the brain – areas that receive input from the eyes, ears, mouth, nose and skin (Tierney and Nelson, 2009). Myelination advances rapidly during early childhood, seen, for example, in the difference between the unstable walking of a toddler compared to the fluid movement of a 5-year-old. Myelination continues through adolescence, progressing to regions of the brain that control higher order thinking, such as memory, perception and feelings. However, like other neuronal growth experiences, this is not simply a process of maturation since a child's experiences affect the rate and extent of myelination (Tierney and Nelson, 2009).

As the brain becomes organised or 'wired', the lower, more primitive areas of the brain, namely the **brainstem** and **midbrain**, develop first (Perry, 2006). These 'lower' regulatory areas govern the bodily functions necessary for life, such as heart rate, respiration, body temperature, appetite and sleep, and are well developed at birth. However, during the first years after birth the higher regions of the brain begin to organise to reflect the child's environment. This includes the **limbic system** and **cerebral cortex** that regulate emotion, language, **executive function** and abstract thought. Given that the brain develops from the 'bottom up', the healthy development of one area is necessary for the healthy development of the next. Bick and Nelson (2015) argue that if adequate signals are not provided for the more basic systems, then the more complex systems such as those that support emotional and cognitive function or memory cannot develop to their full potential.

WHAT DO CHILDREN NEED FOR HEALTHY BRAIN DEVELOPMENT?

Current research suggests that the primary way for children to develop to their full potential is if they experience responsive, nurturing relationships (Shonkoff, 2010). This begins with the child's parents/carers and extends to other key figures, such as relatives, neighbours and early childhood professionals. Indeed, research indicates children need nurturance and stimulation for healthy brain development (Nagel, 2012). Children are active participants in shaping their own development, together with the adults who care for them. They naturally reach out for interaction through eye contact, facial expressions, movement, gestures, sounds and words. Responsive interaction from parents/carers involves tuning in and responding to these cues. By quickly calming a distressed baby or stimulating a restless one, the parent/carer helps the infant regulate his emotions. Mirroring children's vocalisations and gestures, smiling, talking back and forth, singing and cuddling, promote trust and security. This in turn builds healthy brains, including the development of the limbic area and **prefrontal cortex**. Researchers at the Center on the Developing Child (2016) refer to this as 'serve and return' interactions, arguing that if caregivers' responses are inconsistent, inappropriate or absent the developing architecture of the brain may be disrupted and later learning, behaviour and health affected. Other positive factors impacting on young children's neurodevelopment include being sensitive to children's need for sleep and mental relaxation, attention to their health and nutritional needs, appropriate stimulation in the form of typical sensory experiences, engagement with language, opportunities to learn and play, and protection from adversity.

 case study 2.1

'Serve and Return' Interactions

Mum is in the living room; 2-year-old Jamil opens a cupboard and pulls out some plastic pots. Mum places 5-month-old Aaliyah on a blanket. Aaliyah lets out an 'AaaAAAah' and Mum replies with an 'EeeEEEeh'. This continues for a few moments until Aaliyah turns her gaze away. Mum pauses and then Aaliyah turns her head back towards Mum. Mum picks up a rattle and gently shakes it near Aaliyah's face. Aaliyah moves her hands and legs in excitement. Mum places the rattle in her daughter's hand. Jamil bangs two pots together. Mum turns around and remarks, 'You're banging pots'. She gets down on the floor next to Jamil. They bang pots together and laugh. Jamil drops his pot and reaches out for the one Mum is holding. 'You want this one now, do you?' she asks. He nods. Mum passes the pot to Jamil. Meanwhile, Aaliyah lets out a cry as she hits her head with the rattle. 'Oh, sweetie. You hurt yourself.' She picks up Aaliyah and cuddles her. 'It's alright now', she says, in a soothing tone.

1. Find examples of when:
    a. The child 'serves' with a bid for the parent's attention and the parent 'returns' with a timely and congruent response.
    b. The parent provides appropriate stimulation.

2. Give reasons for why a parent might:
   a. Miss a child's cues for attention, or signs of interest.
   b. Fail to respond in a nurturing way to a child's distress.

BIOECOLOGICAL INFLUENCES ON CHILDREN'S DEVELOPMENT

Thus far, we have considered the influence of parents/carers on children's healthy neuro-development. However, bioecological systems theory (Bronfenbrenner and Ceci, 1994) helps us to understand that development and learning are influenced not just by the gene–environment interaction that goes on in the immediate context of the child's home, but also by other, wider environments over the course of time (see Chapters 1 and 8 for further discussion). In addition to the influence of the family, proximal environments (micro/mesosystem) that can have a positive impact on children's neurodevelopment include high-quality early childhood settings as well as bi-generational Early Intervention Programmes (EIPs) that support parents/carers in caring for, stimulating and responding sensitively to their children. The Guatemalan Nutrition Intervention, the Jamaican Stimulation Trail, the Bucharest Early Intervention Project (see below) and the Nurse–Family Partnership in the USA and the UK (see Chapter 17) are examples of EIPs that have attenuated the effects of adversity on children's developing brains and bodies. At a community (exosystem) level, safe neighbourhoods, access to family planning, health care, adult education, mental health and substance abuse services can strengthen the ability of families to provide nurturing care. Finally, at a socio-political (macrosystem) level, government policies can create an enabling environment. For example, policies related to housing, employment, parental leave, immigration, poverty alleviation, free early childhood education, and coordination between sectors can all impact on parents' capacity to provide nurturing care. It is for this reason that researchers from the medical, developmental and neuroscience communities, as well as international organisations such as Unicef and the World Health Organisation, are arguing that action needs to be taken at every level to counter adversity, foster healthy brain development and promote protective influences for young children (see, for example, the 2016 *Lancet* 'Early Childhood Development' series).

 — reflection point 2.1

What role do early childhood professionals have in ensuring children have the nurturing care they need to support their brain development?

THE EFFECTS OF STRESS

Stressful experiences can be beneficial or harmful to children's developing brains. Stress responses are necessary for survival as they prepare the body to deal with threat. Scientists at the National Scientific Council on the Developing Child (2014) differentiate between three types of stress.

'Positive' stress, such as meeting new people or starting preschool, is characterised by short-term physiological responses such as brief elevations in heart rate, blood pressure and stress hormones, such as adrenalin and **cortisol**. For children who experience consistent, responsive care, these physiological effects are buffered and return to their normal baselines. The result is the development of a healthy stress system that turns on when needed and off when the stressful experience has passed. 'Tolerable' stress refers to events that have the potential to disrupt children's brain architecture, such as bereavement, divorce, natural disasters or injury. Although these situations are serious, if the activation of the stress response is time-limited and buffered by supportive relationships, these stressors will not cause lasting damage to the brain.

By contrast, 'toxic' stress refers to strong and extended activation of the stress response without the buffering presence of a supportive adult. Risk factors for toxic stress include the sustained absence of 'serve and return' interactions, chronic neglect and abuse (see Chapter 13 for further discussion), enduring parental mental illness or substance abuse, exposure to family violence or war, extreme poverty, and a combination of these factors. When cortisol levels remain elevated over long periods of time, it can literally be toxic to brain architecture. This can affect myelination and lead to reduced volume in the **hippocampus**, **cerebellum** and prefrontal cortex, causing difficulties in learning, memory and executive functioning. Toxic stress can have long-term effects too, increasing susceptibility to ill health in adulthood such as cardiovascular disease, **diabetes** and mental health difficulties. When cortisol levels remain high for prolonged periods, the brain can become less sensitive to its effects, such that it becomes harder for the stress response to 'shut down'. Behaviourally, this can result in hyperarousal of the stress response system, where children can be highly sensitive to situations others may find non-threatening, and ready to respond with a 'fight or flight' reaction. While toxic stress has a deleterious influence on children's brains, EIPs that support responsive parent–child interactions, coupled with prevention efforts that promote parental mental health and target the causes of stress, have been found to mitigate some of the long-term effects on neural structure and function (Thompson, 2014). This is due to the brain's plasticity.

 action point 2.1

Public health campaigns such as 'Change for Life' and 'Smokefree' increase societal awareness of healthy lifestyle choices. Create a list of possible public health campaigns that could help prevent prenatal and postnatal neurotoxic exposure and thereby protect children's early brain development.

PLASTICITY AND EARLY EXPERIENCES

Plasticity refers to the brain's capacity to change its structure in response to experience by reorganising neural pathways in the brain. Neuroplasticity occurs throughout the lifespan, although it is greatest early in life and tends to decrease with age. Wills at al. (2008) argue that since the brain is plastic it is highly adaptable and can be influenced by positive experiences such as responsive caregiving, appropriate sensory stimulation and good nutrition. However, this plasticity means it is also vulnerable to negative experiences such as sensory deprivation, stress and malnutrition. Greenough, Black and Wallace (1987) identify two types of plasticity: 'experience-expectant' and 'experience-dependent'. Both types of plasticity occur concurrently until early adulthood, with development being driven more strongly by experience-expectant processes, and learning by experience-dependent processes (Galvan, 2010).

Experience-expectant development is associated with the concept of sensitive periods and is premised on the idea that the brain 'expects' typical sensory inputs from the environment at particular times in order to hardwire for particular capacities. This includes patterned light, sound, language, opportunities to move and manipulate objects and responsive carers. Each of these inputs are (or should be) common to all members of the species. Therefore, providing the infant receives appropriate care, experience-expectant development should occur naturally. However, if children fail to receive these types of stimulation during sensitive periods of development then brain growth can be impaired, particularly in the areas of vision, hearing, language and responses to social cues (National Scientific Council on the Developing Child, 2007). For example, if a baby is deprived of patterned light during the first year of life, perhaps as a result of cataracts that are not removed early enough, those parts of the brain responsible for vision will shut down, synapses will die off and function may be lost permanently. Similarly, if an infant experiences socio-emotional deprivation where they either have no primary carer, as in the case of the Romanian orphans (see Spotlight on Research 2.1), or carers who are unresponsive or threatening, then the attachment process is disrupted and the child's ability to form healthy relationships later in life may be impaired. Bick and Nelson (2015) posit that the majority of sensitive periods occur during early childhood. This makes the input received (or not received) particularly during the first three years critical for ongoing development.

Experience-expectant experiences *must* happen in order for certain areas of the brain to develop, and in most cases they do, barring highly aberrant conditions. However, experience-dependent experiences *might* happen depending on the unique experiences an individual has. The neural connections that are established depend entirely on the quality of the environmental input. For example, if a young child is raised in a vocabulary-rich environment then her language may be more developed than a child who is raised in a more restricted language environment. Experience-expectant plasticity underlies our ability to learn, remember and modify our behaviour. Skills that are developed through repetition and practice, such as learning to read or play a musical instrument, are examples of experience-dependent plasticity. Furthermore, experience-dependent plasticity, although strongest during childhood, is not associated with sensitive periods but occurs throughout life. The same process applies to negative experiences. As Glaser (2014) suggests, if a child is exposed to a great deal of aggression, then the part of the brain that is learning to respond to aggression will develop well, whereas the areas of the brain that respond to positive affection will develop less well. Therefore, since experiences are specific to the individual, every brain is wired differently. However, whilst the brain is adaptive to maltreating environments, because of plasticity this is not entirely determinative. The good news is that plasticity means the brain can recover from maltreatment or compensate for damage to some extent if the individual goes on to experience a supportive environment. This is especially the case early in life when development is most plastic and responsive to stimulation.

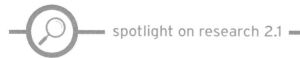

The Bucharest Early Intervention Project (BEIP)

Beginning in 2000, BEIP is a longitudinal study of children abandoned at birth and placed in state-run orphanages in Bucharest, Romania. These children experienced severe psycho-social deprivation due to low adult–child ratios, unresponsive care and a lack of sensory, cognitive and linguistic stimulation (Nelson et al., 2014). The research sought to examine the effects of early institutionalisation on brain development, and to study the impact of high-quality foster care as an intervention for institutional care. A baseline assessment of 136 infants was conducted and then half the children (aged 5–31 months) were randomly assigned to foster care, whilst the other half remained in institutional care. A sample of 72 never-institutionalised children was recruited as an in-country comparison group. Children have been seen for follow-up assessments at 30, 42 and 54 months, 8 years, 12 years and 16 years.

As reported by Nelson et al. (2014), the study found that early institutionalisation leads to profound difficulties in cognition and language development, attachment, brain activity and structure, high incidences of psychiatric disorders and impairment. However, children assigned to foster care show improvements in cognitive function, language and socio-emotional development. In terms of brain activity, previously institutionalised children who were placed in foster care before the age of 2 show electroencephalogram (EEG) activity (electrical activity in the brain) that resembles the never-institutionalised children, whereas children placed after 2 years look virtually identical to currently institutionalised children. This would suggest that there are sensitive periods for regulating recovery. That is, the earlier an institutionalised child is placed into responsive family settings, the better the recovery. Indeed, for brain activity and attachment, children placed in foster care prior to 24 months had significantly better outcomes than children placed after 24 months. Thus, nurturing parent–child relationships can attenuate the effects of adversity, particularly if this occurs before brain processes become entrenched and in turn harder to rewire (Tierney and Nelson, 2009). Simply put, intervention that occurs as early as possible is likely to lead to the healthiest outcomes in the long term.

NEUROMYTHS

The notion of plasticity and particularly the concept of 'sensitive' or 'critical' periods have been widely misinterpreted, giving rise to the neuromyth that brain development is effectively closed by the age of 3. This can lead to a sense of determinism: that the first three years determine the rest of life. Furthermore, parents can feel burdened with guilt if they fail to make the most of these 'critical windows of opportunity' for learning. The issue at stake here is an oversimplification of research findings and confusion between experience-expectant and experience-dependent plasticity. No evidence exists of a sensitive period for experience-dependent plasticity. Indeed, experience-dependent plasticity occurs throughout life. So, although the general principle 'the earlier the better' applies for experience-expectant processes, such as some aspects of emotional development and the ability to see and hear effectively, 'the window of opportunity for most domains of development remains open far beyond age 3, and we remain capable of learning ways to 'work around' earlier impacts well into the adult years' (Center on the Developing Child, 2016: 16).

Another neuromyth arising from this misunderstanding of learning windows is the idea that parents/carers need to provide 'enriching experiences' that train and stimulate young children's brains. An example of this involves playing Mozart sonatas or 'Baby Einstein' videos to babies in an effort to boost their cognitive function. 'Brain-based' toys and educational programmes such as 'Brain Gym' are other examples of 'enrichment activities', in which it is hoped that extra stimulation will lead to increased synaptic connections. However, there is little evidence that special enrichment activities promote advanced development, beyond that of the everyday sensory inputs and learning experiences a child usually receives within the context of responsive relationships (Shonkoff, 2010; Nagel, 2012).

THE CO-OPTION OF NEUROSCIENCE INTO POLICY

Shonkoff and Levitt (2010) argue that early childhood policy and practice have much to gain from advances in neuroscience. Brain research explains the causes, mechanisms and functional states of adverse brain development outcomes (the 'Why'). Early childhood professionals and the public policy community can take these insights to develop more effective approaches to prevention and intervention (the 'What' and the 'How'). However, it is also clear that neuro-scientific knowledge is at an early and provisional stage, and whilst 'neuroscientists may know the limits of their research, such caveats are not what policymakers and proselytisers wish to hear' (Wastell and White, 2012: 407–8). Consequently, some findings have been popularised, misrepresented and co-opted to justify particular strategies. For example, Allen's (2011) Early Intervention report to the UK government displays the powerful image of a brain scan of a 'normal child' compared with that of a 'severely neglected child'. There is no explanation of what 'normal' means and very little information about the research methodology, except that this was a case of 'extreme neglect' in a Romanian orphanage. Whilst commendable for advancing an agenda of early intervention for disadvantaged children, it seems that neuroscience is being drawn upon for its persuasive value rather than its explanatory capacity (Edwards et al., 2015).

Misinterpretations can easily translate into policy objectives, with implications for early childhood practice. For example, Twardosz (2012) argues that the 'critical' window of the first three years creates a 'now or never' imperative that portrays parents and teachers in a race against time so that synapses are not lost. Furthermore, a focus on early childhood risks missing children who would benefit from help later in their lives. Caution also needs to be exercised when applying neuroscience to parenting policies. An emphasis on parents as the sole providers of nurturing care, without a concomitant focus on alleviating the structural conditions that cause stress in families, such as socio-economic disadvantage, can lead to policies that pathologise parents. Burman's (2007) suggestion to adopt a critical approach to developmental research that has normative and moral assumptions hidden in it is apposite here.

In spite of this, neuroscientific findings have led to important changes in thinking, practice and policy that have had beneficial effects for young children. For example, there is greater appreciation for the role of experience in children's brain development, which has helped to dispel the belief that how the brain develops depends on the genes you are born with. An understanding that biology is not destiny underscores the significant role early childhood professionals play in supporting children and their families. We now have important evidence that demonstrates the role environmental factors such as nutrition, nurturing care and stimulation play in shaping children's development. Indeed, neuroscientific findings have been used to improve outcomes in children's learning and behaviour. For example, research studies such as the BEIP have led to policy changes that prohibit the institutionalisation of children under the age of 2, and helped create more government-sponsored foster care in Romania. Moreover, neuroscientific evidence used in combination with empirical data from a number of evaluations of successful EIPs, has propelled an increased global commitment to early childhood development, as seen in the 2030 Sustainable Development Goals (see Chapter 18). Undoubtedly, the co-option of neuroscience into early childhood policy is set to continue. It is up to parents, early childhood students, professionals and policy-makers to critically examine the effects of this, which can be both beneficial and unhelpful for young children and their families.

SUMMARY

- Development occurs as a complex interaction between genetic factors and the environment a child experiences. Brain development processes include neural development and migration, myelination, synaptic formation and pruning.
- Responsive, nurturing care from parents/carers is the principal factor in promoting young children's healthy brain development. Other positive environmental factors include protection from toxins, attention to children's prenatal and postnatal health, proper nutrition, typical sensory experiences, engagement with language, and opportunities to learn and play.
- One of the ways early childhood professionals can apply evidence from neuroscience to promote children's healthy brain development is by engaging in positive 'serve and return' interactions with children and supporting parents/carers to do the same.
- Plasticity refers to the brain's capacity to change its structure in response to experience: both positive and negative. Development tends to be driven by experience-expectant processes and learning by experience-dependent processes.
- Neuroscience is a field in its infancy. It can be easily misinterpreted, leading to 'neuromyths'. Neuroscience can also be co-opted to support policy agendas. This can have beneficial as well as misleading effects.

 online resources

Make sure to visit https://study.sagepub.com/fitzgeraldandmaconochie for selected SAGE videos (with questions), SAGE journal articles, links to external sources and flashcards.

FURTHER READING

Center on the Developing Child at Harvard Site (2017). [online] Available at: http://developing child.harvard.edu [Accessed 9 March 2017].

This website synthesises interdisciplinary research findings on children's brain development. It contains research reports and accessible multimedia resources such as short videos and interactive modules.

Conkbayir, M. (2017). *Early Childhood and Neuroscience: Theory, Research and Implications for Practice*. London: Bloomsbury.

This book draws on psychological theory and neuroscience to provide an overview of early childhood development and its application to policy and practice.

REFERENCES

Allen, G. (2011). *Early Intervention: Next Steps*. London: Cabinet Office.

Bick, J. and Nelson, C. A. (2015). Early Adverse Experiences: What Does the Latest Brain Research Tell Us? In: *A Good Start: Advances in Early Childhood Development*. The Hague: Bernard Van Leer Foundation, pp. 10–13.

Bronfenbrenner, U. and Ceci, S. J. (1994). Nature–Nurture Reconceptualized in Developmental Perspective: A Bioecological Model. *Psychological Review*, 101(4): 568–86.

Burman, E. (2007). *Deconstructing Developmental Psychology*. Hove: Routledge.

Center on the Developing Child (2016). *From Best Practices to Breakthrough Impacts: A Science-Based Approach to Building a More Promising Future for Young Children and Families*. [online] Available at: http://developingchild.harvard.edu/resources [Accessed 9 March 2017].

Edwards, R., Gillies, V. and Horsley, N. (2015). Brain Science and Early Years Policy: Hopeful Ethos or Cruel Optimism? *Critical Social Policy*, 35(2): 167–87.

Galvan, A. (2010). Neural Plasticity of Development and Learning. *Human Brain Mapping*, 31(6): 879–90.

Glaser, D. (2014). The Effects of Child Maltreatment on the Developing Brain. *Medico-Legal Journal*, 82(3): 97–111.

Greenough, W. T., Black, J. E. and Wallace, C. S. (1987). Experience and Brain Development. *Child Development*, 58(3): 539–59.

Lancet, The (2016). *Advancing Early Childhood Development: From Science to Scale*. [online] Available at: www.thelancet.com/series/ECD2016 [Accessed 9 March 2017].

Moore, D. S. (2015). *The Developing Genome: An Introduction to Behavioral Epigenetics*. Oxford: Oxford University Press.

Nagel, M. C. (2012). *In the Beginning: The Brain, Early Development and Learning*. Camberwell: ACER Press.

National Scientific Council on the Developing Child (2007). *The Timing and Quality of Early Experiences Combine to Shape Brain Architecture: Working Paper 5*. [online] Available at: http://developingchild.harvard.edu/resources [Accessed 9 March 2017].

National Scientific Council on the Developing Child (2014). *Excessive Stress Disrupts the Architecture of the Developing Brain: Working Paper 3*. [online] Available at: http://developing child.harvard.edu/resources [Accessed 9 March 2017].

Nelson, A. C., Fox, N. A. and Zeanah, C. H. (2014). *Romania's Abandoned Children: Deprivation, Brain Development and the Struggle for Recovery*. Cambridge, MA: Harvard University Press.

Perry, B. D. (2006). Applying Principles of Neurodevelopment to Clinical Work with Maltreated and Traumatized Children. In: N. Boyd Webb (ed.), *Working with Traumatized Youth in Child Welfare*. New York: The Guildford Press, pp. 27–52.

Shonkoff, J. P. (2010). Building a New Biodevelopmental Framework to Guide the Future of Early Childhood Policy. *Child Development*, 81(1): 357–67.

Shonkoff, J. and Levitt, P. (2010). Neuroscience and the Future of Early Childhood Policy: Moving from Why to What and How. *Neuron*, 67(5): 689–91.

Simpkins, C. A. (2013). Brain Development through the Life Span. In: C. A. Simpkins and A. M. Simpkins (eds), *Neuroscience for Clinicians: Evidence, Models and Practice*. New York: Springer, pp. 151–64.

Thompson, R. A. (2001). Development in the First Years of Life. *Future of Children*, 11(1): 21–33.

Thompson, R. A. (2014). Stress and Child Development. *Future of Children*, 24(1): 41–59.

Tierney, A. L. and Nelson, C. A. (2009). Brain Development and the Role of Experience in the Early Years. *Zero to Three*, 30(2): 9–13.

Twardosz, S. (2012). Effects of Experience on the Brain: The Role of Neuroscience in Early Development and Education. *Early Education and Development*, 23(1): 96–119.

Twardosz, S. and Bell, M. (2012). Introduction to the Special Issue on Neuroscience Perspectives on Early Development and Education. *Early Education and Development*, 23(1): 1–3.

Wastell, D. and White, S. (2012). Blinded by Neuroscience: Social Policy, the Family and the Infant Brain. *Families, Relationships and Societies*, 1(3): 397–414.

Wills, K. E., Gilkerson, L. and Klein, R. (2008). Building the Brain. In: L. Gilkerson and R. Klein (eds), *Early Development and the Brain*. Washington, DC: Zero to Three, pp. 1–57.

CHILDREN AS THINKERS: PHILOSOPHY FOR CHILDREN

BY FUFY DEMISSIE

The chapter is written in a way that it is easy to understand.

The way the different theories were interpreted and linked to how children think has given me a more in-depth understanding. I found the way Vygotsky's and Piaget's theories were linked to children's thinking particularly helpful and can confidently use these ideas in my future study.

Whether you are a nursery nurse or a teacher, critical thinking is an essential skill in the observation of children to make sense of what we see children do, say or react to. I really liked how the learning features in the chapter help you develop your critical skills and get a clearer understanding of the topic. The further reading section also has great additional articles to expand your knowledge.

BUKOLA OYELADE
BA (HONS) EARLY CHILDHOOD STUDIES
UNIVERSITY OF EAST LONDON

learning outcomes

By actively reading this chapter and engaging with the material, you will be able to:

- identify the links between self-regulation and critical and creative thinking
- compare pedagogical approaches to promote critical and creative thinking
- appraise the role of the adult in promoting critical and creative thinking.

INTRODUCTION

The topic of young children's thinking is a vast and well-researched area of early childhood education. This chapter draws on some of these key ideas and findings to examine the characteristics of, and pedagogies for, creative and critical thinking. After a brief survey of some of the key theories and perspectives, the chapter outlines the main features of creative and critical thinking, their role in early childhood education, the strategies used to promote them and the ways in which a philosophical approach can strengthen and extend the educator's role.

THEORIES AND PERSPECTIVES ON YOUNG CHILDREN'S THINKING

Thinking is a mental act used by human beings to make sense of, and act on, their environment. It involves processes such as perception, memory and reasoning. Through recent work in developmental psychology and Piaget's and others' detailed observations, we have a good understanding of how young children's thinking develops. Piaget's theory of young children's intellectual (**cognitive**) development has been particularly influential. He argued that children build **schemas** or understandings about the world based on their play and interactions with the environment. In the sensori-motor (0–2 years) stage, they learn as they act on the physical world (e.g. repeatedly pushing objects off a table, or putting toys in their mouths), and in the pre-operational stage (2–7 years) they begin to think in images and symbols and engage in symbolic play, before they gradually start to develop their logical and abstract thinking in the concrete operational (7–11 years) and formal operational stage (11+ years). This process of change and development occurs through the twin processes of **assimilation** (integrating new experiences) and **accommodation** (altering schema/concepts about the world), until **equilibrium** is reached (Piaget, 1936/1963).

In contrast, Piaget's contemporary Vygotsky argued that age doesn't necessarily determine how children think. Instead, interactions with adults can extend their actual capacity for thinking to surpass age-related expectations. Research by Athey (1990) and Nutbrown (1994) has shown that familiar and relevant contexts and adult interactions can influence the levels of children's thinking. Similarly, when Hughes adapted Piaget's three mountains experiment (an attempt to demonstrate 4-year-olds' **egocentricity**) he found that in meaningful and familiar contexts, 4-year-olds showed non-egocentric behaviours (Donaldson, 1978/1987).

Recent research in developmental psychology gives further insight into the nature of and types of thinking that constitute young children's **cognitive development**. In particular, the concept of **self-regulation** has been important for early childhood educators (Whitebread, 2012). Self-regulation is the ability to monitor our learning, recognise our misconceptions and mistakes and know how to address or change them. The process of reflecting on thinking is also known as **metacognitive awareness**. Nelson and Narens' model identifies two levels of metacognition (1990). The 'object' level is where the thinking occurs (e.g. working out sums), whilst the 'meta' level is the process of 'thinking about our thinking' (i.e. reflecting on whether we achieved our goals, used the best strategy or made any avoidable mistakes). Depending on the success of the action, the process of self-monitoring (meta-level thinking) may lead, in the future, to self-regulating behaviour so that alternative approaches to working out the sum may be used.

 spotlight on research 3.1

Whitebread and Colleagues (2007)

In one two-year longitudinal study, Whitebread and his colleagues (2007) examined the meta-cognitive and self-regulatory ability of 400 3–5-year-olds; 32 educators were involved, chosen because of their expertise and willingness to participate in the study. The observational study focused on formal or informal peer-tutoring activities, and collaborative activities such as joint problem-solving, playing games, re-enacting stories or other kinds of imaginative play. The children worked alone, in small groups and with or without adults. The activities were video recorded and analysed using the following categories: metacognitive knowledge (of the task and personal factors affecting their performance), metacognitive regulation (such as monitoring, planning) and emotional regulation (monitoring and control of learners' emotions during task). From an initial sample of 582 events that suggested evidence of metacognitive behaviours (such as planning, monitoring, evaluation), 60 were selected for a detailed analysis using the analytical model above.

The highest levels of metacognition and regulation were evident when children worked in pairs or in groups rather than individually. Examples of regulatory behaviours included monitoring others' behaviour: 'No ... you can't go until the light is green'; attempts at guiding others' actions as well as non-verbal behaviours used to draw others' attention to the task in hand and to suggest possible solutions. The authors concluded that, in contrast to popular views, young children are 'capable of meta-cognitive and self-regulatory behaviours' (p. 15). More specifically, they found evidence of high levels of metacognitive activity in collaborative contexts with little adult involvement. Nonetheless, they also argue that further research is needed into different types of adult involvement to examine whether some types of intervention are more likely to facilitate high levels of metacognitive activity.

Self-regulating behaviours, such as delayed gratification and the associated thinking skills, are widely considered to be associated with enabling learning behaviours such as independence, positive relationships and self-confidence (Whitebread, 2012). Whitebread et al.'s (2007) study did not show the positive impact of adults on metacognitive activity. However, the EPPE study (Sylva et al., 2004) has shown that educators who engage children in shared sustained thinking have a significant impact on children's learning. Regardless, the role of the adult is significant, whether in terms of providing an enabling environment (such as collaborative tasks) or in the skilful use of language to extend and deepen children's learning. In the next section, we look at two types of thinking (creative and critical) that are considered to be important characteristics of self-regulating learners.

 reflection point 3.1

Focus on your reading so far (or on another activity you have recently undertaken or regularly do) and reflect on the thought processes that accompanied the task:

- What was the 'object' level, i.e. what did you think about?
- Focusing on the 'meta' level, did you have any specific aims (e.g. to highlight the key points) and did you achieve them?

CRITICAL AND CREATIVE THINKING IN EARLY CHILDHOOD

There is an emerging consensus, in western contexts at least, that those who can make links and connections between their learning (think creatively) and are able to evaluate and appraise their experiences (think critically) learn more deeply and more meaningfully (Veenman et al., 2004; Wang et al., 1990; Whitebread and Pino Pasternak, 2010). Critical and creative thinking have distinctive features. First, they are ways of thinking that are not subject/curriculum specific, and involve specific skills (evaluating, problem solving) as well as dispositional aspects (curiosity, open-mindedness). Moreover, they are often seen as good preparation for dealing with and living in an uncertain and complex world (Craft, 2002). In the early childhood classroom, critical and creative thinking have a more immediate relevance as they are natural characteristics of a play-based learning environment. In the following section, I summarise the key aspects of creative and critical thinking, their place in a range of early childhood curricula and the strengths/limitations of a range of pedagogical approaches (such as Shared Sustained Thinking and Forest School).

CRITICAL THINKING

Critical thinking is a contested concept with different views about its definition and key characteristics (Ennis, 1996). It is generally seen as a form of reflective thinking that requires skills in appraising/evaluating information to make a judgement or a decision. As suggested already, aspects of critical thinking (in the broadest sense at least) are needed to make sense of, and respond to, the things that we hear, see, smell, touch and feel. Thus, good critical thinkers are able to identify problems, decide, infer (through deducing, judging and explaining), consider, reason and predict (Ennis, 1996; Lipman, 2003).

The early years setting is ideally set up to facilitate learning through critical and creative thinking. In the water tray, sand pit or the wooden block area, children are constantly engaged in evaluating, predicting and revising their schemas about how objects and materials behave in different contexts. It is a learning environment that has changed little since Robert Owen's (1777) early infant schools and Frobel's kindergartens (1852). Both recognised and promoted the idea that the best learning happens when young children are given the opportunity to experiment with materials and make sense of their experiences. The same philosophy is also evident in Montessori nurseries, where children are encouraged to learn by experimenting and investigating materials and resources within a carefully structured environment (Giardiello, 2013). Although the early pioneers did not explicitly advocate critical thinking, they actively promoted the type of environment that nurtured children's evaluation, prediction and **inference** skills.

CREATIVE THINKING

Creativity is traditionally associated with individuals' ability to create unique products/outcomes, such as artwork, musical lyrics/compositions or structures (Craft, 2002). In the early childhood curriculum, it is fostered through music, drama/movement and art. But, more recently, creativity is also being seen as a process or way of thinking. Creative thinking is a meaning-making process that involves imaginative thinking or 'possibility thinking' that can be applied in any context to generate possibilities and illuminate new connections and understandings. According to Craft, its key features are posing questions, play, immersion (children's deep involvement), innovation (connections between ideas), risk taking, being imaginative and self-determination (Craft, 2002; Wegerif et al., 2015).

Similar to critical thinking, creative thinking also plays an important role in young children's meaning-making process (Robson et al., 2012). Their innate curiosity leads them to ask 'what if?' questions that generate ideas, help find new ways to do things and help them make links and notice patterns in their experiences. From their imaginative play with words, sounds, rhymes and objects, young children experiment and investigate to make sense of their world.

CRITICAL AND CREATIVE THINKING

Critical and creative thinking emphasise different parts of the thinking process. The former (critical) is the reflective and evaluative aspect, the latter (creative) the generator of playful ideas and possibilities (Nickerson, 1999). However, these ways of thinking are also inter-connected. For example, constructing a tower with wooden bricks is likely to involve both creative (*what if I use this brick instead of the other?*) and critical thinking (*which one is the best shape, least likely to fall down?*). Moreover, both arise from, and are driven by, curiosity and enquiry. It is through asking 'what?', 'why?' and 'how?' that we are able to evaluate, infer and predict, and through 'what if?' questions that we can find connections between ideas or consider different ways of approaching a problem.

Creative and critical thinking are similarly affected by different curriculum expectations and policy contexts. For example, in England, we see contradictory expectations for 0–5- and 5–8-year-olds. Whilst educators' practice in nurseries is largely informed by a play-based **pedagogy** that champions creative and critical thinking, the over-5s are increasingly taught in formal contexts with little room for play and exploration. In contrast, in Scandinavian countries (where formal schooling starts at age 6/7), young children continue to learn in play-based contexts, whilst Chinese early childhood settings adopt a more formal and structured curricula where critical and creative thinking are less prominent. These differences show that the early childhood curriculum is a **social construction**, where views about children and what they should learn are reflected in curricula, pedagogy and policy.

reflection point 3.2

From your own everyday experience, recall an example of when you utilised critical and/or creative thinking:

- How was the experience similar/different to the examples described above?
- What do you think are the challenges in using these thinking approaches in early childhood contexts?

THE THINKING CHILD IN EARLY YEARS CURRICULA

Early educationalists did not always agree about the aims and purposes of educating young children. John Locke (1632–1704) argued that schooling should train young children to think and reason, whilst, for Rousseau, formal education had little relevance for the youngest children (Giardiello, 2013). Through the influence of Piaget's and Vygotsky's work, however, thinking is now a key part of many early childhood curricula. In the following are included summaries of early childhood curricula in relation to critical and creative thinking.

The Reggio Emilia curriculum is an early childhood programme for 0–6-year-olds that is based on a view of children as capable and competent, and whose ideas are highly valued. The creative arts are seen as an important context for developing children's thinking (through work with artists and provision of the Art Room). In addition, through project-based work children's interests and problems and questions form the basis of teaching and learning activities. The 'pedagogista' (educator) is a co-enquirer and co-constructor who also scaffolds the children's learning by documenting it and providing the appropriate resources and learning environments (Malaguzzi, 1993).

Early Years Foundation Stage (EYFS): England's EYFS is a play-based curriculum for the 0–5 age range that outlines the early learning goals for seven areas of learning. In its latest version (DfE, 2017), it champions critical and creative thinking as characteristics of effective learning and as aspects that 'underpin learning and development across all areas'. According to the EYFS, children learn most effectively when they are learning actively, and thinking critically and reflectively about their choices and experiences.

High Scope: this approach originated in the USA and has been highly influential. It is a pedagogy for 3–6-year-olds that aims to cultivate the self-regulating learner. Through the framework of 'plan-do-review', children are encouraged to plan their daily activities, reflect on what they learn and plan the next stages of their learning (Schweinhart and Weikart, 1993).

THE ENGLISH NATIONAL CURRICULUM 5–7

This is a statutory document that specifies the knowledge and skills that 5–7-year-olds must gain in maths, English, science, music, computing, geography, history and physical education. Unlike the EYFS, it does not state how children learn best, or suggest specific pedagogies or approaches. Nonetheless, recent curriculum changes appear to put a much higher emphasis on reasoning in the Mathematics curriculum (DfE, 2015).

 reflection point 3.3

- Can a 'creative' approach to learning in early childhood education co-exist with a formal curriculum such as the National Curriculum? Jot down possible reasons for and against.
- Based on what you have read so far about critical and creative thinking, can you see any relevance/significance for music, geography or history in the curriculum?

PEDAGOGIES FOR CRITICAL AND CREATIVE THINKING

Early childhood educators have used a range of approaches to nurture and promote young children's thinking. The following section outlines their key aspects and in some cases provides relevant research.

Resourcing the learning environment: Planning the physical environment to enhance children's learning has always been a key part of early childhood education. To promote thinking and enquiry, educators provide carefully selected resources such as **treasure baskets** and sensory artefacts, role-play areas, outdoor resources, mark making, and creative areas and construction spaces. Broadhead and Burt's influential (2012) work on **playful pedagogies** and the learning environment showed how open-ended resources with no pre-determined purpose (such as empty cardboard boxes, wooden blocks and milk crates) improve the quality and depth of children's play and engagement.

Broadhead and Burt's (2012) one-year study in a primary school in the north of England investigated the impact of open-ended play on young children's learning and development. The project involved a lead researcher and the teachers at the school. Through interviews and video recordings (that both teachers and children watched and discussed), they gathered data about the staff's experience of setting up an outdoor space stocked with open-ended resources such as boxes and crates rather than traditional outdoor toys. The children created flexible spaces (the 'whatever you want it to be places') where they began to take a lead in their learning. This led to staff valuing these type of resources as the children began to engage in deeper and more immersive play characterised by continual 'problem solving and problem setting' (Broadhead and Burt, 2012).

Playing in the woods: Until recently (in the UK context at least), the concept that children could learn from building fires, willow structures and outdoor cooking would have seemed a strange idea. Yet, the Forest School approach, an idea originating from Scandinavian countries, is gaining in popularity. Children visit outdoor woodland areas where they climb trees and play in the mud and streams to explore and engage with the natural world. Its underlying philosophy is supported by the 'loose parts theory' (Nicholson, 1971). Loose parts theory proposes that the degree of flexibility in the learning/play environment affects children's play and their thinking. In structured and fully finished environments (such as home corners), children are less likely to engage in critical and creative thinking because they already know the limits and possibilities of the play resources. In contrast, unpredictable environments with open-ended resources are likely to lead to richer play and more flexible thinking (Broadhead and Burt, 2012).

Thinking with others: During 'Sustained Shared Thinking' (SST), two or more individuals work together in an intellectual way to solve a problem, clarify a concept and evaluate an activity to develop and extend understanding (Siraj-Blatchford et al., 2002). SST is a pedagogy strongly influenced by Vygotsky's view that the educator can extend young children's capacity for thinking. Through open questions that encourage dialogue, educators facilitate thinking by focusing on children's genuine interests and adopting a collaborative rather than a didactic approach. Examples of open questions include recapping: 'so you think that…'; inviting children to elaborate: 'tell me more'; offering own experience: 'I like to cook as well', and so on. Through use of these types of questions, the unexpected discovery of a spider, for example, or a dilemma or problem in the classroom can become ideal contexts for sustained shared thinking episodes.

Solving the problem: Thinking Actively in a Social Context (TASC) is a problem-solving framework that is used with older children (5–8-year-olds). It encourages children to engage in a systematic problem-solving approach that is similar to standard design protocols. For example, if the task is to build a LEGO car, first they gather their ideas (what do we know?), then outline aims, generate ideas, decide on the best idea, implement the plan, evaluate, communicate their findings and reflect on what they learnt in a presentation to their peers (Wallace, 1993).

 reflection point 3.4

Consider the different ways educators support critical and creative thinking:

- What similarities and differences do you notice between them?
- To what extent did your early educational/growing up experiences encourage risk taking, open-ended resources or adults who interacted with you as equals?

CRITICAL PERSPECTIVES ON PEDAGOGIES FOR CRITICAL AND CREATIVE THINKING

All the strategies outlined above have an important role in promoting children's creative and critical thinking. Well-resourced and carefully chosen resources and, at times, risky and challenging environments can stimulate children to think and learn in new ways. Moreover, structured frameworks such as TASC can be useful in making the process of thinking more explicit for children.

Teaching for creative and critical thinking nonetheless has its challenges. For example, SST requires adults to be open-minded thinkers who also model and enact the dispositions and skills that we want children to develop. In addition, adopting genuinely collaborative partnerships can be difficult when adults are more used to directing and managing children's learning. Furthermore, relying on the resources and the environment to foster children's critical and creative thinking also has its challenges. 'Thinking friendly' resources (such as milk crates, cardboard boxes) do not necessarily lead to enquiry and reflection unless children are encouraged to ask questions and/or their attention is drawn (through modelling and interactions) to the language of critical and creative thinking. The best-resourced environment also requires adults who are good at listening, asking open-ended questions and modelling thinking language. In the same way, structured frameworks such as TASC also need adults who can extend children's thinking through sensitive interactions and modelling.

 action point 3.1

Record a short episode of your own talk with children and reflect on the extent to which your engagement and interactions extended children's language and thinking (ensure that you ask for permission first!):

- What kinds of comments/questions did you make/ask?
- Who talked the most? You or the child/children?
- Did you notice examples of children using language for thinking, such as 'if... then', 'first, second'?

BROADER ISSUES IN THINKING PEDAGOGIES

One of the challenges of the pedagogy of thinking is that popular perspectives of effective thinking take a narrow view of thinking. According to Lipman (2003), to think well is not just a matter of applying the right skills (e.g. inferring, analysing), but also involves knowing/ understanding when and how to apply them. That is, good thinkers not only know the strategies for effective thinking, but are also aware of how context (including their own biases and assumptions) affects judgements about right/wrong or effective/less effective. As Sternberg concludes, 'we can teach children to think, but if we do not teach them how to think ethically, our teaching them to think may not benefit society at all' (cited in Wegerif et al., 2015: 13).

Another debate relates to the tendency to see thinking purely in terms of intellectual outcomes. If education, in the broadest sense, means equipping children with the skills and dispositions to become effective citizens, then the emotional or affective aspects of thinking should be equally valued. Children who are taught to reflect on what is good or bad about their and others' behaviour, or have the sensitivities and skills to negotiate and manage classroom squabbles, are more likely to be effective, self-regulating learners. High Scope's approach to conflict resolution for preschoolers is predicated on these principles; children are taught to evaluate and reflect on incidents and invited to suggest possible solutions. Similarly, Payley's landmark work on young children's fantasy play was matched by her passion for creating fair and inclusive classrooms. In her widely read books, such as *You Can't Say You Can't Play* (1993), she reports on how she used her pupils' stories as contexts for reflection on fairness and equity in the classroom, and her strategies for helping them to think through the problems (e.g. name calling, exclusion) and seek possible solutions.

WHAT CAN THE PHILOSOPHICAL EDUCATOR OFFER?

A philosophical approach entails the use of reasoning and questioning to clarify the way we use ideas/concepts (such as fairness, justice) to make sense of the world. The idea that philosophy can improve children's thinking was originally put forward by Lipman (2003) who devised the Philosophy for Children (P4C) approach to teaching thinking. He argued that improvement in children's thinking was best achieved through establishing a community of learners where educators nurtured the critical and creative thinking aspects but also the caring (listening and valuing) and collaborative (responding and supporting) modes of thinking. This also meant that the adult acts as a **facilitator** who guides the discussion through careful questioning rather than imposing their own agenda.

Lipman's main argument was that children who learn how to employ collaborative and caring thinking are more likely to be effective critical and creative thinkers. P4C is a holistic pedagogy of thinking that is underpinned by the 4Cs (critical, caring, collaborative and caring thinking) (see Figure 3.1). Using stimuli (such as a story, a picture, an artefact) as a starting point, children generate questions that form the basis of the discussion as they seek to 'address' one of the questions. Thus, the role of the adult is multi-faceted: to create a caring and collaborative environment for dialogue and discussion, whilst, at the same time, encouraging and modelling the different modes of thinking that include: critical (seeking reasons, justifying, questioning assumptions), creative (seeing connections, finding examples), caring (being open to changing ideas, taking interest) and collaborative (building on each other's ideas) thinking to 'answer' their questions. The enquiry question may arise from an issue/problem that relates to, for example, a classroom topic, the motives of a fairytale character, or a story or video clip that centres on an idea or concept that is connected to the children's experience.

THE P4C METHODOLOGY

1. Ground rules: students and facilitators jointly construct desired behaviours (such as listening, building on ideas) during the enquiry.
2. Stimulus: the facilitator presents the stimulus (a story, a photo, a video clip) for the enquiry.
3. Question raising/suggestion: based on the stimulus, the participants, individually or in pairs, generate questions for the enquiry.
4. Voting: the facilitator invites the participants to choose the question they would most like to discuss.

5. First thoughts: the facilitator starts by inviting the participants to share their first thoughts/answers to the question.
6. Building the dialogue: the facilitator invites and encourages participants to identify concepts, define meanings and question/challenge positions and assumptions.
7. Last words: the facilitator draw the enquiry to a close by inviting each participant to offer their last thoughts on the question. (SAPERE, 2010)

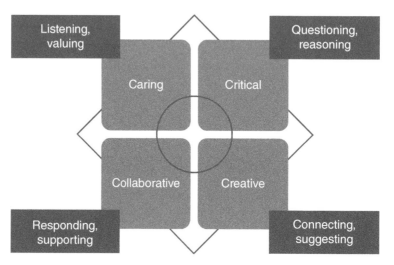

Figure 3.1 The 4 Cs

Source: Phillipson and Wegerif (2017); adapted from SAPERE (2010)

The P4C methodology (stimulus, questions, voting and dialogue) works best with children who are confident in using language for communication. However, with the right scaffold, 4- and 5-year-olds can take part in philosophical enquiry. Gardner, a key figure in P4C, advises that for the younger age range (and for older children new to philosophy) in particular, it is important to create a safe environment where children are motivated to express their ideas and are ready to use any aspect of the learning environment as a context for dialogue and inquiry (Gardner and Splitter, 1995).

Concrete experiences and familiar characters (such as those in fairytales), supplemented by dance, stories and artwork are also beneficial. Further, the adult needs to help children articulate their ideas and to make logical connections: 'the teacher not only carries responsibility for modelling inquiry, she must be prepared to repair and refocus the conversation so as to make it possible for the inquiry to proceed' (1995: 157).

Educators can also start with thinking games (such as 'would you rather..?') that are designed to support reasoning (see Stanley, 2012). The children's TV programme *What's the Big Idea?*, on the BBC's CBeebies, is a good example of a developmentally appropriate resource. Each episode focuses on Hugo's attempt to clarify his understanding, meanings and implications of concepts such as 'Grown-ups' or 'Love' using aspects of the 4Cs. Spontaneous enquiries (see below) can also be highly effective in developing critical and creative thinking.

case study 3.1

Implementing P4C

The author visited a classroom of 3–5-year-olds to mentor and support the class teacher in implementing P4C. On the second visit, the children showed me the toy robots they had collected as part of their learning about 'people who help us'. When I invited them to tell me about one of the robots, one of the boys confidently claimed, 'I think he is a boy'. This suggested the concepts of gender/identity as a possible line of enquiry. I responded by asking 'How do you/we know it is a boy?' Some of their suggestions included: 'he has a round head', 'it's a superhero' and 'it doesn't have eyelashes'!

I suggested that we test this theory. I encouraged some boys and girls to stand up and asked the rest if the suggested criteria (no eyelashes, round head) were evident. When we looked closer, we could see that everyone (boys and girls) had eyelashes, round heads and that no one was a superhero! Some of the boys looked a bit disappointed to find that their assumptions had been successfully challenged. Our enquiry was brought to a satisfying end when one of the girls exclaimed 'we don't know if it is a boy or a girl!'

1. Describe the role of the adult in this exchange.
2. Evaluate the success or otherwise of the interaction and identify possible reasons why.
3. What types of questions could you use to challenge children's thinking further?

This section has shown that adopting a philosophical approach can be a useful addition to educators' strategies for supporting critical and creative thinking. This is not to discount the value of existing approaches (such as Forest School). Indeed, P4C and SST have much in common as they both involve the collaborative co-construction of knowledge based on children's interests. What a philosophical approach offers, as illustrated in SAPERE's professional development programme, is a clear structure and conceptual framework for making sense of the approaches educators use already (such as SST). For example, by drawing children's attention to important concepts (such as heroes, family) educators have a way to encourage critical and creative thinking. In conclusion, whilst critical and creative thinking remain a priority for early years curricula, attention paid to educators' skills and confidence is needed. A philosophical approach can be a way of strengthening and enriching our pedagogies for nurturing self-regulating learners.

SUMMARY

- Self-regulation is seen as key to learning and development. Nurturing young children's critical and creative thinking are important means of enhancing their abilities to self-regulate their behaviour and learning.
- Developing young children's creative and critical thinking is a feature of a range of influential early years curricula. Consequently, educators have developed pedagogical approaches to implement their curricula aims.

- The level and quality of adults' interaction styles can influence children's willingness and confidence to articulate and develop their thinking. Providing an environment and context that promote creative and critical thinking needs to be supplemented by high-quality interactions. Adopting a philosophical approach to dialogue and interaction can be a useful tool in negotiating the challenging task of facilitating authentic dialogue with children.

online resources

Make sure to visit https://study.sagepub.com/fitzgeraldandmaconochie for selected SAGE videos (with questions), SAGE journal articles, links to external sources and flashcards.

FURTHER READING

Stanley, S. (2012). *Why Think? Philosophical Play from 3–11*. London: Continuum.

Stanley provides a wealth of material to support educators' skill in supporting dialogue in the early years classroom. She uses everyday playful activities (such as role play) to show how adults can encourage children to think philosophically about the scenarios and problems that arise in their play.

Whitebread, D. (2012). *Developmental Psychology and Early Childhood Education: A Guide for Parents and Practitioners*. London: Sage.

This book argues that developing children's independence and self-regulation skills is of fundamental importance. It provides in-depth insight from research and theory to highlight the pedagogical approaches (such as relationships and cognitive challenges) that are most likely to encourage young children's learning and development.

REFERENCES

Athey, C. (1990). *Extending Thought in Young Children: A Parent–Teacher Partnership*. London: Chapman.

Broadhead, P. and Burt, A. (2012). *Understanding Young Children's Play: Building Playful Pedagogies*. New York: Routledge.

Craft, A. (2002). *Creativity and Early Years Education: A Lifewide Foundation*. London: Continuum.

Department for Education (DfE) (2015). National Curriculum in England: Primary Curriculum. [online] Available at: www.gov.uk/government/publications/national-curriculum-inengland-primary-curriculum [Accessed 7 October 2017].

Department for Education (DfE) (2017). Early Years Foundation Stage (EYFS). [online] Available at: www.gov.uk/early-years-foundation-stage [Accessed 7 October 2017].

Donaldson, M. (1978/1987). *Children's Minds*. London: Fontana.

Ennis, J. (1996). *Critical Thinking*. London: Prentice Hall.

Gardner, S. and Splitter, L. (1995). *Teaching for Better Thinking: The Classroom Community of Enquiry*. Melbourne: ACER.

Giardiello, P. (2013). *Pioneers in Early Childhood Education: The Roots and Legacies of Rachel and Margaret McMillan, Maria Montessori and Susan Isaacs*. London: Routledge.

Lipman, M. (2003). *Thinking in Education*. Cambridge: Cambridge University Press.

Malaguzzi, L. (1993). The Hundred Languages of Children. In: C. Edwards, L. Gandini and G. Forman (eds), *The Hundred Languages of Children: The Reggio Emilia Experience in Transformation*, 3rd edn. Norwood, NJ: Ablex, p. 2.

Nelson, T. and Narens, L. (1990). Metamemory: A Theoretical Framework and New Findings. *Psychology of Learning and Motivation, 26*: 125–73.

Nicholson, S. (1971). How NOT to Cheat Children: The Theory of Loose Parts. *Landscape Architecture, 62*: 30–4.

Nickerson, R. (1999). Enhancing Creativity. In: R. Sternberg (ed.), *Handbook of Creativity*. New York: Cambridge University Press: 392–430.

Nutbrown, C. (1994). *Threads of Thinking: Young Children Learning and the Role of Early Education*. London: Paul Chapman.

Payley, V. (1993). *You Can't Say You Can't Play*. Harvard, NJ: Harvard University Press.

Phillipson, N. and Wegerif, R. (2017). *Dialogic Education: Mastering Concepts through Thinking Together*. London: Routledge.

Piaget, J. (1936/1963). *The Origins of Intelligence in Children*, 18th edn. New York: W.W. Norton.

Robson, S., Rowe, V. and Hargreaves, D. (2012). Observing Young Children's Creative Thinking: Engagement, Involvement and Persistence. *International Journal of Early Years Education, 20*(4): 349–64.

Schweinhart, L. and Weikart, D. (1993). *A Summary of Significant Benefits: The High Scope Perry Pre-School Study through Age 27*. Ypsilanti, MI: High Scope Press.

Siraj-Blatchford, I., Sylva, K., Muttock, S., Gilden, R. and Bell, D. (2002). *Researching Effective Pedagogy in the Early Years (REPEY)*. DfES Research Report No. 365. London: HMSO.

Society for the Advancement of Philosophical Enquiry and Reflection in Education (SAPERE) (2010). *Handbook to Accompany the Level 1 Course*, 3rd edn. Oxford: SAPERE

Stanley, S. (2012). *Why Think? Philosophical Play from 3–11*. London: Continuum.

Sylva, K., Melhuish, E., Sammons, P., Siraj, I. and Taggart, B. (2004). *The Effective Provision of Pre-school Education (EPPE) Project*. Nottingham: DfES.

Veenman, M., Wilhelm, P. and Beishuizen, J. (2004). The Relation between Intellectual and Metacognitive Skills from a Developmental Perspective. *Learning and Instruction, 14*: 89–109.

Wallace, B. (1993). *Thinking Actively in a Social Context (TASC): Theory and Practice*. Oxford: AB Academic Publishers.

Wang, M. C., Haertel, G. and Walberg, H. (1990). What Influences Learning? A Content Analysis of Review Literature. *Journal of Educational Research, 84*: 30–43.

Wegerif, R., Li, L. and Kaufman, J. (2015). *The Routledge International Handbook of Research on Teaching Thinking*. London: Routledge.

Whitebread, D. (2012). *Developmental Psychology and Early Childhood Education*. London: Sage.

Whitebread, D. and Pino Pasternak, D. (2010). Metacognition, Self-regulation and Meta-knowing. In: K. Littleton, C. Wood and J. Kleine Staarman (eds), *International Handbook of Psychology in Education*, 2nd edn. Bingley, UK: Emerald, pp. 673–712.

Whitebread, D., Bingham, S., Grau, V., Pino Pasternak, D. and Sangster, C. (2007). Development of Metacognition and Self-regulated Learning in Young Children: The Role of Collaborative and Peer-assisted Learning. *Journal of Cognitive Education and Psychology, 3*: 433–55.

CHILDREN AS LEARNERS: MULTIMODAL PERSPECTIVES ON PLAY AND LEARNING

BY KAREN DANIELS AND ROBERTA TAYLOR

Prior to reading this chapter, I had some knowledge of children's play and learning but had not previously heard the term multimodal interaction. However, the chapter provided a clear explanation of the terms which aided my understanding.

Due to my previous job role as a Flying Start Playgroup Leader, I was able to link the behaviours that were identified in the chapter with what I have observed in practice. For example, observing children carrying out behaviours that they had clearly observed at home and then demonstrating these during their play. The chapter case studies provide extra insight into what these interactions might look like within a setting, whilst the action points give you clear pointers for how to look for these behaviours in your settings.

KELLY HARRIS
BA (HONS) EDUCATION AND EARLY
CHILDHOOD STUDIES
CARDIFF METROPOLITAN UNIVERSITY

learning outcomes

By actively reading this chapter and engaging with the material, you will be able to:

- identify the multiple semiotic resources children draw on in their meaning making
- analyse young children's multimodal interaction
- evaluate the use of space and resources in early childhood settings
- identify and understand key research in the field of multimodal communication.

INTRODUCTION

Children learn, make meaning and communicate in many different ways. If we want to better understand how children learn, it is essential that we consider the many ways that children make meaning and the multiple **modes** through which they express meaning. This chapter examines children's use of multiple and varied **semiotic resources** and modes used during the process of meaning making. By this we mean the way that children's face-to-face communication is an embodied act which is realised through posture, gesture, gaze, facial expression, touch (haptics) as well as spoken language. The chapter sets out some main principles from the **social semiotic perspective** (Kress, 2010) on communication and demonstrates the multiple modes which children employ in their collaboration and communication.

A founding principle of this perspective on communication is that meaning is always made in context. Attention to the places where children are learning is therefore necessary. For this reason, an **ethnographic approach** is taken to understanding young children's activity. The chapter presents a **multimodal** analysis framework alongside examples from videoed classroom observation of children's interaction in order to illustrate this. Socio-cultural and social constructivist perspectives on learning and play are explained. Some examples of children's use of space, materials and narrative play are put under a multimodal lens through the employment of **ethnographically contextualised multimodal discourse analysis**. The data presented illustrates the multiple modes involved in meaning making and discusses what a multimodal perspective on communication contributes to understandings of young children's language, communication and play.

From a semiotic perspective, this chapter explores children's cultural knowledge and their use of **intertextual** references from their home and community experiences, in order to see how children draw on these in their collaboratively constructed **play texts**. A multimodal perspective on children's interaction can contribute to understandings of children's learning experiences and provide nuanced understandings of the ways in which very young children learn, play and participate.

 **action point 4.1**

Having gained consent from parents and children, choose one play space that the children seem to like and use the most as a focus to carry out an observation. You may wish to film, or take photographs at intervals, as well as making notes on what is taking place. Turn your attention in particular to what happens to the space you are observing, and what happens to the resources. With colleagues, discuss the following:

- How do children use the space?
- What sort of activity takes place there?
- How do they move within and across that space?
- What meanings do they ascribe to the objects and spaces that they play in?
- What changes do they make to the spaces and materials?
- What does this tell you about their interests and shared experiences?

MULTIMODAL THEORY OF COMMUNICATION: WHAT IT IS AND WHY IT IS IMPORTANT FOR PLAY AND LEARNING

Action point 4.1 will have focused attention on the way that children make meanings as they play with objects and materials. A social semiotic perspective regards children's interaction, or 'talk', as the communication of meaning achieved through the employment of a multimodal ensemble of resources, such as posture, gaze and gesture. From birth, children communicate through gaze and facial expression, and pre-verbal toddlers through gesture, such as finger pointing to communicate interest. This view of communication has its origins in Halliday's (1978) view of language as a social semiotic, or, in other words, a tool to make meaning. Jewitt, Bezemer and O'Halloran (2016) make the point that while Halliday developed this approach for the study of language, he was clear that language is one among many modes of meaning making. Kress and Van Leeuwen (2001) outlined an approach for understanding all communication as multimodal. They argued that in the twenty-first century the emergence and rapid development of new ways of communicating using new technology required a re-evaluation of the assumed dominance of spoken and written word as primary, or dominant, forms of communication. This position has enabled the examination of the contribution of multiple modes to face-to-face interaction as well as print, written and digital texts. Sociolinguists and linguistic anthropologists have long been interested in the work of gesture, gaze and posture in communication. What distinguishes Multimodal Theory of Communication is the principle that while language may at times be dominant, at other times it is not, and that by *not* privileging language the researcher, early childhood practitioner and/or parent/carer is able to see more clearly the contributions of other modes (Taylor, 2006; Daniels, 2016). From the multimodal perspective of interaction, meaning is made by the child through the use of the most apt sign from within their interest and repertoire. Kress (2010) describes aptness as a 'best fit' of form and meaning. Attention to all aspects of communication, including the use of material artefacts, such as toys and the ways that children position themselves and their toys in space, can enable the practitioner to have a deeper understanding of the ways in which children are co-working to construct knowledge. Supporting the development of spoken language is an important goal for early childhood practitioners. However, observing children's communication as multimodal opens up new ways of understanding the multiple modes and how these shape children's play and early learning experiences. Below (see case studies 4.1 and 4.2) we can see how observing from a multimodal perspective can open up new ways of seeing how children and adults interact and co-construct meanings. This in turn offers new possibilities for evaluating the nature of our interactions with children and the ways in which the learning environment can support and influence, or conversely, limit children's play and meaning-making activity. If we only attend to the mode of speech, we will miss much of what takes place in children's interaction. Using multimodal analysis to examine children's interaction provides a more comprehensive insight into how children communicate through different modes, and, moreover, better understanding of how children select the modes that are most apt for what they wish to communicate. This insight has benefits for parents, practitioners and researchers in understanding and responding effectively in interactions with children.

SOCIO-CULTURAL AND SOCAL CONSTRUCTIVIST THEORIES OF LEARNING

In addition to the principle that meaning making is always multimodal, is the condition that all meaning is made in context. Bakhtin (1981) proposed that communication cannot take place in isolation; in other words, communication is a community-based act. Bakhtin wrote primarily about language but his words can be understood in relation to other modes. Here he speaks about language: 'Words exist in three aspects: the *neutral* form found in a dictionary, as *another's* word imbued with the resonances of another speaker, and as *my* word with my expression' (Bakhtin, 1981: 49).

Furthermore, when used in communication words are not neutral but are loaded with connotation from previous usage. The touching of an artefact, such as a toy, or a gesture or a 'look', can be used by a child to construct meaning based on their prior experience. The point here is that meaning is not made in isolated moments, but builds on previous moments. As Bakhtin (1999: 124) reminds us, 'any utterance is a link in a very complexly organised chain of other utterances'. It is for this reason that any close analysis of children's moments of interaction should be undertaken as part of extended contextualising observation.

If we are to work from the principle that meanings are always made in context, we also need a theory of learning which coheres with that position. Socio-cultural and social constructivist theories work from the notion that meaning is constructed by people mediated through cultural tools such as language or drawing (also constructed by people). Theorists such as Vygotsky (1986) argue that learning is social – in other words, each person constructs their own understanding through their interaction with others. This does not mean children do not learn from artefacts such as books or sand trays but that these are cultural tools manufactured by people with intent or design which communicate meaning (and thus are social). Rather than a behaviourist view of learning, whereby children learn in response to a stimulus and when they are rewarded, Vygotsky's view of learning is a social one. This theory also recognises the ways in which children reach for higher mental functions when they are supported by a knowledgeable other. For Vygotsky, it is the **zone of proximal development (ZPD)**, the space between what a child can do for themselves and what they can achieve with support, where learning takes place.

Broadly, Vygotsky believed that as children acquire language they learn to develop thought. He believed that this process relies on social interaction combined with internal thought processes. In testing Piaget's (1970) theory of **egocentric speech**, he concluded that children need the feeling of being understood, and the contact and social interaction within a group to voice their egocentric speech (1986: 251). His notion of the zone of proximal development proposes that cognitive development is founded on dialogue with a teacher or an adult which supports the child's learning. The teachers' use of questions and rephrasing can aid this development. This concept was extended by Bruner's (1975) notion of **scaffolding** where the teacher extends a child's learning by focusing on the skill to be acquired. Mercer (1995) further extended this by proposing that teacher-led dialogue and directed group activity between children can fulfil this function through exploratory talk. Alexander (2000) writes of a shift in focus from the 'act of instruction' to the 'process of learning'. He gives as evidence the psychologist Bruner's move from a 'solo intra-psychic' view of knowing and learning to one which engages with the relationship between learning and culture (Alexander, 2000: 556).

In this section, we have explored the multiplicity of ways that children communicate and make meaning as they play and engage with the world and people around them. Such communication is inherently social and contingent on interaction with others.

YOUNG CHILDREN, LEARNING AND SYNAESTHETIC ACTIVITY

There is considerable recent interest in play and meaning making as semiotic (Flewitt, 2005; Rowe, 2008; Wohlwend, 2011). Researchers working from a semiotic perspective are expanding the line of research by exploring the connections between modes of communication, in order to more fully understand the multimodal nature of children's meaning making.

Social semiotics aims to investigate human meaning-making practices in specific social and cultural circumstances as text and meaning are constructed. According to Kress (1997), social semiotic theory insists that all signs and messages are always multimodal. This means that no sign or message ever exists in just one single mode. Kress presents the example of the young child who draws a series of circles to represent a car. The child has drawn an analogy of wheels, and turning, and movement in order to represent something that is culturally significant to that child. Here then the child is interpreting movement and image. This text will probably also be accompanied by talk – for example, a child talking about what they are doing, or expressing this to another person. This example illustrates how when texts and signs are collaboratively created, there is an interplay of communication which will draw on a range of modes. These acts of text creation also draw on cultural meanings. Kress (1997) describes how, as children are drawn into participating in culture, what is available to them becomes more and more that which the culture values and in turn makes readily available to the child. Furthermore, the texts the child encounters or creates are always **agentic**: the child acts in a transformative way upon the signs they encounter, and therefore children become the agents of their own cultural and social making. 'Agent' in this context refers to the ways in which children actively take up the meaning-making practices available and integrate these into their own repertoire. For example, in case study 4.1, we can see how Sam is moving and using the objects around him that are taken from his experience of what a person might do in an office.

Working from a social semiotic perspective, Kress (1997) has shown how children in early childhood are predominantly guided by **synaesthetic activities** which draw on all their senses and use visual, kinaesthetic, three-dimensional and gestural modes. This meaning making emerges prior to a child's use and mastery of the alphabetic code. Kress (1997) describes the role of material objects that children engage with in order to express their ideas and make meaning collaboratively in order to engage in **peer culture**. In children's activities, such as role play and narrative play, young children participate and innovate with the culture around them and explore the possibilities of the social and cultural world. Such activity involves the orchestration of multiple modes.

OBSERVING CHILDREN'S MULTIMODAL INTERACTIONS

When an educator is engaged in the observation and analysis of children's interaction, several different accounts of the activity are generated. The interaction itself takes place in real time and is spontaneous and fleeting. Field notes, or observational notes, can be written contemporaneously, or soon after, and offer a partial and subjective account of what took place. The video recording is similarly partial and subjective. Its gaze and what it records are within the control of the observer and the choice of camera direction taken. The transcription of that film record is also subjective. The researcher makes decisions about what to include in the transcript based on their interest, for example children's multimodal forms of communication. The reliability of the analysis of children's interaction depends on the rigour applied to the data through the use of a methodologically sound framework. Combining observational notes and multimodal transcription can support close analysis and generate new understandings of children's communication in play and learning.

As illustrated in the previous section, children's communication takes place in context. The researcher or observer in the room is necessarily part of that context and contributes through their presence. Daniels (2016) explains how, when videoing children in an early childhood setting with a handheld camera, her voice can be heard from time to time as she interacts with the children at play. Taylor (2014) makes the point that whilst the researcher in the room is not necessarily an insider to the children's world, they can be seen to be an insider to what is unfolding at a particular moment. The knowledge of and familiarity with the setting are what allow for ethnographic interpretation of video data during the transcription and analysis later. Observing children's activity closely in this way helps practitioners to evaluate the learning environment and the ways in which children use the space and materials. It can also support practitioners in gaining insights into young children's play interests and preferred modes of communication.

reflection point 4.1

How might the participant observer influence the field of research and the data she generates?

TRANSCRIBING AND ANALYSING OBSERVATIONAL DATA

In order to uncover the ways in which children make meaning through multiple modes, a framework for analysis of video-recorded data needs to be used. Each researcher will choose a framework suitable for their particular research questions and interests, and there are many different examples in published research (Norris, 2004; Flewitt, 2005; Jewitt et al., 2016).

The framework presented here is based on Halliday's (1994) functional perspective on grammar and the metafunctions (interpersonal, ideational and textual) of communication. Put simply, each interaction comprises functions related to the people involved (interpersonal), the subject matter (ideational) and the actual modes employed (textual). This framework endeavours to make the *familiar* exchanges of child-to-child discourse *strange*, through the use of the multimodal analytic tool which focuses on contextually understood micro-instantiations of classroom interaction. This involves a multimodal transcription grid, which can include gaze, gesture, posture/movement and spoken language, and a microanalysis of the work of cohesive devices in the textual metafunction. It is important that this is understood through the ethnographic contextual data generated by observation and participation in conjunction with an understanding of the children and their community.

spotlight on research 4.1

Children's Emerging Literacy Practices

Table 4.1 is a sample analysis taken from Karen's year-long ethnographic study (Daniels, 2018) into young children's emerging literacy practices. Here, Karen transcribed children's multimodal activity while they played at the writing table. Two girls, Mia (aged 4 years and 8 months) and Chanelle (5 years, 1 month), are writing on the paper strip at the writing table, and it appears that they are playing at being the teacher and a pupil.

Table 4.1 Mia and Chanelle play

Time	Speech	Gaze	Gesture	Movement
0:52		C: Looking at paper strip		C: Writes a cursive 't' on the strip
				M: Moves away to bookcase and picks up more strips
0:58	M: 'Right!'	M: Selects a strip with two letters already written on (t and i)	M: Pushes the strip towards C	M: Hands a pen to C
				C: Picks up pen
1:00		C and M: Looking at strip of card		M: Places cards with t i l in front of C
				C: Holding pen in right hand, poised to write
1.02		C: Looks towards M	C: Puts left hand forefinger on pen, then touches card with forefinger	
		M: Looks to J	Touches paper with pen and writes i	
			M: Points to next letter on strip	
1:11	Joshua: 'Where you got those from?'	M: Looks back to C	M: Points to bookcase	Appears and stands behind M and C
				J: Moves away
1:13	M: 'Over there ...'		C: Writes l, l	
	C: 'Done'			

Source: Daniels, 2018

In the multimodal transcript in Table 4.1, it is noticeable how the communication that takes place is predominantly by movement of objects, and gesture. The arrangement of resources and access to them in turn are shaping the communication and possibilities for participation that take place. Analysis of this transcription takes place in conjunction with the ethnographic contextualising field notes. It takes account of the ideational metafunction through considering the purpose and functions of the communicative acts. It examines the interpersonal function by considering the relationships, power, status and interests of the children and adults involved. The textual metafunction is considered though the cohesive devices used. In short, textual cohesion is achieved through the use of cohesive devices of Repetition, Reference Conjunction, Substitution, Omission, Metaphor and Idiom, and Intertextual Referencing (Salkie, 1995). Of these, repetition, reference and intertextual reference can be particularly useful tools for taking the data apart and examining what is taking place.

Repetition: Repetition of a word, a gaze or a gesture can signify attention and accommodation in interaction. It is a primary tool for cohering ideas and meanings within a text.

(Continued)

Reference: In linguistics, this relates to the use of pronouns such as him or her, this or that, but reference can be achieved through the direction of gaze or through a gesture such as pointing.

Intertextual reference: This is the way in which we refer to other prior texts as a tool for making meaning. Think of it as a communicative short cut. Children might reference a story or film they like to invoke particular narratives, such as *The Lion King* for strength.

Observing Children in Early Years Settings

Observing children's multimodal activity can support practitioners' understandings of children's multimodal communication in play and consider their developing confidence in expressing their ideas and thinking. In the examples, we can see Chanelle and Mia playing out a narrative of teacher and pupil, or Sam in case study 4.1 playing out a narrative of being busy at work in the office.

Maybin notes the way that intertextual reference in children's interaction is apparently 'automatic' and 'the cognitive processing involved must happen at a relatively unconscious level' (2006: 157-8). Observing children through a multimodal lens has the potential to show how children make intertextual links with their prior experience.

From considering interaction multimodally and not privileging speech, Roberta was able to demonstrate postural **intertextuality** (Taylor, 2006). Five boys aged 6-7 were talking around a desk in a classroom about an exciting football match they had watched on television the previous night. As they talked, they leaned in together, drew diagrams on their whiteboards and then got up from the table and enacted the moves they had seen during the match. They dived to the floor as a goalkeeper saving a goal and they held poses such as the striker with his extended foot and arms to the side. These poses were not from the live television recording of the match itself but the kind of poses captured in the football magazines popular with children interested in football. An essential part of the meaning making of this text was the communication of striker as hero through the poses taken up. Similar postural intertextuality was identified during the Playground Games in the Digital Age project (Marsh and Bishop, 2013), where children adopted the postures, gestures and manner of gaze in enacting a talk show in the playground. (2013: 44). They describe how a boy enacting the role of Jeremy Kyle, a daytime television talk show host, dropped to his knee holding out a microphone in an inviting manner to his 'show's participant' in the 'studio', an area of the playground. This was a posture seen on the television and then enacted as part of play. The posture itself was part of the meaning being invoked and represented.

 action point 4.2

Find a time to carry out close observation. Look for examples of children using reference through pointing or the direction of their gaze. Look for ways that children make links between their experiences in their play. You might consider how they bring intertextual references, for example story characters, into their play. They might draw on experiences of everyday life too. Look for repetition across the words and phrases, or gestures that children make. Reference and repetition make it possible for children to draw on past experience and communicate their meanings and share these with other children.

Case studies 4.1 and 4.2 are episodes taken from Karen's year-long ethnographic research study where she observed children's expanding communicative repertoires from a semiotic perspective. As you read these, you might ask:

1.   What kinds of postures do you see children adopting in their play meaning making?
2.   Which cultural texts do you see them referencing?
3.   How can an understanding of this aid the educator in encouraging play?

 case study 4.1

Batman and a Day in the Office

Figure 4.1 was taken in an early childhood education and care setting for children aged 0–5. Sam, dressed as Batman, is playing in the 2–3s room. Sam is 3 years of age.

He has been organising the resources in the role-play area into an office (like his dad's), having now transported writing materials from the writing table. A multimodal transcription and analysis of his activity show how much of his communication was embodied, and gestural, and involved the organisation of space and resources as he set up his office. The holding of the pencil, scratching of his head, writing on the pad, answering of the telephone and the orchestration of gesture and movement that took part were all done with an air of authority. This observation shows important aspects of Sam's development. Long before Sam is literate, he shows his understanding of the way that literate behaviours are integrated into life and ways of being. In playing at being literate, he arranges spaces and objects associated with literacy. At one point, another child comes to join in with the play and Sam's body instructs him what he can and cannot do in the office, again assuming an air of authority.

Figure 4.1   Sam, dressed as Batman

case study 4.2

Making Superheroes

Liam, Tumbikani and Josh are making superhero puppets (see Figures 4.2 and 4.3). They are standing their puppets on a low table and talking about them. Tumbikani and Josh are having a discussion about which superhero is 'in charge'. The multimodal transcription in Table 4.2 shows how the children are simultaneously using spoken language and the objects and materials around them to explore the social world of the superheroes, and are negotiating a hierarchy of superpowers. The modal quality of the materials around them inflects their practices. Josh invents the superpower of a magic orange cape, due to the colour of the felt. Abstract ideas such as the hierarchy of the superheroes is represented in the lining up of the puppets. The children here are creating an imaginary world where superheroes are 'in charge' on their own planets, and they are possibly exploring classroom hierarchies that exist in children's peer cultures and in the wider world.

Figure 4.2   Making superheroes

Figure 4.3   Lining-up superheroes

Table 4.2 Multimodal transcription of making superheroes

Time	Speech	Child activity with puppet	Gesture/Gaze
0:5	T: 'I am in charge!'	Holding puppet in right hand, standing it upright	Liam looks to T's superhero
0: 8	J: 'No!!!'	L: Wrapping cape on his puppet	T: Puts left hand over face
0: 16	T: 'On my planet, I'm in charge' L: (echoes) 'My planet, I'm in charge' T: 'I'm in charge … a bit you' J: 'Can it fly?' T: (singing) 'Doooooo'	L: Wraps string round cape, leaves table T: Waves puppet in circles over his head T: Stands puppet upright on table	L: Looks to T T: Eyes following puppet
0:25	J: 'Does it have powers?' J: 'It has orange superpower. I have orange power' T: 'You don't have orange powers!! What colour powers do you have?' J: 'Errrr' T: 'Errr' J: 'Like new powers. Orange cape' T: 'So I'm the leader … I the leader, you are the leader on me. And you at the back of him'	J: Stands puppet alongside T's J: Twirls the puppet between his fingers L: Returns and stands puppet alonside other two Boys line up superheroes	

Source: Daniels, 2018

From carrying out a multimodal analysis of children's activity, we are better placed in seeing how the learning environment is supporting children's learning and development. Attention is also brought to the multiple modes that children draw on when they communicate, and the ways in which their activity is stimulated by the spatial and material environment, children's histories and shared experiences in order to make meaning. The children here are drawing on a range of texts, such as their experience of superheroes and of a 'person in the office'. Simultaneously, they use their available semiotic tools to explore classroom relationships, and they play with the spaces and materials in the classroom.

KEY RESEARCH IN THE FIELD OF MULTIMODAL COMMUNICATION

Observing children's activity as they access the learning environment, and the ways in which they combine spaces and materials with communicative resources for meaning making, can provide valuable insights into their early learning. It can help practitioners and researchers assess how far the learning environment and adult support are facilitating children's repertoires for meaning making. It can also provide insights into children's concerns and interests, and enable practitioners to react flexibly to children's learning needs. Below are examples of researchers who have observed children's multimodal meaning making in a variety of settings.

KAREN WOHLWEND

Karen Wohlwend's work (2011) examines play as an embodied meaning-making process, where children use their bodies, toys, props and drawings to create play texts and take part in cultural practices. She observes how children's play actions produce valued ways of belonging in the classroom community. Focusing on children's play performances of popular media characters, such as superheroes and princesses, Wohlwend describes how children try out pretend identities and create imagined worlds. Such pretence, according to Wohlwend, has real effects on children's friendships and their participation in peer cultures.

Understanding young children's communication and play as multimodal can provide a way of valuing what young children bring to their experience and the ways in which they investigate the meaning-making possibilities of the environment. In addition, by observing children's multimodal activity in settings, we are better able to evaluate the impact of the learning environment.

DEBORAH WELLS-ROWE

Deborah Rowe (2008) observed how 2-year-old children participated in writing activities in a preschool. She examined how adults and children co-authored texts together, noting that a large proportion of children's talk involved verbal or gestural descriptions of their intentions. Rowe noted five key patterns of activity: 'the joint negotiation of textual intentions in face-to-face interaction; the forceful nature of the pedagogical mode of address; children's use of existing resources to take up roles as writers; changes in participation; and children's agency in shaping their participation as writers' (Rowe, 2008: 387).

This chapter has suggested that by examining children's interactions from a social semiotic perspective, taking note of how they make meaning multimodally, insights into children's interests and repertoires for making meaning and communicating can be gained.

SUMMARY

- Young children draw on the modes of posture, gesture and gaze in order to make meaning.
- Children's communication can facilitate our understanding of the ways in which young children make meaning. A multimodal perspective offers a view of learning that is linked to children's expanding repertoires for making meaning through multiple modes and media.
- A multimodal perspective can help support the development of inclusive practice as we value the experiences and communicative repertoires that children bring from home and community settings, and while speech is valued, it is seen as part of an orchestration of communicative modes.

- Research using multimodal analysis is a developing field that offers a way of exploring how young children use multiple modes to communicate meaning.

online resources

Make sure to visit https://study.sagepub.com/fitzgeraldandmaconochie for selected SAGE videos (with questions), SAGE journal articles, links to external sources and flashcards.

FURTHER READING

Daniels, K. (2016). Exploring Enabling Literacy Environments: Young Children's Spatial and Material Encounters in Early Years Classrooms. *English in Education*, 50(1): 12–34.

This article examines how young children collaboratively assign meanings to the spaces and materials they encounter in an early years classroom.

Flewitt, R. (2005). Is Every Child's Voice Heard? Researching the Different Ways 3-year-old Children Communicate and Make Meaning at Home and in a Pre-school Environment. *Early Years*, *25*(3): 207–22.

This article considers the multiple modes that children use to communicate and share meanings and stresses the importance of being sensitive to children's communicative strategies.

Taylor, R. (2006). Actions Speak as Loud as Words: A Multimodal Analysis of Boys' Talk in the Classroom. *English in Education*, *40*(3): 66–82.

This article examines the ways in which children communicate using a range of different modes in order to share ideas and learn together.

REFERENCES

Alexander, R. (2000). *Culture and Pedagogy: International Comparison in Primary Education*. Oxford: Blackwell.

Bakhtin, M. (1981). *The Dialogic Imagination*. Austin, TX: University of Texas Press.

Bakhtin, M. (1999). The Problem of Speech Genres. In: A. Jaworski and N. Coupland (eds), *The Discourse Reader*. London: Routledge.

Bruner, J. S. (1975). The Ontogenesis of Speech Acts. *Journal of Child Language, 2*: 1–40.

Daniels, K. (2016). Exploring Enabling Literacy Environments: Young Children's Spatial and Material Encounters in Early Years Classrooms. *English in Education*, 50(1): 12–34.

Daniels. K. (2018). *Movement, Meaning and Affect: The Stuff Early Childhood Literacies are Made Of*. Sheffield Hallam University. [online] Available at: http://shura.shu.ac.uk/21513

Flewitt, R. (2005). Is Every Child's Voice Heard? Researching the Different Ways 3-Year-Old Children Communicate and Make Meaning at Home and in a Pre-school Environment. *Early Years*, *25*(3): 207–22.

Halliday, M. A. K. (1978). *Language as a Social Semiotic*. London: Edward Arnold.

Halliday, M. A. K. (1994). Language as Social Semiotic. In: J. Maybin (ed.), *Language and Literacy in Social Practice*. Clevedon: Multilingual Matters/The Open University.

Jewitt, C., Bezemer, J. and O'Halloran, K. (2016). *Introducing Multimodality*. London: Routledge.

Kress, G. (1997). *Before Writing: Rethinking Paths to Literacy*. London: Routledge.

Kress, G. (2010). *Multmodality: A Social Semiotic Approach to Contemporary Communication*. London: Routledge.

Kress, G. and Van Leeuwen, T. (2001). *Multimodal Discourse: The Modes and Media of Contemporary Communication*. London: Arnold.

Marsh, J. and Bishop, J. C. (2013). *Changing Play: Play, Media and Commercial Culture from the 1950s to the Present Day*. Maidenhead: Open University Press.

Maybin, J. (2006). *Children's Voices: Talk, Knowledge and Identity*. Basingstoke: Palgrave Macmillan.

Mercer, N. (1995). *The Guided Construction of Knowledge: Talk Amongst Teachers and Learners*. Clevedon: Multilingual Matters.

Mercer, N. (2000). *Words and Minds: How We Use Language to Think Together*. London: Routledge.

Norris, S. (2004). *Analyzing Multimodal Interaction: A Methodological Framework*. London: Routledge.

Piaget, J. (1970). Piaget's Theory. In: P. H. Mussen (ed.), *Carmichael's Handbook of Child Development*. New York: Wiley, pp. 703–32.

Rowe, D. (2008). The Social Construction of Intentionality: Two-Year-Olds' and Adults' Participation at a Preschool Writing Center. *Research in the Teaching of English*, *42*(4): 387–434.

Salkie, R (1995), *Text and Discourse Analysis*. London: Routledge.

Taylor, R. (2006). Actions Speak as Loud as Words: A Multimodal Analysis of Boys' Talk in the Classroom. *English in Education*, *40*(3): 66–82.

Taylor, R. (2014). Multimodal Analysis of the Textual Function in Children's Face-to-Face Classroom Interaction. In: A. Maiorani and C. Christie (eds), *Routledge Series on Multimodality: Multimodal Epistemologies – Towards an Integrated Framework*. Abingdon: Routledge.

Vygotsky, L. (1986). *Thought and Language* (ed. A. Kozulin). London: The MIT Press.

Wohlwend, K. E. (2011). *Playing their Way into Literacies: Reading, Writing, and Belonging in the Early Childhood Classroom*. New York: Teachers College Press.

CREATIVITY, CURIOSITY AND RESILIENCE

BY SARAH RAWDING

The learning outcomes set out clear expectations about what I would achieve from reading the chapter.

I found the explanations and examples of each of the three learning dispositions very useful and clear. The case study was a good way to reflect on my own practice and consider how I have hindered children or helped them to develop their skills. I have worked in settings where they have not allowed children to 'transport' objects from different areas; upon reflection this was hindering their curiosity and creativity but at the time I followed the setting's beliefs of 'keeping things tidy'.

The reflection point and action point allowed me to think of things from a different perspective and reflect on my own practice and how I can improve this in order to develop the children's skills and knowledge. I am thankful for literature that allows me to do this.

I am keen to share my knowledge gained from this chapter with my co-workers!

ANNETTE BENNETT
FDA EARLY YEARS
SHEFFIELD HALLAM UNIVERSITY

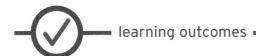

learning outcomes

By actively reading this chapter and engaging with the material, you will be able to:

- recognise the importance of the process of learning as well as outcomes
- locate curiosity, creativity and resilience as dispositions integral to positive and lifelong learning
- review the role of adults in supporting children's dispositions
- compare educational approaches towards dispositions.

INTRODUCTION

Lifelong learning is the potential for an individual to learn throughout the lifespan. It starts from the premise that learning is not limited to childhood and formal education as knowledge and understanding are subjective and infinite, and learning a continuous process. For individuals to have the relevant skills to adapt to a society characterised by change, they need to have a positive attitude towards learning and developing. Positive attitudes towards learning are integral to successful lifelong learning, and for a positive attitude there must be a motivation, drive or desire to learn, to change, reflect and adapt.

To develop a lifelong learning approach, individuals need to know how to learn. '**Learning power**' or capacity to learn consists of **dispositions**, values and attitudes towards learning (Deakin-Crick et al., 2004). Integral to learning power are **resilience**, **reciprocity**, resourcefulness and reflectiveness. These are the four 'R's' which influence whether an individual is ready and willing to learn, and equip individuals with learning power (Claxton, 2002). Enthusiasm and motivation for learning are also essential to learning power as children learn best when they are intrinsically motivated, when they are driven and when they are engaged. This chapter will consider some of the key learning dispositions which enable children to develop learning power and become positive learners, able to reach their potential throughout the spectrum of subjects within the education system and to develop a lifelong learning approach. The focus will be on three dispositions: **curiosity**, **creativity** and resilience, although it is acknowledged that many other dispositions are also important.

PRIORITIES OF EDUCATION

The focus of many Western twenty-first century education systems is not on attitudes and motivations to learn but on attainment in subjects. There is an emphasis on achieving external outcomes as opposed to nurturing qualities (Sterling, 2010). This can be seen in England with the focus on ongoing assessment and evaluation of progress towards goals. This formal assessment begins as early as 2 years of age, with a developmental progress check towards expected levels. Later, at the end of the Early Years Foundation Stage, children's progress towards the Early

Learning Goals, 'knowledge, understanding and abilities … progress against expected levels, and … readiness for Year 1' (DfE, 2017: 14), is assessed. A range of formal and statutory assessments continue at each key stage throughout a child's school life, categorising and labelling children in terms of their knowledge and understanding of academic subjects. The education system focuses heavily on outcomes of learning and the process of learning becomes a mere means to an end, where successful learning equates often simply to assessment success (Claxton, 2007).

Development takes place within the early years at a rapid rate and the first five years are characterised by 'phenomenal learning capacities' (McDowall Clark, 2016: 44) (see Chapter 2 for further discussion). Positive and negative habits developed in early childhood can have a lasting and enduring effect, so it makes sense to help children to develop positive habits towards learning, giving them sound building blocks to begin a process of lifelong learning. By supporting children to develop positive approaches or dispositions to learning, they will be equipped with the underpinning skills and capacities to cope with, adjust to and prepare for the acquisition of knowledge and understanding required for success in such an outcome-orientated system.

WHAT ARE DISPOSITIONS FOR LEARNING?

Bertram and Pascal (2002) identify dispositions as one of the key elements of effective learners. They are central to Claxton's (2002) concept of learning power and affect engagement with learning opportunities (Buckingham Shum and Deakin-Crick, 2012). Educational achievement is linked to specific dispositions towards learning (Watkins and Noble, 2013). A child who is supported to solve problems using novel and innovative methods is likely to approach future issues in original and resourceful ways. A child who is actively encouraged to seek out experiences and be inquisitive about the world will uncover new and exciting things to learn. A child who bounces back and moves forward after making a mistake or not achieving a goal will be more positive when facing future challenges. This links back to Claxton's (2002) four R's outlined previously. According to Katz (1985), the acquisition of knowledge and skills and dispositions to learn should be mutually exclusive as one is not desirable or useful without the other. If children become masters of their own knowledge, they will experience the intrinsic rewards associated with internal motivations for learning. This will be discussed further later in the chapter.

 reflection point 5.1

When working with young children, it is important to recognise yourself as a fellow learner. Think about your own incentives for learning. What motivates you? Thinking specifically, why are you reading this textbook? Is your drive to read an internal one? Or is it external? Are you reading for a particular goal? To be able to reach a specific mark in an assignment or task, or to support you to review practice? Consider whether you are more likely to read and understand material that you are interested in and curious about.

Dispositions to learn have been defined in many ways. They are patterns of behaviour, 'habits of mind that dispose the learner to interpret, edit and respond to experiences' (Carr, 1997: 2), habits of thought (Resnick, 1987) and 'proclivities' that determine the directions we take (Perkins, 1995: 275). A common theme here is that dispositions are habits, inclinations or tendencies, so we may infer that if positive 'habits' or dispositions can be instilled early it is likely that these will endure.

The range of dispositions relevant to learning is vast. With the wide range of attributes identified in the literature, it is difficult to be specific about which dispositions are essential to promote a positive approach to learning. According to Claxton (2007), effective learners are (in addition to various other competencies) curious and resilient, adventurous, imaginative and creative. Curiosity is a critical motivation on human behaviour (Lowenstein, 1994) and, as young children are naturally curious, this is regarded as a significant disposition to promote learning. Young children demonstrate creativity in their approach to learning, and creativity is increasingly being regarded as an essential disposition within society – for learners, for the workforce and ultimately for the economy. Finally, resilience gives learners the motivation to overcome challenge and to persist in the face of failure. These three dispositions will now be explored.

CURIOSITY

Natural curiosity is one of the driving forces behind the rapid early development of young children (Robinson, 2008), defined as the 'engine of intellectual development' (Engel, 2011: 632). Babies have innate curious tendencies and an inbuilt drive for discovery (Nutbrown and Page, 2008), demonstrated through their ability, even at a few days old, to show preferences through gaze (Gopnik et al., 1999). As they gain increasing control over their bodies, they demonstrate curiosity through sensory interactions with objects. This curiosity continues as children become mobile and independent.

Children are more likely to engage in learning opportunities in a deep and meaningful way if they are interested. Interests allow opportunities for spontaneous, participative inquiry, exploration and interpretation of ideas (Hedges and Cooper, 2016). Young children are drawn to new and novel experiences that spark their interest and which offer further learning opportunities as 'the curious amongst us ... lean in to get a closer look' (Shonstrom, 2016: 150). Research shows that when children have high levels of involvement (Laevers, 2005), they are more likely to be interested, motivated and show enthusiasm for learning (Bishop, 2006). The satisfaction of involvement comes from the exploratory drive or natural intrinsic curiosity of the child, and learning focused on discovery can lead to discovery in itself becoming a reward for learning (Bruner, 1974), leading to a positive spiral where curiosity can be regarded as both a cause and an effect of effective learning. A child's innate curiosity initially drives them to seek out and experience new and interesting experiences, which enable deep-level learning (Deakin Crick, 2007) and which serve as a motivator for children to seek further curious encounters.

 action point 5.1

Next time you are observing a child, consider the ways in which they are demonstrating curiosity about an activity, an object or an experience. Think about the ways in which you would define curiosity - would you use terms such as inquisitive? Nosey? Questioning?

(Continued)

Can you see a link between a child's interest and their curiosity?
Does a child's behaviour, their body language, facial expression, use of language or response, change when they are curious?

Research indicates that curiosity reduces over time, and, as children move through the formal education system, this natural and innate tendency diminishes. Shonstrom (2016) identifies 'killers of curiosity' which serve as obstacles to learning. The education system is one such obstacle where 'teachers ... have to work within a system that ... places quantitative results before qualitative analysis ... [and] competencies over curiosity' (Shonstrom, 2016: 155).

RESILIENCE

There is no universal definition of resilience – like other dispositions, it has been described in a variety of ways, but is generally viewed as the ability to cope with everyday life (Hill et al., 2007), the capacity to adapt, to recover, to 'bounce back' (Glover, 2009), to be able to persist with problems and challenges, to tolerate not knowing and to cope with making mistakes (Fuller, 2001). Mayr and Ulich (2009) maintain that resilient children have a proactive approach to problem solving and are persistent, curious and autonomous. It appears that to be resilient children require a range of sub-dispositions such as persistence, adaptiveness and curiosity, highlighting again that the distinction between dispositions is not clear. As one of the four R's of learning power (Claxton, 2002), resilience is central to the willingness and ability to learn. It enables learners to engage with situations, which may be complex and unpredictable, to take on challenges, to persist and to recover from setbacks (Wells and Claxton, 2002).

Taket, Nolan and Stagnitti (2014) regard resilience as a capacity which can be developed and strengthened, implying that it is more than a biological trait or 'innate toughness'. They found that families promote the development of resilience in young children through building problem-solving skills and supporting peer relationships. This supports the findings of Masten et al. (1995) that resilience can be enhanced through supportive relationships with adults, and Knight (2007) who identified the interplay between internal/personal and environmental factors in the development of resilience. Knight maintains that protective factors are more important than risk factors, and if these can be enhanced then so can resilience. This perspective, that resilience is not a fixed trait, but one which can be developed or weakened through experience, has important implications for educational programmes considering the value of developing resilience in children.

CREATIVITY

As with curiosity and resilience, creativity is difficult to define and measure (Craft, 2002). It is acknowledged that creativity is a desirable attribute for the workforce in our fast-paced, competitive and ever-changing twenty-first century society because creative people bring fresh ideas and new approaches to problems. In the literature, creativity has been linked with many attributes such as motivation, curiosity and commitment (Brolin, 1992) and with determination and perseverance (Dacey and Lennon, 1998). Sternberg (2003) views creativity as novel thinking where valuable ideas are produced through analysing and redefining problems under the premise that risks and mistakes are allowed and uncertainty accepted.

One of the issues raised in the literature is whether creativity is a personality trait or results from social factors and experience. Brolin (1992) refers to a 'creative personality' where individuals display motivation, endurance, commitment, curiosity and a willingness to take risks. In contrast, other perspectives (Brooker, 2011; Noyes, 2004) indicate that creativity is affected by the social environment and that learning in a supportive and appropriate environment with sensitive interactions can enhance a creative approach. Creativity is not considered by all to be a stable and enduring trait and, often, by the time children have moved through the education system, creativity has diminished.

Like curiosity, there are certain factors that can impede creativity – these include oversupervision, overemphasis on external rewards and time pressures (Amabile, 1988). The negative impact of externally motivated rewards on creativity has been explored in studies of education systems characterised by extrinsic motivation, such as in Hong Kong (Moneta and Sui, 2002), and within educational frameworks which focus heavily on adult-led and outcome-orientated assessment, as opportunities to demonstrate and strengthen creativity are limited. Another challenge is that teachers and educators traditionally promote behaviours such as obedience and good manners which are believed to suppress creativity (Saracho, 2012). 'Ideal learners' are characterised by conformity, so unique and novel approaches to problem solving do not match notions of the conforming individual (Benjamin, 1984). Cropley and colleagues (2010) maintain that creativity can be trained if teachers are aware of what to look for, supporting Williams et al.'s (2001) perspective that creativity can be cultivated – although, 'to engender creativity first we must value it' (Sternberg and Lubart, 1991: 614).

 spotlight on policy 5.1

The Statutory Guidance for the Early Years Foundation Stage (EYFS)

Practice in education is influenced and constrained by policy. Pedagogical approaches are framed by guidelines and frameworks. In England, 'effective' early years practice is outlined in the Statutory Guidance for the Early Years Foundation Stage (EYFS) (DfE, 2017). The EYFS identifies three prime and four specific areas of development that children should work towards by the end of the Foundation Stage. In addition, the **characteristics of effective learning** refer to the ways in which children engage with the environment and others, and these underpin the prime and specific areas. Development Matters (Early Education, 2012) is practice guidance used in many UK ECEC settings to outline the expected development and skills of children under 5. Although practitioners are encouraged to support children to explore and be curious about objects, events and people, to support them to take risks with new experiences, to problem solve, learn by trial and error, show

(Continued)

persistence and 'bounce back' after difficulties, the EYFS falls short of explicitly encouraging a focus on dispositions.

The Te Whãriki approach of New Zealand (Ministry of Education, 1996) is a holistic curriculum which promotes learning and development within a sociocultural context. The approach is founded on a vision that children 'grow up as competent and confident learners and communicators, healthy in mind, body and spirit, secure in their sense of belonging and in the knowledge that they make a valued contribution to society' (p. 4).

In addition to knowledge and skills, Te Whãriki upholds that children need dispositions to tackle new challenges and that there are close links between knowledge, skills and attitudes which help children to develop dispositions that encourage learning. Dalli (2011) found that the Te Whãriki curriculum was emergent and fluid, and practitioners have opportunities to identify 'possibilities for learning'. In addition, Cherrington (2016) found that practitioners used the language of Te Whãriki throughout practice, referring to dispositions and regarding children as confident and competent learners. This research highlights how policy and guidance can have a direct impact on the discourse used by practitioners, which influences the pedagogical approach taken. This has implications for practice to promote dispositions within the UK where dispositions are secondary and implied in policy rather than explicit. Thinking more broadly, the approach towards education and learning is constrained and directed by wider sociocultural factors which influence the broader aims of education and pedagogical approaches. In China, for example, where conformity is valued, creativity is not classed as a desirable trait and can lead to social isolation due to its association with unpredictability (Zhang et al., 2016). It is important to remember that the sociocultural context in which education takes place has a strong influence on how dispositions are defined, interpreted and valued.

---

 reflection point 5.2

Consider the ways in which different curriculum models such as the EYFS and Te Whãriki promote motivations to learn. How do they differ in their focus on process or outcome of learning and how does this fit in more broadly with the political or cultural approach to education within that society?

HOW DO EXTERNAL INFLUENCES AFFECT DISPOSITIONS?

One of the key aims of early childhood education should be to develop and promote dispositions for learning which enable children to enter school with positive attitudes to learning and development (Sylva, 1994), as a child's perception of their own potential is most influential in the early years for future success (Fuller, 2001). Early socialisation experiences develop and shape dispositions, with both the environment and interactions between children and adults having a lasting impact (Bertram and Pascal, 2002; Noyes, 2004). From this perspective, dispositions are socially situated and a product of experience (Brooker, 2011) which can be learned and taught (Resnick, 1987). Katz (1992) maintains that dispositions are not static and fixed entities but fluid and variable and can be strengthened or weakened by approaches to learning, warning that it is difficult to redevelop dispositions which have been extinguished. For positive dispositions to be utilised and applied, they must be supported, promoted and reinforced through opportunity and encouragement, making the environment and interactions that take place fundamental and giving adults a key role in nurturing and strengthening dispositions (Katz, 1992). Practitioners who are sensitive to children's interests and inquiries can tune into curiosity and motivations to learn (Hedges and Cooper, 2016).

For adults to support dispositions in children, they must consider the process of learning. In Carr and Claxton's (2004) terms, they should move away from a focus on the 'content curriculum' and attend to the 'learning curriculum', i.e. the 'how' rather than the 'what' or 'how much' (Claxton, 2007). However, with the constraints of prescriptive and assessment-focused curriculums, this remains a challenge for effective practice.

It is pertinent here to consider Laevers' (2005) work to create a 'process orientated child monitoring system' which focuses on the process of learning transferable core competencies as opposed to emphasising context, outcome and superficial learning. Motivations or intrinsic drives to learn are central to this approach and involvement in this context is linked to the exploratory drive which can be related to curiosity. For Laevers (2005), the exploratory drive guarantees lifelong learning, highlighting the key role of education to maintain and fuel intrinsic motivations. The Leuven scale has been used successfully in settings to assess levels of 'involvement' and 'wellbeing' – considered necessary factors for deep-level learning and development – demonstrating how a more balanced approach between process and outcome can be made; however, more generally, disputes over the measurement and assessment of concepts linked with process, such as dispositions, remain.

WHAT ARE THE CHALLENGES OF A DISPOSITION APPROACH?

One of the key challenges of a disposition approach is that the concept itself is abstract and lacking a unified and agreed definition (Sadler, 2002). Without clear and specific definitions, concepts such as creativity, curiosity and resilience are almost impossible to measure and assess, making them difficult to promote within education. Blaiklock (2008: 84) refers to the 'slippery nature of dispositions' and raises questions about whether these could or should be a focus for assessment and education. Diez (2006: 68) points out that dispositions can 'leak out in action' and can be interpreted through observations of children's behaviours, however interpretations would depend on practitioners having the skills and knowledge to understand the importance of dispositions and to know what to look for. It is clear from the literature that there is considerable overlap between dispositions such as creativity, curiosity and resilience. This implies that dispositions are 'combinations of attributes' which coexist and cannot be viewed, or measured, independently.

'If the development of positive learning dispositions is to be accepted as a legitimate and feasible educational aim then these ideas have to be translated into workable methods for their assessment' (Carr and Claxton, 2002: 10). This has been achieved to some extent with the development of instruments and measuring tools (Mayr and Ulich, 2009), including self-assessment approaches (Deakin-Crick et al., 2004) and observation frameworks (Fumoto et al., 2012). However, for a disposition approach to be successful, language focused around the process of learning is also necessary (Claxton, 2007) for practitioners to consider the personal qualities required for learning (Deakin-Crick and Yu, 2008). A discourse of disposition, similar to that highlighted by Cherrington (2016) and found in the Leuven scale, would enable dispositions to be at the forefront of practice. It is clear that there are serious challenges to utilising a disposition approach in education, but also evident that a shift towards valuing the processes of learning as well as outcomes can enable learners to be supported to develop the attitudes to learning which enable them to gain the learning power necessary for lifelong learning.

 case study 5.1

Supporting Play

Charlie (aged 40 months) is digging using a small spade to find a range of interesting objects which have been buried in the sand. Charlie has found three items already and has carefully removed these from the sand tray and placed them in a small bucket by his side. Charlie has been engaged in this activity for over 10 minutes when something catches his attention at the other side of the room and he moves away. Charlie shortly returns to find that another child is now in his space and all the spades are being used. Charlie watches for a moment then runs off towards the home corner. He opens one of the cupboards and picks up a spoon. Charlie returns to the sand tray and commences digging using the spoon. A practitioner looks over and sees Charlie using the spoon in the sand and says, 'no Charlie, the spoon belongs in the home corner, please put it back'. Charlie returns the spoon but when he comes back to the sand tray he notices another child has tipped out his bucket of objects back into the sand. Charlie starts to cry and the practitioner who has observed this goes over to Charlie and suggests that she help him find the items and put them back in the bucket. She hands Charlie a spade and the bucket and leads him back to the sand tray.

1. In what way was Charlie being creative, curious and resilient in his play?
2. In what way did the practitioner discourage Charlie's creativity?
3. How could the practitioner have enhanced creativity further?
4. How did the practitioner support Charlie to be resilient?

SUMMARY

- The concept of disposition is difficult to define, assess and measure, although there is agreement that children who are supported to develop positive dispositions will approach future learning opportunities in a more positive way.
- There are strong links between dispositions of curiosity, creativity and resilience which are interwoven and are key to successful and engaged learning.

- Pedagogical approaches may promote or discourage a focus on the process of learning, highlighting challenges to effective practice in curricula which prioritise outcomes of learning.
- Dispositions contribute to the development of positive habits for learning and should be promoted, encouraged and enhanced by sensitive and supportive adults who are aware of the importance of the process of learning to enable children to succeed within the education system and beyond.

online resources

Make sure to visit https://study.sagepub.com/fitzgeraldandmaconochie for selected SAGE videos (with questions), SAGE journal articles, links to external sources and flashcards.

FURTHER READING

Chappell, K., Cremin, T. and Jeffrey, B. (2015). *Creativity, Education and Society: Writings of Anna Craft*. London: Institute of Education Press.

This text is a useful and interesting collection of the work of Anna Craft who was a leading scholar on the subject of creativity and possibility thinking.

Shonstrom, E. (2016). *Wild Curiosity: How to Unleash Creativity and Encourage Lifelong Wondering*. London: Roman and Littlefield.

This is an inspiring text which explores motivations for learning and some of the wider societal factors which may extinguish these motives.

Watkins, M. and Noble, G. (2013). *Disposed to Learn: Schooling, Ethnicity and the Scholarly Habitus*. London: Bloomsbury.

This text draws on the work of Bourdieu to explore the impact of cultural diversity on dispositions to learn and learner outcomes.

REFERENCES

Amabile, T. (1988). A Model of Creativity and Innovation in Organisations. *Research in Organisational Behaviour, 10*: 123–67.

Benjamin, L. (1984). Creativity and Counselling. Highlights: An ERIC/CAPS Factsheet. Ann Arbor, MI: School of Education, University of Michigan. [online] Available at: http://files. eric.ed.gov/fulltext/ED260369.pdf [Accessed 2 July 2018].

Bertram, T. and Pascal, C. (2002). What Counts in Early Learning? In: O. Saracho and B. Spodek (eds), *Contemporary Perspectives in Early Childhood Curriculum*. Greenwich, CT: Information Age.

Bishop, G. (2006). True Independent Learning: An Andrological Approach – Giving control to the learner over choice of material and design of the study session. *Language Learning Journal*, *33*: 40–6.

Blaiklock, K. (2008). A Critique of the Use of Learning Stories to Assess the Learning Dispositions of Young Children. *New Zealand Research in Early Childhood Education Journal*, *11*: 77–87.

Brolin, C. (1992). Creativity and Critical Thinking: Tools for Preparedness for the Future. *Krut*, *53*: 64–71.

Brooker, L. (2011). Developing Learning Dispositions for Life. In: T. Waller, J. Whitmarsh and K. Clark (eds), *Making Sense of Theory and Practice in Early Childhood*. Maidenhead: Open University Press, pp. 83–101.

Bruner, J. (1974). *Beyond the Information Given: Studies in the Psychology of Knowing*. London: Allen and Unwin.

Buckingham Shum, S. and Deakin-Crick, R. (2012). *Learning Dispositions and Transferrable Competencies: Pedagogy, Modelling and Learning Analytics*. 2nd International Conference on Learning Analytics and Knowledge (29 April–2 May, Vancouver, BC). ACM Press: New York.

Carr, M. (1997). Learning Stories: Position Paper 5. Project for Assessing Children's Experiences. Department of Early Childhood Studies, University of Waikato.

Carr, M. and Claxton, G. (2002) Tracking the Development of Learning Dispositions. *Assessment in Education*, *9*(1): 9–37.

Carr, M. and Claxton, G. (2004). A Framework for Teaching Learning: Learning Dispositions. *Early Years International Journal of Research and Development*, *24*(1): 87–97.

Cherrington, S. (2016). Early Childhood Teachers' Thinking and Reflection: A Model of Current Practice in New Zealand. *Early Years*. [online] Available at: http://dx.doi.org/10.1080/095751 46.2016.1259211 [Accessed 2 July 2018].

Claxton, G. (2002). *Building Learning Power: Helping Young People become Better Learners*. Bristol: TLO.

Claxton, G. (2007). Expanding Young People's Capacity to Learn. *British Journal of Educational Studies*, *55*(2): 115–34.

Craft, A. (2002). *Creativity and Early Years Education*. London: Continuum.

Cropley, D. H., Cropley, A. J., Kaufman, J. C. and Runco, M. A. (2010). *The Dark Side of Creativity*. New York: Cambridge University Press.

Dacey, J. and Lennon, K. (1998). *Understanding Creativity: The Interplay of Biological, Psychological and Social Factors*. New York: Creative Education Foundation.

Dalli, C. (2011). A Curriculum of Open Possibilities: A New Zealand Kindergarten Teacher's View of Professional Practice. *Early Years*, *31*(3): 229–43.

Deakin-Crick, R. and Yu, G. (2008). Assessing Learning Dispositions: Is the Effective Lifelong Learning Inventory Valid and Reliable as a Measurement Tool? *Educational Research*, *50*(4): 387–402.

Deakin-Crick, R., Broadfoot, P. and Claxton, G. (2004). Developing an Effective Lifelong Learning Inventory: The ELLI Project. *Assessment in Education*, *11*(3): 248–72.

Deakin Crick, R. (2007). Learning How to Learn: The Dynamic Assessment of Learning Power. *The Curriculum Journal*, *18*(2): 135–153.

Department for Education (DfE) (2017). *Statutory Framework for the Early Years Foundation Stage*. London: The Stationery Office.

Diez, M. E. (2006). Assessing Dispositions: Context and Questions. *New Educator*, *2*(1): 57–72.

Early Education (2012). *Development Matters in the Early Years*. London: DfE/Early Education.

Engel, S. (2011). Children's Need to Know: Curiosity in Schools. *Harvard Educational Review*, *81*(4): 625–45.

Fuller, A. (2001). A Blueprint for Building Social Competencies in Children and Adolescents. *Australian Journal of Middle Schooling*, *1*(1): 40–8.

Fumoto, H., Robson, S., Greenfield, S. and Hargreaves, D. (2012). *Young Children's Creative Thinking*. London: Sage.

Glover, J. (2009). *Bouncing Back: How can Resilience be Promoted in Vulnerable Children and Young People?* Essex: Barnardos. [Online] Available at: www.barnardos.org.uk/bouncing_back_resilience_march09.pdf [Accessed 2 July 2018].

Gopnik, A., Meltzoff, A. and Kuhl, P. (1999). *How Babies Think*. London: Weidenfeld and Nicolson.

Hedges, H. and Cooper, M. (2016). Inquiring Minds: Theorising Children's Interests. *Journal of Curriculum Studies*, *48*(3): 303–22.

Hill, M., Stafford, A., Seaman, P., Ross, N. and Daniel, B. (2007). *Parenting and Resilience*. York: Joseph Rowntree Foundation.

Katz, L. (1985). Dispositions in Early Childhood Education. *ERIC/EECE Bulletin* 18. Urbana, IL: ERIC Clearinghouse on Elementary and Early Childhood Education.

Katz, L. (1992). *What Should Young Children be Learning?* Urbana, IL: ERIC Digest.

Knight, C. (2007). A Resilience Framework: Perspectives for Educators. *Health Education*, *107*(6): 543–55.

Laevers, F. (2005). *Deep Level Learning and the Experiential Approach in Early Childhood and Primary Education*. Leuven: Research Centre for Experiential Education.

Lowenstein, G. (1994). The Psychology of Curiosity: A Review and Reinterpretation. *Psychological Bulletin*, *116*(1): 75–98.

McDowall Clark, R. (2016). *Childhood in Society for the Early Years*, 3rd edn. London: Learning Matters/Sage.

Masten, A., Coatsworth, D., Neemann J., Gest, S., Tellegen, A. and Garmexey, M. (1995). The Structure and Coherence of Competence from Childhood to Adolescence. *Child Development*, *66*: 1635–59.

Mayr, T. and Ulich, M. (2009). Social-Emotional Well-being and Resilience of Children in Early Childhood Settings: PERIK – An empirically based observation scale for practitioners. *Early Years*, *29*(1): 45–57.

Ministry of Education (1996). *Te Whāriki: Early Childhood Curriculum*. Wellington, NZ: Learning Media.

Moneta, G. and Siu, C. (2002). Trait Intrinsic and Extrinsic Motivations, Academic Performance and Creativity in Hong Kong College Students. *Journal of College Student Development*, *43*(5): 664–83.

Noyes, A. (2004). Video Diary: A Method for Exploring Learning Dispositions. *Cambridge Journal of Education*, *34*(2): 193–209.

Nutbrown, C. and Page, J. (2008). *Working with Babies and Children from Birth to Three*. London: Sage.

Perkins, D. (1995). *Outsmarting IQ: The Emerging Science of Learnable Intelligence*. New York: The Free Press.

Resnick, L. (1987). *Education and Learning to Think*. Washington, DC: National Academies Press.

Robinson, M. (2008). *Child Development from Birth to Eight*. Maidenhead: Open University Press.

Sadler, D. (2002). Learning Dispositions: Can We Really Assess Them? *Assessment in Education*, *9*(1): 45–51.

Saracho, O. (2012). *Contemporary Perspectives on Research in Creativity in Early Childhood Education*. Charlotte, NC: Information Age Publishing.

Shonstrom, E. (2016). *Wild Curiosity: How to Unleash Creativity and Encourage Lifelong Wondering*. London: Rowman and Littlefield.

Sterling, S. (2010). Learning for Resilience or the Resilient Learner? Towards a Necessary Reconciliation in a Paradigm of Sustainable Education. *Environmental Education Research*, *16*(5–6): 511–28.

Sternberg, R. (2003). Creative Thinking in the Classroom. *Scandinavian Journal of Educational Research*, *47*(3): 325–38.

Sternberg, R. J. and Lubart, T. I. (1991). Creating Creative Minds. *The Phi Delta Kappan*, *72*(8): 608–14.

Sylva, K. (1994). School Influences on Children's Development. *Journal of Child Psychology and Psychiatry*, *34*(1): 235–70.

Taket, A., Nolan, A. and Stagnitti, K. (2014). Family Strategies to Support and Develop Resilience in Early Childhood. *Early Years*, *34*(3): 289–300.

Watkins, M. and Noble, G. (2013). *Disposed to Learn: Schooling, Ethnicity and the Scholarly Habitus*. London: Bloomsbury.

Wells, G. and Claxton, G. (2002). *Learning for Life in the 21st Century*. Oxford: Blackwell.

Williams, W., Markle, F., Brigockas, M. and Sternberg, R. (2001). *Creative Intelligence for School: 21 Lessons to Enhance Creativity in Middle and High School Students*. Needham Heights, MA: Allyn & Bacon.

Zhang, G., Chan, A., Zhong, J. and Yu, X. (2016). Creativity and Social Alienation: The Costs of Being Creative. *The International Journal of Human Resource Management*, *27*(12): 1252–76.

PART 2
CHILDREN INTERACTING

GO TO
https://study.sagepub.com/fitzgeraldandmaconochie *for free access to SAGE videos on topics covered in this book*

CHILDREN AS COMMUNICATORS

BY TANYA RICHARDSON

Before reading the chapter, I was aware that children start communicating prior to birth and that this develops further once they are born; however, I was not aware of the huge impact the outdoors has on their communication skills.

The key theories discussed are compared clearly and the summary table of the different approaches acts as a reminder, saving you time from doing in-depth research on each theorist separately.

The chapter helped me to reflect on what I observe during my own placement and work experience – for example when children get upset they try to imitate what has happened as well as trying to explain with words. This has enabled me to understand them better when they are trying to speak whilst crying.

JENNIFER TO
BA EARLY CHILDHOOD STUDIES
UNIVERSITY OF NORTHAMPTON

learning outcomes

By actively reading this chapter and engaging with the material, you will be able to:

- identify key theories on how children's communication is developed and enhanced
- debate ways that communication is impacted on by other aspects of development
- investigate social and cultural influences on children's communication development
- question the impact of the digital age on children's communication
- evaluate ways that children can be supported to become confident and competent communicators in a diverse society.

INTRODUCTION

Children communicate in many ways: through posture, facial expressions, body language, the expression of emotion (see Chapter 4 for further discussion). This communication develops as children grow and learn, with babies learning to communicate their needs through cries and gestures, progressing to cooing and babbling and, eventually, around the age of 18 months to 2 years old, children experience what is often referred to as the verbal explosion or the 'spurt in vocabulary' (Berk, 2009: 376). Irrespective of how children choose to communicate, it is recognised that speech and language are crucial to a child's outcomes in later life, and therefore language development is particularly important when thinking about communication (Bercow, 2008; Field, 2010). This chapter explores communication from the perspective of the child's holistic development and environmental factors that impact on language.

IS CHILDREN'S COMMUNICATION DEVELOPED THROUGH NATURE OR NURTURE?

When considering speech and language development, it is important to establish what is meant by this and analyse theory within this area to develop a broad understanding. Barrett (1999: 1) provides a definition for spoken language as 'a code in which spoken sound is used in order to encode meaning'. There is ongoing debate over whether the ability to speak and communicate is a learned behaviour, from the behaviourist perspective (Skinner, 1957); or is a skill that, from a nativist perspective, is 'etched into the structure of the brain' (Berk, 2009: 359).

Chomsky (1965), a highly regarded theorist in the area of speech and language development, was an advocate for development within this area being a product of processes within the brain. Chomsky claimed that all children are born with the innate ability to communicate and converse using spoken language. He argued that this was the only explanation for young children learning such a wide range of vocabulary, and how they learnt to apply that vocabulary, in such a short amount of time (Skinner et al., 1973). Chomsky (1965) argued that all children are born with a Language Acquisition Device (LAD), an area within the brain which he believed to be pre-programmed to absorb and compute the components of language. Research has been undertaken that shows that children's ability to learn language is universal and not specifically culturally linked. Children speaking different languages have been found to be mastering similar sounds at similar points within their development (Slobin, 1971) and this goes some way to reinforcing Chomsky's theory, that language acquisition is a natural phenomenon and develops in a pre-determined order (see Chapter 2 for further discussion on early brain development).

In contrast to Chomsky's theory, Skinner (1957) holds that the ability to communicate is a learned behaviour. He argues that language is taught to children by adults who repeat sounds and support meanings, so that young children are able to develop the skills of communication and expand their vocabulary. This theory is reinforced when researching cases where extreme neglect has occurred and social interaction has been absent or severely reduced (Koluchova, 1972). Children progress only once they receive a level of interaction from those who already have the skills required. Skinner's theory, that the ability to communicate using language is a learned behaviour, holds some credibility in these situations.

In more recent times, building on the theories of Skinner and Chomsky, scientific research has acknowledged that the development of the brain has an important and vital part to play in speech and language learning. Robinson (2003) asserts that the left hemisphere of the brain is deemed to be the most crucial in the development of the finer points of speech, in learning and recalling correct vocabulary, for example. At around the age of 18 months, the left side of the brain becomes more dominant. This is usually the stage of a child's life when the 'verbal explosion' takes place. It could be argued therefore that an element of nativist development is occurring within this area. This is a reasonable conclusion as a child cannot learn to develop one side of their brain to be more dominant than the other. This therefore gives some support to Chomsky's theory and to his notion of a language acquisition device.

However, given the variance seen in levels of speech and language in young children, this is unlikely to provide a full explanation. What seems more likely, with regards to speech and language development, is that it is a combination of behaviourist and nativist theories. It was argued by Lenneberg (1967) that speech and language development is indeed a combination of the two. He held that the acquisition of speech and language is a natural ability that all are born with, but that this development cannot happen successfully without support and example from more experienced language users. Tomasello (2003) expands on this theory further and asserts that for children to acquire language they need to engage in a social process, but this can only be enhanced once the innate development has happened. This usage-based theory works on the principle that children need first to have the physical ability to communicate and can, only then, apply their social knowledge of how to use this language within situations, and hence expand their range of vocabulary.

The conclusion that can be drawn from this plethora of research is that children, most significantly, require social interaction in order to develop a competence in language and its application. Furthermore, there is a requirement to build on the predisposed skills that are present at birth. However, this cannot happen without interaction from other people. This illustrates the importance of children receiving encouragement and support from an early age, to maximise their development with regards to communication, speech and language.

action point 6.1

Compare and contrast the different approaches in Table 6.1 to evaluate the contribution of biology/genetics and the environment on language development.

Table 6.1 Theorists and their contributions

Theorist	Life span	Theoretical approach	Contributions to the theory of speech and language development
Noam Chomsky	1928–present	Nativist	Chomsky believes that children are biologically pre-programmed to develop language skills and this will happen irrespectively. Chomsky theorised that children are all born with a Language Acquisition Device (LAD) that enables their brains to develop the required skills to be able to speak and communicate.
B.F. Skinner	1904-1990	Behaviourist	Skinner argued that speech develops as a result of positive reinforcement from adults. An example of this is when parents express delight at the child making sounds. Skinner believed that children continue to develop in order to gain further praise and encouragement.
Jean Piaget	1896-1980	Cognitive	Piaget believed that children explore the world through movement and the use of their senses (sensori-motor stage) and that language develops as a result of this exploration. This theory gives an emphasis to the requirement of an appropriate environment.
Lev Vygotsky	1896-1934	Social interactionist	Vygotsky built on the theory from Piaget, by arguing that in addition to the cognitive aspects there is also a need that children interact with others in order to develop speech and language.
Jerome Bruner	1915-2016	Social interactionist	Bruner introduced the concept of scaffolding – aiding development with the use of a more knowledgeable other. He asserted that language is developed by the supporting relationship of a significant other.

HOW DOES CHILDREN'S COMMUNICATION FIT WITH OTHER AREAS OF DEVELOPMENT?

Speech, language and the skills required for communication do not develop in isolation and need other areas of development to be encouraged alongside so that the child can develop holistically; meaning that one aspect of development can, and does, influence others. An example of this is physical development. It is reported that physical movement and use of the voice are neurologically linked (McGilchrist, 2009), and when children are being active they are more likely to use their voice. It could be argued that an increase in physical activity means that children then have a greater ability to gesture, to point, to move around more and to access things that particularly interest them. This therefore can enhance children's speech and language development by aiding the extension of vocabulary (Campos et al., 2000). The more children are able to move, the more they have to talk about. Interestingly, verbal explosion, as discussed earlier, usually occurs at a time when children are becoming more physically active. Piaget and Inhelder (1969) asserted that for a child to be able to enhance their language, they first need to be able to locate themselves in their environment and reach the realisation that they co-exist – with other people and with objects. This relates to a child's sense of self and therefore can be associated with their social development. If it is important that a child is physically active in order to develop their communication skills, social interaction is also crucial. It could therefore be assumed that if a child is disadvantaged in one of these areas, their language development could also be affected. Bedford, Pickles and Lord (2015) have indeed found some connection between these areas, acknowledging that reduced physical ability appears to impact on the development of language.

Figure 6.1 shows language as the centre piece of a child's holistic development, and it is theorised that language is indeed pivotal to all other aspects of a child's development, and the other aspects of development impact, in turn, on the child's development with regards to communication. This offers more credibility to the point made earlier in this chapter that an environment, and the people within that environment, can impact on children's speech and language development.

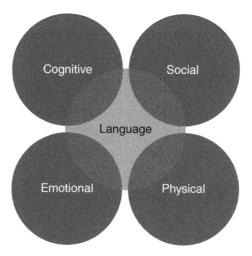

Figure 6.1 The pivotal role of language in holistic development

reflection point 6.1

Observe a child/group of children around the age of 2 to 3 years old and reflect on how communication/language links with other aspects of their development. Observe where the child(ren) communicate(s) the most. To assist, you may find it helpful to consider the questions below.

Do you think that children need to use other skills in order to maximise their language skills? Are those that are more physical speaking more? If a child is communicating a lot, is that helping other areas of their development? What happens to a child who is struggling with one area of their development - does it impact on their language? Do you agree with the concept that all areas of development are intrinsically linked? Explain why.

WHAT INFLUENCE DO SOCIAL AND CULTURAL SITUATIONS HAVE ON COMMUNICATION?

Whilst recognising that holistic development can impact on a child's communication, it is also noted that the economic and social factors that a child is exposed to can influence this area of development. Research by Hart and Risley (1995) found that a child's parents' influence was so significant that, by the age of 3, children whose parents were considered to be of a higher socio-economic class, had a much larger repertoire of vocabulary than children whose families were reliant on the state benefit system. The difference in words heard by children from the two types of family was up to 300 spoken words per hour. Calculating this over a 12-month period, children with the higher socio-economic background would hear 11 million words, in comparison to those from families at the other end of the spectrum, who would hear just three million words per year. A note of caution is needed here. With any studies that include socio-economic status as a variable, it may be possible to make broad generalisations but we should avoid applying these to individual families. However, thinking broadly, this could obviously have an influence on children's speech and language development. It was discussed earlier in this chapter how important social interaction is to communication, and the social interaction within the family environment is especially significant. Gross (2012) agrees with Hart and Risley (1995) and states that children from areas of social deprivation are more likely to be starting their school lives with communication skills below that of their peers (Gross, 2012). Sosu and Ellis (2014) have found a 13-month difference with regards to vocabulary acquisition in children at the age of 5, when comparing children from areas of deprivation to their peers from more economically affluent areas. Irrespective of socio-economic background however, it is noted that what parents do with their children has an impact on their development (Tizard and Hughes, 1984). Hart and Risley (1995), Sosu and Ellis (2014) and Tizard and Hughes (1984) therefore show some agreement with interactionist theories (Bruner, 1983), which argue that children need interaction with others, alongside the inborn ability to communicate, to be able to develop to the best of their abilities within this area.

As a response to the research detailed above, early years practitioners within England need to demonstrate an awareness of the importance of speech and language development for all children and with particular thought for disadvantaged children. Ofsted (2015: 11) reported that this should be the prime area of concern for those children eligible for the two-year funding (additional access to ECEC offered by the English government for 2-year-olds in disadvantage). Ofsted report that 'every interaction (is used) as an opportunity to develop children's speech, language and vocabulary' (2015: 11). It could be said, though, that it is not just interaction with others that is needed to stimulate development in communication, but also interaction with the material environment.

Marshall and Lewis (2013) recognise the family home as being an important influence on speech and language development; the environment itself, as well as what happens within that environment. Participants in Marshall and Lewis' study believed that the home's physical environment was an important influence, particularly in regards to 'space, cleanliness, sound (including television), activities available to the child, toys/play and resources available outside of the home' (2013: 347). The development of communication has also been found to have strong links with the level of responsiveness shown by the child's mother (Tamis-LeMonda et al., 2001). Researchers also found that the maternal responsiveness given to a child at the age of 13 months was an accurate indication of how children will develop their use of **expressive language**, how they will show **syntactic development** and how they will be able to recollect past events in the correct context. This shows that although research (Hart and Risley, 1995; Sosu and Ellis, 2014) indicates that the socio-economic situation of a family is important with regards to speech, language and communication development, it is not purely that factor which determines how a child develops. Tamis-LeMonda, Bornstein and Baumwell (2001) show that interaction between the mother and child is also important with regards to language acquisition, but it could be said that this is the case for parents per se. The EPPE project (Sylva et al., 2003: 6) found that what is important with regards to parents is not what qualifications or background they have, but what they do with their children.

From a practitioner's perspective, therefore, what is important is that the family situation is taken account of, but also a high-quality ECEC environment and high quality within the child's family relations are strived for. A child's speech and language development needs quality interactions and experiences in which they can engage and that they can learn from. Consideration therefore needs to be given to how early years practice can support this and how practitioners can assist all parents in supporting this aspect of their child's development.

HOW DOES THE DIGITAL AGE INFLUENCE CHILDREN'S COMMUNICATION?

England is reportedly becoming a digital nation, with today's young reportedly accessing, on average, two hours of television, and more if using other devices, screen time a day (Yelland, 2011; Ofcom, 2017). Interestingly though, although children are accessing digital devices at a young age within England, children are still accessing literature, with 99.7% of children reporting that they have access to books within their homes, and with children reporting to own an average of 89 books (Formby, 2014). It is known that when adults and children look at books together, this has a significant positive impact on a child's communication (Doyle and Bramwell, 2006). It is therefore important not to just give children access to books but also to encourage social interaction alongside these books. Formby (2014) found that 73% of children reportedly have access to a touchscreen device, and although children of a lower socio-economic status are less likely to have one (63% compared to 73%), those who do have a digital device are twice as likely as their peers to access books on that device. Building on the point discussed earlier in this chapter, that children from a lower socio-economic background reportedly have lower language abilities (Hart and Risley, 1995), this continues to emphasise the importance of social interactions, and of the encouragement of communication development by engaging with others. It is neither possible nor desirable to stop the influence of the digital world, however what is pertinent is that the crucial aspect that needs to remain is the social interaction alongside these digital devices. This social interaction is that which aids communication and language development (Tomasello, 2003).

 case study 6.1

Language Development

A parent comes to see you in your setting with concerns over Paul, her 3-year-old son. She is worried because he does not communicate when she takes him out anywhere. Mum reports that at home her son spends a lot of his time in his bedroom alone, playing on his games console. He is an only child. Dad lives with them, although he has to work long hours and is not home often. They do not eat meals together as a family and, apart from coming to the setting, Mum has stopped taking him anywhere else because he does not communicate when they are there.

1. Using the learning from this chapter so far, what suggestions could you make on how this family could help their son Paul's language development?
2. What could you do in the setting to help?

HOW CAN CHILDREN BE SUPPORTED TO BECOME CONFIDENT AND COMPETENT COMMUNICATORS IN A DIVERSE SOCIETY?

Smidt (2013) believes that to learn to communicate appropriately means that children have to master interaction with others in particular contexts or social situations. She states that a child's dialogue can only be constructed successfully once the social interactions that children are exposed to meet their inner meanings and the **cultural symbols** that the children have previously been exposed to. This reinforces the notion that the environment, and the experiences that are provided within that environment, will provoke development of a child's communication skills. Therefore, it is likely, that children who are given a wider range of experiences, and are exposed to a wider range of environments from a young age, will have a greater vocabulary and an increased wish to communicate. Ferguson et al. (2013) believe that the physical environment that a child is exposed to has an impact on their socioemotional and cognitive development, and this impact is shown throughout a child's whole life. It is therefore crucial that children have access to a communication-enhancing and stimulating environment. Thinking back to case study 6.1, this emphasises that providing access to environments that Paul would enjoy could be an important and useful strategy.

This communication-enhancing and stimulating environment should provide opportunities for children to express their views and opinions and to collaborate in their play and learning (Claxton and Carr, 2004) and should reflect children's interests so that they have the desire, and the disposition, to talk and hence to learn (Curtis and Carter, 2003). Jarman (2007) argues that a specific area is necessary to encourage children to communicate, which is cosy and inviting, although it is argued that this should occur throughout a setting, and not be restricted to certain areas. It is important to consider how communication, opportunities to talk, read, discuss and play should be woven throughout a setting.

When considering the impact of environment on a child's communication, children should be able to access outdoor environments and natural environments (e.g. Forest Schools) as well as the traditional indoor classroom environment. It is recognised that the outdoors is beneficial for children's physical development (BERA/TACTYC, 2014; Fjørtoft, 2004) and for creative development (Knight, 2011), but it is also acknowledged that the outdoors can help children to communicate (Richardson, 2014). Research undertaken by the Department for Children, Schools and Families (DCSF) (2007) found that children can speak up to five times as much when engaged in outdoor play. It has also been found that the quality of speech is improved when children are given access to Forest School environments (Richardson and Murray, 2017). What is important therefore is that enhancing and stimulating environments are provided within different contexts to enable every child to develop to their maximum potential.

As well as providing stimulation, it is important that a child's environment should be culturally relevant (Marshall and Lewis, 2013). Within England, approximately a fifth of children have English as an additional language (EAL) (NALDIC, 2016). The EYFS statutory guidance (DfE, 2017) states that children should be given the opportunity to develop their home language whilst in the setting as well as being encouraged to develop a 'good standard in English language' (DfE, 2017: 9). With regards to assessing a child's development within this area, the DfE (2017) states that children should primarily be assessed on their capabilities in English and, then, if appropriate, should be assessed in their home language with the support of parents/carers. It is recognised that practitioners who work with children with EAL need a different set of skills and level of knowledge than when dealing with children who have English as a first language (see Chapter 15 for further discussion). A recurring theme to support communication is how social interaction is an essential component and whether children speaking a different language to their peers could provide a barrier to this social development. It is therefore worth considering how practitioners can support development within these areas.

action point 6.2

Each ECEC setting will have a connection with a speech and language therapist. To explore this further, try to speak to the therapist and find out some information about their services – what do they offer parents and children? What is required before a child can be referred for support? What can be done in practice to help? How does the support differ for children who do not speak English as their first language?

SUMMARY

This chapter has discussed children as communicators, and has explored key theory and research to be able to conclude the following:

- Children develop communication through interaction with others and by interacting with their environments. Although children need to be born with the physical ability to communicate, they also have a need to be nurtured to fully develop within this crucial area of communication.
- Children develop holistically but communication and language development is the centre piece to other areas – all areas are intrinsically linked to one another.
- Based on the fact that social development is crucial to language development, it is imperative that children have the right start in life – that parents, practitioners and peers provide an environment that is supportive and that reflects a child's culture and community. This should result in them feeling comfortable, and encourage them to thrive.
- Although children have increasing access to digital devices, this does not necessarily have a negative effect on communication and language, however it remains important to maintain social interaction alongside this digital access.
- Children need access to a wide range of opportunities and environments and when considering early years practice, consideration needs to be given to providing children with the enriching experiences that they deserve. Children with English as an additional language need practitioners to support and encourage their development in a way that supports their needs.

 online resources

Make sure to visit https://study.sagepub.com/fitzgeraldandmaconochie for selected SAGE videos (with questions), SAGE journal articles, links to external sources and flashcards.

FURTHER READING

ICan (2017). [online] Available at: www.ican.org.uk [Accessed 23 July 2017].

This children's communication charity website provides resources for parents/carers and practitioners and deals with speech and language from birth to 16 years old.

Communication Trust (2017). [online] Available at: www.thecommunicationtrust.org.uk [Accessed 23 July 2017].

The Communication Trust, a network of over 50 not-for-profit organisations, provides a wealth of information on this website. It is designed for anyone who may be involved in speech and language development for children and young people.

Hayes, C. (2016). *Language, Literacy and Communication in Early Years*. Northwich: Critical Publishing.

This book details language acquisition and considers how language ability impacts on literacy and learning, set in a political and sociological context.

REFERENCES

Barrett, M. (1999). *The Development of Language*. London: Psychology Press.

Bedford, R., Pickles, A. and Lord, C. (2015). Early Gross Motor Skills Predict the Subsequent Development of Language in Children with Autism Spectrum Disorders. *Physical Therapy*, *91*(7): 1116–29.

BERA/TACTYC (2014). Early Years Policy Advice: Learning, Development and Curriculum. [online] Available at: www.bera.ac.uk/wp-content/uploads/2014/02/Early-Years-Summary-Learning-Development-and-Curriculum.pdf [Accessed 22 February 2017].

Bercow, J. (2008). *The Bercow Report: A Review of Services for Children and Young People (0–19) with Speech, Language and Communication Needs*. Nottingham: DCSF Publications.

Berk, L. (2009). *Child Development*, 8th edn. London: Pearson Education.

Bruner, J. (1983). *Child's Talk: Learning to Use Language*. Oxford: Oxford University Press.

Campos, J., Anderson, D., Barbu-Roth, M., Hubbard, E., Hertenstein, M. and Witherington, D. (2000). Travel Broadens the Mind. *Infancy*, *1*(2): 149–219.

Chomsky, N. (1965). *Current Issues in Linguistic Theory*. The Hague: Mouton.

Claxton, G. and Carr, M. (2004). A Theoretical Framework for Teaching Learning: Learning Dispositions. *Early Years International Journal of Research and Development*, *24*(1): 87–97.

Curtis, D. and Carter, M. (2003). *Designs for Living and Learning*. St Paul: Red Leaf.

Department for Children, Schools and Families (DCSF) (2007). *Confident, Capable and Creative: Supporting Boys' Achievements*. Nottingham: DCSF Publications.

Department for Education (DfE) (2017). *Statutory Framework for the Early Years Foundation Stage*. [online] Available at: www.foundationyears.org.uk/files/2017/03/EYFS_STATUTORY_FRAMEWORK_2017.pdf [Accessed 14 April 2017].

Department for Education (DfE) (2014). *Statutory Framework for the Early Years Foundation Stage*. London: DfE Publications.

Doyle, B. and Bramwell, W. (2006). Promoting Emergent Literacy and Social-Emotional Learning through Dialogic Reading. *The Reading Teacher*, *59*(6): 554–64.

Ferguson, K., Cassells, R., MacAllister, J. and Evans, G. (2013). The Physical Environment and Child Development: An International Review. *International Journal of Psychology*, 48(4): 437–68.

Field, F. (2010). *The Foundation Years: Preventing Poor Children Becoming Poor Adults. The report of the Independent Review on Poverty and Life Chances*. London: HM Government.

Fjørtoft, I. (2004). Landscape as Playscape: The Effects of Natural Environments on Children's Play and Motor Development. *Children, Youth and Environments*, 14(2): 21–44.

Formby, S. (2014). *Parent's Perspectives: Children's Use of Technology in the Early Years*. London: National Literacy Trust.

Gross, J. (2012). The National Perspective: How Are We Doing? In: M. Gascoigne (ed.), *Better Communication: Shaping Speech, Language and Communication Services for Children and Young People*. London: RCSLT.

Hart, B. and Risley, T. (1995). *Meaningful Differences in the Everyday Experience of Young American Children*. Baltimore, MD: Brookes Publishing Co.

Jarman, E. (2007). *Communication Friendly Spaces*. London: Basic Skills Agency.

Knight, S. (2011). *Risk and Adventure in Early Years Outdoor Play: Learning from Forest Schools*. London: Sage.

Koluchova, J. (1972). Severe Deprivation in Twins: A Case Study. *Journal of Child Psychology and Psychiatry and Allied Disciplines*, 13(2): 107–14.

Lenneberg, E. (1967). *The Biological Foundations of Language*. New York: Wiley.

McGilchrist, I. (2009). *The Master and his Emissary: The Divided Brain and the Making of the Western World*. London: Yale University Press.

Marshall, J. and Lewis, E. (2013). 'It's the Way You Talk to Them': The Child's Environment – Early years practitioners' perceptions of its influence on speech and language development, its assessment and environment targeted interventions. *Child Language Teaching and Therapy*, 30(3): 337–52.

NALDIC (2016). Research, Publications and Statistics. [online] Available at: https://naldic.org.uk/the-eal-learner/research-and-statistics [Accessed 21 May 2018].

Ofcom (2017). Children and Parents: Media Use and Attitudes Report. [online] Available at: www.ofcom.org.uk/__data/assets/pdf_file/0020/108182/children-parents-media-use-attitudes-2017.pdf [Accessed 20th June 2018].

Ofsted (2015). *Teaching and Play in the Early Years: A Balancing Act?* Manchester: Ofsted Publications.

Piaget, J. and Inhelder, B. (1969). *The Psychology of the Child*. London: Routledge and Kegan Paul.

Richardson, T. (2014). *Speech and Language Development in a Forest School Environment: An Action Research Project*. London: SAGE Research Methods Cases. [online] Available at: http://srmo.sagepub.com/view/methods-case-studies-2013/n342.xml [Accessed 22 January 2017].

Richardson, T. and Murray, J. (2017). Are Young Children's Utterances Affected by Characteristics of their Learning Environments? A Multiple Case Study. *Early Child Development and Care*, 187(3–4): 457–68.

Robinson, M. (2003). *From Birth to One: The Year of Opportunity*. Buckingham: Open University Press.

Skinner, B. (1957). *Verbal Behaviour*. New York: Appleton-Century-Crofts.

Skinner, D., Bruce, D. and Oates, J. (1973). *Generative Linguistics: Language Acquisition – Language and Cognition*. Bletchley: Open University Press.

Slobin, D. (1971). *Psycholinguistics*. London: Scott, Foresmann and Co.

Smidt, S. (2013). *The Developing Child in the 21st Century: A Global Perspective on Child Development*. London: Routledge.

Sosu, E. and Ellis, S. (2014). How Can we Close the Attainment Gap between Pupils from High- and Low-Income Families in Scotland? [online] Available at: www.jrf.org.uk/report/closing-attainment-gap-scottish-education [Accessed 22 December 2016].

Sylva, K., Melhuish, E., Sammons, P., Siraj-Blatchford, I., Taggart, B. and Elliot, K. (2003). *The Effective Provision of Pre-school Education (EPPE) Project: Findings from the Pre-school Period*. London: The EPPE Office.

Tamis-LeMonda, C., Bornstein, M. and Baumwell, L. (2001). Maternal Responsiveness and Children's Achievement of Language Milestones. *Child Development*, *72*(3): 748–67.

Tizard, B. and Hughes, M. (1984). *Young Children Learning*. Oxford: Blackwell Publishing.

Tomasello, M. (2003). *Constructing Language: A Usage-based Theory of Language Acquisition*. London: Harvard University Press.

Yelland, N. (2011). Reconceptualising Play and Learning in the Lives of Young Children. *Australasian Journal of Early Childhood*, *36*(2): 4–12.

CHILDREN'S FRIENDSHIPS

BY CARON CARTER

Sections in this chapter were well explained and straight to the point. My favourite features are the reflection points, chapter summary, further reading and learning outcomes. The learning outcomes gives you an overview of what the chapter will cover. This way you know straight away what to expect.

The chapter summary is great to refresh your memory if you don't want to read the whole chapter again and can come in handy for revision. The further reading section gives you additional materials if you would like to gain greater insight into friendships.

JULIA KOZIRKO
BSC (HONS) PSYCHOLOGY AND EARLY
CHILDHOOD STUDIES
UNIVERSITY OF SUFFOLK

 learning outcomes

By actively reading this chapter and engaging with the material, you will be able to:

- explain how different disciplines define friendship
- understand what friendship means to young children
- develop your knowledge of children's peer culture
- identify some of the challenges and demands of children's friendships
- critically evaluate intervention strategies used to support children's friendships.

INTRODUCTION

This chapter explores the phenomenon of children's friendships. It begins by defining what friendship is and how different **disciplines** define this concept. Then it moves to what friendship means for children. Children have various types of friendships, including imaginary friends and their siblings. This chapter also explores the everyday challenges of friendship and how children manage this. Finally, the chapter concludes by outlining two intervention programmes used in schools to encourage sustainable friendships.

WHAT IS FRIENDSHIP? WHEN DOES IT START?

Friendship is a field that has been researched since 1933 (Koch, 1933; Moreno, 1943; Sullivan, 1953; Gronlund, 1959). Many researchers have tried to define exactly what friendship is. Bukowski (1996) states that friendship has 'liking' at its core. Children like each other, are attracted to each other and enjoy spending time in one another's company. Dunn (2004: 13) echoes this idea of children liking to do things together and views friendship as 'understanding and sharing the other person's interests and ideas, as well as mutual affection and support'. Dunn notes that this definition can include toddlers and preschoolers, although there is evidence to suggest that babies do interact with each other from as early as a few months (Howes, 1996). Doherty and Hughes (2009: 37) drew on the work of Newcomb and Bagwell (1995) to define friendship further. They came up with four features of friendship to help with their definition (Table 7.1).

Table 7.1 Features of friendship

Reciprocity - where both friends enjoy playing together

Intense social activity - involves extended play periods, requiring effort to establish and maintain games

Conflict resolution - where friends solve problems, negotiate and compromise together

Effective task performance - this overlaps with all three features above, but results in a joint outcome

Friendship is often most visible during the toddler and preschool years when children form a common bond around an area of interest (Doherty and Hughes, 2009). For example, if two children enjoy playing alongside one another in the construction area, this shared interest can bring about a friendship. As children get older, the features or qualities of friendship shift. Older children view intimacy, loyalty and confidence as part of a **reciprocal relationship** (Dunn, 2004).

Other disciplines define friendship in different ways (Bagwell and Schmidt, 2011). This section will look at how the disciplines of **psychology** and **sociology** describe friendship.

PSYCHOLOGY

The field of psychology labels children's relationships as either **vertical** or **horizontal**. Vertical relationships have a power imbalance and these might be relationships with parents or teachers. Horizontal relationships are defined as those that are more equal. Peer relationships would be described as horizontal. A significant amount of research on children's friendships was carried out in the field of psychology during the 1980s and 1990s. The method most commonly used to collect data was known as **'socio-metric' testing**. Children were asked to name the children they liked to play with and, even in some cases, those they did not like to play with (Coie et al., 1982). This data was used to categorise children into status groups (Table 7.2).

Table 7.2 Categories of peer acceptance

Popular	These children are selected most frequently as they are most liked.
Rejected	These children are selected in relation to negative nominations and are least liked by their peers.
Neglected	These children are not selected as either most liked or least liked. They are often overlooked by their peers.

Source: Adapted from Rubin et al. (1992)

These categories were then studied and researched further to come up with characteristic behaviours to accompany each category. For example, children who were classed as **'rejected'** often demonstrated inappropriate and disruptive behaviours. This resulted in other children physically moving away from them. These children were more likely to become isolated or remain in the rejected category throughout their school years (Coie and Dodge, 1983; Dodge, 1983). The children who were classed as **'popular'** were liked by their peers and displayed more co-operative behaviours. Today, this type of research may be unethical, particularly if children are asked to nominate children they do not like to play with. Nevertheless, this study raised the profile of research on children's friendships in the field of psychology.

SOCIOLOGY

In the field of sociology, friendship research focuses on how children build their own **peer culture** and make sense of the world. For instance, Corsaro (2003) used an **ethnographic** lens to study friendship and look at how children define it themselves (see Spotlight on Research 7.1). Corsaro spent an extended period of time in the field and attempted to become one of the children to try to understand the children's perspectives on friendship and peer culture. This research considered how children draw on and adapt the rules and routines of the adult world to produce their own distinct peer culture. This process was coined '**interpretive reproduction**'. As Bagwell and Schmidt (2011: 8) explain, 'the children themselves define their relationship rather than an outsider's view' being used. The sociologist's role is to study how children make meaning about their friendships and then portray this in the most authentic means possible (for more information on this, see Carter and Nutbrown, 2016).

spotlight on research 7.1

William Corsaro's Ethnographic Research

William Corsaro started to study children's peer culture in 1988. Previous research focused on **individualism** and Corsaro decided to move away from this towards an interpretive approach. He was interested in how children take information from the adult world and interpret and internalise this in their own way. Former research had started this thinking (Piaget, 1968; Damon, 1977; Vygotsky, 1978; Selman, 1980). Corsaro felt that children had been underestimated and could work together and collaboratively with their peers. Corsaro (1992: 160) sought to examine how children use the adult world to create their own distinct peer culture, coined 'interpretive reproduction'. Peer culture was defined as 'a stable set of activities or routines, artefacts, values and concerns [where] children produce and share interaction with peers' (Corsaro and Eder, 1990: 197). Some of Corsaro's research (2003) was carried out using an ethnographic approach so that he could immerse himself in the children's peer culture and enter their secret world.

IDENTIFYING FRIENDSHIPS

Howes (1996) argues that children under 2 years old are identified by teachers and parents as friends. Similarly, research indicates that by 12 months of age children could select a particular friend from their peer group to interact with (Howes, 1983). Other research has been conducted to try to determine friendship within the early years. Hartup (1989) collected data with toddlers, focusing on behaviour rather than verbal means of displaying friendship. Children's preference and proximity to one another were used to define friendship. In this case, a friendship was defined by children wanting to play closely alongside one another.

Another way of determining friendship has involved asking parents to look at the weekly or daily interactions of their children with others (Ladd and Golter, 1988). Parents can be highly influential in relation to who children become friends with. This is often because of a friendship that develops between parents and the frequency of opportunity they have to be together.

For example, in Ladd and Golter's research, one **dyad** had mothers who had become friends during pregnancy, had visited each other's homes regularly and then had attended the same childcare setting from six months old. Rubin and Sloman (1984) argue that mothers can also be quite selective about which children they allow their child to play with. In the current climate, children play out in the street less and there are more concerns about safety. Gill (2007) argues that a 'risk-averse' attitude impacts on children's opportunities for free play.

 action point 7.1

Create a list of factors that could encourage or inhibit children's friendships.

THE EARLY YEARS FOUNDATION STAGE AND FRIENDSHIPS

Play has a pivotal role to play in the development of children's friendships. Dunn (1983) notes the significance of shared play opportunities in the formation of new friendships. Such friendships also act as a buffer at times of transition to new settings or school (Ladd, 1990). Through co-operative play, children have the opportunity to develop social skills and problem solve. The Early Years Foundation Stage (EYFS) notes the importance of play in children's social learning and development (DfE, 2017). This starts with a focus on healthy positive attachments with key adults as a foundation for developing future friendships with peers (Carter, 2013).

 reflection point 7.1

What could practitioners/teachers do to support a child who is finding it difficult to make friends independently?

The EYFS allows practitioners to focus on the needs of individual children and be creative in terms of how they **scaffold** and **facilitate** children's friendship learning. By knowing the child well and working as a team, support for children can be effective. Developing practitioner knowledge of children's peer culture would also be of help when thinking about strategies and ideas to help children. This can be done by looking at research in the field and discussing as a staff team how this might influence practice. Children often have specific rules and practices within their peer culture that adults are not always aware of (Carter and Nutbrown, 2016).

TYPES OF FRIENDS

Research suggests that children report having several types of friends (Carter and Bath, 2016; Carter and Nutbrown, 2016). Carter (2013) asked children to draw pictures of their friends and talk about them. The children in this study drew pictures of school friends, community friends, sibling friends and even imaginary friends. The picture in Figure 7.1 shows this.

Figure 7.1   Gwyneth with her friends, including her cuddly object friend

   The presence of imaginary friends and sibling friends was rather unexpected. These will be explored further.

IMAGINARY FRIENDS

Imaginary friends can be defined in two ways – first, as **invisible companions** (Svendsen, 1934); and second and more recently, as **animated** or **personified objects** (Singer and Singer, 1990; Taylor, 1999). This section will focus on **imaginary** friends as **object friends**. These objects come in various forms but in Carter's (2013) research they were cuddly toys, small pocket toys and LEGO figures. The presence of such friendships amongst children aged 5–7 was unexpected as typically their presence occurs in the preschool years (Fraiberg, 1959; Piaget, 1962; Manosevitz et al., 1973). Pearson et al. (2001) studied imaginary friends with 5–12-year-olds and found that 25% of these children still had imaginary friends. Taylor et al. (2004) also found that 31% of 6- and 7-year-olds in their study still reported playing with imaginary friends. As children get older, they tend to hide this from adults (Taylor et al., 2004). This may be because children sense adult or peer disapproval, or perhaps the imaginary friends just fizzle away.

In early research, the presence of an imaginary friend was viewed negatively, indicating poor social skills (Hurlock and Burnstein, 1932; Svendsen, 1934; Harter and Chao, 1992). More recently, children's views have started to be considered and the values and benefits of having an imaginary friend are now being explored (Gleason and Hohmann, 2006; Taylor et al., 2013; Carter and Bath, 2016). Children with imaginary friends appear to have a higher interest in fantasy play, increased levels of **social cognition** and co-operation with adults and peers (Connolly and Doyle, 1984). Gleason (2004: 205) found that imaginary friends were being used as **social rehearsal** for play with real friends. He argues: 'This extra social rehearsal may even mean that children with imaginary companions are particularly adept at forming and maintaining peer relationships in comparison with other children.'

Carter and Bath (2016) argue that imaginary object friends have a place in the classroom. Children often like to bring objects into school that can be viewed by the child as an extension of themselves. In studies by Dreyfus (1997) and Carter and Bath (2016), some children felt the close proximity of an object was affording them extra confidence during the acquisition of new skills. Others used objects to entice other children to make friends.

SIBLING FRIENDS

Some children in the study drew their siblings as their friends (Carter, 2013; see Figure 7.2).

The distinction between a friendship with a sibling and that with a peer, is that there is not always an element of choice. As children get older, especially as they enter adolescence, there is more choice (Blumstein and Kollock, 1988; Berscheid, 1994). For some children, relationships with siblings can be hostile and ambivalent, whilst others will have a positive friendship with a sibling (Dunn, 1996; Dunn et al., 1994).

A positive friendship with a sibling can be beneficial. Lamarche et al. (2006: 376) claim that social benefits include 'emotional support, security, companionship, co-operation, competitiveness and sharing mutual experiences'. A sibling friendship can also act as a source of comfort and support during times of adversity, including parental disharmony, divorce, stress and the introduction of a step-parent (Hetherington, 1988; Jenkins, 1992; Caya and Liem, 1998).

CHALLENGES AND DEMANDS OF FRIENDSHIP

Children are able to report their everyday friendship experiences (Carter, 2005, 2013; Carter and Nutbrown, 2016). This section will share a few of these experiences to highlight the commonplace challenges and demands of friendship that children face. This will be of interest to early childhood and school settings who may wish to evaluate their practice in the light of children's views and perceptions.

Commentary: 'My friends are, Louis's my brother and he helps me make my toy models and I've got my toy bunny rabbit and I play with him when I get home.'

Figure 7.2 Max's picture of his cuddly object friend, and his sibling

PLAYING ALONE

In Carter's (2005) study, some children described having no one to play with and feeling lonely. This made some children feel unhappy. Bob spoke about this after being asked; 'If you had no one to play with and were lonely, how would this make you feel?'

Bob:	'It made me feel sad when I was lonely when I wasn't a playground friend.'
Researcher:	'So when you weren't a playground friend you were lonely?'
Bob:	'Yes. I had no one to play with. I was always at the friendship stop and no one saw me.'
Researcher:	'OK, could you get help from anyone or did you stay lonely?'
Bob:	'No.'
Researcher:	'How did you feel?'
Bob:	'I just felt bored and annoyed. I felt annoyed having no one to play with.'
Researcher:	'Could you tell anyone?'
Bob:	'No.'

Having the skills to make and maintain friendship was important to avoid being alone (Renshaw and Brown, 1993). Dunn (2004) noted that children with few or no friends were more likely to feel lonely. Children who were categorised as 'rejected' are reported as being most lonely (Asher and Paquette, 2003). However, Asher (1990) argues that 'rejected' children can still avoid loneliness if they can make and sustain a friendship with just one classmate. Having just one friend is sufficient to protect children from being lonely. Supporting children to make and maintain friendships would therefore be significant to ECEC settings and schools. This would include nurturing a realistic expectation of friendship, acknowledging that conflict and negotiation are part and parcel of a healthy friendship (Sapon-Shevin et al., 1998).

Some children did report the desire to play alone sometimes if they chose to do so. 'Choice' was the operative word here. If they wanted to play alone that was OK and did not make them feel sad or lonely:

> *Elsa: You could sometimes play with yourself because if you're in the playground you always find something to do, like if you've got a climbing frame you could go on the climbing frame, if you've got hopscotch on the floor you could do hopscotch.*

As well as choice being significant, the frequency of playing alone was also imperative. Whilst playing alone was OK if you chose to, some children suggested this was inadvisable if it was a frequent occurrence. Elsa advised just playing alone for one playtime and no more. Ultimately, it is essential for practitioners and teachers to listen to children in instances like this and to respect the fact that sometimes children will want time to play alone.

ACCESS TO PLAY

As stated earlier in this chapter, play is pivotal to children's friendships. Friendships often begin through a shared interest or desire to play with the same things. Therefore, play is important to making and keeping friends. Being able to access play will be important to successful friendship formation. Within a school setting, play opportunities are reduced and usually arise at playtime. Children recounted the need to get out into the playground quickly in order to be able to access play scenarios (Carter, 2013). If children had to stay behind at playtime, or went to the toilet, games to play would have been established and therefore it would be difficult or even impossible to access these. Within children's peer culture there seems to be a notion of a number of roles or parts to distribute when establishing a game. They call the games, 'a 2-er game' or 'a 3-er game' (Carter, 2013; Carter and Nutbrown, 2016). For example, 'a 2-er game' of horses will have two parts for the two children playing the game. Children use this concept of a game with a number of parts to include or exclude children. If a child approaches and would like to play, sometimes they will create a part for them, but, more often, once a game has started, they will say they cannot play because the game only has, for instance, two parts.

The following is Isla's commentary that goes with her picture in Figure 7.3. She is explaining how you try to enter an established game that only has two parts. She then talks about how it

Figure 7.3 Isla: the 2-er game

feels when someone asks if they can play with you and how that interruption to your play or activity can feel:

> *This is a two-er game with two girls. Zack feels upset and sad. Try to make friends with another boy or girl. Please, please, may I play with you? Children should ask before started a game as might make them forget what game they are playing. My friend interrupts, Jessica, I feel a bit upset and forget what game I'm playing. If I'm making buns I would say yes because I would want to do that. She always wants to play with me and I don't always want to and that makes me a bit upset. Sometimes I like playing on my own or with Grace.*

FRIENDSHIP STRATEGIES
PLAYGROUND FRIENDS

Schools use a number of strategies to support children to make and maintain friendships. One such strategy is '**playground friends**'. This intervention strategy focuses on trying to achieve a positive playtime experience for all children. The idea is that individual children apply for a position as a 'playground friend' (see Figure 7.4). This role entails supporting other children with their playground challenges and dilemmas. For example, playground friends are asked to help children think of games to play, play with children who have no one to play with, and bring out and put away playground equipment. This strategy also aims to give 'playground friends' additional skills, including confidence, self-esteem, problem solving, a sense of responsibility and moral values (Mosley and Thorp, 2002).

This is a useful strategy for promoting inclusion and can work well to support children. However, children need to be supported to carry out this role. There should be training and ongoing provision to make this a success for all (Carter, 2005).

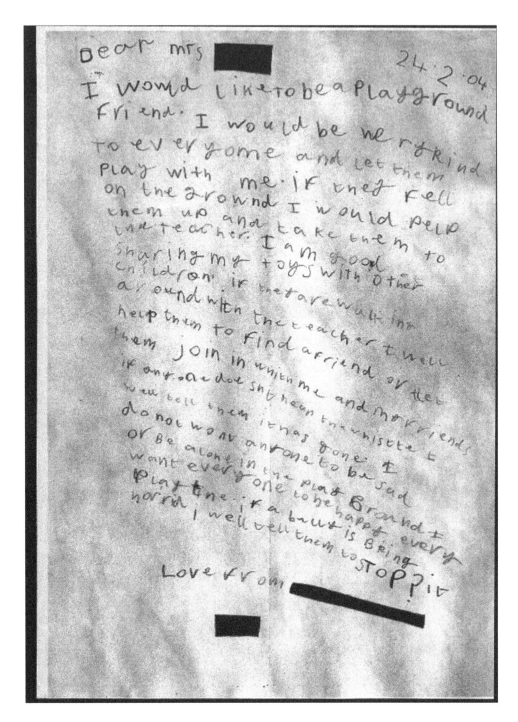

Figure 7.4 Letter of application for the role of playground friend

case study 7.1

Sonia: How to Do the Right Thing?

Sonia had just become a playground friend. She was a good role model to others and teachers felt she was a positive influence on other children. When she was asked about how she was finding the playground friend role, she said that it had been difficult. The role had threatened her own established friendships. This is what Sonia said:

On the first day I had to look after someone and we were playing a really good game and we didn't have anywhere to fit her in. I had to just keep her by my side and she helped me in the game. There was a lot of people in the game and all the characters that we could think of were being used up. (Carter, 2005: 35)

1. What should the school do to support Sonia to carry out this role?
2. What changes could be made to practice?
3. If 'playground friends' training was implemented, what might be the content of these sessions?

CIRCLE OF FRIENDS

This intervention strategy was initially devised to support children with special educational needs (SEND) who were finding friendships and social interactions challenging (Barrett and Randall, 2004). A small number of children volunteer to participate and become a '**circle of friends**' for a specific child. The 'circle of friends' meeting takes place periodically, once a term or half term, and is facilitated or chaired by an adult. The session starts by going around the circle, asking each child to state positive aspects that this child has achieved and celebrating these. Then the meeting moves on to what has been challenging for the specific child. The circle or group then give support and suggest strategies that the child could use and implement to improve their current situation. Newton et al. (1996) report on the success of this strategy for children.

Shotton (1998) noted that for some children this approach would be inappropriate. This was because the focus of the sessions singled out one child, including the circle of children talking about them in their absence. Shotton was interested in finding ways to support children who were defined as 'neglected' or ignored by their peers. These children are often quiet and sensitive about their lack of friends. Usually, this results in them being withdrawn. Consequently, Shotton (1998) took Newton et al.'s (1996) approach and adapted it so the session was facilitated in a more subtle manner. All children in the class were asked to volunteer for the circle sessions with the focus being 'on the needs of everyone in the class to establish and maintain friendships'. In this way, no single child was identified or singled out.

reflection point 7.2

1. How may the 'circle of friends' intervention strategy support children?
2. Rosenthal and Gatt (2011: 121) argue that many caregivers and teachers 'believe it inappropriate to intervene or interfere in children's play'. However, if children are struggling with friendships – for example, because they are shy, withdrawn or aggressive – is there a place to guide and support?

SUMMARY

- Different disciplines define friendship in slightly different ways. Friendship has specific features and means different things to children depending on their stage of development.
- Children have different types of friends, including imaginary friends, school friends, community friends and sibling friends.
- Children's peer culture has specific rules, routines and practices as seen, for example, in children's '2-er' or '3-er' games. Adult knowledge of children's peer culture practices can enhance practice.
- Children face friendship challenges and demands on an everyday basis. For example, playing alone is sometimes OK and access to play scenarios is vital for friendship success. Exploring these demands and challenges can help children.
- Friendship intervention strategies like 'playground friends' and 'a circle of friends' can be used to support children with friendship issues. However, they have benefits and limitations and these need to be considered when putting such strategies into practice.

online resources

Make sure to visit https://study.sagepub.com/fitzgeraldandmaconochie for selected SAGE videos (with questions), SAGE journal articles, links to external sources and flashcards.

FURTHER READING

Corsaro, W. A. (2015). *The Sociology of Childhood*, 4th edn. London: Sage.

This book draws on children and childhood from a sociology perspective. Part three is on children's cultures and has four relevant chapters.

Kernan, M. and Singer, E. (eds) (2011). *Peer Relationships in Early Childhood Education and Care*. London: Routledge.

This book reports on research on children's peer culture. There is a focus on diversity and children's agency within children's peer relationships.

Theobald, M. (ed.) (2017). *Friendship and Peer Culture in Multilingual Settings*. Bingley: Emerald.

This book reports on research into children's friendships in multilingual settings. The aim is to expand knowledge in this area and consider how to apply this to practice.

REFERENCES

Asher, S. R. (1990). Recent Advances in the Study of Peer Rejection. In: S. R. Asher and J. D. Coie (eds), *Peer Rejection in Childhood*. Cambridge: Cambridge University Press, pp. 3–14.

Asher, S. R. and Paquette, J. A. (2003). Loneliness and Peer Relations in Childhood. *Current Directions in Psychological Science*, *12*(3): 75–8.

Bagwell, C. L. and Schmidt, M. E. (2011). *Friendships in Childhood and Adolescence*. Guilford: Guilford Publications.

Barrett, W. and Randall, L. (2004). Investigating the Circle of Friends Approach: Adaptions and Implications for Practice. *Educational Psychology in Practice*, *20*(4): 353–68.

Berscheid, E. (1994). Interpersonal Relationships. *Annual Review of Psychology*, *45*: 79–129.

Blumstein, R. and Kollock, P. (1988). Personal Relationship. *Annual Review of Sociology*, *14*: 467–90.

Bukowski, W. M., Newcomb, A. F. and Hartup, W. W. (1996). Friendship and its Significance in Childhood and Adolescence: Introduction and Comment. In: W. M. Bukowski., A. F. Newcomb and W. W. Hartup (eds), *The Company they Keep*. Cambridge: Cambridge University Press, pp. 1–15.

Carter, C. (2005). What are Children's Perceptions and Experiences of Being a Playground Friend? M.Ed dissertation, University of Sheffield.

Carter, C. (2013). Children's Views and Perceptions of their Friendship Experience. PhD thesis, University of Sheffield.

Carter, C. and Bath, C. (2016). The Pirate in the Pump: Children's Views of Objects as Imaginary Friends at the Start of School. *Education 3–13 46* (3): 335–344.

Carter, C. and Nutbrown, C. (2016). A Pedagogy of Friendship: Young Children's Friendships and How Schools can Support Them. *International Journal of Early Years Education 24*(4): 395–413.

Caya, M. L. and Liem, J. H. (1998). The Role of Sibling Support in High-Conflict Families. *American Journal of Orthopsychiatry*, *68*(2): 327–33.

Coie, J. D. and Dodge, K. A. (1983). Continuities and Changes in Children's Social Status: A Five-Year Longitudinal Study. *Merrill-Palmer Quarterly*, *29*: 261–82.

Coie, J. D., Dodge, K. A. and Coppotelli, H. (1982). Dimensions and Types of Social Status: A Cross-Age Perspective. *Developmental Psychology*, *18*(4): 557–70.

Connolly, J. and Doyle, A. B. (1984). Relation of Social Fantasy Play to Social Competence in Preschoolers. *Developmental Psychology*, *20*: 797–806.

Corsaro, W. A. (1992). Interpretive Reproduction in Children's Peer Cultures. *Social Psychology Quarterly*, *55*(2): 160–77.

Corsaro, W. (2003). *We're Friends, Right? Inside Kids' Culture*. Washington, DC: Joseph Henry.

Corsaro, W. A. and Eder, D. (1990). Children's Peer Cultures. *Annual Review of Sociology*, *16*: 197–220.

Damon, W. (1977). *The Social World of the Child*. San Francisco: Jossey-Bass.

Department for Education (DfE) (2017). Statutory Framework for the Early Years Foundation Stage. [online] Available at: www.foundationyears.org.uk/files/2017/03/EYFS_STATUTORY_ FRAMEWORK_2017.pdf [Accessed 8 August 2017].

Dodge, K. A. (1983). Behavioral Antecedents of Peer Social Status. *Child Development*, *54*: 1386–99.

Doherty, J. and Hughes, M. (2009). *Child Development: Theory and Practice 0–11*. Harlow: Pearson Education.

Dreyfus, H. (1997). The Current Relevance of Merleau-Ponty's Phenomenology of Embodiment. Paper presented at the International Focusing Institute 'After Postmodernism' Conference, University of Chicago, 14–16 November. [online] Available at: www.focusing.org/apm_ papers/dreyfus2.html [Accessed 2 July 2018].

Dunn, J. (1983). Sibling Relationships in Early Childhood. *Child Development*, *54*(4): 787–811. [online] Available at: www.jstor.org/stable/1129886 [Accessed 8 August 2017].

Dunn, J. (1996). Arguing with Siblings, Friends and Mothers: Developments in Relationships and Understanding. In: D. I. Slobin., J. Gerhardt., A. Kyratzis and J. Guo (eds), *Social Interaction, Social Context and Language: Essays in Honor of Susan Ervin-Tripp*. Mahwah, NJ: Erlbaum, pp.191–204.

Dunn, J. (2004). *Children's Friendships: The Beginnings of Intimacy*. Oxford: Blackwell Publishing.

Dunn, J., Slomkowski, C. and Beardsall, L. (1994). Siblings Relationships from the Preschool Period through Middle Childhood and Early Adolescence. *Developmental Psychology*, *30*(3): 315–24.

Fraiberg, S. H. (1959). *The Magic Years*. New York: Scribner.

Gill, T. (2007). *No Fear: Growing Up in a Risk Averse Society*. London: Calouste Gulbenkian Foundation.

Gleason, T. R. (2004). Imaginary Companions and Peer Acceptance. *International Journal of Behavioural Development*, *28*(3): 204–9.

Gleason, T. R. and Hohmann, L. M. (2006). Concepts of Real and Imaginary Friendships in Early Childhood. *Social Development*, *15*(1): 128–44.

Gronlund, N. E. (1959). *Sociometry in the Classroom*. New York: Harper.

Harter, S. and Chao, C. (1992). The Role of Competence in Children's Creation of Imaginary Friends. *Merrill-Palmer Quarterly*, *38*: 350–63. [online] Available at: http://psycnet.apa.org/ psycinfo/1993-09152-001 [Accessed 8 August 2017].

Hartup, W. W. (1989). Social Relationships and their Developmental Significance. *The American Psychologist*, *44*(2): 120–6.

Hetherington, E. M. (1988). Parents, Children, and Siblings: Six Years after Divorce. In: R. Hinde and J. S. Hinde (eds), *Relationships within Families: Mutual Influences*. New York: Clarendon Press/Oxford University Press, pp. 311–31.

Howes, C. (1983). Patterns of Friendship. *Child Development*, *54*: 1041–53.

Howes, C. (1996). The Earliest Friendships. In: W. M. Bukowski., A. F. Newcomb and W. W. Hartup (eds), *The Company They Keep: Friendship in Childhood and Adolescence*. Cambridge: Cambridge University Press, pp. 66–86.

Hurlock, E. B. and Burnstein, M. (1932). The Imaginary Playmate: A Questionnaire Study. *Journal of Genetic Psychology*, *41*: 380–91.

Jenkins, J. (1992). Sibling Relationships in Disharmonious Homes: Potential Difficulties and Protective Effects. In: F. Boer and J. Dunn (eds), *Children's Sibling Relationships*. Hillsdale, NJ: Erlbaum, pp. 125–38.

Koch, H. (1933). Popularity in Preschool Children: Some Related Factors and a Technique for its Measurement. *Child Development*, *4*(2): 164–75. [online] Available at: www.jstor.org/stable/1125594 [Accessed 8 August 2017].

Ladd, G. W. (1990). Having Friends, Keeping Friends, Making Friends, and Being Liked by Peers in the Classroom: Predictors of Children's Early School Adjustment? *Child Development*, *61*: 1081–100.

Ladd, G. W. and Golter, B. S. (1988). Parents' Management of Preschoolers' Peer Relations: Is it Related to Children's Social Competence? *Developmental Psychology*, *24*(1): 109–17.

Lamarche, V., Brendgen, M., Boivin, M., Vitaro, F., Pérusse, D. and Dionne, G. (2006). Do Friendships and Sibling Relationships Provide Protection Against Peer Victimization in a Similar Way? *Social Development*, *15*(3): 373–93.

Manosevitz, M., Prentice, N. and Wilson, F. (1973). Individual and Family Correlates of Imaginary Companions in Preschool Children. *Developmental Psychology*, *8*: 72–9.

Moreno, J. L. (1943). *Who Shall Survive? A New Approach to the Problem of Human Interrelations*. Washington, DC: Nervous and Mental Disease Publishing.

Mosley, J. and Thorp, G. (2002) *All Year Round: Exciting Ideas for Peaceful Playtimes*. Cambridge: LDA, A Division of McGraw-Hill Children's Publishing.

Newcomb, A. F. and Bagwell, C. L. (1995). Children's Friendship Relations: A Meta-Analytic Review. *Psychological Bulletin*, *117*: 306–47.

Newton, C., Taylor, G. and Wilson, D. (1996) Circles of Friends: An Inclusive Approach to Meeting Emotional and Behavioural Needs. *Educational Psychology in Practice*, *11*: 41–8.

Pearson, D., Rouse, H., Doswell, S., Ainsworth, C., Dawson, O. and Simms, K., et al. (2001). Prevalence of Imaginary Companions in a Normal Child Population. *Child: Care, Health and Development*, *27*: 12–22.

Piaget, J. (1962). *Play, Dreams and Imitation*. London: Routledge and Kegan Paul.

Piaget, J. (1968). *Six Psychological Studies*. New York: Vintage Books.

Renshaw, P. D. and Brown, P. J. (1993). Loneliness in Middle Childhood: Concurrent and Longitudinal Predictors. *Child Development*, *64*: 1271–84.

Rosenthal, M. and Gatt, L. (2011). Training Early Years Practitioners to Support Young Children's Social Relationships. In: M. Kernan and E. Singer (eds), *Peer Relationships in Early Childhood Education and Care*. New York: Routledge, pp. 113–26.

Rubin, K. H., Coplan, R., Nelson, L. J., Cheah, C. S. L. and Lagace-Seguin, D. G. (1992). Peer Relationships in Childhood. In: M. H. Borastein and M. E. Lamb (eds), *Developmental Psychology: An Advanced Textbook*. Hillsdale, NJ: Lawrence Erlbaum Associates, pp. 451–502.

Rubin, Z. and Sloman, J. (1984). How Parents Influence their Children's Friendships. In: M. Lewis (ed.), *Beyond the Dyad*. New York: Plenum, pp. 115–40.

Sapon-Shevin, M., Dobbelaere, A., Corrigan, C. R., Goodman, K. and Mastin, M. C. (1998). Promoting Inclusive Behaviour in Inclusive Classrooms. In: L. H. Meyer, H. Park, M. Grenot-Scheyer, I. S. Scwartz and B. Harry (eds), *Making Friends*. New York: Paul H. Brookes Publishing.

Selman, R. (1980). *The Growth of Interpersonal Understanding*. New York: Academic Press.

Shotton, G. (1998) A Circle of Friends Approach with Socially Neglected Children. *Educational Psychology*, *14*(1): 22–5.

Singer, D. and Singer, J. (1990). *The House of Make-Believe*. Cambridge, MA: Harvard University Press.

Sullivan, H. S. (1953). *The Interpersonal Theory of Psychiatry*. New York: Norton.

Svendsen, M. (1934). Children's Imaginary Companions. *Archives of Neurology and Psychiatry*, *32*: 985–99.

Taylor, M. (1999). *Imaginary Companions and the Children Who Create Them*. New York: Oxford University Press.

Taylor, M., Carlson, S. M., Maring, B. L., Gerow, L. and Charley, C. M. (2004). The Characteristics and Correlates of Fantasy in School-age Children: Imaginary Companions, Impersonation and Social Understanding. *Developmental Psychology*, *40*: 1173–87.

Taylor, M., Sachet, A. B., Maring, B. L. and Mannering, A. M. (2013). The Assessment of Elaborated Role-Play in Young Children: Invisible Friends, Personified Objects, and Pretend Identities. *Social Development*, *22*(1): 75–93.

Vygotsky, L. S. (1978). *Mind in Society*. London and Cambridge, MA: Harvard University Press.

CHAPTER 8

CHILDREN WITHIN THE FAMILY CONTEXT

BY EUNICE LUMSDEN

The chapter has made me reflect on the significant impact that families and parents have on the individual child. As educators, we have a responsibility to understand what family support and intervention looks like in practice. Intervention and support are often delayed, mainly due to the sector's knowledge and understanding in this area. This chapter clearly outlines the complexities that we face as educators today, supported by clear definitions and action points.

Having worked with practitioners who needed support due to family situations, early childhood settings need to have support systems in place for all those in their care. This chapter encourages the reader to reflect on their own experiences which is a really powerful starting point.

The chapter was particularly good at outlining how family events could impact on children from the same family in different ways. Being able to empathise with a family's situation and understand the 'why?' to a child's behaviour unlocks so many doors – this chapter is key to being able to do this.

NICOLA MASTERS
MA EARLY YEARS
UNIVERSITY OF NORTHAMPTON

learning outcomes

By actively reading this chapter and engaging with the material, you will be able to:

*   explain the child in the context of their family, community and society
*   appraise how Bronfenbrenner's *chronosystem* and *chaotic-system* support an appreciation of the factors that affect development over the life course
*   critically discuss the complexities of parenting and family support
*   apply learning about parenting and family support to early childhood education and care (ECEC).

INTRODUCTION

This chapter introduces Early Childhood students to the importance of knowing and critiquing the child within the context of their family, community and wider society. The discussion considers the uniqueness of every child and family, the influence early parenting can have on lifelong outcomes and the broader policy context. There will be consideration of the complexities of parenting, parenting capacity and family support, including the different responsibilities of the birth, legal and parenting parents. The work of Bronfenbrenner (2005) provides a theoretical framework to support the description, application and critique of the child and the systems in which they operate. It will be assumed that when the term 'family' is used it includes all family members, adults and children, and, where appropriate, the case study of the Gordon family supports the application of theory to practice.

INTRODUCING URIE
BRONFENBRENNER (1917–2005)

As discussed throughout the book, the work of Bronfenbrenner has had a profound influence on how the **ecology** of a child's development is impacted on at different levels: *meso, micro, exo and macro* (Lumsden, 2012). His work was initially visualised as concentric and interconnected circles, often referred to as nested systems (as discussed in the introduction). Many people continue to draw on the early representations of his work to consider the issues that support or impede child development. However, it is the final iteration of his work that offers a framework to support a deeper critique of the child within the context of their family, community and society.

Bronfenbrenner claimed to be his greatest critic, contending that further research was needed to understand how society affects human development. For him, if his initial theories were right, why did the 'chaos' he saw in society exist? He extended his theory, arguing that development needed to be understood over the life course (*chronosystem*). This system supported understanding of how events over time can influence individual development. While the *chronosystem does* provide greater understanding, for example the impact of bullying or child abuse, it still did not explain the 'chaos' in society. In the final stages of his life, he saw the new challenge as finding a model to support researchers in understanding the events that act as barriers to human development, the *chaotic-system* (Figure 8.1).

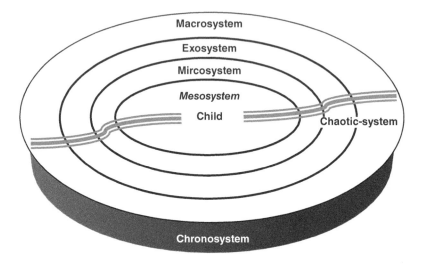

Figure 8.1   Impact of the chaotic-system

Source: Based on Bronfenbrenner's human bioecological theory which visualises the inclusion of the chaotic-system (Lumsden, 2012)

This model has the flexibility to support understanding of the factors that impact on development across the life course, including marital breakdown, sudden death, long-term health issues, changes in policy and natural disasters. For professionals, the *chaotic-system* provides a model of how constant changes in policy nationally and locally shape their work, as well as specific events in the family.

THE FAMILY

 action point 8.1

Draw your own family tree.

Who have you included and why?

How much do you know about your family?

Are there any people you would like to include who are not related by birth, marriage or adoption but who you class as 'your family'?

How have your experiences influenced you and your choice to study early childhood?

Definitions about what a parent or family is are fluid, have a cultural context and evolve over time, mirroring wider societal changes (Dolan et al., 2006; Frost, 2011). In other words, they are socially constructed and impacted on by all the systems identified by Bronfenbrenner (2005). The term family can be interpreted more broadly to include membership of a community with a shared vision and beliefs (Llewellyn et al., 2014). Understanding is also shaped by our own subjective experiences of 'family'. Children in the same family with the same parents and shared experiences have different perceptions and memories of their family life.

 reflection point 8.1

How difficult or easy was the exercise in action point 8.1?

Are there gaps you need to find out about?

How has your own experience influenced the person you are?

How do your personal experiences of family life inform your professional practice in ECEC?

The term family is often used as though families are homogenous. That is both misleading and problematic and it is vital that the uniqueness of families is recognised and respected.

 case study 8.1

The Gordon Family

This case study outlines the complexity and generational patterns that can be found in some families, with intergenerational themes of domestic violence, anti-social behaviour and professional engagement with the family.

(Continued)

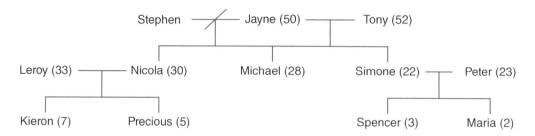

Figure 8.2 The Gordon family tree

The Gordon family comprises of two generations, as illustrated in the family tree in Figure 8.2. Jayne married Stephen and had two children: Nicola, now aged 30, and Michael, 28. Stephen died in a motorbike accident when the children were 5 and 3 years old respectively. Jayne then married Tony and they had Simone. After her birth, Tony adopted Nicola and Michael so that, in law, all three children were full siblings and had the same father.

The relationship between Jayne and Tony was volatile and concerns had been expressed about parenting and anti-social behaviour which led to intermittent involvement with social workers. Jayne also experienced depression following the birth of each child and sporadic episodes throughout their childhood.

Nicola had two children in her late teens, Kieron and Precious. She is married to Leroy, their father. Kieron and Precious both had periods in the care of the local authority because of child protection issues.

Michael is in prison for drug offences; he has never married.

Simone is married to Peter and has two children, Spencer and Maria. Her marriage is particularly volatile and she and the children spend time in and out of women's refuges, but she always returns to her husband.

Applying Theory to Practice

Nicola, Michael and Simone have all experienced challenges that appear to have impacted on their adult lives. Using the Bronfenbrenner framework, compile a list of factors you think have influenced their experiences.

As case study 8.1 illustrates, family life is complex, parenting styles vary and ongoing and specific events can have intergenerational consequences (*chronosystem* and *chaotic-system*). For the Gordon family, there were one-off events, such as the death of Jayne's partner, and a culmination of events including domestic violence, maternal depression, episodes in care of the local authority and relationship difficulties. As adults, Michael has become addicted to drugs and been imprisoned, Nicola has struggled with parenting and the thread of domestic violence is evident in Simone's marriage (*mesosystem* and *microsystem*).

The support for the family is also affected by chances at the *exo-* and *macrosystem* levels. For example, when Michael, Nicola and Simone were children, domestic violence was dealt with by the police; it certainly was not seen as a child protection issue. It is only recently that practice has changed (DfE, 2015). Childcare was predominantly seen as the role of the mother, and fathers were often excluded from family support (Ferguson and Hogan, 2004). There is now considerable evidence about the vital role of fathers (DWP, 2017a) and an increasing numbers of fathers are lone parents. However, fathers generally receive little support and their own mental health needs can be ignored (Khan, 2017).

Additionally, the Adverse Childhood Experience (ACE) study in North America has found an association between ACEs and health and social problems as an adult (Felitti et al., 1998). ACEs include domestic violence, drug and alcohol misuse and mental health issues. The findings of the American study have been reinforced in the UK (Ford et al., 2016; Public Health Wales, 2016). In the Gordon family, Michael and Nicola share the same birth father and their development may have been influenced by his early death. Their sister Simone did not experience the same early trauma, however all three of them shared life in a family environment of domestic violence, though how this affected them would have been different depending on, for example, exposure to the violence and their age.

In summary, every child's experience of family life is unique and the different academic disciplines provide theoretical perspectives to help us 'make sense' of the family, family life and the relationships within the family and wider society. Those studying early childhood need to draw on the different perspectives to develop their interdisciplinary knowledge and apply this to practice. The work of Bronfenbrenner provides a framework to support this.

While he was a psychologist, his work drew on a range of disciplines to support understanding of human development and led to his final call for greater understanding of the *chaotic-system*. Sociology offers a lens here, providing different perspectives about the centrality of the family to wider society, the political context of 'family' and how family life has evolved, as well as individual positioning within family structures (Llewellyn et al., 2014). Broadly, we are all situated within a family structure that is positioned and influenced by the society in which we live. This structure is not solid, rather fluid, embracing all different types of families, including lone parents, same-sex parents, married couples, cohabiting couples and families where there is much more gender sharing of parental tasks (Frost, 2011; Frost et al., 2015).

Bronfenbrenner (2005) was also concerned about how social policy added to the 'chaos'. In England, psychological research into infant mental health has embraced neuroscience (see Chapter 2) and social policy. Research into infant mental health and the impact of maternal mental health across the life course has gained prominence, not only for the individual but for society as a whole. Here, research evidence meets the political imperative for targeted, evidence-based practice that has a strong economic argument and places responsibility with parents for their child's outcomes (Heckman, 2013; WAVE Trust, 2013; APPG, 2015; Macvarish et al., 2015). Put simply, it is argued that investing in early childhood has huge economic benefits for every layer of society. As Sally Davies (Chief Medical Officer, England) stated in the foreword to the *1001 Critical Days* manifesto (Leadsom et al., 2013: 2): 'Those who suffer multiple adverse childhood events achieve less educationally, earn less, and are less healthy, making it more likely that the cycle of harm is perpetuated, in the following generation.'

However, this recognition is not new. Pringle and Naidoo (1975: 169) argued that, while there was no empirical evidence, we know enough to stop the 'vicious circle of the emotional or intellectually deprived children of today becoming tomorrow's parents of yet another generation of deprived children'.

What is different now is the research evidence supporting the importance of early childhood and the political rhetoric in policy reports about intervening early in families in need (Allen, 2011; DWP, 2017a). However, there is still a lack of consistent political action to embed systemic change that lasts longer than the political term of five years. Moreover, responsibility for the needs of children and families across their life course is vested in a number of governmental departments and there is no one minister with overall responsibility.

PARENTING

As the previous discussion has illustrated, families are all different and comprise of complex relationships. The responsibilities parents have are enshrined in legislation (Children Act 1989, in England and Wales; Children (Scotland) Act 1995; Children (Northern Ireland) Order 1996). However, how parents engage with these is influenced by their own beliefs and experiences. Research has identified four types of parenting styles – **authoritarian**, **authoritative**, **permissive** and **neglectful**, with authoritative parenting identified as achieving the best outcomes. This involves providing a nurturing and warm environment alongside 'clear rules and guidelines' (Frost et al., 2015: 79).

One way of understanding the different roles and responsibilities of being a parent is by considering it in relation to three areas, 'birth parent', 'legal parent' and 'parenting parent' (Table 8.1). These are influenced by cultural variations in child-rearing practices, for example the different roles of the mother and father, and the role of grandparents and community elders. The 'Parenting Parent' aspects can be shared with others, especially young children who attend ECEC settings.

If the Gordon family is considered, Jayne is the birth parent, legal parent and parenting parent of Nicola, Michael and Simone, whereas Tony is the birth parent of Simone, and became the legal parent of Nicola and Michael through a step-parent adoption and did not become their parenting parent until he married Jayne. The parenting parent role may have been affected by Jayne's maternal mental health.

Table 8.1 Types of parents

Birth Parent	Legal Parent	Parenting Parent
Life	Parental responsibility	Love
DNA	Register birth	Affection
Eye colour	Register death	Care
Hair colour	Application for passport	Empathy
Hereditary diseases	Permission to travel abroad	Support
Predisposition to certain health conditions	Permission for operations	Education
	Marriage under 18 (not Scotland)	Looks after when ill
Predisposition to certain skills (e.g. art and music)	Joining armed forces under 18	Puts child's needs first

Birth Parent	Legal Parent	Parenting Parent
Religion	Meet basic needs (shelter, warmth, food)	Home
		Experiences
	Keep child safe	Opportunities
	Provide formal education	Boundaries
		Discipline
		Guidance
		Advice
		Financial support

 reflection point 8.2

How many of these tasks in the 'Parenting Parent' column of Table 8.1 take place in ECEC settings?

What training have you had in relation to these?

Are these tasks discussed with parents?

With a policy direction aimed at increasing free childcare hours (up to 30 hours for working parents who meet the defined criteria), what are the implications for ECEC settings in relation to the parenting parent tasks?

Actually assessing parental capacity to fulfil their responsibilities is difficult, and defining what is good-enough parenting is multifaceted, socially constructed and subjective. However, those involved in supporting families have to make assessments about parenting capacity as part of their day-to-day work, especially when children are deemed in need under the respective legislation of the four nations of the UK.

The work of Kellett and Apps (2009) is particularly useful here. Their research considered how health visitors, paediatricians, family support practitioners and teachers assessed the support needed by parents. There was a specific focus on how the 54 practitioners who participated in in-depth interviews viewed '"good", "good enough" and "risky" parenting' (Kellett and Apps, 2009: 1). Their findings suggested that practitioners really struggled with the terms, and Table 8.2 provides the elements that emerged about what was seen as 'good-enough parenting', 'risky parenting' and the challenges of establishing clear boundaries between them. For example, some reported parenting that was emotionally warm but also evidenced physical neglect. Therefore, the research suggested that 'emotional responsiveness and warmth were necessary but not sufficient criteria for good enough parenting' (Kellett and Apps, 2009: 46).

Table 8.2 Assessing 'good-enough' parenting

Good-enough Parenting	Risky Parenting	Challenges
Basic care and safety	Putting self before child	Differences in parenting styles
Love and affection	Lack of parental control	Cultural and ethnic differences in child-rearing practices
Putting children's needs first	Lack of routine and order	
Providing routine and consistent care	Neglecting child's basic needs	Socio-economic differences
Engaging with support services (if difficulties experienced and acknowledged by parents)	No or limited engagement with support services	Areas seen as 'good-enough parenting' may also have elements of risky parenting

Source: Based on Kellett and Apps (2009: 46)

The research also highlighted that training on different parenting styles, the impact of culture, ethnicity and social class and different approaches to assessing need, is limited. Health visitors and family workers talked about 'assessment', whereas paediatricians and teachers used the words 'observation' or 'triggers for concern'. The latter two professional groups also put the focus on the child rather than their families. Interestingly, the more experienced professionals described their assessments and observations as drawing on 'gut instincts', 'a kind of interface where professional and personal factors and objective and subjective observations met' (Kellett and Apps, 2009: 45).

The assessment of parenting capacity is important in identifying the right support for the child and family, including whether a court order needs applying for if the child is deemed to be at risk of significant harm. There are three main types of assessments: early help which is non-statutory, and needs assessment and child protection, both of which are statutory (Lumsden, 2018). They are completed using an assessment framework, based on the work of Bronfenbrenner, that investigates parental capacity, the development needs of the child and the family in the context of the environment in which they live (DfE, 2015).

SUPPORTING FAMILIES

As the previous discussion has illustrated, parenting is complex and the 'parenting parent' responsibilities can be fulfilled by a range of people in the *mesosystem*, including those working in ECEC. Moreover, every family is unique, with their parenting style being influenced by a range of factors, and the collective and individual needs of family members will all be different. Not all families require support beyond the universal services provided for all, and their informal networks of family and friends. For others, more formal help is needed, in the short, medium or long term. This section is therefore concerned with wider support services for families and the contentious area of when the state should intervene in family life (*macrosystem*).

For those studying early childhood, it is important to know and be able to critique the continuum of the widest aspects of universal child welfare, the nature of family support and the specifics of child protection (see Chapter 13). They also need to appreciate at what point 'support' transitions into 'formal intervention' through the legislative and statutory frameworks of the four nations of the UK. As Herring (2017) contends, the greatest power a state has is to remove a child from their family. However, this should only happen when there is no alternative, and, as reinforced by the Human Rights Act 1998, wherever possible, the privacy of the family should be maintained (Herring, 2017).

Furthermore, the nature of family support can mean different things for different agencies and in different situations. For example, a key worker in ECEC may see their role as supporting the family with transition or specific aspects of development, whereas the health visitor has a specific focus on child health and the social worker on supporting a family to meet a child's needs to prevent them being received into the care of the local authority. In fact, Featherstone (2004: 63) describes 'family support' as an 'ambiguous and elastic concept', and, according to Dolan et al. (2006: 13), there is 'no dominant theoretical underpinning apparent in the literature that attempts to address the thorny question of what is family support'.

The work of Frost et al. (2015) has much to commend itself to support understanding of the 'conceptual tussle' of family intervention. Their critique of this area is compelling, highlighting the real tensions between the notion of 'Early Help' (Munro Report, DfE, 2011), 'Early Intervention' (Allen, 2011), prevention and Family Support (Frost et al., 2015: 37). Arguably, these debates become more complicated at times of austerity when the policy direction of travel at a national and local level is for more targeted approaches rather than universal services. The requirement for cost-effective, evidenced-based interventions and randomised research trials with families is becoming more prevalent. The Early Intervention Foundation (EIF) uses the following criteria to evaluate family services – 'strength of evidence', 'implementability' and a 'cost benefit analysis' (Asmussen et al., 2016: 19).

In practice, four levels of need, where families may require support, have been identified, though the terminology and thresholds for accessing services may vary across localities in the UK (DfE, 2015):

- **Universal** – services such as education and health that are available to all.
- **Early Help** – services that may provide short-term support, for example support with welfare benefit claims.
- **Targeted** – when more specific support is needed, for example support with a parenting issue.
- **Specialist** – when support is required to address specific areas, such as child abuse or child mental health.

The level of need then shapes the type of assessment undertaken, as discussed in the previous section, and assessment of the nature of support is provided.

 action point 8.2

Using the information in case study 8.1, about Nicola, Leroy and their children, make a list of the levels of different support they may have needed under the four headings of universal, early help, targeted and specialist.

As well as universal education and health services, Nicola and Leroy would have received targeted and specialist support. They would have experienced both statutory and non-statutory assessments to assess need, whether the children were facing significant harm and what type of support, individually and collectively, the family needed.

As the discussion has illustrated, family support is complicated and one way of critiquing it is by considering the principles underlying it (Dolan et al., 2006). Action point 8.3 draws on the work of Dolan and colleagues.

 action point 8.3

Ten Practice Principles of Family Support

Dolan et al. (2006: 16) define family support as:

both a style of work and a set of activities that reinforce positive informal social networks through integrated programmes. These programmes combine statutory, voluntary, community and private services and are generally provided to families within their own home and communities. The primary focus of these services is on early intervention aimed at promoting the health, wellbeing and rights of all children, young people and their families. At the same time, particular attention is given to those who are vulnerable and at risk.

How does this definition help you understand the continuum of family support?

Does it still have currency in supporting the understanding of contemporary debates about family support?

With a greater focus on targeted support, what role should ECEC have in supporting families?

Underpinning this definition are ten principles:

1. Working in partnership is an integral part of family support. Partnership includes children, families, professionals and communities.
2. Family support interventions are needs-led and strive for the minimum intervention required.
3. Family support requires a clear focus on the wishes, feelings, safety and wellbeing of children.
4. Family support services reflect a strengths-based perspective which is mindful of resilience as a characteristic of many children's and families' lives.
5. Family support promotes the view that effective interventions are those that strengthen informal support networks.
6. Family support is accessible and flexible in respect of location, timing, setting and changing needs, and can incorporate both child protection and out of home care.
7. Families are encouraged to self-refer, and multi-access referral paths will be facilitated.
8. Involvement of service users and providers in the planning, delivery and evaluation of family support services is promoted on an ongoing basis.
9. Services aim to promote social inclusion, addressing issues around ethnicity, disability and rural/urban communities.

10. Measures of success are routinely built into provision so as to facilitate evaluation based on attention to the outcome for service users and thereby facilitate ongoing support for quality services based on best practice.

Do you really understand each principle?

Do you agree with them?

Would you add any more?

Discuss these principles with a fellow student or colleague and arrange them in order of significance. Is your understanding of the principles the same?

How can these principles support the work of ECEC settings?

These principles support the understanding that not all families need formal engagement with services; when they do, it should be in partnership, accessible and clearly evaluated. With more children accessing ECEC, there is a need for settings to really focus on how they support families and ensure their staff are fully trained in all aspects of working with families, especially given the drive to reduce the number of workless families (DWP, 2017a). There is a clear direction of travel for greater focus on targeted, evaluated interventions as the Troubled Families Programme in England discussed, as Spotlight on Policy 8.1 illustrates.

 spotlight on policy 8.1

The Troubled Families Programme

This flagship programme was launched in England in 2012. It was underpinned by 'payment by results' and aimed at families viewed as a problem to the community and authorities, with intergenerational multifaceted needs typified by poor parenting, anti-social behaviour, substance misuse and worklessness (DCLG, 2012). The overarching aim was to reach 120,000 'troubled families', providing individual support, and to change their lives by May 2015. The success criteria included:

- children back into school
- reducing criminal and anti-social behaviour
- parents on the road back to work
- reducing the costs to the tax payer and local authorities.

It was the first time there had been a systematic approach to addressing the multifaceted needs of some families, with payment to local authorities through a targeted approach where funding was linked to targets being met. There were 152 different local programmes. However, concerns were expressed about flaws in the data that underpinned the programme and the language used to describe those involved (Frost et al., 2015).

There has been considerable debate about the first phase of the programme, with the government hailing it at different points as being a success, however an independent review found that the aims had not been met (Day et al., 2016; DCLG, 2016). There had been some changes to families participating but these could not be attributed solely to being involved in the programme. The differences in how local authorities managed the programme, the impact of scaling up interventions and other variations meant that there was a lack of evidence to draw conclusions. Furthermore, the payment by results framework had been contentious, with concerns about how some had administered it. Additionally, some local authorities expressed concern about the target-driven nature of the programme meaning they were constrained in actually reaching families with preschool children.

The research did highlight some achievements, including:

- raising the profile, leading to local authorities supporting the programme
- the progamme led to some local areas undertaking system reform
- improved data collection at a local level
- some families reported improved financial management, and having a key worker was positive for 76% of families.

Before the evaluation was completed, phase two of the initiative started. This phase runs until 2020 and has three main aims: to reach 400,000 families and 'make work an ambition for all troubled families'; to transform local services to ensure 'a whole family approach'; and to evidence to tax payers that this targeted approach 'lowers costs and savings for the tax payer' (DCLG, 2017: 6). The 2018 evaluations showed progress in terms of the number of families being supported and where significant progress had been made in terms of agreed 'improvement goals' (MHCLG, 2018).

In April 2017, the government reaffirmed its commitment to the programme, acknowledging the findings from the first phase, which it had learnt from, and stating that it was putting measures in place to review payment by results and how the programme is evaluated. Furthermore, there is recognition of new research evidence that reinforces the 'overlapping disadvantages experienced by workless families and the significantly poorer outcomes faced by their children' (DCLG, 2017: 23). As a result of this, the programme will be delivered in conjunction with the *Improving Lives: Helping Workless Families* initiative (DWP, 2017a, b, c). Alongside this initiative was the move to 30 hours free childcare in September 2017 in England for eligible parents.

Bronfenbrenner's framework supports the understanding of this programme. Over time, information has emerged which challenged the initial data used to support the initiative and the second phase was started before the finding of 'no impact' from the first phase had been made public. Furthermore, with a political desire to get people into work, the *chaotic-system* enables understanding of the challenges ahead. Four different government departments are responsible for related policies which impact on the child in their family and community. The DWP is responsible for the *Improving Lives: Helping Workless Families* initiative, the MHCLG (formerly the DCLG) for the Troubled Families programme, the DfE for ECEC, education and social work and the professionals that work within them. Finally, the DoH has specific priority areas for early childhood. All these areas have different secretaries of state, ministers and civil servants, all of which can change at any moment, bringing with it instability and uncertainty.

reflection point 8.3

Do you think the Gordon family would be classified as a 'troubled family'?

What do you think the advantages and disadvantages are of a targeted rather than universal approach to all families?

What are the implications for ECEC provision of policy initiatives aimed at getting workless families into work?

How do you think the *chronosystem* and *chaotic-system* support understanding of the Troubled Families programme and subsequent developments?

SUMMARY

- Children's lives are complex, as they interact with families and the broader community at different levels. The chapter suggested a theoretical framework to 'make sense' of how interdisciplinary perspectives enable a critique of the factors influencing a child's development over their life course.
- All families are unique, as is the experience of those within them, and they may include other groups or individuals that are not related by birth. Through reference to Bronfenbrenner's chronosystem and chaotic-system, the chapter emphasised the dynamic, complex and broad nature of children's lives and provided a framework to continually appraise this to respond effectively to each child and family.
- Support for families depends on specific needs and is underpinned by a number of principles, including the relationship between the state and the family. Parenting is complex and elements of the role can be undertaken by other people or institutions, such as ECEC settings.
- For families requiring support, there has been a shift towards more targeted approaches with a focus on getting workless families into the workplace. It is important to critique this shift and consider how research is being used to support the political rhetoric.

online resources

Make sure to visit https://study.sagepub.com/fitzgeraldandmaconochie for selected SAGE videos (with questions), SAGE journal articles, links to external sources and flashcards.

FURTHER READING

Frost, P. N., Abbott, S. and Race, T. (2015). *Family Support: Prevention, Early Intervention and Early Help*. Cambridge: Polity Press.

This book effectively critiques how parents and the family have been constructed in recent policy narratives.

Macvarish, J., Lee, E. and Lowe, P. (2015). Neuroscience and Family Policy: What Becomes of the Parent? *Critical Social Policy, 35*(2): 248–69.

This journal article critiques the impact of research into brain development on the positioning of parents in policy narratives.

REFERENCES

All Party Parliamentary Group (APPG) (2015). Conception to the Age of 2: First 1001 Days – Building Great Britons. [online] Available at: www.1001criticaldays.co.uk/buildinggreatbrit onsreport.pdf [Accessed 11 April 2017].

Allen, G. (2011). *Early Intervention: The Next Steps – An independent report to Her Majesty's Government*. London: Cabinet Office.

Asmussen, K., Feinstein, L., Martin, J. and Chowdry, H. (2016). Foundations for Life: What Works to Support Parent Child Interaction in the Early Years – Report overview. [online] Available at: www.eif.org.uk/wp-content/uploads/2016/07/FFL-Overview-document-FINAL-1. pdf [Accessed 11 April 2017].

Bronfenbrenner, U. (ed.) (2005). *Making Human Beings Human: Bioecological Perspectives on Human Development*. London: Sage.

Day, L., Bryson, C., White, C., Purdon, S., Bewley, H., Sala, L. K. and Portes, J. (2016). National Evaluation of the Troubled Families Programme: Final Synthesis Report. [online] Available at: www.gov.uk/government/uploads/system/uploads/attachment_data/file/560499/Troubled_ Families_Evaluation_Synthesis_Report.pdf [Accessed 12 April 2017].

Department for Communities and Local Government (DCLG) (2012). Listening to Troubled Families: A Report by Louise Casey. [online] Available at: www.gov.uk/government/uploads/ system/uploads/attachment_data/file/6151/2183663.pdf [Accessed 12 April 2017].

Department for Communities and Local Government (DCLG) (2016). The First Troubled Families Programme 2012 to 2015: An Overview. [online] Available at: www.gov.uk/ government/uploads/system/uploads/attachment_data/file/560776/The_first_Troubled_ Families_

Department for Communities and Local Government (DCLG) (2017) Supporting Disadvantaged Families – Troubled Families Programme 2015-2020: Progress so Far. [online] Available at: https://assets.publishing.service.gov.uk/government/uploads/system/uploads/attachment_ data/file/611991/Supporting_disadvantaged_families.pdf [Accessed 27 Sep 2018].

Department of Education (DfE) (2011). The Munro Review of Child Protection: Final Report – A child-centred system. London: The Stationery Office. [online] Available at: www.gov.uk/ government/uploads/system/uploads/attachment_data/file/175391/Munro-Review.pdf [Accessed 11 March 2017].

Department for Education (DfE) (2015). Working Together to Safeguard Children: A Guide to Inter-agency Working to Safeguard and Promote the Welfare of Children. [online] Available at:

www.gov.uk/government/uploads/system/uploads/attachment_data/file/592101/Working_Together_to_Safeguard_Children_20170213.pdf [Accessed 11 March 2017].

Department for Work and Pensions (DWP) (2017a). Improving Lives: Helping Workless Families.[online]Availableat:www.gov.uk/government/uploads/system/uploads/attachment_data/file/605836/improving-lives-helping-workless-families-web-version.pdf [Accessed 12 April 2017].

Department for Work and Pensions (DWP) (2017b). Improving Lives: Helping Workless Families – An evidence resource on family disadvantage and its impact on children. [online] Available at: www.gov.uk/government/uploads/system/uploads/attachment_data/file/605988/evidence-resource-improving-lives-helping-workless-families-web-version.pdf [Accessed 12 April 2017].

Department for Work and Pensions (DWP) (2017c). Improving Lives: Helping Workless Families – Analysis and research pack at a glance: Contents. [online] Available at: www.gov.uk/government/uploads/system/uploads/attachment_data/file/605989/analysis-research-pack-improving-lives-helping-workless-families-web-version.pdf [Accessed 12 April 2017].

Dolan, P., Canavan, J. and Pinkerton, J. (eds) (2006). *Family Support as Reflective Practice*. Philadelphia: Jessica Kingsley Publishers.

Featherstone, B. (2004). *Family Life and Family Support: A Feminist Analysis*. Basingstoke: Palgrave Macmillan.

Felitti, V., Anda, R., Nordenberg, D., Williamson, D., Spitz, A., Edwards, V., et al. (1998). Relationship of Childhood Abuse and Household Dysfunction to Many of the Leading Causes of Death in Adults: The Adverse Childhood Experiences (ACE) Study. *American Journal of Preventive Medicine*, 14: 245–58.

Ferguson, H. and Hogan, F. (2004). *Strengthening Families through Fathers: Developing Policy and Practice in Relation to Vulnerable Fathers and their Families*. Waterford, Ireland: The Centre for Social and Family Research, Waterford Institute of Technology.

Ford, K., Butler, N., Quigg, Z. and Bellis, M. (2016). Adverse Childhood Experiences (ACEs) in Hertfordshire, Luton and Northamptonshire. Liverpool: Liverpool John Moores University. [online] Available at: www.cph.org.uk/wp-content/uploads/2016/05/Adverse-Childhood-Experiences-in-Hertfordshire-Luton-and-Northamptonshire-FINAL_compressed.pdf [Accessed 9 August 2017].

Frost, N. (2011). *Rethinking Children and Families: The Relationship between the Child, the Family and the State*. London: Continuum International Publishing Group.

Frost, P. N., Abbott, S. and Race, T. (2015). *Family Support: Prevention, Early Intervention and Early Help*. Cambridge: Polity Press.

Heckman, J. (2013). James Heckman Changes the Equation for American Prosperity. [online] Available at: https://heckmanequation.org/assets/2014/05/F_Heckman_Brochure_041515.pdf [Accessed 8 April 2017].

Herring, J. (2017). *Family Law*, 8th edn. Harlow: Pearson Education.

Kellett, J. and Apps, J. (2009). Assessments of Parenting and Parenting Support Need: A Study of Four Professional Groups. [online] Available at: www.jrf.org.uk/file/39455/download?token=s9R7btS2&filetype=full-report [Accessed 11 April 2017].

Khan, L. (2017). *The Impact of Fathers on Children's Mental Health*. Centre for Mental Health. [online] Available at: www.centreformentalhealth.org.uk/briefing-50-fatherhood [Accessed 13 March 2017].

Leadsom, A., Field, F., Burstow, P. and Lucas, C. (2013). The 1001 Critical Days: The Importance of Conception to the Age of Two Period. [online] Available at: www.andrealeadsom.com/downloads/1001cdmanifesto.pdf [Accessed 12 March 2017].

Llewellyn, A., Agu, L. and Mercer, D. (2014). *Sociology for Social Workers*, 2nd edn. Cambridge: Polity Press.

Lumsden, E. (2012). The Early Years Professional: A New Professional or a Missed Opportunity? PhD thesis, University of Northampton.

Lumsden, E. (2018). *Child Protection in the Early Years: A Practical Guide*. London: Jessica Kingsley Publications.

Macvarish, J., Lee, E. and Lowe, P. (2015). Neuroscience and Family Policy: What Becomes of the Parent? *Critical Social Policy*, 35(2): 248–69.

Ministry of Housing, Communities and Local Government (MHCLG) (2018). Supporting disadvantaged families: annual report of the Troubled Families Programme 2017 to 2018. Available at: https://assets.publishing.service.gov.uk/government/uploads/system/uploads/attachment_data/file/694362/CCS207_CCS0318142796-1_Un_Act_Troubled_Families_AR_2017-18_Accessible__2_.pdf [Accessed 8th June 2018].

Pringle, M. and Naidoo, S. (1975). *Early Child Care in Britain*. London: Gordon and Breach.

Public Health Wales NHS Trust (2016). Adverse Childhood Experiences and their Association with Chronic Disease and Health Service Use in the Welsh Adult Population. Cardiff: Public Health Wales. [online] Available at: www.wales.nhs.uk/sitesplus/documents/888/ACE%20Chronic%20Disease%20report%20%289%29%20%282%29.pdf [Accessed 9 August 2017].

WAVE Trust (2013). Conception to the Age of 2: The Age of Opportunity. London: WAVE Trust. [online] Available at: www.wavetrust.org/sites/default/files/reports/conception_to_age_2_-_the_age_of_opportunity_-_web_optimised.pdf [Accessed 10 March 2017].

SUPPORTING PLAY

BY PHILIPPA THOMPSON

I like that the chapter explores various concepts of 'play' and has introduced me to new and relevant perspectives. It has helped me to understand the role of play in early years education and contextualise play in its many forms.

The author discusses the 'use' of play in learning and development through the frameworks of policy, sociology and education. The case studies provided help you to link the theoretical perspectives that are discussed with the application of these in practice. You are also encouraged to apply some critical thinking skills to the topic of play, play work and play learning.

I would highly recommend this chapter.

NAOMI SALMON
BA (HONS) EARLY
CHILDHOOD STUDIES
UNIVERSITY OF EAST LONDON

 learning outcomes

By actively reading this chapter and engaging with the material, you will be able to:

- explain the range of key perspectives that lead to definitions of play
- identify the key dilemmas and debates for early childhood practitioners when advocating for play
- apply evidence to support the idea that play is politically influenced
- discriminate between different perspectives on the role of the adult in play
- critically evaluate the justifications for the 'use' of play in early childhood practice.

INTRODUCTION

The title of this chapter, Supporting Play, suggests that in the field of early childhood education and care (ECEC) play needs advocates or 'supporters' as well as knowledgeable practitioners. The chapter outlines how play has been constructed in early childhood as important and yet still fails to convince those who create policy and curriculum of its value. It provides a historical overview of how play has been conceptualised and how perhaps the dominant discourses that influence play require updating and understanding in practice. This will enable those currently in practice to become more effective advocates for play and to promote positive outcomes for young children. There are many differing perspectives on play and these will be explored in this chapter through a consideration of a range of disciplines. Since Early Childhood is a multidisciplinary field, it is important to pull together the fields of psychology, play work, education, health, social care and children's rights when looking at the notion of play. In a current climate of English policy where children are perceived as '**becomings**' rather than '**beings**' (Samuelsson and Carlsson, 2008) and play is considered an 'interference' to children's academic outcomes, it is essential that those working in the field truly understand the notion of play and why they consider it important.

Throughout the chapter, the reader will consider how research has developed over time and how definitions and perceptions have potentially become muddled. Understanding what play is, how it has developed in terms of theoretical underpinnings and the politics involved, support early childhood practitioners to engage in an educated debate. The discussion of how play is often 'used' as a vehicle for learning or considered as a tool for assessment (Glick Gross, 2006) in some early childhood practice, when others value it in its own right (Rinaldi, 1998; Else, 2009), is also important. Many working in ECEC settings will acknowledge that play is essential but the practice may state otherwise. Young children can lack autonomy and may be presented with adult-directed 'play', for example creating a painting for a display that is encouraged to look the way the adult determines rather than having their own ideas valued. Rather than being quick to criticise, it is important to understand why practitioners may feel it is necessary to work in this way with young children. Finally, this chapter will consider ways in which the role of the adult can be understood from a theoretical perspective to enable advocates for play to understand their role further.

WHAT IS PLAY?

There is a wealth of literature on play and 'being playful' (Howard and McInnes, 2010) and this can be overwhelming to those trying to determine a single definition. As well as the literature, there is also personal experience of play that can have an influence on our choices of literature and definition. This creates a complex point of thinking, and, as a consequence, play is not easily defined nor easily explained. However, if practitioners wish to be advocates then broad definitions or understandings need to be created. This brings to mind a suggestion by Leonardo Da Vinci (McCurdy, 1956: 19), that those who love practice without theory are like a sailor who boards a ship without a rudder and a compass, and can never be certain where he is going. It could be argued that this aptly describes the current position of play in early childhood practice.

Many working in ECEC have a firm belief that play is an essential part of good practice (Thompson, 2012). Existing definitions of play are plentiful and provide a starting point for anyone searching for their own. Play is suggested as being intrinsically motivated and a process rather than a product (Hughes, 2001; Bruce, 2010). Other key words attached to play are fun, innocent and natural (Grieshaber and McArdle, 2010). Hughes (2001: 56) argues that 'play is a fundamental learning mechanism'. There are many other suggestions but, in order to develop our own understanding, a consideration of historical perspectives from a range of fields is necessary.

HISTORICAL PERSPECTIVES ON PLAY

Whilst developing our perspectives on play, it is important to understand where these come from and how they are grounded in research. Much of the practice in early childhood settings that is guided by policy is still built on ideas from the perspective of developmental psychology dating back to the 1930s and beyond (see Tables 9.1 and 9.2). This section will consider the work of key play theorists and how their ideas have evolved into the present day. There are many others that have also been influential and this is to be considered a starting point for further research.

Table 9.1 Key theorists of play

Theorist	A brief synopsis of key ideas
Plato (428/427 BC - 348/347 BC)	Made links between play and education with a suggestion that regulation of play would enable a more stable society (D'Angour, 2013).
Rousseau (1712-1778)	Identified 'pointless' questioning and testing by adults of young children and felt that by interrupting their play much of the thinking and reasoning were lost. Pioneered observations of play to make decisions about children's knowledge and understanding (Frost, 2010; Thompson, 2012).

Theorist	A brief synopsis of key ideas
Pestalozzi (1746–1827)	Suggested that children have moments of 'readiness' when they can take on new ideas and concepts. Felt adults should identify and follow children's interests, giving them time to process and develop. Opposed the belief that there was one 'right' answer to questions and believed rote learning should be discouraged (Nutbrown et al., 2008; Frost, 2010; Thompson, 2012).
Froebel (1782–1852)	Framed play as 'a tool for learning' within the discourse of 'respect' for the individual child (Manning, 2005; Thompson, 2012). He developed the idea of 'gifts and occupations' to develop learning through play and a key focus of this was mathematical learning. The term 'structured play' is often associated with Froebel.
Isaacs (1885–1948)	Main contribution was the observation of children's play to promote the understanding of children's thoughts and ideas (Howard and McInnes, 2010; Thompson, 2012). Used the controversial phrase 'children's work is play' and was an advocate for the importance of social interactions.
Vygotsky (1896–1934)	Encouraged a move away from the constraints of developmental stages and promoted the skilful use of observations by adults. Social interactions were a key focus and he is best known for the idea of the **'zone of proximal development' (ZPD)**. ZPD has more recently been referred to in a review (Tickell, 2011) of the then Early Years Foundation Stage in England (DCSF, 2008).
Piaget (1896–1980)	Attempted to provide play with more status by providing developmental stages of play, i.e. practice play, symbolic play and games with rules. Whilst these have been challenged in current research, his concepts of assimilation and accommodation do however provide a higher status for play when it is being challenged as 'purposeless' (Nolan and Kilderry, 2010; Smidt, 2010; Thompson, 2012).

Table 9.2 More recent theories of play (1932 to present day)

Parten	Developed types of play that still shape some of the thinking around practice today. These types were: 'Unoccupied, Solitary, Onlooker, Parallel, Associative and Co-operative' (Sawyer, 1997). These would now be considered as 'social contexts for play' (Fisher, 2013: 140) and often a source of confusion in practice.
Sutton-Smith	Considered evolutionary aspects of play and challenged the notion that play is considered important for children, but somehow seen as frivolous for adults. He lists play in categories that include pastimes and hobbies rather than a focus from a particular discipline (Sutton-Smith, 2009).
Bruce	Best known for her development of the 12 features of free-flow play. Suggests that if practitioners have an understanding of the features of play then their planning, observation and analysis of play become more informed (Bruce, 2010; Thompson, 2012).
Bilton, Knight, Maynard and Tovey	Key advocates of play in the outdoors, encouraging practitioners to consider spaces for play and risky play.

(Continued)

Hughes	Play worker who considers play as a 'fundamental learning mechanism' (Hughes, 2001: 56). He frames play as having 16 differing types that support workers to reflect on play and its process with children of school age (4 yrs +). Traditional education notions of 'role play' are challenged and practitioners are encouraged to look more closely for elements such as dramatic play, imaginative play or socio-dramatic play. 'Deep play' challenges practice to consider that play can have a 'darker' side that needs to be explored.
Moyles	Considers play and playful pedagogies within the context of policy and the role of reflective practitioners. 'Pure play', 'playful learning', 'playful teaching' and the role of the practitioner within each of these are explored (Moyles, 2010), along with the question of whether 'pure play' is really achievable in an early childhood setting. Suggests that play provides opportunities for deeper learning.
Nutbrown	Work developed on schemas and play, moving forward from the work of Athey. Encourages practitioners to consider brain development and 'patterns of behaviour'. Other key areas are family literacy, inclusion and children's perspectives. A key advocate for early childhood as an academic discipline.
Broadhead, Wood	Both have developed perspectives of play over time from a standpoint of early childhood education, policy and curriculum. Playfulness, pedagogy, sociability and co-operation have dominated their work, and the political consideration of play is a key element.

PLAY AND EDUCATION

'Learning through play' is a phrase often heard in early childhood settings across the UK. With this comes the debate between practitioners and politicians in terms of whether children should be playing freely (Broadhead et al., 2010; Bruce, 2010; Moyles, 2010) or whether their play should be 'purposeful' (DfE, 2017: 9). What is concerning for play advocates is that for play to be valued in the sector, it must have the words 'learning' or 'development' attached as if to show there is a meaningful outcome. The current Early Years Foundation Stage (EYFS) (DfE, 2017) poses the ultimate dilemma in terms of children's play. One of four of the overarching principles suggests, in terms of children's play, that 'every child is a *unique child*, who is constantly learning and *can be* resilient, capable, confident and self-assured' (p. 6). Such use of language could suggest that children are not able to be these things without the support of a more structured curriculum. This takes us away from the construct of children as 'beings' but rather suggests they are 'becomings' (Samuelsson and Carlson, 2008). If this is the starting point for practitioners, it is no wonder they feel pressure to harness children's play and use it to create a measurable outcome.

 spotlight on practice 9.1

The EYFS

Practitioners are faced with a difficult choice when working with the EYFS. They may be advocates for play but the language of the curriculum tells them how it should be done and determines that part of the role of the adult is to prepare children to be ready, at age 5 or 6 years, to leave play behind.

Consider the following statement taken from the EYFS (DfE, 2017):

1.8. Each area of learning and development *must be* implemented through *planned, purposeful play* and through a mix of *adult-led and child-initiated activity. Play is essential for children's development*, building their confidence as they learn to explore, to think about problems, and relate to others. *Children learn by leading their own play, and by taking part in play which is guided by adults.* There is an ongoing judgement to be made by practitioners about the balance between activities led by children, and activities led or guided by adults. Practitioners must respond to each child's emerging needs and interests, guiding their development through warm, positive interaction. As children grow older, and as their development allows, it is expected that the balance will gradually shift towards more activities led by adults, to *help children prepare for more formal learning, ready for Year 1.* (DfE, 2017: 6)

At first glance, the wording can seem to be in support of play in early education but there are questions to be raised by those in practice in ECEC. Whilst considering their own pedagogical approach, practitioners should critically reflect on the underlying political ideologies contained within policy documents such as the EYFS. The underpinning values contained therein shape how play is defined and how practitioners are expected to work with young children. Those who have studied current research in ECEC may find it problematic to combine their understanding of early childhood theory and the practice of more formal education. They will be continually required to justify an approach in early childhood which supports the role of open-ended play and the knowledgeable practitioner.

Children can also have awareness of the adult's agenda. It therefore should be questioned whether the play seen in some early childhood settings is what the adult expects of the child rather than what he/she would choose to do. Grieshaber and McArdle (2010) studied children's perceptions of play in three early childhood settings. They provide evidence that young children recognise that adults make most of the rules for play and are therefore constructing an idea of play that is acceptable for the adult rather than the child. Practitioners also need to consider whether their definitions of play are based on pre-conceived **constructs of childhood**. If they start with the perception that children are vulnerable or 'sponges' to soak up information, they are unlikely to value play in the same way as those who consider children 'rich and competent' (Rinaldi, 1998). Attitudes to risk and adventure outdoors will also differ as a result of these different perceptions.

 case study 9.1

Playing at Home

Tom, aged 4 years, is in his bedroom and tips a large container of metal cars out onto the floor. The cars have been collected from various car boot sales as well as being gifts, as part of a collection of 'Hot Wheels' cars. He then attaches a single plastic track with a clamp to a low

(Continued)

shelf which provides a slide and 'loop the loop' for the cars to go down. For the next 15 minutes, he sorts the cars according to colour and places them together. He sings to himself as he does this. Dad pops in and out of the room putting clothes away but Tom does not pay any attention to this and continues to sort and classify.

Once the cars are sorted into groups and lined up, Tom slides them one by one in groups down the ramp and watches to see if they 'loop the loop'. If they make it round the loop, Tom places them to his left. If they don't make it round, he puts them back in the container. He then begins to put the 'made it' cars into a line, dependent on how far they travelled once they left the loop and the final piece of track. He places the one that travels the furthest at the front of the line and then the next etc. This line constantly changes dependent on the distance travelled and where the car is perceived to have come. He continues to sing during his play and this play continues for another 50 minutes until he is called to have some lunch by Dad.

Tom has continued to play with his cars, with more added over time and has found different ways to sort and classify through time, speed, distance and other categories. From the age of 3 years, he used notebooks and pens to represent these categorisations and continues to do so at the age of 12 years, in a more sophisticated scientific/mathematical way.

1.   Would you consider this case study an example of 'pure play' or playful learning? (Moyles, 2010). Give reasons for your answer.
2.   Take a range of starting positions to analyse this case study, e.g. health, social work, industry, education. What do you think you learn about the child through this?
3.   Think of an early childhood setting where you have experience of this age group:

   a.   Give reasons why this play experience may not have been witnessed there (think about resources, environment, time, gender, etc.).
   b.   How could ALL (see question 2) professionals work with families to engage with the knowledge and understanding already gained from home and family life (**funds of knowledge**)?

4.   What do you consider to be the 'measurable outcomes' of this play? Return to the different positions suggested in Question 2 when considering your answer.

IS PLAY POLITICAL?

There are many influences and perspectives on play and it is necessary to examine these to develop a critical understanding. Bronfenbrenner considered this as the wider environment that influences the development of the child – this includes the **macrosystem** which involves the political and economic culture a child grows up in (Gray and MacBlain, 2012). In 1967 the Plowden Report was published by CACE. In its review of primary education in England, the report authors stated, 'at the heart of the educational process lies the child' (p. 7). This had a significant impact on how child-centred play and exploration were celebrated and valued in ECEC. Its role in provoking national discussion in research and policy must not be underestimated. Over the next five decades, play, learning and policy became more entangled as educational standards and methods were measured for political gain. Play struggles to provide the measurable outcomes required due to its very nature of being intrinsically motivated and child-led. Play is often perceived as 'low status' in educational discourses and therefore a lack of confidence and training in the value of play as a 'learning medium' are evident (Howard et al., 2006: 392).

Rather than the status of play being increased by political educational developments, it has rather been diminished in recent years. For example, in a speech by schools minister Nick Gibb (2017) he dismisses the notion of child-centred pedagogies and hails 'teacher-led instruction' as the way to 'raising standards'. Five years prior to this, Moss (2012) raised the debate that practice in ECEC was becoming too formalised to satisfy attainment targets and league tables. Moss termed this **schoolification** and raised concerns about the impact on early childhood practice. He suggested that confidence in practitioners' own **pedagogy** (their theoretical approach to facilitating children's play) was being diminished and that ECEC appears to have become part of the political global 'game' of achievement. As Roberts-Holmes (2015) suggests, the pedagogy of our youngest children is being subsumed by that of the 'wider school performativity culture'.

There are many challenges to overcome if you are an advocate for play but perhaps these also help to create further thinking and research. This could enable those passionate about the benefits of play to convince others that, whilst appreciating the requirement for high standards in ECEC, the inflexible use of measurement or **datafication** (Roberts-Holmes, 2015) is not the right path. Challenging a deep understanding of the range of pedagogies is required. Practitioners need to be able to synthesise their approaches to enable the young children they are working with to play, whilst supporting a '**bi-directional relationship**' between play and the curriculum' (Wood, 2007: 130).

Here lie the challenges for those working with young children in ECEC. Those that prefer to understand children's play through the discourse of developmental and educational psychology can rely on the 'ages and stages' model that helps to provide reasons and explanations for children's play. It also allows for a process of measurement widely used in health and education. However, the dangers of this are that play is used as a process for completing 'tick lists' rather than a process to be understood and supported.

Play will continue to be a political tool whilst early childhood is funded by government. Politicians require outcomes to demonstrate it is money well spent. Despite the **United Nations Convention on the Rights of the Child (UNCRC)** (UN, 1989: Article 31) stating 'that every child has the right to rest and leisure, to engage in play and recreational activities appropriate to the age of the child', play is still not high on the agenda of policy makers.

Whilst the field of ECEC may struggle with the dilemma of such a **consumerist** approach, positive outcomes should also be considered. Wood and Hedges (2016) put forward the notion that once outcomes are a requirement, then issues such as diversity, equality and equity are addressed and potentially this can lead to an improved style of provision. This is an area worthy of further research for those concerned about the 'factory'-like state of our current early childhood services (Moss, 2012).

action point 9.1

Familiarise yourself with the UNCRC (1989) Article 31, and General Comment 7. List the Articles that you feel have a resonance with play and suggest why you think this (see Further Reading below).

WHAT ROLE DOES THE ADULT PLAY?

This section will consider the variety of roles that can be considered to support or possibly hinder the development of play. The adult will be considered from four differing perspectives with a brief explanation on how this can impact on young children's play:

1. Adult as learner
2. Adult as co-constructor
3. Adult as facilitator
4. Adult as intruder

ADULT AS LEARNER

When an adult considers young children's play, they can do so from the perspective of wanting to know more and understand what the meaning of the play is that they see evolving in front of them. Placing themselves in the role of the learner creates a position in which to consider how play is being framed in the setting: perhaps as a tool for learning; a tool for assessment; a context for the observation of development (Glick Gross, 2006); or a vehicle for delivering predetermined outcomes (Chesworth, 2016). Whilst considering their practice, this leads to the enquiring adults, who in their quest to discover how they perceive play, will observe and learn from the children. As has been demonstrated, play is an extremely complex and contested notion and the adult as learner may become the adult as campaigner, advocating for changes to policy as well as practice.

ADULT AS CO-CONSTRUCTOR

Playful adults can participate as **co-constructors** of meaning with young children when equal partners in play. A depth of understanding of early childhood theoretical perspectives enables adults to support children's ideas and construct theories and understanding together. The outcomes of the Effective Provision of Pre-School Education (EPPE) project findings (Sylva et al., 2003) suggested that sustained adult–child interactions led to higher attainment and quality provision for young children. The phrase 'sustained shared thinking' was used to describe quality interactions where 'two or more individuals "work together" in an intellectual way to solve a problem, clarify a concept, evaluate activities, or extend a narrative' (Siraj-Blatchford, 2010, cited in Peters and Davis, 2011: 7). This suggests that the adult should play an integral part in the play of young children. However, this is framed in the context of providing evidence that quality practice will achieve outcomes from play, so here the adult has a vision of 'the playing-learning child' (Samuelsson and Carlsson, 2008).

ADULT AS FACILITATOR

The 'facilitator' is a definition of the role of the adult that can often be heard in English ECEC practice. It appears to support those working with children in education settings in particular to feel a justification for observing play rather than 'butting' in. Peters and Davis (2011) also discovered a reluctance for practitioners in New Zealand to let go of the role of 'facilitator' (where good quality resources were provided and changed according to the needs of the children) and to become the co-constructor, instead perhaps listening and talking with the children and developing the idea of **working theories**. The language involved and the role of the adult in play are complex and intertwined. It is important that those from a range of disciplines consider how their roles may contrast or complement each other.

ADULT AS INTRUDER

Adults must also consider the fact that they may not be wanted when children are playing. This is particularly noticeable when children are outdoors, engaged in more risky play. The adult (parent or practitioner) can become intruder and protector (or in fact over-protector) suddenly engaging in a 'power' role, asking children to 'be careful' and stopping them from climbing any higher. This can often interrupt the flow of play and lead to anger and frustration. A consideration of why adults feel the need to question children during their play needs to be explored as this interference with children's play can be to its detriment (Fisher, 2016). Many practitioners feel duty bound to demonstrate that everything they do with the child will have a measurable outcome due to current educational demands for data.

 reflection point 9.1

What was your starting position when thinking about the role of the adult in play? Has your position altered after reading this section? Explain why.

Consider the roles of the following people – how would you define their role as an adult working with young children?

a. Allergy nurse in a children's hospital
b. Room leader in a baby room
c. Social worker working on a complex child protection case.

As can be seen from the above discussion, the role of the adult in ECEC is an extremely complex one. There are many disciplines with a range of approaches and the strong focus on early education can sometimes ignore the positive interactions occurring in other fields such as Health. However, young children deserve all those to be flexible and have a good understanding of the importance of the voice of the child.

SUMMARY

- Play is a complex concept to define but those working or studying in the field of ECEC must consider not only their understanding of play but also their justification for giving it value and status.
- In addressing the key definitions of play, adults will need to consider the key dilemmas and debates that can arise when the issue of play is considered.
- To fully engage with the issues of play, professionals need to engage with parents, research and policy in a meaningful way. The acknowledgement of wider global perspectives, such as the economy, has an impact on the positional stance of governments and policy makers with regards to play.
- The role of the adult in play must be considered critically and from a reflective stance to truly consider a position on play.
- A consideration of the 'use' of play within early childhood will lead professionals, students and researchers to underpin the reasons for why and how play is an integral part of working with young children.

 online resources

Make sure to visit https://study.sagepub.com/fitzgeraldandmaconochie for selected SAGE videos (with questions), SAGE journal articles, links to external sources and flashcards.

FURTHER READING

Moyles, J. (2014). *The Excellence of Play*. Maidenhead: Open University Press.

This book draws on a range of authors to provide an overview of the many differing perspectives involved in play and pedagogy. It considers (amongst many) the difficulties for adults in negotiating curriculum and play; new approaches to play in the digital age; children as researchers; the development of theories of play; and challenges the reader to consider their own position on play in early childhood.

Soler, J. and Miller, L. (2003). The Struggle for Early Childhood Curricula: A Comparison of the English Foundation Stage Curriculum, Te Whāriki and Reggio Emilia. *International Journal of Early Years Education, 11*(1): 57–68.

Whilst this article is not focused on play, it considers the issues that surround our thinking in this field. It is helpful when thinking about play to look at international perspectives in comparison to our own dilemmas and debates.

REFERENCES

Broadhead, P., Howard, J. and Wood, E. (eds) (2010). *Playing and Learning in the Early Years: From Research to Practice*. London: Sage.

Bruce, T. (2010). Play, the Universe and Everything! In: J. Moyles (ed.), *The Excellence of Play*. Maidenhead: Open University Press, pp. 185–98.

Central Advisory Council for Education (CACE) (1967). *Children and their Primary Schools*. The Plowden Report. London: HMSO.

Chesworth, L. (2016). A Funds of Knowledge Approach to Examining Play Interests: Listening to Children's and Parents' Perspectives. *International Journal of Early Years Education*, 24(3): 294–308.

D'Angour, A. (2013). Plato and Play: Taking Education Seriously in Ancient Greece. *American Journal of Play*, 5(3): 293–307.

Department for Children, Schools and Families (DCSF) (2008). *Statutory Framework for the Early Years Foundation Stage*. London: HMSO.

Department for Education (DfE) (2017). *Statutory Framework for the Early Years Foundation Stage: Setting the Standards for Learning, Development and Care for Children from Birth to Five*. Ref. DFE-00169-2017. London: DfE. http://www.nationalarchives.gov.uk/doc/open-government-licence/version/3/

Else, P. (2009). *The Value of Play*. London: Continuum.

Fisher, J. (2013). *Starting from the Child: Teaching and Learning in the Foundation Stage*. Maidenhead: Open University Press.

Fisher, J. (2016). *Interacting or Interfering? Improving Interactions in the Early Years*. Maidenhead: Open University Press.

Frost, J. L. (2010). *A History of Children's Play and Play Environments: Towards a Contemporary Child Saving Movement*. Abingdon: Routledge.

Gibb, N. (2017). Speech: Nick Gibb – The evidence in favour of teacher-led instruction, 24 January. [online] Available at: www.gov.uk/government/speeches/nick-gibb-the-evidence-in-favour-of-teacher-led-instruction [Accessed 7 June 2018].

Glick Gross, M. (2006) The Role of Play in Assessment. In: D. P. Fromberg and D. Bergen (eds), *Play from Birth to Twelve: Contexts, Perspectives and Meanings*, 2nd edn. Abingdon: Routledge, pp. 223–32.

Gray, C. and MacBlain, S. (2012). *Learning Theories in Childhood*. London: Sage.

Grieshaber, S. and McArdle, F. (2010). *The Trouble with Play*. Maidenhead: Open University Press.

Howard, J., Jenvey, V. and Hill, C., (2006). Children's Categorisation of Play and Learning Based on Social Context. *Early Child Development and Care*, 176(3-4): 379–93.

Howard, J. and McInnes, K. (2010). Thinking through the Challenges of a Play-based Curriculum: Increasing Playfulness via Co-construction. In: J. Moyles (ed.), *Thinking about Play: Developing a Reflective Approach*. Maidenhead: Open University Press, pp. 30–44.

Hughes, B. (2001) *Evolutionary Playwork and Reflective Analytic Practice*. London: Routledge.

McCurdy, E. (ed.) (1956). *The Notebooks of Leonardo da Vinci* (Vol. 1). New Delhi: Prabhat Prakashan.

Manning, J. P. (2005). Rediscovering Froebel: A Call to Re-examine his Life and Gifts. *Early Childhood Education Journal*, *3*(6): 371–6.

Moss, P. (ed.) (2012). *Early Childhood and Compulsory Education: Reconceptualising the Relationship (Contesting Early Childhood)*. London: Routledge.

Moyles, J. (2010). Practitioner Reflection on Play and Playful Pedagogies. In: J. Moyles (ed.), *Thinking about Play: Developing a Reflective Approach*. Maidenhead: Open University Press, pp. 13–29.

Nolan, A. and Kilderry, A. (2010). Postdevelopmentism and Professional Learning: Implications for Understanding the Relationship between Play and Pedagogy. In: L. Brooker and S. Edwards (eds), *Engaging Play*. Maidenhead: Open University Press, pp. 108–21.

Nutbrown, C., Clough, P. and Selbie, P. (2008). *Early Childhood Education: History, Philosophy, Experience*. London: Sage.

Peters, S. and Davis, K. (2011). Fostering Children's Working Theories: Pedagogic Issues and Dilemmas in New Zealand. *Early Years: An International Journal of Research and Development*, *31*(1): 5–17.

Rinaldi, C. (1998). Projected Curriculum Constructed through Documentation: Progettazione. In: C. Edwards, L. Gandini and G. Forman (eds), *The Hundred Languages of Children: The Reggio Emilia Approach – Advanced reflections*. Norwood, NJ: Ablex, pp. 113–25.

Roberts-Holmes, G. (2015). The 'Datafication' of Early Years Pedagogy: 'If the Teaching is Good, the Data should be Good and if there's Bad Teaching, there is Bad Data'. *Journal of Education Policy*, *30*(3): 302–15.

Samuelsson, I. P. and Carlsson, M. A. (2008). The Playing Learning Child: Towards a Pedagogy of Early Childhood. *Scandinavian Journal of Educational Research*, *52*(6): 623–41.

Sawyer, R. K. (1997). *Pretend Play as Improvisation: Conversation in the Preschool Classroom*. Hillsdale, NJ: Psychology Press.

Smidt, S. (2010). *Playing to Learn: The Role of Play in the Early Years*. Abingdon: Routledge.

Sutton-Smith, B. (2009). *The Ambiguity of Play*. London: Harvard University Press.

Sylva, K., Melhuish, E., Sammons, P., Siraj-Blatchford, I., Taggart, B. and Elliot, K. (2003). *The Effective Provision of Pre-school Education (EPPE) Project: Findings from the Pre-school Period*. London: Institute of Education, University of London and Sure Start.

Thompson, P. (2012). Play in Early Years Education. In: J. Kay (ed.), *Good Practice in the Early Years*. London: Continuum, pp. 13–44.

Tickell, C. (2011). *The Early Years Foundations for Life, Health and Learning. An independent report on the Early Years Foundation Stage to Her Majesty's Government*. Ref. D16 (8857)/0311.

United Nations (UN) (1989). *United Nations Conventions on the Rights of the Child (UNCRC)*. Adopted by the United Nations Assembly, 20 November. Geneva: United Nations.

Wood, E. (2007). Reconceptualising Child-Centred Education: Contemporary Directions in Policy, Theory and Practice in Early Childhood. *FORUM: for Promoting 3–19 Comprehensive Education*, *49*(1–2): 119–34.

Wood, E. and Hedges, H. (2016). Curriculum in Early Childhood Education: Critical Questions about Content, Coherence, and Control. *The Curriculum Journal*, *27*(3): 387–405.

PART 3
SUPPORTING CHILDREN

GO TO
https://study.sagepub.com/fitzgeraldandmaconochie *for free access to SAGE videos on topics covered in this book*

INCLUSION AND PARTICIPATION

BY PENNY BORKETT

My favourite aspects of the chapter are the case studies, how inclusion works in practice and the historical perspective on inclusion.

The historical perspective helps to put the issue into context. This is especially useful if you are using the information as reference for an assignment.

The case studies get you applying the information to everyday practice, which is useful if reflection is needed in an assignment.

Inclusion is now high on the agenda for many settings who are reflecting on the way that children participate in their learning and how they provide new opportunities. This chapter was insightful in covering these aspects.

RUTH OWEN
BA (HONS) EARLY CHILDHOOD STUDIES
UNIVERSITY OF EAST LONDON

learning outcomes

By actively reading this chapter and engaging with the material, you will be able to:

- define the notions of diversity, inclusion and participation
- describe the policy context of young children's inclusion and participation
- critically evaluate the dilemmas and challenges of inclusive practice
- apply theoretical models of participation to practice
- critically evaluate the dilemmas and challenges of children's participation in practice.

INTRODUCTION

This chapter will outline some of the evolving concepts and principles of **inclusion** and **participation** and how these relate to early childhood education and care (ECEC). It will introduce and discuss policies that postulate the 'uniqueness' of children and the responsibility of adults to ensure all children have a voice in matters that relate to them. Theories of inclusion, particularly around cultural **diversity**, and models of children's participation in decision making will be evaluated.

WHAT IS INCLUSION?

The term inclusion has evolved over the years and is a much contested and elusive concept. Nutbrown and Clough (2009) state that 'there are as many versions of inclusion as there are settings, practitioners, children and families' (p. 194). They go on to suggest that in the past inclusion particularly related to including children with **special educational needs** (SEN) in **mainstream schools** and removing barriers to learning, but as time has moved on the concept has broadened. Inclusion now relates to **equality of opportunity** for all children whatever their gender, ability, ethnicity, culture, faith or **socio-economic group**. Perhaps one way to begin to understand the notion of inclusion is to consider its antonym: exclusion. Exclusion is the act of not allowing someone to belong or to take part in an activity on the basis of some condition, circumstance or attitude. For example, a group of preschool boys might exclude the girls from playing in the block play area on account of their gender, or a local authority might exclude a child from attending their school of choice on account of a lack of resources. By contrast, inclusion is about increasing participation for all children (and adults) and eliminating social exclusion.

Corbett (2001) suggests that in order to begin considering inclusion, one needs to examine who it is that is excluded from society. She goes on to suggest that it is often **disabled children**, and those from different cultures and ethnic minorities, as well as bilingual children and those living in areas of deprivation, who are excluded from full participation in society. Corbett (2001) states that inclusion should be seen as an **emancipatory** concept that relates to the empowerment of people and the celebration of difference and diversity. Similarly, Pascal and Bertram (2009) view inclusion as being about **democracy** and a voice for all, whilst stating that inclusion should relate to all children, particularly those who may be 'silenced' either through ability or language.

action point 10.1

Observe a group of children at different points during the day. Record instances when children are included and/or excluded from social activities. Reflect on the reasons for why these instances may have occurred, and any ethical dilemmas this may reveal. What action could you/did you take to support inclusion and challenge exclusion?

Barr and Truelove (2015) argue that specific resources can be used to encourage inclusion in early childhood settings in order that all children gain a sense of belonging. They suggest this may be through providing specific toys, or by using texts in different languages, signs, symbols and photographs. All of these should be viewed as prompts to encourage children to participate in activities. Devarakonda (2013), however, suggests that some practitioners may view **inclusion** as idealistic and something 'utopian' and hard to deliver. Ainscow, Booth and Dyson (2006) discuss some of the challenges of inclusive practice in an educational climate where successive governments have endorsed a '**standards-driven**' educational climate. This seeks to increase **attainment levels**, particularly around the areas of literacy, numeracy and science. They argue that in this kind of educational arena, inclusion may not be seen as a high priority, since including children with emotional, behavioural or cognitive difficulties may lower a school's **educational standards** which are presented through league tables and used to 'advertise' the effectiveness of a school. Thus, the standards agenda can conflict with an inclusion agenda. In order to begin to understand where views of inclusion have come from, it is important to consider some of the history of education and where inclusion fits within it.

THE HISTORICAL PICTURE OF INCLUSION

In 1978, the then Conservative Prime Minister Margaret Thatcher ordered an evaluation of the education of children with **disabilities** and medical needs (Her Majesty's Stationery Office, 1978). This was led by Mary Warnock, a philosopher in the fields of English, morality and education. This then led to the formation of the 1981 Education Act. One of the recommendations was that, where possible, children with SEN, rather than being educated in institutions away from the communities in which they lived, should be taught in mainstream schools. A second proposal was that the families should work together with other professionals involved with the child to draw up a '**statement of educational need**' (p. 5). This statement should clearly set out the needs of the child and steps that need to be put in place in mainstream or **special schools** to accommodate them.

In 2001, the Labour government produced the first **SEN Code of Practice** that brought guidance for both parents and professionals working with children with SEN (DfES, 2001). Estelle Morris was the Secretary of State who chaired the writing of this and explained that the Code sought to 'promote a consistency of approach to meeting children's special educational needs which placed the rights of children at the heart of the process' (2001: 1).

This guidance related to the services that should be available for families and the way that **multi-agency** teams (professionals from two or more separate disciplines such as health, education and social care) should work together. The Code also set out recommendations in terms of the many education provisions for children with SEN. The review stressed the importance of **early intervention** for very young children who are either born with an **impairment**, or do not develop at the same rate as their peers.

However, in somewhat of a U-turn from the position outlined in her 1978 Report, Warnock (2005) suggested that educating children with SEN in mainstream schools was not as effective as had been hoped. She felt that inclusion was having an impact on other children in schools who did not have special needs and that, at times, the needs and behaviours of children with SEN were not able to be met in mainstream school. Critiquing this view, Norwich (in Warnock and Norwich, 2010) responded by arguing that Warnock's revised ideas about inclusion deny the importance of social learning and the stigmatisation and isolation that some children experience by being placed in special schools. In 2006, the House of Commons conducted another review of special educational needs (SEN). The then head of the Office for Standards in Education, Children's Services and Skills (**Ofsted**) Miriam Rosen stated that 'the debate over provision has for too long focused on an unhelpful interpretation of inclusion as a place (that is, special or mainstream) rather than on what the pupils achieve' (House of Commons, 2005: 5)

Some of the recommendations of this review were:

- a more child-centred approach to the education of children with SEN where, if the child was able, they had a voice in the school provision offered to them
- staff working alongside children with SEN should be able to access more training
- there should be more funding for training for the SEN workforce.

In 2014, the Conservative and Liberal Democratic coalition government produced an updated Code of Practice that brought SEN and disability together, thus becoming the SEND Code of Practice (DfE and DoH, 2014). Within this document, the educational statement has become an **'education, health and care plan'** (p. 14) and the role of early intervention is emphasised.

FROM EDUCATIONAL NEEDS TO EDUCATIONAL RIGHTS

These changing discourses and policies highlight the debates and dilemmas surrounding inclusion, particularly in relation to the development of a more just and equitable education system. Inspired by practitioners from the preschools of Reggio Emilia in Italy, some childhood disability scholars have argued that Warnock's original conception of 'special educational needs' emphasises a deficit model of childhood, i.e. that disabled children are 'needy'. They prefer to use the term 'children with educational rights' as this supports a strong and positive image of children (Runswick-Cole and Hodge, 2009; Maconochie and Swim, 2017). Furthermore, they assert that the current SEND Code of Practice should be replaced by a *Code of Practice for Educational and Health Rights*, to move away from the current deficit model of special educational needs and disability.

 spotlight on policy 10.1

Inclusion in Early Childhood Policy

Principles of social inclusion in general, and educational inclusion in particular, have featured prominently in UK early childhood policy over the last two decades. Tackling the social exclusion of young children and their families, particularly those living in areas of high social disadvantage, was a key component of New Labour's Every Child Matters (HM Treasury, 2003) agenda. The development of **Sure Start** programmes and children's centres was seen as one element towards the goal of ending child poverty and affording families with children under the age of 5 opportunities to participate in health, childcare and nursery education, early intervention, employment and social care services. However, as Fitzgerald and Kay indicate (2013), policies evolve and shift because of changes in society (such as the economic downturn beginning in 2007/8); changes in government (from New Labour 1997–2010, to the Coalition 2010–2015, and the Conservatives from 2015 onwards); and different priorities and political ideologies. As a consequence of these factors, the ring-fence that prevented Sure Start funding from being used for other purposes was removed, resulting in many Sure Start centres closing down, merging or being restructured (Lupton and Thomson, 2015).

In terms of early childhood education and care, inclusion is an important element in all the curriculum frameworks of the devolved governments of the UK. One of the four main principles of the Early Years Foundation Stage (EYFS) framework is the concept of the 'unique child'. Practitioners are expected to value the diversity of all individuals, not just those with particular needs. Since the inception of the EYFS in 2008, it has gone through several revisions. Nevertheless, the notion of the 'unique child' remains and it is vital that practitioners recognise this uniqueness and understand the differences between cultural groups. The latest version (DfE, 2017) states that 'the EYFS seeks to provide equality of opportunity and anti-discriminatory practice, ensuring that every child is included and supported' (p. 5).

Similarly, the Foundation Stage of the Northern Ireland Curriculum also stresses the importance of providing equality of opportunity and access for all. It outlines a number of ways teachers can address individual children's needs, celebrate cultural diversity and enable the fullest participation of all children (CCEA, 2007). Likewise, the Foundation Phase Framework for children in Wales aged 3–7 states that early childhood settings and schools should develop approaches that support the ethnic and cultural identities of all children, encourage the use of children's home language for learning, enable disabled children to access all areas of provision, and work to reduce environmental and social barriers to inclusion (Welsh Government, 2015). Finally, the Getting it Right for Every Child policy in Scotland promotes 'being included' as one of the eight indicators of children's wellbeing. This involves children 'having help to overcome social, educational, physical and economic inequalities, and being accepted as part of the community in which they live and learn' (Scottish Government, 2012: 3).

THE ROLE OF PRACTITIONERS IN ENSURING INCLUSION

According to The Centre for Inclusive Education (see www.csie.org.uk), inclusion is not something that one person in a setting, such as the **special educational needs co-ordinator** (SENCO), should be responsible for. Booth and Ainscow propose that it takes a 'whole setting approach' to ensure that every child feels included (2006: 3). The *Index for Inclusion* (Booth and Ainscow, 2006) is a tool used by early childhood and school settings to evaluate how inclusive their provision is by examining their principles, ethos and practices. The aim is to ensure that every child is able to feel welcomed and that they belong in the setting, where inclusion is valued as a fundamental right for all children, and where 'barriers to learning' (p. 4) are removed in order that children are able to have a voice in all aspects of the setting.

An important aspect of inclusion is the right for all children to have a voice in decisions that affect them. However, not all children are able to communicate through speech, and so for a child with a communication impairment, **learning difficulties**, or who may be bilingual, this may be a difficult concept. So it is vital that children who struggle with communication should be given other strategies in order that they might express their views. Ring (2009) focuses on the role of drawing and how this can enable children to have a voice. Other methods, such as Makaton, Rebus or Picture Exchange Communication systems, can enable children to have a voice through signs used alongside language, or through symbols and photographs placed in the educational environment (Borkett, 2012). As children become accustomed to seeing signs and symbols used alongside speech and the written word, they begin to make links to communication.

 case study 10.1

Recognising the Many Languages of Children

Sunnyside Nursery has a diverse group of children aged 6 months to 4 years who attend each day, including babies, preverbal children, children with English as an additional language, and disabled children. The setting has made a commitment to recognise the many different 'languages' the children use to communicate, including observing children's body language, utilising children's home languages and offering children non-verbal methods to express their views. Some of the children have difficulties with verbal forms

(Continued)

of communication so photographs and symbols are used with all the children in order to facilitate choice and language. One of the most popular activities is singing time. Initially, the practitioners offered children a box full of toys that related to nursery rhymes. The children were encouraged to choose a toy and then the group would sing a song related to the toy (e.g. a duck for the nursery rhyme 'Five little ducks went swimming one day'). As the children have become more proficient in choosing, the objects have been replaced with photographs and then symbols. This has enabled all children to 'have a say' in the songs chosen.

Use this case study to reflect on your own experience:

1. How do you enable children in your setting to have a voice?
2. Do you rely purely on verbal forms of communication or do you use other methods to encourage children to express their views?
3. What more could you do in your setting to enable children to have a voice?

A concept which has woven through the first part of this chapter relates to the child as a democratic being who has opinions and the right to be listened to. The next part of the chapter focuses particularly on this right and the notion of 'participation', which is used widely in early childhood practice.

WHAT DOES CHILDREN'S PARTICIPATION MEAN?

Like inclusion, the term 'participation' is contested as it is dependent on cultural interpretation and context (Kanyal, 2014). Maconochie (2013) asserts that there are two forms of participation and sometimes these are conflated, which can lead to confusion. Social participation is the idea that children are taking part in some kind of activity and being included. On the other hand, political participation involves children being seen as active agents, expressing their views, influencing decision making and bringing about change. Of course, children cannot participate in the political sense of the term, without social participation. Distinctions are also drawn between 'participation' and 'consultation'. Consultation simply involves listening to children but not necessarily acting on their views. However, participation concerns the direct involvement of children in decision making and influencing change (Thomas, 2007).

Moss (2007) argues that when early childhood practitioners support children to express their views and participate in decision making, they are opening up a democratic space that celebrates diversity and makes practice more inclusive. Shier (2001) suggests that the notion of children's participation can become problematic if practitioners do not view children as having rights. He discusses the need for age-appropriate techniques to be used that recognise both the verbal and non-verbal language of children. However, in order to do this effectively, Paige-Smith and Rix (2011) suggest three theoretical starting points:

- all children are viewed as competent and able
- children have access to their own activities and space and are given the time and opportunity to be involved in conversations with their peers and practitioners
- children are seen as democratic beings who have the right to be listened to.

If participation is to be meaningful, practitioners need to guard against privileging the views of certain groups of children, such as verbally articulate or confident children, and excluding others. Indeed, research suggests that babies, preverbal and disabled children and those from ethnic minority and migrant groups face particular barriers to participation on account of their differences and perceived abilities (Maconochie, 2013).

POLICY CONTEXT OF YOUNG CHILDREN'S PARTICIPATION

Much of the impetus for children's participation has stemmed from the children's rights movement, in particular Article 12 of the United Nations Convention on the Rights of the Child (UNCRC; UN, 1989). Article 12 articulates the right of children to be heard and to have their opinions taken into account in accordance with their age and maturity. This right is revolutionary in international law since it disaggregates the child's views, interests and feelings from their family and other sources of authority (Maconochie, 2013). However, the article has been seen as problematic when applied to young children since they are often assumed to be lacking the capacity to make decisions. As a consequence, the UN issued General Comment 7 in 2005, stressing that Article 12 applies to both younger and older children. It states:

> As holders of rights, even the youngest children are entitled to express their views … they make choices and communicate their feelings, ideas and wishes in numerous ways, long before they are able to communicate through the conventions of spoken or written language. (p. 7)

 reflection point 10.1

1. How might babies, toddlers and young children express their views, make choices and affect change (a) at home; (b) in their early childhood setting; and (c) in their local neighbourhood?
2. What potential dilemmas could arise when children's views conflict with adults' views?
3. Some people believe that young children should be protected from making decisions on account of their developmental immaturity. Others argue that children should be encouraged to exercise their right to make decisions as early as possible. What do you think?

In addition to the UNCRC, the Every Child Matters (ECM) (HM Treasury, 2003) programme has also contributed to the participatory agenda in the UK. Within ECM there was an injunction that policies and services should be shaped by and responsive to the needs of children and should involve children and families in local and national decision making. This was exemplified in the 'Positive Contribution' outcome and associated aim that children should 'engage in decision-making and support the community and environment' (HM Treasury, 2003). Parton and Berridge (2011) argue that since then, the UK government has continued to promote a child-centred framework for the child welfare system. For example, social workers and health care professionals should listen to children's views and involve them in decisions about their care, health and protection. Indeed, some of the forms practitioners complete in the course of an assessment ask about children's wishes and feelings (HMG, 2015). Similarly, Ofsted inspectors in schools and early childhood settings should also be cognisant of the views of children and parents when undertaking assessments of the quality of care and educational provision.

THEORETICAL MODELS OF PARTICIPATION

Much of the theoretical discussion about children's participation has involved different models of participation. Arnstein (1969) first developed a 'ladder of participation' in relation to adult involvement in community development. Hart (1992) adapted this for children and a number of variations on this have since followed. Hart's eight-step ladder starts with rungs of 'manipulation', 'decoration' and 'tokenism' where children are not consulted, moving up towards the middle stages where children are consulted but their participation in decision making is limited. The final rungs represent full participation where children are involved in decision making, either on their own or shared with adults. For example, children, like adults, could exercise power to make decisions about aspects of the running of an early childhood setting, such as the design of the outdoor play area.

In 2001 Shier introduced his 'Pathway to Participation' (see Figure 10.1) to be used alongside Hart's ladder. It moves away from the view of participation being hierarchical to it being a series of five pathways. This model particularly relates to the adult's role in supporting participation. It is based around five levels of participation:

- Children are listened to.
- Children are supported to express their views in whichever way they choose.
- Children's views are taken into account.
- Children are involved in the decision-making process.
- Children share power and are responsible for making decisions which affect them.

Many ECEC practitioners have used this model as a tool to evaluate their practice with children, with the aim of making their work more democratic.

Many of these models are based around similar principles which encourage children to participate in democratic processes and to be empowered through the choices that they make. There is an expectation that they are listened to, heard and involved in projects of their choosing. However, many of these models have a tendency to focus on the needs of teenagers and young people and less on the needs of young children. Consequently, Lancaster (2006) devised a framework for evaluating the participatory practice of early childhood settings, called RAMPS.

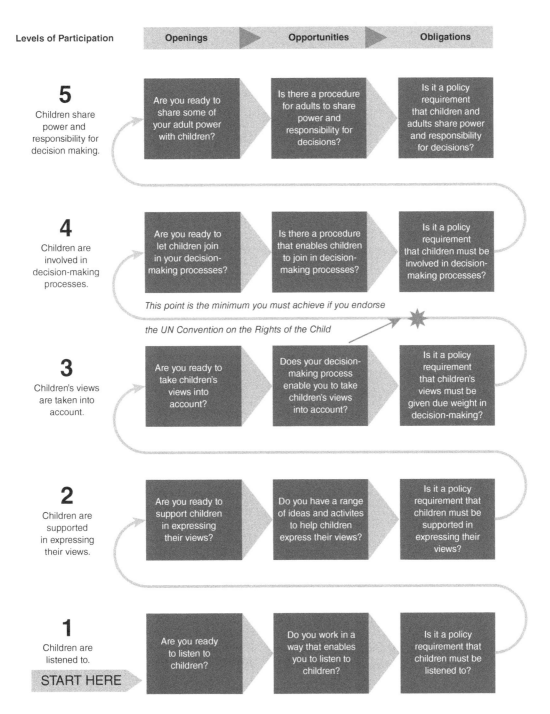

Figure 10.1 Pathway to Participation

Source: Shier (2001)

In this, she suggests, similarly to Paige-Smith and Rix (2011), that there needs to be:

- **R**ecognition that the many languages of young children are valued, listened to and heard
- **A**llocating areas and space where children can express their views and feelings through different mediums
- **M**aking time for children to participate. This requires that practitioners are intentional about seeking children's views and involving them in decision making
- **P**roviding choice to children so that they become arbitrators of their own play
- **S**ubscribing to a **reflective practice**. When adults reflect on their practice, question their assumptions and share with others, especially with children, their practice is more likely to be participatory.

Figure 10.2 brings Lancaster's concepts into a circular diagram with the intention that it is seen as a continuous cycle of participation.

Figure 10.2 Using Lancaster's RAMPS (2006) as a cycle of participation

Source: based on Lancaster (2006)

Maconochie (2013) points out that whilst these models are a useful starting point for thinking about young children's participation, they have also been critiqued on a number of counts. First, in their attempts to be universally applicable, they ignore diversity amongst children and young people and present children as an undifferentiated group. Second, they fail to consider adequately children's participation in their different social, political and historical contexts. These two points have led both Hart (2008) and Shier (2010) to criticise their own models for their normativity and cultural bias, being conceived primarily from their experience in the USA and the UK with older children, and their current misuse as a comprehensive tool for understanding and evaluating participation.

EXAMPLES OF PARTICIPATION IN ECEC PRACTICE

One of the ways participation is often encouraged in ECEC settings is through the use of **continuous provision** whereby activities are available throughout the day for children to access and for them to choose what they want to involve themselves with. Children are encouraged to choose when they have a snack and what it is they eat and drink. Furthermore, in some settings, children are able to choose whether they play indoors or outdoors and for how long. All of these opportunities support children in making their own choices, thus recognising them as a valued citizen in their own lives, whether that be at school, in an ECEC setting, at home or in their community. Children who are listened to by practitioners and other adults and are encouraged to be autonomous, democratic citizens will grow up to see themselves as valued people within society.

SUMMARY

- The notions of 'diversity', 'inclusion' and 'participation' are contested. In this chapter, 'diversity' refers to difference, and celebrating the 'uniqueness' of every child; 'inclusion' refers to enabling all children to be fully included in their educational settings and in society at large; and 'participation' refers to the direct involvement of children in decision making about matters that affect their lives.
- A number of policies have promoted young children's inclusion and participation. This includes the UNCRC, the ECM agenda and the early childhood curriculum frameworks of the devolved governments of the UK.
- One of the dilemmas of inclusive practice is whether disabled children should be educated alongside their non-disabled peers or in separate placements. Another challenge concerns the conflict between the 'standards agenda' and the 'inclusion agenda'.
- Many ECEC practitioners have used theoretical models of children's participation as a tool to evaluate their practice with children, with the aim of making their work more democratic.
- There are a number of challenges to participatory work with young children. Babies, preverbal and disabled children and those from ethnic minority and migrant groups face barriers

to participation on account of their perceived abilities. Potential dilemmas include whether children should be protected from making decisions or encouraged to exercise their right to make decisions as early as possible.

 online resources

Make sure to visit https://study.sagepub.com/fitzgeraldandmaconochie for selected SAGE videos (with questions), SAGE journal articles, links to external sources and flashcards.

FURTHER READING

Devarokonda, C. (2013). *Diversity and Inclusion in Early Childhood: An Introduction*. London: Sage.

This book provides an overview of current research, policy and practice as it relates to the inclusion of young children. It examines issues of race, gender, culture, disability and special educational needs.

Percy-Smith, B. and Thomas, N. (eds) (2010). *A Handbook of Children and Young People's Participation*. Abingdon: Routledge.

This book examines theoretical definitions of children's participation alongside examples of ways children have participated in decision making and policy development in their diverse contexts across the world.

REFERENCES

Ainscow, M., Booth, T. and Dyson, A. (2006). Inclusion and the Standards Agenda: Negotiating Policy Pressures in England. *International Journal of Inclusive Education*, 10(4–5): 295–308.

Arnstein, S. (1969). Eight Rungs on the Ladder of Citizen Participation. *Journal of the American Institute of Planners*, 35(4): 216–24.

Barr, K. and Truelove, L. (2015). Play and the Achievement of Potential. In: J. Moyles (ed.), *The Excellence of Play*, 4th edn. Maidenhead: Open University Press, pp. 35–48.

Booth, T. and Ainscow, M. (2006). *Index for Inclusion: Developing Play, Learning and Participation in Early Years and Childcare*, 2nd edn. Bristol: Centre for Studies on Inclusive Education.

Borkett, P. A. (2012). 'Diversity and Inclusion in the Early Years'. In: J. Kay (ed.). *Good Practice in the Early Years*. London, Continuum, pp.91-115.

Corbett, J. (2001). *Supporting Inclusive Education: A Connective Pedagogy*. London: RoutledgeFalmer.

Council for the Curriculum Examinations and Assessment (CCEA) Belfast (2007). The Northern Ireland Curriculum Primary. [online] Available at: http://ccea.org.uk/sites/default/files/docs/curriculum/area_of_learning/fs_northern_ireland_curriculum_primary.pdf [Accessed 5 November 2017].

Department for Education and Skills (DfES) (2001). *Special Educational Needs Code of Practice*. London: DfES. [online] Available at: www.gov.uk/government/publications/special-educa tional-needs-sen-code-of-practice [Accessed 4 November 2017].

Department for Education (DfE) (2017). *Statutory Framework for the Early Years Foundation Stage*. London: DfE. [online] Available at: www.gov.uk/government/uploads/system/uploads/attach ment_data/file/596629/EYFS_STATUTORY_FRAMEWORK_2017.pdf [Accessed 4 November 2017].

Department for Education (DfE) and Department of Health (DoH) (2014). *SEND Code of Practice: 0 to 25*. London: DfE. [online] Available at: www.gov.uk/government/publications/send-code-of-practice-0-to-25 [Accessed 4 November 2017].

Devarakonda, C. (2013). *Diversity and Inclusion in Early Childhood: An Introduction*. London: Sage.

Fitzgerald, D. and Kay, J. (2013). *Understanding Early Years Policy*, 4th edn. London: Sage.

Hart, R. (1992). *Children's Participation: From Tokenism to Citizenship*. Florence: Unicef.

Hart, R. (2008). Stepping Back from 'the Ladder': Reflections on a Model of Participatory Work with Children. In: A. Reid, B. Jensen, J. Nikel and V. Simovska (eds), *Participation and Learning: Perspectives on Education and the Environment, Health and Sustainability*. Dordrecht: Springer, pp. 19–31.

Her Majesty's Government (HMG) (2015). *Working Together to Safeguard Children*. London: DfE. [online] Available at: www.gov.uk/government/publications/working-together-to-safeguard-children--2 [Accessed 4 November 2017].

Her Majesty's Stationery Office (HMSO) (1978). The Warnock Report: Report of the Committee of Enquiry into the Education of Handicapped Children and Young People. [online] Available at: www.educationengland.org.uk/documents/warnock/warnock1978.html [Accessed 4 November 2017].

HM Treasury (2003). *Every Child Matters*. [online] Available at: http://webarchive.national archives.gov.uk/20130401151715/http://www.education.gov.uk/publications/eOrdering-Download/DfES10812004.pdf [Accessed 20 March 2017].

House of Commons (2005). *Special Educational Needs: Third Report of Session 2005–2006*. London: The Stationary Office Ltd.

Kanyal, M. (ed.) (2014). Models of Participation. In: M. Kanyal (ed.), *Children's Rights 0–8: Participating in Education and Care*. London: David Fulton, pp. 63–88.

Lancaster, Y. P. (2006). *RAMPS: A Framework for Listening to Young Children*. London: Daycare Trust.

Lupton, R. and Thomson, S. (2015). *The Coalition's Record on the Under Fives: Policy Spending and Outcomes*. Social Policy in a Cold Climate Research Report 4. London: LSE/CASE.

Maconochie, H. (2013). Young Children's Participation in a Sure Start Children's Centre. Sheffield Hallam University. [online] Available at: http://shura.shu.ac.uk/7437 [Accessed 2 July 2018].

Maconochie, H. and Swim, T. (2017). Early Intervention. In: T. Swim (ed.), *Infants and Toddlers: Caregiving and Responsive Curriculum*, 9th edn. Belmont, CA: Wadsworth Cengage Learning, pp. 240–60.

Moss, P. (2007). Bringing Politics into the Nursery: Early Childhood Education as a Democratic Practice. *European Early Childhood Education Research Journal*, 15(1): 5–20.

Nutbrown, C. and Clough, P. (2009). Citizenship and Inclusion in the Early Years: Understanding and Responding to Children's Perspectives on Belonging. *International Journal of Early Years Education*, 17(3): 191–206.

Paige-Smith, A. and Rix, J. (2011). Researching Early Intervention and Young People's Perspectives Using a 'Listening to Children' Approach. *British Journal of Special Education*, *38*(1): 28–36.

Parton, N. and Berridge, D. (2011). Child Protection in England. In: N. Gilbert, N. Parton and M. Skivenes (eds), *Child Protection Systems: International Trends and Orientations*. Oxford: Oxford University Press, pp. 60–85.

Pascal, C. and Bertam, T. (2009). Listening to Young Citizens: The Struggle to Make Real a Participatory Paradigm in Research with Young Children. *European Early Childhood Education and Research Journal*, *17*(2): 249–62.

Ring, K. (2009). Supporting Playful Drawing: The Role of the Adult in Early Years Foundation Stage Settings. Paper presented at TACTYC: Inspiring Practice in Early Education conference, November. [online] Available at: https://tactyc.org.uk/pdfs/2009conf_Ring.pdf [Accessed 7 June 2018].

Runswick-Cole, K. and Hodge, N. (2009). Needs or Rights? A Challenge to the Discourse of Special Education. *British Journal of Special Education*, *36*(4): 198–203.

Scottish Government (2012). *A Guide to Getting It Right for Every Child*. Edinburgh: Scottish Government. [online] Available at: www.gov.scot/Resource/0045/00458341.pdf [Accessed 5 November 2017].

Shier, H. (2001). Pathways to Participation: Openings, Opportunities and Obligations – A new model for enhancing children's participation in decision-making. *Children and Society*, *15*(2): 107–17.

Shier, H. (2010). Pathways to Participation Revisited: Learning from Nicaragua's Child Coffee Workers. In: B. Percy-Smith and N. Thomas (eds), *A Handbook of Children and Young People's Participation: Perspectives from Theory and Practice*. Abingdon: Routledge, pp. 215–29.

Thomas, N. (2007). Towards a Theory of Children's Participation. *International Journal of Children's Rights*, *15*(2): 199–218.

United Nations (UN) (1989). *The United Nations Convention on the Rights of the Child (UNCRC)*. Geneva: UN. [online] Available at: https://downloads.unicef.org.uk/wp-content/uploads/2010/05/UNCRC_united_nations_convention_on_the_rights_of_the_child.pdf?_ga=2.256348812.601248384.1510181207-2058859752.1510181207 [Accessed 8 November 2017].

United Nations (UN) (2005). *Implementing Child Rights in Early Childhood, General Comment 7*. Ref. OHCHR CRC/C/GC/7. Geneva: UN. [online] Available at: www2.ohchr.org/english/bodies/crc/docs/AdvanceVersions/GeneralComment7Rev1.pdf [Accessed 8 November 2017].

Warnock. M. (2005). *Special Educational Needs: A New Look*. London: Philosophy of Education Society of Great Britain.

Warnock, M. and Norwich, B. (2010). *Special Educational Needs: A New Look* (ed. L. Terzi). London: Continuum.

Welsh Government (2015). *Curriculum for Wales: Foundation Phase Framework* (revised 2015). Cardiff: Welsh Government. [online] Available at: http://gov.wales/docs/dcells/publications/150803-fp-framework-en.pdf [Accessed 5 November 2017].

CHILDREN'S PUBLIC HEALTH

BY PAMELA DEWIS

I had some understanding of the social determinants of health before reading this chapter, but it gave me a much more in-depth understanding of the topics. I found the chapter easy to read but challenging enough that I was prompted to pause to think about the content. The case study was very enlightening; it was fascinating to see how one setting used data analysis and evidence-based approaches to target bullying. I identified this as an area I would like to do more research on.

It was also very interesting reading about the effects that devolution has had on data collection for the UK as a whole, as this was something I had not considered before.

The further reading that was signposted was very useful for gaining further knowledge on the topic from reliable sources, in particular the World Health Organization website.

AISHA ALI
BA (HONS) EARLY CHILDHOOD STUDIES
UNIVERSITY OF EAST LONDON

learning outcomes

By actively reading this chapter and engaging with the material, you will be able to:

- identify what is known about the state of health of the UK's early childhood population
- apply knowledge of major social determinants of health in early childhood to early childhood education and care practice
- question the application of approaches to promoting health in early childhood settings that do not take account of major social determinants of health.

INTRODUCTION

The focus of this chapter is **child public health** (**CPH**). A rapidly developing field and subspecialty of public health and **paediatrics**, CPH is concerned with the distribution of health and illness across entire childhood populations. CPH is also concerned with investigating factors that influence children's health (**health determinants**) and ways in which children's health can be improved through effective **health promotion** (Blair et al., 2010). Although, over time, health in early childhood has improved significantly in the UK, recent years have witnessed a decline in progress relative to that of other European nations. Moreover, stark inequalities exist between the health of young children from disadvantaged backgrounds and those living in more affluent circumstances. Children's health is influenced by a range of interrelating factors, commonly referred to as health determinants, some of which are hugely detrimental, although potentially modifiable. **Health inequalities** and poverty both represent a case in point. While early education and care professionals can do little to impact poverty, they are, however, ideally placed to mitigate health inequalities and thus contribute hugely to improvements in health in the UK. Focusing on available data sets relevant to the early childhood age range, and drawing on a recent report, this chapter presents an overview of **health indicators** relevant to early childhood in the UK. Subsequently, it explores wider determinants of health than those operating at the level of the individual, and culminates in discussion relevant to the potential contribution of ECEC professionals to ensuring environments conducive to health.

WHAT IS KNOWN ABOUT THE STATE OF HEALTH OF YOUNG CHILDREN IN THE UK?

It is widely accepted that health is a contested concept; impossible to definitively define. Indeed, according to Green et al. (2015), the task of defining health has been compared to shovelling smoke. Furthermore, health is widely recognised nowadays as a subjective state. In other words, being healthy means different things to different people (including children). These two factors combined – and superimposed by an absence, until relatively recently, of composite measures of positive health – have made it very difficult to assess the health of populations by any other means than focusing on the absence of illness. Thus, of necessity, there has long existed a tradition in public health practice to focus on assessing population-level health by means of looking at levels of ill health (Green et al., 2015). Such an approach holds with a negative view of health as the absence of illness as opposed to other conceptions where health is viewed as a positive state of wellness. However, efforts to measure health as a positive (and subjective) state are gaining momentum (Green et al., 2015), the most significant example being the establishment in 2010 of the 'Measuring National Wellbeing' programme (ONS, 2010).

A landmark report by the Royal College of Paediatrics and Child Health (RCPCH), namely the State of Child Health Report (SoCHR) (RCPCH, 2017) describes the current state of health of the UK's childhood population across 25, mainly negative, health indicators. The report concludes that children's health in the UK is a major cause for concern, especially when compared to that of other European countries, and that there exists an alarming gap between the health of children from affluent and those from **deprived backgrounds**.

The report acknowledges that the health of children, including young children, in the UK has vastly improved over recent decades, largely on account of public health measures and medical advancements. It warns, however, that across the childhood age range, progress is slowing down, and that the UK lags behind Europe across a range of health indicators. In respect of early childhood, it shows that infants and young children are suffering and indeed dying unnecessarily, and that this is much more so in young children from deprived backgrounds.

Beginning with a focus on mortality (death) data, much of the ensuing section of the chapter draws heavily on the SoCHR (RCPCH, 2017) to highlight major areas of concern relevant to health in early childhood in the UK. Implicit in the discussion and indeed in any further reference to mortality data, is acknowledgement of the deeply upsetting nature of death occurring in childhood and the need, therefore, to remember that behind every individual statistic there existed someone's child, and that the pain of their loss continues to affect the families and friends concerned.

Although fortunately a rare event in childhood, especially in the **minority world**, mortality is the most commonly presented statistic of child health (Blair et al., 2010). It is generally accepted, however, that mortality data provide an extremely limited view of the true state of health of a childhood population, not least on account of how rarely mortality occurs in this age group. On the other hand, notwithstanding this shortcoming, it is the gathering of mortality data across generations that has developed our understanding of the extent to which, and how, child health has improved in the minority world over time (Blair et al., 2010). Moreover, the gathering of child mortality data also enables international comparisons where comparable countries can learn from each other how best to improve children's health (Wolfe et al., 2014).

Fortunately, far fewer children die nowadays in the UK, and indeed the world, than ever before and the situation continues to improve (Wolfe et al., 2014). **Infant mortality** in particular has reduced massively over recent centuries. In the 1840s, around 15% of babies died before their first birthday compared to 0.4% in 2011 (ONS, 2015). By way of a cautionary note, however, progress in reducing the number of deaths occurring in early childhood and indeed childhood more generally, has slowed over the past 20 years (in some cases by half as much as the progress between 1990 and 2000), particularly when compared to that of other European nations. The UK has the fifth highest infant mortality rate out of 19 European countries and, every year, an estimated 2,000 additional children, amounting to five potentially avoidable child deaths every day, die in the UK compared to Sweden, the best-performing country in this respect (Wolfe et al., 2014).

action point 11.1

1. Find out why death occurring in childhood has become such a rare event in the UK compared to the situation in the 1800s.
2. Try to gain an understanding of why the UK lags behind much of Europe in respect of reducing the number of deaths occurring in early childhood.

Mortality rates and cause of death in early childhood vary by age group. According to the SoCHR (RCPCH, 2017), infant mortality – which continues to account for most deaths occurring in early childhood, particularly in the first month after birth (the **neonatal period**) – was 2,517 across England and Wales in 2014 (RCPCH, 2017). For the UK as a whole, the number of infant deaths occurring in 2014 was 3,014, of which 2,103 (70%) occurred during the neonatal period (Parliamentary Office of Science and Technology (POST), 2016).

Similar to infant mortality rates in England and Wales since the middle of the nineteenth century, the number of deaths occurring in childhood beyond the first year of life has also declined, especially over recent decades. For example, in 2014, the mortality rate for children aged 1 to 14 years fell by 64%, from 28 deaths per 100,000 in 1984 to 10 per 100,000 in 2014. Focusing on the younger age group, the mortality rate for children aged 1 to 4 years fell by 67% over the same period, from 42 deaths per 100,000 in 1984 to 14 in 2014 (ONS, 2014). The SoCHR (RCPCH, 2017) conveys that the number of deaths occurring between the ages of 1 and 9 years in 2014 was 838 across the UK: 761 in England and Wales, 28 in Northern Ireland and 49 in Scotland (RCPCH, 2017). However, on account of the absence of a UK-wide system for comparable (with other European nations) analysis and interpretation of child mortality data, currently there is no way of establishing how the UK compares to other European nations in this particular respect.

The report, besides using mortality data to delineate the state of child health in the UK, employs **morbidity** data for the same purposes. Focusing across the childhood age range, the report contains a number of key messages relevant to long-term conditions as an aspect of morbidity. Many of these are relevant to early childhood. Asthma, for example, a condition that can manifest in children as young as 3 years of age, is highlighted as being more prevalent and causing more hospital admissions and deaths in the UK than almost anywhere else in Europe. Moreover, in some areas of the country, children are dying unnecessarily from asthma on account of a lack of high-quality care (Pearson, 2008; Royal College of Physicians, 2014).

With regard to early childhood in particular, the SoCHR (RCPCH, 2017) conveys morbidity data relevant to unhealthy teeth and gums and to hospital admissions resulting from non-intentional injury. In respect of the former, it is stated that notwithstanding its highly preventable nature, up to 41% of 5-year-olds in the UK have signs of tooth decay, with higher rates affecting deprived populations. In terms of preventable events, the report states that in 2014–15, there were 45,168 non-intentional injury-related hospital admissions across England, Scotland and Wales in the under-5 age group, and this continues to blight the lives of young children as a major cause of illness and often serious disability.

Although not an example of morbidity as such, rather an important health indicator, long-term '**overweight and obesity**', as is common knowledge, presents major risks to health and to the future of society. Indeed, the SoCHR (RCPCH, 2017: 41) cautions that: 'The childhood obesity epidemic presents one of the greatest health threats both to children and their future and the UK's future. This threat is now universal across all countries, rich and poor.'

Notwithstanding this threat, the past decade has seen little by way of improvement in the proportion of children who are at a healthy weight in the UK. During early childhood, throughout England, Scotland and Wales, children's weight at school entry is monitored as a matter of routine. Drawing on the data generated, the SoCHR (RCPCH, 2017) shows that across all three nations, more than one in five children during their first year of primary school are overweight or obese. Northern Ireland is excluded from this particular comparison on account of a lack of data relating specifically to the age group in question. What is known, however, is that 9% of children between the ages of 2 and 15 years in Northern Ireland are obese, and 16% are overweight (Baker, 2017). According to Public Health England (PHE) (2016), out of the 34 **Organisation for Economic Co-operation and Development** (**OECD**) countries, the UK ranks ninth for overweight prevalence (including obesity) in children aged 2–19 years. This latter comparison does include Northern Ireland.

Besides its portrayal of morbidity relevant to physical health in early childhood, the SoCHR (RCPCH, 2017) also presents some children's mental health-related data, albeit limited in comparison. This disproportionate emphasis on physical health supports Lamb's (2015) claim that, all too often, children's mental health fails to attract the attention it warrants. On the plus side, however, Chapter 5 (of the report) draws on data from the most recent **Childline** review (National Society for the Prevention of Cruelty to Children (NSPCC), 2015) which goes part way at least to presenting a picture of mental health issues affecting early childhood. Even more positive is that the data in question arise from children's subjective accounts of issues that concern them, and therefore provide an insider perspective of the situation at hand. According to the NSPCC (2015), the number of children, 11 years of age and under, having received counselling from Childline, relative to older age groups, is low (13%). However, they report a slight increase (3%) on the previous year's report. Consistent with the previous year, on the other hand, is that one out of every four children in this age group contacted them about bullying (5,496 calls). Other commonly reported issues include: family relationships (3,791 calls), friendship problems (2,143 calls), school/education problems (1,565, which saw a 17% increase on the previous year), physical abuse (1,485) and low **self-esteem**/unhappiness (1,321 calls).

 case study 11.1

The Friendly Schools: Friendly Families Initiative

The first-of-its-kind anti-bullying initiative for schools, 'Friendly Schools: Friendly Families' (FSFF) is an approach developed through extensive research with Australian children and adolescents. It is both nationally and internationally renowned as a comprehensive, evidence-based approach to promoting children's health and wellbeing that can substantially reduce bullying behaviour (Friendly Schools, 2014).

The initiative utilises a whole-school approach which aims to enable schools to assess their pupils' social and emotional wellbeing, assess the efficacy of existing strategies, identify any areas in need of improvement and apply evidence-based strategies as appropriate to address any gaps. In so doing, FSFF helps schools build their own capacity for change. The intervention package includes a range of evidence-based products to assist in all aspects of the process, which have been tested and found to be effective in a range of Australian schools. In keeping with a whole-school approach, the central tenet of the FSFF initiative is to bring together entire school communities to foster and sustain a friendly, supportive and safe school culture.

In respect of bullying more specifically, FSFF sets out to raise awareness of the issue, improve communication about bullying, foster adaptive responses to bullying, encourage support for children who are bullied and encourage peer and adult rejection of bullying behaviour. As a means of protecting children from bullying, the initiative advocates, based on relevant research, fostering qualities such as resilience, positive self-esteem, empathy, social skills, self-management skills, decision-making skills and conflict resolution.

1. What, in your view, are the attributes of the FSFF initiative that makes it particularly appropriate for schools to choose as an intervention strategy?
2. Look again at the NSPCC data above – in your view, how could the initiative contribute to improving the current situation?

Other child mental health data is available from a major survey conducted in 2004, the findings of which are reported by Green et al. (2005). The 2004 survey revealed that one in ten children and young people between the ages of 5 and 16, and 7.7% (340,000) of children aged 5–10 years living in the UK, suffer from a diagnosable mental health disorder, which amounts to around three children in every school classroom. A report from the Children's Commissioner (2017) for England found that 20–25% of children with a mental health condition receive support and the vast amount of resources is spent on children with the severest needs. This is despite clear evidence that early intervention is both cost efficient and more likely to prevent the escalation of symptoms. The most prevalent diagnostic categories were found to be **conduct disorders**, anxiety, depression and **hyperkinetic disorders** (Green et al., 2005). More recently, however, and with reference to early childhood specifically, according to Earle (2013) there is a 10% prevalence rate for 3-year-olds with emotional and behavioural problems, and a further study showed 7% of children aged 3–4 years as having severe behaviour problems.

At this juncture, it is important to note something very significant. The health of young children from deprived backgrounds in the UK is worse than that of children living in more affluent circumstances and this applies to all the health indicators discussed. According to Rough et al. (2013), this alarming gap between the health of rich and poor children in the UK appears to be widening. In the succeeding section, it will become clear that such health inequalities contribute massively to the slowing down in improvements to child health in the UK, and to the nation's poor performance in ensuring the health of its childhood population when compared to other European and OECD countries. For a more detailed analysis of child health inequalities, see BMA (2013), listed in further reading.

Based on your reading of the chapter so far, consider how ECEC practitioners could contribute to improvements in the state of health in early childhood in the UK.

What particular issues should they focus on and how?

How might they establish the extent to which the above issues apply in their particular locality?

HOW CAN ECEC PROFESSIONALS USE THEIR KNOWLEDGE OF MAJOR HEALTH DETERMINANTS TO CONTRIBUTE TO IMPROVEMENTS IN CHILD PUBLIC HEALTH?

Prerequisite to answering this question is the need to introduce the remaining two key concerns of CPH and public health more generally: the interacting factors that shape population-level health and wellbeing (health determinants) and ways in which individuals, professionals, organisations and society as a whole can influence, for the good, health determinants that are modifiable (Blair et al., 2010).

Health determinants include biological/hereditary factors (genotype) and psychosocial factors: behaviours; material circumstances and the social environment (factors that influence development of the **phenotype**). The Commission on Social Determinants of Health (CSDH) (2008) explains how these influencing factors are in turn influenced by individuals' social position, and that moreover social position is itself influenced by a range of factors. These include: education; occupation; income; gender; ethnicity and race; factors which are affected by the general socio-economic, cultural and environmental contexts in which they operate. This emphasis in CPH on biological as well as social determinants of health aligns with Bronfenbrenner's ecological systems theory that healthy development is dependent on the genome's interaction with subsystems of the ecosystem (see Chapter 1). Marmot and Bell (2012: 10) contextualise social determinants of health, as described by the CSDH (2008), as 'the conditions in which people are born, grow, live, work and age' and fervently maintains, based on a raft of rigorous **epidemiological** evidence, including the renowned millennium cohort study, that disparities in the quality of these conditions are at the very root of inequalities in health and consequent poorer health outcomes for the least favoured in society. Put simply, health inequalities result from inequalities in society. In other words, positive health influences are not evenly distributed across society and therefore neither is positive health. Marmot (2010) further posits that, in view of the persistent socio-economic inequalities affecting the UK, including inequalities in early education, housing and neighbourhood conditions, employment and working conditions and, more generally, access to equal participation in the benefits of society, that there should continue to be health inequalities is no mystery, and the situation is unjust.

According to Marmot and Bell (2012), the socio-economic inequities affecting the UK do not bode well for the health of the UK's early childhood population (or the population as a whole, given the well-known fact that poor health in early childhood is a strong predictor of poor health throughout childhood and into adulthood). By way of illustration: according to Roberts et al. (2016), children living in countries where there are wide gaps between rich and poor people are more likely to die than their counterparts living in countries where wealth is shared more equitably. Moreover, they portray a synergistic relationship between the slowing down of the decline in infant mortality in the UK, starting around 1990, and a coinciding rise in income inequality. To add to this what can only be described as a bleak situation, absolute poverty (poverty is another major determinant of health, e.g. Duncan et al., 2010) is increasing in the UK (MacInnes et al., 2013) and as many as 30% of households lack sufficient income to secure an acceptable standard of living (Joseph Rowntree Foundation, 2017). In 2016, the Child Poverty Act was repealed and with it a legal requirement on government to reduce levels of poverty.

Determinants of health, including health inequalities, begin their influence before birth (through their effect on mothers' health) and accrue over a lifetime, with particular significance attached to the early years (Marmot, 2010). Likewise, the importance of what happens in early childhood forms a focal part of the recommendations of a number of reviews into health inequalities, including 'Fair Society, Healthy Lives: The Marmot Review' (Marmot, 2010). In fact, the review made the early years its priority objective in its recommendations to the government, arguing that good foundations during very early childhood are crucial to reducing health inequalities across the life course (Marmot, 2010).

By now it should be possible to infer how ECEC professionals can use their knowledge of major health determinants to contribute to improvements in CPH. In essence, the increased susceptibility of infants and young children to harmful social determinants of health – the root cause of major health concerns – coupled with ECEC professionals having regular and direct access to young children and their main caregivers, demands an approach to improving health in early childhood that goes beyond didactic health education. Moreover, social determinant-focused efforts to promote health in early childhood should concentrate, first and foremost, on contributing to the prevention of serious health concerns pertinent at the local level and making use of the best available evidence on effectiveness. Local-level health needs and determinants, including those pertaining to young children, are assessed through the undertaking, led by **health and wellbeing boards**, of **joint strategic needs assessments (JSNA)**. These joint assessments culminate in the development of local **health and wellbeing strategies** which set out priorities for action based on the findings of the joint strategic needs assessment. National child health promotion guidelines must also be consulted in respect of informing strategic priorities for improving young children's health locally.

 action point 11.2

Find your local 'health and wellbeing strategy'. This should involve nothing more than an Internet search. Using the document, draw up a summary of how ECEC professionals specifically could contribute to its success.

THE POTENTIAL BENEFITS TO CHILDREN'S HEALTH OF ACTION ON THE WIDER DETERMINANTS OF HEALTH

Practice guidance relevant to early childhood across the UK (England: Statutory Framework for the Early Years Foundation Stage; Wales: Foundation Phase Framework; Scotland: Early Years Framework; Northern Ireland: Learning to Learn Framework), although different in name and other less significant aspects, share a focus in the main on promoting health in early childhood settings through interventions that aim to bring about changes in health-related parenting behaviour. Behaviour change is also the focus targeting children specifically. One example of this is Public Health England's Eatwell Guide (which replaces the Eatwell Plate). Such interventions focus on traditional health education as opposed to approaches to improving health that take account of wider social determinants; that is, approaches that aim to make the healthy choice the easy choice, a phrase famously coined by the World Health Organisation (WHO) in its Ottawa Charter of 1986. Although traditional health education is delivered with the best of intentions, it fails to acknowledge parents' understanding of their impact, their desire to do well by their children and the often difficult circumstances (negative health determinants) in which they parent. Moreover, this type of approach does not recognise the fact that unhealthy habits are adopted as coping strategies to negotiate the conditions that preclude healthy living, and that thus no amount of health education, in the absence of action on wider determinants, will bring about change.

 spotlight on organisations 11.1

World Health Organisation (WHO)

Based in Geneva, the WHO is a specialised agency of the United Nations, working in 150 countries. It is concerned with public health across the lifespan, at an international level. Established in 1948, the organisation's overall aim is the attainment by all people of the highest possible state of health by means of directing and coordinating health within the United Nations. The WHO (2017) sets out to achieve its aims by means of:

- providing leadership on matters critical to health and engaging in partnerships where joint action is needed
- shaping the research agenda and stimulating the generation, translation and dissemination of valuable knowledge
- setting norms and standards and promoting and monitoring their implementation
- articulating ethical and evidence-based policy options
- providing technical support, catalysing change and building sustainable institutional capacity
- monitoring the health situation and assessing health trends.

The WHO website provides a raft of information and guidance on a wide range of health topics, including health promotion. The health topics most relevant to this particular chapter are 'child health' and 'social determinants of health'. In fact, the organisation's A-Z of health topics is extensive, including data, publications, initiatives, evidence-based practice and much, much more. The WHO's work on health and development also carries huge relevance as does its focus on evidence-based health-promotion practice. The website has a wealth of public health data pertaining to children, as well as evidence-based information and strategies for promoting health.

CPH recognises that effective action to improve the state of child health must focus on modifiable health determinants operating across all subsystems of the ecosystem. Based on the work of the **Carnegie Task Force** on meeting the needs of young children, Rough et al. (2013) conclude that, of factors likely to protect against health inequalities, effective educational interventions and family support appear to offer the best methods – clearly a key area of practice for ECEC professionals at the micro and meso levels. They identify that support can be interpersonal or emotional, practical or financial, and that there exists a body of scientific evidence that, to be effective, 'interpersonal' support is reliant on supporters' ability to enable parents to feel a sense of belonging and to feel less criticised and less vulnerable, and that this can be achieved through working in a way that is 'accepting, encouraging, valuing and empowering' (Rough et al., 2013: 50). These underlying principles of effective interpersonal support can be used to underpin early childhood professionals' encounters with parents, regardless of whether or not their remit is to deliver educational and family support interventions specifically. Furthermore, evidence-based and user-informed guidance for use by **children's centres**, whose core purpose, as is well known, is to reduce inequalities in health and other positive outcomes, can also be used to inform any aspect of ECEC practice (Bowers et al., 2012).

The determinants-level approach is closely aligned to the principles underpinning a settings approach to promoting and protecting health, which recognises that health is created and lived in settings. The settings approach holds that besides their direct impact on health, settings experienced during day-to-day life are also places where individuals make choices about health and health-related behaviours (Green et al., 2015). According to Green et al. (2015), Kickbusch (1996: 5) asserts that the settings approach provides a renewed 'focus from the deficit model of disease to the health potentials inherent in the social and institutional settings of everyday life'. This is very much in keeping with the whole-school approach outlined in the FSFF case study; an approach that could easily be applied, and indeed is in many areas, in ECEC settings.

The settings approach, however, is not without its drawbacks. These are summed up by Green et al. (2015) thus: not all settings will reach disadvantaged and vulnerable groups, hence the approach could run the risk of furthering health inequalities if this were not dealt with effectively; the settings approach requires buy-in from everyone involved; it is a resource-intensive approach; it demands new ways of working and associated professional expertise; and, finally, because change takes time, momentum could be lost. Notwithstanding these drawbacks, Green et al. (2015) cite Hancock (1999) as hailing the approach to be one of the most successful approaches from the WHO Ottawa Charter on health promotion, and Kokko et al. (2014: 495) as claiming the approach as one of the 'fundamental international foundations of health promotion'.

SUMMARY

- It is clear that young children's health in the UK has vastly improved over time; however, progress has slowed and children in the UK fare worse compared to those from other high-income countries in Europe, across a range of health indicators. Also, there are stark inequalities in children's health in the UK, meaning that infants and children are suffering, and indeed dying, unnecessarily.
- ECEC professionals have an important role to play in improving young children's health. This is because what happens in the early years lays the foundations for health in later childhood and in adulthood. To be effective in this role, they must have regard for the wider determinants of health and for the more traditional approaches to health education, as well as for the importance of evidence-based approaches, local child health-related intelligence, policy recommendations and guiding principles for effective interpersonal relationships with parents.
- Approaches to promoting young children's health that do not take account of the major social determinants of health fail to tackle the root causes of poor health. Moreover, they assume a deficit in parents' understanding of health and ignore the fact that for many parents, and for a variety of reasons, the healthy choice is seldom the easy one.

 online resources

Make sure to visit https://study.sagepub.com/fitzgeraldandmaconochie for selected SAGE videos (with questions), SAGE journal articles, links to external sources and flashcards.

FURTHER READING

Bowers, A., Strelitz, J., Allen, J. and Donkin, A. (2012). *An Equal Start: Improving Outcomes in Children's Centres*. London: UCL Institute of Health Equity.

This document highlights the outcomes children's centres should strive for to give all children an equal start. It draws on different perspectives as an evidence base for good practice recommendations suitable across ECEC settings.

British Medical Association (BMA) Board of Science (2013). *Growing up in the UK: Ensuring a Healthy Future for Our Children*. London: BMA.

Available online, this report examines the state of the health of children growing up in the UK, with particular reference to major health determinants.

Green, J., Tones, K., Cross, R. and Woodall, J. (2015). *Health Promotion: Planning and Strategies*, 2nd edn. London: Sage.

Chapter 10 in this book provides an excellent resource for anyone interested in adopting a settings approach to health promotion.

REFERENCES

Baker, C. (2017). *Briefing Paper: Obesity Statistics*. London: House of Commons Library. [online] Available at: http://researchbriefings.files.parliament.uk/documents/SN03336/SN03336.pdf [Accessed 17 August 2017].

Blair, M., Stewart-Brown, S., Waterston, T. and Crowther, R. (2010). *Child Public Health*, 2nd edn. Oxford: Oxford University Press.

Bowers, A., Strelitz, J., Allen, J. and Donkin, A. (2012). *An Equal Start: Improving Outcomes in Children's Centres*. London: UCL Institute of Health Equity.

British Medical Association (BMA) Board of Science (2013). *Growing up in the UK: Ensuring a Healthy Future for Our Children*. London: BMA.

Children's Commissioner (2017). Briefing: Children's Mental Healthcare in England. [online] Available at: https://www.childrenscommissioner.gov.uk/wp-content/uploads/2017/10/Childrens-Commissioner-for-England-Mental-Health-Briefing-1.1.pdf [Accessed 24th June 2018].

Commission on Social Determinants of Health (CSDH) (2008). *CSDH Final Report: Closing a Gap in a Generation: Health Equity through Action on Social Determinants of Health*. Geneva: World Health Organisation.

Duncan, G., Ziol-Guest, K. M. and Kalil, A. (2010). Early-Childhood Poverty and Adult Attainment, Behavior, and Health. *Child Development*, *81*(1): 306–25.

Earle, J. (2013). Emotional and Behaviour Problems. In: *Growing Up in the UK: Ensuring a Healthy Future for our Children*. London: BMA Board of Science, pp. 121–48.

Friendly Schools (2014). Home page. [online] Available at: http://friendlyschools.com.au/fsp [Accessed 7 January 2017].

Green, H., McGinnity, Á., Meltzer, H., Ford, T. and Goodman, R. (2005). *Mental Health of Children and Young People in Great Britain, 2004*. London: ONS. [online] Available at: http://content.digital.nhs.uk/catalogue/PUB06116/ment-heal-chil-youn-peop-gb-2004-rep2.pdf [Accessed 16 December 2016].

Green, J., Tones, K., Cross, R. and Woodall, J. (2015). *Health Promotion: Planning and Strategies*, 2nd edn. London: Sage.

Joseph Rowntree Foundation (2017). Households below a Minimum Income Standard. [online] Available at: www.jrf.org.uk/report/households-below-minimum-income-standard-200809-201415 [Accessed 13 July 2017].

Kokko, S., Green, L.W. and Kannas, L. (2014). A review of settings-based health promotion with applications to sports clubs. *Health Promotion International*, *29*(3): 494–509.

Lamb, N. (2015). Forward from Norman Lamb, Minister of State for Care and Support. In: *Future in Mind: Promoting and Protecting Our Children and Young People's Mental Health and Wellbeing*. London: DoH, p. 3.

MacInnes, T., Aldridge, H., Bushe, S., Kenway, P. and Tinson, A. (2013). *Monitoring Poverty and Social Exclusion*. York: Joseph Rowntree Foundation. [Online] Available at: file:///C:/Users/dspd/Desktop/MPSE2013.pdf [Accessed 16 December 2016].

Marmot, M. (2010). *Fair Society, Healthy Lives*. The Marmot Review. London: Institute of Health Equity.

Marmot, M. and Bell, R. (2012). Fair Society, Healthy Lives. *Public Health*, *26*(1): S4–S10.

National Society for the Prevention of Cruelty to Children (NSPCC) (2015). *Always There When I Need You: Childline Review – What's affected children in April 2014 to March 2015*. London: NSPCC. [online] Available at: www.nspcc.org.uk/globalassets/documents/annual-reports/childline-annual-review-always-there-2014-2015.pdf [Accessed 16 December 2016].

ONS (Office for National Statistics) (2010). Well-being. [online] Available at: www.ons.gov.uk/peoplepopulationandcommunity/wellbeing [Accessed 10 April 2018].

ONS (Office for National Statistics) (2014). Childhood Mortality in England and Wales: 2014. [online] Available at: www.ons.gov.uk/peoplepopulationandcommunity/birthsdeathsand-marriages/deaths/bulletins/childhoodinfantandperinatalmortalityinenglandandwales/2014 [Accessed 31 March 2017].

ONS (Office for National Statistics) (2015). How Has Life Expectancy Changed Over Time? [online] Available at: http://visual.ons.gov.uk/how-has-life-expectancy-changed-over-time [Accessed 14 January 2017].

Parliamentary Office of Science and Technology (POST) (2016). *Infant Mortality and Stillbirth in the UK*. London: POST. [online] Available at: http://researchbriefings.parliament.uk/ResearchBriefing/Summary/POST-PN-0527 [Accessed 2 February 2017].

Pearson, G. (2008). *Why Children Die: A Pilot Study 2006 (South West, North East and West Midlands, Wales and Northern Ireland)*. London: The Confidential Enquiry into Maternal and Child Health.

Public Health England (2016). Childhood obesity international comparisons data factsheet. [online] Available at: https://khub.net/documents/31798783/32038776/Child+obesity+international+comparisons+data+factsheet/1aa529dc-8411-401c-a4f0-f216b28257b9?version=1.1 [Accessed 25 June 2018].

Roberts, J., Donkin, A. and Marmot, M. (2016). Opportunities for Reducing Socioeconomic Inequalities in the Mental Health of Young People: Reducing Adversity and Increasing Resilience. *Journal of Public Mental Health*, *15*(1): 4–18.

Rough, E., Goldblatt, P., Marmot, M. and Nathansona, V. (2013) 'Inequalities in Child Health'. In BMA Board of Science (eds.) *Growing up in the UK: Ensuring a healthy future for our children*. London: BMA, pp. 37-56

Royal College of Paediatrics and Child Health (RCPCH) (2017). *State of Child Health Report (SoCHR)*. London: RCPCH.

Royal College of Physicians (RCP) (2014). *Why Asthma Still Kills: The National Review of Asthma Deaths (NRAD) – Confidential enquiry report*. London: RCP.

Wolfe, I., Macfarlane, A., Donkin, A., Marmot, M. and Viner, R. (2014). *Why Children Die: Death in Infants, Children and Young People in the UK – Part A*. London: RCPCH.

World Health Organisation (WHO) (2017). Home page. [online] Available at: www.who.int/en [Accessed 7 January 2017].

THE POLITICS OF CHILDREN'S SERVICES

BY MARIE LAVELLE

This chapter has given me an insight into how politics and things such as taxation and social welfare influence a child, their family and practitioners. This understanding will help in my studies, as it will allow me to recognise how social inequalities can impact children and their development.

I found the action point around the currency of legislation particularly useful, as I have never really thought to note whether legislation or policy is still in use or consider why it may not be.

I really enjoyed the page on Bronfenbrenner (p.182) as it explains the ecological model of human development and has helped me understand this in a way I haven't previously.

LEANNE MOORE
BA (HONS) EARLY CHILDHOOD STUDIES
UNIVERSITY OF PLYMOUTH

 learning outcomes

By actively reading this chapter and engaging with the material, you will be able to:

- describe how policy is formed in the devolved countries of the UK
- identify key political drivers of child- and family-focused policy
- critically explore the value of political intervention in the lives of children and families
- identify how government operates at a distance and the role of policy discourse in this process
- consider the ways practitioners can exercise agency to challenge policy and campaign for doing things differently.

INTRODUCTION

The years 2016 – 19 may go down in history for the level of political turbulence. The British electorate's vote to leave the European Union, the ensuing political fall-out, the change of prime minister and subsequent 'snap' election which resulted in a hung parliament and minority government, have left politics in the UK, at the time of writing this chapter, uncertain. Within the UK, the loss of public services – attributed not just to austerity but also to **political ideologies** around the role of the state in society – and the threat of continuing and worsening child poverty have implications for children, families and those who work with and support them. Whilst it might seem strange to start this chapter with a general overview of the current political landscape, the following discussion of politics and children's services sits within this and hence is coloured and textured by these (and past) events. The introduction of these wider political forces is a deliberate provocation to encourage you to engage in wider **macro-political** debates.

To begin this chapter, the formation of policy and legislation will be examined. Undoubtedly, you will have a good idea of how governments are elected and the impact of their policy, ideology and subsequent legislation. If not, see the further reading suggestions at the end of the chapter. However, what is often missing are the stages in between and the subtle ways in which policy and politics are **enacted** (Ball, 2015). The political interest in children and early years is explored, which has often come with unintended consequences for children, their parents and for early years settings as practitioners too have become a site of concern. The work of philosopher Foucault, sociologists Miller and Rose, Moss and others will be useful in exploring this. Underpinning these deliberations will be the work of Bronfenbrenner, who recognised how wider social forces impact on children's everyday experiences.

POLITICS IN AND BEYOND THE NURSERY: BRONFENBRENNER

Bronfenbrenner's ecological model of human development, itself a model with political begin-nings, demonstrates the interconnection between children, family, practitioners and policy/government, at local, national and global levels (Meadows, 2010). For Bronfenbrenner, chil-dren are not just affected by **proximal** factors, such as interactions with their parents, siblings and other important people, but also **distal** influences. Seemingly distant factors such as polit-ical ideologies and the resulting policy direction and law are enacted in society on its citizens, including children. Poverty, for example, is often positioned at a distance from children as opposed to other factors which might be closer to the child and their development, such as parent behaviour (Axford, 2010) or the emphasis on school readiness (see Chapter 16 for fur-ther discussion). Yet policy such as taxation (macro-level), welfare reform, the housing crisis which might feel more distant or distal, also impact on children and the quality of their lived experiences.

> The understanding of human development demands going beyond the direct observation of behaviour on the part of one or two persons in the same place; it requires examination of multi-person systems of interaction not limited to a single setting and must take into account aspects, as aspects of the environment beyond the immediate situation containing the subject.
> (Bronfenbrenner, 1977: 512)

If the work of Bronfenbrenner is to be taken seriously, equal consideration needs to be given to macro-level, big politics debates.

The interconnectedness of systems has been embedded in programmes to support children and families in both the UK and the USA. Bronfenbrenner, along with psychologists Maine and Zigler, were key instigators of the **Head Start** programme in the USA. They recognised wider social factors bore an equal, if not greater, burden on children's lives than influences which lay close to the child. These ideas were influential in the development of the 1997–2010 Labour government's Sure Start Local Programme (Glass, 1999) and subsequent children's centres in England. Yet, in a time of increasing **neoliberalism**, disadvantage is often placed at the level of the individual, these **discourses** percolate into practice, often unnoticed and normalised, and hence structural factors are often neglected in the solutions to social prob-lems. Dealing with factors closer to children, manipulating the parent–child interaction for example, placing emphasis on school readiness to improve the future economic productivity of the child, are politically and pragmatically do-able as opposed to taking bolder steps to reduce inequality such as tackling the distribution of wealth (Axford, 2010) (see Chapter 11 for further discussion of this).

Yet the ecological model is also a dynamic model, one in which children (and those who work with them) have some agentic capacity, capable of influencing other systems within the model. Hence, its use within this book is a timely reminder of the importance of looking at and challenging what might seem the unmovable structural forces which affect children, and challenging neoliberal explanations that position the cause of social issues at the level of the individual child, parent, practitioner or indeed setting.

POLITICS IN THE NURSERY: THE ROLE OF PRACTITIONERS

The call to 'bring politics into the nursery' (Moss, 2007: 5) is not new. Politics has, over the last 30 years, been firmly embedded and very much present in the nursery (the term 'nursery' is used here in keeping with Moss, to include all ECEC settings). However, the willingness of practitioners (in the nursery) to engage in the big 'P' or macro-politics which lie outside the nursery, is less obvious.

 reflection point 12.1

Consider your own political perspective.
    What political values do you hold? Where do they come from? Do you talk politics in your setting? Why does this matter?

We all have our own values and beliefs about the society we live in, 'we are all ideologists' as Freeden (2003: 1–2) says: 'we have understandings of the political environment of which we are part, and have views about the merits and failings of that environment'. It is through the ideologies we hold that we interpret and give meaning to 'facts'. Ideologies are therefore perspectival, contingent and constructed, and whilst they are not 'real' they shape reality. Political parties are therefore formed around shared understandings, and common ideologies and their policies will reflect the political ideologies of that political party, often value-laden with historical underpinnings. Political parties campaign for their election based on promises published in their party manifesto, setting out its prospective legislative agenda. Current societal, national and global anxieties and issues will also influence the direction of policy making, as will influences from special interest groups, lobbyists and the media. Political ideologies mean each party will have a different view of the solutions to societal problems, or whether in fact something is a problem or not (Bacchi, 2009). However, policy development is not as linear, logical or straightforward as is frequently presented. It is not formed from a single rational strategy but from a complex mixture of different influences (Cairney, 2012). Spotlight on Policy 12.1 illuminates how policy and legislation are moulded by these different political ideologies, with consequences for children and families.

 spotlight on policy 12.1

The Life Cycle of a Policy: The Child Poverty Act 2010

In the final days of the Labour government, the enshrining in law of the drive to eradicate poverty was an attempt to leave a legacy of commitment for any succeeding government. From

(Continued)

the outset of the 1997 Labour government, there was concern for high levels of unemployment, wage inequality and reduced social mobility, and the growing evidence of the impact of poverty on life chances. With one in four children at the time experiencing relative poverty, the UK had one of the highest child poverty rates in the developed world, second only to the USA. In 1999, Tony Blair announced the aim of eradicating child poverty by 2020. Despite attempts to quarter the numbers of children in poverty by 2004/5 and the 2010 target being missed, the Child Poverty Act began its passage through Parliament. On 25 March 2010, the Child Poverty Act 2010 was given Royal Assent.

However, in May 2010, just two months after the Act gained Royal Assent, the coalition government, formed between David Cameron's Conservative Party and Nick Clegg's Liberal Democrat Party, led to new political ideologies informing policy. The Act was amended in 2010 with some refocus on social mobility. In 2012 there was growing criticism from the right-wing think tank Centre for Social Justice headed by Iain Duncan Smith. One of the criticisms being the definition of poverty being inadequate along with a refocusing on the 'root causes of poverty', namely welfare and unemployment. In 2013 the first State of the Nation report from the Commission concluded that it was unlikely that the targets for reducing child poverty set out in the Act would be met. Between 2010 and 2015 the focus was targeted on families where it was suggested worklessness was 'normal', hence the focus switched to tackling 'troubled families', of which 120,000 were initially identified, see Chapter 8 for further discussion. The 2015 Conservative government, with a small majority in Parliament, pushed through welfare reform. The 2016 Welfare Reform and Work Act abolished the Child Poverty Act, and sections 1 to 11, 15, 17 and 19-25 were repealed. This meant that the targets for reducing and abolishing child poverty were removed, along with the need to report the number of children living in poverty. However, following protests and campaigning from groups and MPs, the need to report on child poverty rates was reinstated. The 2016 Welfare Reform and Work Act, it is said, will be responsible for an increase in future child poverty.

PARTIES AND THEIR IDEOLOGIES

Conservativism (often referred to as 'the right') is associated with conserving the traditional, preserving such things as the idea of 'the family' and a view that the state should not interfere in everyday life. Between 1979 and 1997 when the Conservative government was in power, greater emphasis was placed on the role of the free-market. As a result, there was a move to deregulation, with much of the state-owned assets sold off and greater emphasis placed on the market to regulate and the rise of the individual within this. The current Conservative government (2015–) has continued to pursue this political ideological agenda in reducing the role of the state and welfare in society. It has also continued the commitment to increasing early years funding for 3-year-olds, however there has been concern from providers that the costs of the 30-hour offer are not being covered adequately in the funding provided. There is concern many small providers may go out of business or have to increase their fees, for provision not covered by the offer, for parents.

Socialism (and social democracy) is concerned with the collective good and community action, the reduction of poverty, inequality and the promotion of work (or labour). The Labour Party is most associated with this ideology, although at times it has tried to distance itself from socialist values as 'New' Labour sought a 'third way'. Between 1997 and 2010 Labour policies reflected a 'communitarian' approach, one which was about creating social change through an agenda of responsibilisation. For example, Sure Start children's centres not only offered support for families, to level the playing field for children from poorer homes, there was also an expectation that families would engage in and embrace some sort of personal change – attending groups, volunteering or engaging in training for employment.

Whilst liberalism reflects freedom and justice and is the underlying philosophy of modern-day conservativism – free from state intervention – the Liberal Democrat Party has been one which has, it is argued, offered a middle ground, embracing freedom of the individual and wanting to reduce state involvement but with a social justice agenda. The Liberal Democrats shared power with the Conservative Party in the Coalition government in 2010–15.

Whilst this may all seem straightforward, elements of ideologies are often continued from one government to the next with slight twists and turns. The 'third way' of the 1997 Labour government (Giddens, 1998) borrowed from both left and right political ideologies to explain its approach. Here, neoliberal ideals first established by Margaret Thatcher's government (1979–90), which placed responsibility with the individual within a community, continued to be reflected in policy. Liberalism, and the freedom which underpins it, is likely to be an ideology that is the basis for most people's political views, especially with regard to liberating policies such as the freedom to marry whom you want.

DEVOLUTION

Another fact to bear in mind is that policies and laws may be different depending on which country of the UK you are reading about. Devolution refers to the way power to create some new laws and policy is given by the Westminster government to the Welsh Parliament, the Scottish Parliament and the Northern Ireland Assembly. Members of Parliament in the devolved countries also sit in the UK Parliament in Westminster, regardless of which devolved country they come from and can vote on key issues in Parliament. Whilst many elements of law and policy are similar across the different countries of the UK, some are very different. Early Childhood Education and Care (ECEC) is one significant area of devolvement (Fitzgerald and Kay, 2016). However, as Dunlop (2016) highlights in the case of Scotland, ambitious plans for children's services are hindered by the gap created by what is devolved to the Scottish government and what is reserved. For example, education is a devolved area of policy, however other policy, including benefits, social security and employment, are constructed by the UK government. This is reflected across the other countries of the UK, echoing the above discussion about proximal and distal issues.

 action point 12.1

1. Find a piece of legislation or policy which relates to your practice – it might be the Early Years Foundation Stage or something else you are currently using in your writing.

(Continued)

2. Now look at the jurisdiction – who does this apply to? Is it Wales, Scotland, Northern Ireland or England?
3. Is the legislation/policy current? Is it still in use or has the policy been archived?

When studying and exploring political issues in early childhood, be vigilant of the date of publication/reference of different policies and related writings. Governments change (every four to five years or more frequently) and therefore the underlying political approaches, ideologies, aims and strategies also change. Whilst laws may stay the same, for example the enduring Children Act 1989, different governments may subsequently amend these laws so that their own ideological approach is pursued. Therefore, note which government a piece might be referring to (e.g. the Labour government of 1997–2010).

THE ECONOMISATION OF EARLY CHILDHOOD

One way childhood has been constructed, in and through policy, is as a site of **social investment**. Concern for inequality, child poverty and poor social mobility, coupled with the growing evidence of the need to 'intervene' and 'get it right from the start', have given rise to the rationale for the economic resourcing of intervention in the early years. Children, it is clear, are central to the project of what has been termed 'the social investment state', which promotes employment over welfare and the development of skills to furnish this employment over a lifetime, starting with children (Adamson and Brennan, 2014). Accounting for this investment in an era of modernisation of government, American economist and Nobel laureate, Heckman (2007) developed a quotient (an equation) for the returns gained from early investment in children from disadvantaged American homes. For every dollar spent on early childhood education, he calculated a seven dollar saving to the economy in later life. Since the late 1990s, his work has been used as the basis for the need to resource ECEC. These 'calculative technologies' are applied not just within institutions, such as education, but also in the private spheres, such as family life, 'producing new ways of rendering economic activity into thought … linking private decisions with public objectives' (Miller and Rose, 2008: 67).

The need to show how political and economic investment in early childhood is worthy of financial investment was promoted in the modernisation agenda of the Labour government (1997–2010), who fostered the need to evidence the use of early interventions such as Sure Start Local Programmes, the Family Nurse Partnership, Incredible Years, and other projects. In the period of austerity that followed, with reduction in universal services and a more targeted approach to supporting the most vulnerable families and children, this evidencing has been increased and further concentrated on 'harder' rather than 'soft' outcomes (Campbell-Barr et al., 2012). As children's services sit at the interface between state policies and children, it is through early intervention that the state's relationship with children has been configured and reconfigured (Parton, 2011), depending on which political party is governing and the ideology they aspire to. More recently, Conservative ideology has seen a withdrawal of the 'big state', with the state stepping in only when there is a concern for the child or the family; not just when a child might be vulnerable but when there might be a cost in the future. For example, the Troubled Families agenda is often framed in terms of potential savings to the state in the future (for a critical perspective of this, see Crossley, 2017).

For Moss (2013), the increased political and financial interest in ECEC services over the last 30 years is something not only to be celebrated. Instead, Moss is concerned for the dominant rationale that early intervention and investment bring high returns later in terms of education, future employment and contribution to the economy. In other words, the reason for the government provision of these services is concerned with the growth of 'human capital':

> Invest and intervene early, when children are young, apply the correct 'human technologies', and (so the story goes) the problems of the world will be resolved; discontents and dysfunctions will vanish, human capital will soar, and individuals and countries will compete successfully in the global market-place. (Moss, 2017: 3)

Here, neoliberalism pervades our everyday lives through the way it 'configures human beings exhaustively as market actors, always, only, and everywhere as homo oeconomicus' (Brown, 2016: 31). With this comes the acceptance of inequality, for in the market there will be those who have invested in themselves or their children and those who have not; the presence of winners and losers is inevitable and to some extent accepted (Brown, 2016).

Whilst the 'investment' in ECEC has brought benefits for children and families, it has also come with consequences both intended and unintended (Adamson and Brennan, 2014; Lloyd, 2015). For children's services, 'investment' has increased accountability, instrumental approaches to monitoring outcomes for children and the normalising of surveillance of children, parents and practitioners, and is discussed in the next section (see Chapter 22 for further discussion). The 'human technologies' Moss talks about above are multiple, quietly embedded within much of what we do with children and families and therefore often unchallenged. They are 'technologies of government' and ways which 'government operates at a distance' (Latour, cited in Miller and Rose, 2008: 16). In doing so, children's services are spaces where political ideologies and discourses are embodied and embedded in practice. As a result, practitioners too become part of the 'machinery of government' and children and childhood become shaped through neoliberal ideals of what it means to be a good citizen – *homo oeconomicus*. The result has been that childhood has become 'the most intensively governed sector of personal existence' (Rose, 1999: 121).

HOW POWER OPERATES AT A DISTANCE: THE ROLE OF PRACTITIONERS

The reconstruction of childhood as a site of social investment has implications for those working with children. The drive to improve outcomes for young children and promote equality through early intervention emerged from the growing body of evidence of the contextual (the more distal) influences on outcomes for children. At the same time, research began to highlight concerns about the quality of the workforce, the need for this to be professionalised and for expert knowledge to inform the practice of educating and caring for young children. As children's early years were positioned as sacred, the role of parents, although acknowledged as important, was not to be trusted with the raising of the next generation. Indeed, the early years sector has been positioned as redemptive with regard to a whole array of social ills: 'Preschools (and other "children's services") assume the role of social regulation, intended to bring a technical fix to bear on the wider social consequences of the economic deregulation demanded by neoliberalism' (Dahlberg and Moss, 2005: 41).

The 'technical fix' is potentially enacted through standardised frameworks, curricula and guidance – all 'technologies of government'. Standardised testing, teaching standards and quality standards all form the basis on which to measure and ultimately compare. Progress in children's development and learning, quality of provision, to name a few, are utilised to evidence the difference that services, practice and practitioners make. The results are compared against agreed standards or 'norms', seemingly gathered 'objectively' from large data sets and research. Knowledge of populations is gathered not from all-encompassing 'Big Brother' observations, but from a multitude of gazes and assemblages (also discussed in Chapter 22). Through the gathering of information about populations, much of our everyday life is charted, observed and measured. The technologies behind this data gathering can be regarded as part of the machinery of government (Miller and Rose, 2008).

 action point 12.2

Consider the information you gather about children and their families. What is this information used for? Is it used for comparison – perhaps comparing children with other children? Is it used to assess the child against 'normal' progress? Who decides what is 'normal'? What happens if a child is not within the boundary of 'normal'?

Instrumentalist approaches not only lead to a techno-rational practice, they also pull practitioners into performing 'government at a distance'. Miller and Rose (2008) draw on Latour's concept here to expose how measurement of effect in one place (the collecting of data on children's progress, for example) is used to create change elsewhere. Therefore, if children do not meet these minimum standards in terms of their progress, they are regarded as not following a normal expected pattern of development. Practitioners are called on to examine what they do, to 'reflect on' and to 'evaluate' their practice to establish their own failings, regardless of the limitations and external constraints. It is this normalisation constructed within a set of 'truth discourses' on such things as children's development and quality of provision, as two examples, which then categorise the 'other' as 'not normal'. As we can see, a number of interrelated tools of disciplinary power are important: hierarchical observation and the use of normalising judgements (Hoskin, 1990) involve categorising and identifying those who are seen as different in some way. Normalising discourses and categorisation are key features in how government works at a distance. As too is the 'conduct of the conduct' – the **self-surveillance** of reflection and evaluation of practice and supervision ('super-vision'!). These 'technologies of government' and discourses filtrate through a range of routes, not just through local guidance and policy, but also through interactions with other practitioners, parents and children themselves.

ECEC settings provide the opportunity for surveillance not just of children and their development, but also of parents and their family life and of practitioners themselves. Institutions such as these, it might be argued, 'make public the private' (Miller and Rose, 2008). The resulting feeling of being observed both 'autonomises and disindividualises power' (Foucault, 1977: 202), creating a 'visibility trap'. Rather than being subjected *to* power (a top-down power), the individual (child, parent, practitioner) becomes subjected *by* power. It influences how they act, how they think and how they see themselves. For parents, this results in acting how they feel they 'ought' to act; how a 'good parent' would act (Lavelle, 2015). This is also the same for practitioners and teachers, where practice is observed, judged and measured for quality. Teachers are increasingly subjected to the 'walk through' or more formal observation of practice. The rationale for these evaluative practices is often constructed in the discourse of quality and self-improvement, often in the form of continuous professional development. Here policy is not just a top-down process but one which 'effects' and becomes enacted (Ball, 2015: 307), as the truth claims carried in policy have the power to 'create rather than reflect a social reality' (p. 308). For teachers in schools in Ball's work and for practitioners in early years settings under discussion here, policy discourse provides the conduit for self-surveillance and **subjectification** – by and through policy, they create the 'good practitioner'. Hence, policy 'changes what we do (with implications for equality and social justice) and changes who we are (with implications for subjectivity)' (Ball, 2015: 306).

RESISTING, NEGOTIATING: THE POLITICS OF PLAYING WITH POLICY

So, where does this leave ECEC practitioners if we accept the arguments above? How do we reconcile the position I have created, where practitioners, not just children and parents, are rendered 'docile' – the Latin for teachable and therefore governable (Foucault, 1977)? As a nurse and midwife in the 1980s and 1990s, before both were graduate status professions, I look back at how power worked in these large hierarchical organisations. Through the level of work levied at and expected of individuals who worked in them, there was no time to pause and reflect in the everyday work of caring, with the emotional labour it consumed. In some respects, the story here is based on an awareness of the extraordinary power of knowing; knowing how power is operating around us and within us is fundamental to resisting. It is not the intention here to dispute the many ways early years practitioners are challenging and resisting dominant discourses through what Deleuze and Guattari call 'minor or minority politics' (Dahlberg and Moss, 2005). These politics are creative, innovative and stealth-like in their enactment; they may also be personal, local and perhaps hidden, and as a result unknown. Whilst this quiet revolt, this 'down playing of policy' (Ball, 2015), might be possible for some, for others it will not be. For ECEC workers, the challenges are great. In small settings, there are few places to 'hide' from policy, and, as the stakes are high and both the process and the product rendered highly visible through, for example, inspection regimes, the need for compliance is equally great: 'These minor engagements do not have the arrogance of pragmatic politics – perhaps even refuse their designation as politics at all. They are cautious, modest, pragmatic, experimental, stuttering, tentative' (Rose, 1999, cited in Dahlberg and Moss, 2005: 121).

Therefore, it is important that, as practitioners, we not only take notice but also engage in the political issues which shape our own ideologies, and examine where these come from and most of all consider what they do, in terms of how they influence how we work with children and their families. Exposing how power operates through policy and through practitioners, realising that 'we do not *do* policy, policy *does* us' (Ball, 2015: 307), is one of the first steps. However, as 'neo-liberal governmentalities' (Ball and Olmedo, 2013) become normalised into everyday practice, the opportunities for resistance diminish, as they will become embedded in everyday practice.

This chapter started with Bronfenbrenner, therefore it is only right it ends with him too. Whilst macrosystems are often seen as institutional, they are also personal:

> Most macrosystems are informal and implicit – carried around unwittingly in the minds of society's member as ideology ... What place or priority children and those responsible for their care have in such macrosystems is of special importance in determining how a child and his or her caretakers are treated and interact with each other in different types of settings. (Bronfenbrenner, 1977: 515)

If this is the case, an explicit exploration of our own political ideologies is vital.

SUMMARY

The chapter has:

- outlined the way that politics, both at a micro-political and a macro-political level, continues to shape how parents and children are constructed and the work practitioners do to support them
- explored the impact of neoliberalisation on education and early years, hence the need for a 'democratic space' to think differently is even greater
- explored how childhood has been positioned as the site of social investment and questioned whether this has been positive or whether there have been unintended negative consequences
- critically reflected on the implications for practitioners, as they too have become the site of surveillance
- considered the ways that practitioners may exercise agency to resist or to play with policy to be positive advocates for children.

 online resources

Make sure to visit https://study.sagepub.com/fitzgeraldandmaconochie for selected SAGE videos (with questions), SAGE journal articles, links to external sources and flashcards.

FURTHER READING

Beresford, P. (2016). *All Our Welfare*. Bristol: Policy Press.

For an engaging exploration of the changing world of welfare and its impact on children, family and the services that support them.

Fitzgerald, D. and Kay, J. (2016) *Understanding early Years Policy,* 4th edn. London: Sage.

For an explanation of political systems and the impact on children and families. The test asks challenging questions of whether policy represents the perspective of all stakeholders?

Lavelle, M. (2015). 'A storm in a tea-cup? "Making a difference" in two Sure Start Children's Centres', *Children & Society*, 29(6):583–592.

Explores the way policy is enacted in unseen, taken-for-granted ways, within early years practice.

REFERENCES

Adamson, E. and Brennan, D. (2014). Social Investment or Private Profit? Diverging Notions of 'Investment' in Early Childhood Education and Care. *International Journal of Early Childhood, 46*: 47–61.

Axford, N. (2010). Is Social Exclusion a Useful Concept in Children's Services? *British Journal of Social Work, 40*(3): 737–54.

Bacchi, C. (2009). *Analysing Policy: What's the Problem Represented to Be*? Harlow: Pearson Education.

Ball, S. (2015). What is Policy? 21 Years Later: Reflections on the possibilities of policy research. *Discourse: Studies in the Cultural Politics of Education, 36*(3): 306–13.

Ball, S. and Olmedo, A. (2013). Care of the Self, Resistance and Subjectivity under Neoliberal Governmentalities. *Critical Studies in Education, 54*(1): 85–96.

Bronfenbrenner, U. (1977). Toward an Experimental Ecology of Human Development. *American Psychologist, July*, 513–31.

Brown, W. (2016). *Undoing the Demos: Neoliberalism's Stealth Revolution*. New York: Zone Books.

Cairney, P. (2012). *Understanding Public Policy: Theories and Issues*. Basingstoke: Palgrave.

Campbell-Barr, V., Lavelle, M. and Wickett, K. (2012). Exploring Alternative Approaches to Child Outcome Assessments in Children's Centres. *Early Child Development and Care, 182*(7): 859–74.

Crossley, S. (2017). *A Kind of Trouble*. [online] Available at: https://akindoftrouble.wordpress.com/author/akindoftrouble [Accessed 10 April 2017].

Dahlberg, G. and Moss, P. (2005). *Ethics and Politics in Early Childhood Education*. London: Routledge.

Dunlop, A. (2016). A View from Scotland: Early Years Policy in the Four Nations – Common challenges, diverse solutions. *Early Education Journal, 78* (Spring): 10–12, 15.

Fitzgerald, D. and Kay, J. (2016). *Understanding Early Years Policy*, 4th edn. London: Sage.

Foucault, M. (1977). *Discipline and Punish: The Birth of a Prison*. London: Penguin.

Freeden, M. (2003). *Ideology: A Very Short Introduction*. Oxford: Oxford University Press.

Giddens, A. (1998). *The Third Way: The Renew of Social Democracy*. Cambridge: Polity Press.

Glass, N. (1999). Sure Start: The Development of an Early Intervention Programme for Young Children in the United Kingdom. *Children in Society, 13*: 257–64.

Heckman, J. (2007). *Heckman, the Economics of Human Potential*. Available at: https://heckmane quation.org [Accessed 12 March 2017].

Hoskin, K. (1990) Foucault under Examination: The Cryo-educationalist Unmasked. In: S. Ball (ed.), *Foucault and Education: Disciplines and Knowledge*. London: Routledge, pp. 29–53.

Lavelle, M. (2015). A Storm in a Tea-cup? 'Making a Difference' in Two Sure Start Children's Centres. *Children & Society, 29*(6): 583–92.

Lloyd, E. (2015). Early Childhood Education and Care Policy under the Coalition Government. *London Review of Education, 13*(2): 144–56.

Meadows, S. (2010) *The Child as Social Person*. London: Routledge.

Miller, P. and Rose, N. (2008) *Governing the Present: Administering Economic, Social and Personal Life*. Cambridge: Polity Press.

Moss, P. (2007). Bringing Politics into the Nursery: Early Childhood Education as a Democratic Practice. *European Early Childhood Education Research Journal, 15*(1): 5–20.

Moss, P. (2013). Beyond the Investment Narrative. *Contemporary Issues in Early Childhood, 14*(4): 370–2.

Moss, P. (2017). *What Image for Education Services for Children under 6 Years in Troubled Times?* Paper presented at international conference 'La cultura dell'infanzia comerisorsa della città', Pistoia, 31 March–1 April.

Parton, N. (2011). Child Protection and Safeguarding in England: Changing and Competing Conceptions of Risk and their Implications for Social Work. *British Journal of Social Work, 41*(5): 854–75.

Rose, N. (1999). *Powers of Freedom: Reframing Political Thought*. Cambridge: Cambridge University Press.

SAFEGUARDING CHILDREN

BY GINNY BOYD

This chapter has increased my understanding of the differences between safeguarding and child protection, and how the failure to implement these procedures effectively can have a negative impact on children, potentially, for the rest of their lives.

Real-life examples of poor practice, and the negative consequences to the child and the practitioner, help you consider how to make the correct decisions with regards to safeguarding. It allows you to reflect on your own previous practice and gives clear guidance on safeguarding procedures in order to adequately protect the child, whilst recognising that specific procedures differ from school to school. It enlightens you to issues which may seem minor in a setting, but have the potential to be much more serious, and gets you thinking about correct procedures.

This chapter helps you understand your roles and responsibilities as practitioners and why legislation is relevant to early childhood study.

JAMIE AINGE
MA EDUCATION
SHEFFIELD HALLAM UNIVERSITY

 **learning outcomes**

By actively reading this chapter and engaging with the material, you will be able to:

- explain and differentiate between the terms safeguarding and child protection
- recognise practitioners' roles and responsibilities in relation to safeguarding young children
- identify why legislation is both relevant to and influences the safeguarding of children
- critically evaluate the barriers to safeguarding children.

INTRODUCTION

Safeguarding is an essential, if often poorly understood, concept which all practitioners and policy makers need to understand. The subject of safeguarding is vast and thus this chapter aims to provide the reader with an introduction to the subject. This chapter begins by: defining safeguarding and **child protection**; exploring practitioners' roles and responsibilities; providing an examination of relevant legislation and policy; and concludes with a discussion around the complexity of intervening successfully in children's lives.

WHAT IS SAFEGUARDING?

There is some confusion regarding terminology: safeguarding and child protection do not have the same meaning. Child protection is a component, albeit an essential one, of safeguarding, however safeguarding encompasses a wider responsibility on services to take action to promote the welfare of all children and young people. The **statutory guidance** *Working Together to Safeguard Children* (Department for Education, 2018: 7) defines safeguarding and promoting the welfare of children as:

- 'protecting children from maltreatment;
- preventing impairment of children's health or development;
- ensuring that children grow up in circumstances consistent with the provision of safe and effective care; and
- taking action to enable all children to have the best outcome'.

Safeguarding applies to all children under the age of 18, whether they are in settings, the community or the family home. Safeguarding strategies, policies and practice are proactive in intent and focus, their aim being to promote children's health, education, physical safety, emotional wellbeing and development. Given this is such a vast area, there are a plethora of safeguarding policies and practice. Examples include anti-bullying policies in settings (GOV.UK, undated), guidance on tackling obesity in young children (DoH, 2011) (see Chapter 11 for further discussion), the Prevent strategy (Home Office, 2016) (see Chapter 16 for further discussion) and government guidance on supporting children with special educational needs and disabilities

(SEND) (DfE, 2014). As child protection is such a key component of safeguarding, this will be explored in greater detail.

CHILD PROTECTION

Although safeguarding and promoting welfare are broader, child protection is obviously of paramount concern. Safeguarding is proactive and is concerned with all children. In contrast, child protection is reactive, responding to specific concerns regarding individual children. Once those concerns reach the 'threshold', whereby practitioners identify that a child is suffering, or are likely to suffer significant harm, action must be taken to protect that child (DfE, 2018). The lack of a clear and universally agreed understanding regarding what constitutes significant harm continues to cause difficulties for both practitioners and families. This is explored in more detail later in the chapter.

All children are dependent on their caregivers, usually their parents, for their survival, and require shelter, food, comfort, love, clothing, and so on, to meet their needs. Some families need additional support to be able to do this, whilst others cannot provide this and intervention is needed to protect the child: both in terms of their immediate wellbeing and potential longer-term harm. The vast majority of children live in families who are motivated to provide their children with the best care they can. For those children where there are child protection concerns, most remain in the care of their birth family with support offered to assist the family to care for them safely.

Child protection concerns have long been categorised into several different types of abuse, although the precise definitions continue to evolve and develop in accordance with the changes in attitudes, values and understanding in wider society. Regardless of the type of abuse, the key concern is whether the child is at risk of, or is suffering from, significant harm (**Children Act 1989**). The later discussion around the role of the state considers how changes in policy and legislation both influence and are influenced by these changing attitudes.

Child protection concerns are categorised in the following terms – children are at risk of: physical abuse, sexual abuse, neglect and/or emotional abuse. Although these are separate categories, many children are subject to multiple forms of abuse; indeed, emotional abuse is always present to some degree. Definitions for each category of abuse are provided by the government, as detailed in Table 13.1 (DfE, 2018: 103).

Before further discussing the potential long-term damage of abuse and neglect, it needs to be recognised that some children who have experienced abusive environments are able to recover and thrive. It is important this is acknowledged so as not to limit hope, optimism and ultimately the child's aspirations. Why some children recover, yet others become permanently and catastrophically damaged, is still not fully understood and much more research is required.

Table 13.1 Categories of abuse taken from *Working Together to Safeguard Children*

Type of abuse	Definition
Physical abuse	A form of abuse which may involve hitting, shaking, throwing, poisoning, burning or scalding, drowning, suffocating or otherwise causing physical harm to a child. Physical harm may also be caused when a parent or carer fabricates the symptoms of, or deliberately induces, illness in a child.

Type of abuse	Definition
Sexual abuse	Involves forcing or enticing a child or young person to take part in sexual activities.
Neglect	The persistent failure to meet a child's basic physical and/or psychological needs, likely to result in the serious impairment of the child's health or development. Neglect may occur during pregnancy as a result of maternal substance abuse.
Emotional abuse	The persistent emotional maltreatment of a child such as to cause severe and persistent adverse effects on the child's emotional development.

Source: Department for Education (2018)

PRACTITIONERS' ROLES AND RESPONSIBILITIES

Expanding safeguarding beyond the narrower child protection definition necessitates the involvement of the full range of early childhood education and care (ECEC) practitioners. It is clear that any one practitioner is unable to meet all the needs of an individual child and it is necessary for support to come from a variety of sources. These practitioners need to work together and, most importantly, in partnership with the family. This is explored later in the chapter and further in Chapter 17.

Considering the definition of safeguarding, it is clear that without additional intervention some children are unlikely to be able to achieve their potential. This is especially important for ECEC practitioners as the first three years of a child's life are crucially important and influence their short-, medium- and long-term brain development (see Chapter 2). The brain grows faster in the first three years of life, 'pruning' unused synaptic connections, thereby influencing a child's physical, emotional, social and educational development. This provides both the opportunity and the necessity to intervene early to promote the optimum development for the child. Thus, ECEC practitioners are rightly concerned to ensure the children in their charge are supported to enable them to achieve their full potential.

RESPONSIBILITY OF THE STATE: CONTRADICTIONS IN POLICY

By using the government's own definition of safeguarding, it is clear that many of the constraints to enabling children to achieve their best outcomes lie outside the control of individual families. This is particularly evident for families living in poverty. Data demonstrate that there is a relationship between the prevalence and impact of poverty on the life chances of children (Main and Bradshaw, 2016). The 2014–15 data indicate that 3.9 million children in the UK were living in poverty; this equates to 28% of all children (Department for Work and Pensions, 2017).

reflection point 13.1

If safeguarding includes preventing the impairment of children's health and development, what role do practitioners have in supporting both families and communities to obtain improved facilities and resources?

There are a plethora of studies demonstrating the pervasive impact of poverty on all aspects of children's lives (Wickham et al., 2016). Again, this is often evident in unsuitable housing, such as homes which may be damp or overcrowded. If a child is left hungry, it will inevitably affect their ability to learn, however able. Many schools, in response to this, have developed breakfast clubs to ensure children are not hungry when they are trying to learn. There has been a proliferation of food banks, established in recognition that a number of families do not have sufficient resources to enable them to provide enough food for all the family. Even for those in poverty who do get enough food to survive, the quality and nutritional value are more likely to be poor. Cheap food is often high in calories and low in nutritional value, again affecting a child's ability to thrive. Alongside the potential impact on the individual child, studies cite the emotional toll poverty takes on families (Mahony, 2017). This places additional pressure and stress on parents who can be upset and exhausted by not being able to provide for all their children's needs, and by the cycle of debt they can quickly find themselves in.

 spotlight on policy 13.1

Legislation: The Role of the State

With regards to safeguarding, when examining how practitioners work together and with families, the clear operationalisation of policy and legislation can be observed. Enshrined in legislation are the specific statutory duties to safeguard children in relation to settings, the community and the child's home. A range of individual organisations and practitioners have specific responsibilities regarding this. It is important to examine some of the key laws and policies which are relevant to safeguarding.

It is important first to understand the difference between a law and a policy. The process for making a law is time-consuming and lengthy; once a bill (a draft law) has approval from both the House of Lords and the House of Commons, it receives formal approval by the monarch, known as 'Royal Assent', becomes statutory law and is subsequently described as an **Act of Parliament**. All statutory laws must be obeyed by all those in the jurisdiction it covers. This is important as some of the laws apply to all countries within the UK and some will only apply to England and not the devolved nations. Unless otherwise stated, the legislation and policies discussed in this chapter relate to England. There also exists statutory guidance and this must be followed in the same way as statutory law. A policy, by contrast, is not legally binding and sets out what a government hopes to achieve and the methods and principles it will use to achieve them.

So why is legislation relevant and indeed essential to ECEC practitioners? Legislation provides the legal basis for their work with children and their families. The Children Act 1989 was an attempt to bring together the piecemeal legislation concerning safeguarding into one comprehensive law. The Act enshrined a number of principles, for example: the need for the welfare of the child to be of paramount concern; the requirement to work in partnership with families; the concept of **parental responsibility**; and the duty of the local authority (LA) to investigate child protection concerns. The Children Act has been updated, however the principles remain central to current law, policy and practice, and the 1989 Act remains law and needs to be followed in addition to newer legislation, for example the Children Act 2004. Subsequent laws have both clarified and placed additional responsibilities on the LA and other agencies, for example outlining their responsibility towards children with SEND.

A **section 47** investigation, so called because it originates in section 47 of the Children Act 1989, is the name of a specific investigation undertaken by the local authority when there are concerns that a child may be at risk of or is suffering significant harm. There is also a proactive element of the Children Act 1989 as it defines **children in need** (section 17) and confers on the LA the duty to identify and provide support to these children:

> A child in need is defined under the Children Act 1989 as a child who is unlikely to achieve or maintain a reasonable level of health or development, or whose health and development is likely to be significantly or further impaired, without the provision of services; or a child who is disabled. (DfE, 2018)

To aid the implementation of the Children Act 1989, the government publishes guidance on interagency co-operation. The current statutory guidance in England is *Working Together to Safeguard Children* (DfE, 2018) and all agencies and professionals must follow this and indeed have to evidence that they are compliant with it. A crucial aspect of an Ofsted inspection of a setting will focus on safeguarding; for example, checking whether settings are using up-to-date safeguarding policies and procedures, or verifying that staff have attended safeguarding training and completed disclosure and barring service (DBS) checks (Ofsted, 2016). In other jurisdictions of the UK, checks apply but are often known by different names and carried out by different bodies (e.g. Disclosure Scotland).

As well as statutory laws and guidance, the government frequently publishes polices. Changes in government tend to produce changes in policies; an example of this is *Every Child Matters* (ECM) which was introduced by the Labour government in 2003 for England and Wales, following the death of Victoria Climbié. ECM highlighted the importance of both early intervention and effective protection (HM Treasury, 2003). Although the policy was dropped in 2010 with the change in government, a number of practice settings do still use this. Despite the fact that ECM is no longer current government policy, it did influence other developments such as the Children Act 2004 (Davies and Ward, 2012). In Scotland, a similar approach is known as *Getting It Right For Every Child* (GIRFEC) and many of the aims were subsumed into the Children and Young People (Scotland) Act 2014, where the approach still applies.

Building on the requirements of the earlier Children Act 1989, Section 11 of the Children Act 2004 places a duty on a wide range of professionals and agencies to share information and work collaboratively where there are concerns a child may be at risk of or suffering significant harm. The 2004 Act specifically obligates not just those who customarily work with children, but also a wide range of diverse organisations – for example, the Police, the National Health Service (NHS), British Transport Police and Probation Services.

(Continued)

The Children Act 2004 introduced the requirement for all local authorities to establish local safeguarding children's boards (LSCB). The LSCB has a range of statutory functions, including developing local safeguarding policy and procedures and monitoring the effectiveness of local services. LAs have overarching responsibility for safeguarding and promoting the welfare of all children and young people in their area, and it is their statutory duty to promote co-operation between agencies in order to achieve this (DfE, 2018). It is also the responsibility of the LSCB to instigate a **serious case review (SCR)** when a child in their area dies or is seriously injured as a result of suspected abuse or neglect. The purpose of the SCR is to ascertain what led to the tragedy and to identify how professionals and organisations can improve the way they work together to safeguard children (DfE, 2018). SCRs frequently highlight the lack of effective information sharing between agencies, and it is clear that these findings and recommendations directly influenced the Children Act 2004.

It is clear that safeguarding is heavily influenced by political and economic considerations, and inevitably there are contradictions in policy. An example of this is the proposed cut in the Education Services Grant (ESG) – money given to English LAs from central government to meet their legal obligations to support vulnerable pupils in schools. This will mean that, despite legal requirements to provide services, LAs may not have adequate funding and schools may have to pay for these from their own budgets (Lepper, 2017).

Contradictions are also reflected in the changes in the NHS. Government statutory guidance clearly outlines the necessity of taking prompt action to enable all children to achieve the best outcomes, stating that 'Providing early help is more effective in promoting the welfare of children than reacting later' (DfE, 2015: 12). The recent move in responsibility for public health from the NHS to the LA has led to a juxtaposition where despite evidence that early intervention is cheaper and has better outcomes, the current policy is largely contrary to this; for example, the cuts in public sector funding, leading to a reduction in health visitors and the closure of Sure Start programmes and children's centres – all of whom are experts in early intervention.

WHEN IS IT APPROPRIATE TO INTERVENE TO PROTECT CHILDREN?

Although practitioners largely agree about what constitutes extreme abuse, there is a lack of consensus about what constitutes 'good enough' parenting. This inevitably leads to variations in practice for those children who need positive intervention to enable them to achieve their potential. These families are the focus of much discussion and guidance, especially around thresholds and the benefits of early intervention.

Early intervention quite simply refers to offering support to children and their families where there is concern that, in order to meet a child's needs, additional support should be provided. Studies highlighting the success of early intervention are plentiful (DCSF, 2010). Two reported benefits are related to cost and effectiveness. Offering support to families before difficulties become entrenched can make it easier for families to make and sustain the necessary changes.

The developing brain adapts to the environment it finds itself in, thus for children with unreliable caregivers this adaptation, whilst essential for the child's survival, is highly likely to cause significant difficulties in the medium and long term.

Parenting is arguably the most difficult job many people will undertake. Those experiencing difficulties with one child are likely to find these exacerbated with the arrival of further children, therefore making and sustaining positive change can become increasingly difficult. The first child often creates the optimal conditions to make any necessary changes, as the optimism and motivation for a parent to provide the care they can for their child are often at their height (Davies and Ward, 2012).

Early intervention has been cited as cost-effective, as change may be achieved with less intensive support from specialist services. Changing entrenched behaviour is likely to be more time-consuming and requiring of a more specialised response. Davies and Ward's (2012) research illustrates how quickly harm occurs in children, yet conversely how time-consuming and difficult it is to undo this damage. There is a plethora of early intervention strategies, for example the **early help approach**. Using the **Common Assessment Framework** (CAF) to focus on the child should enable ECEC practitioners to promote the early recognition of any difficulties. The CAF offers a holistic structure to assessment and a common language and approach across geographical areas and practitioners (DCSF, 2009). It covers three domains: the child's development needs, parental capacity to respond appropriately and the impact and influence of the family and the environment.

BARRIERS TO SAFEGUARDING

Evidence highlights that notwithstanding the raft of laws, policies and guidelines, too many children are left for too long experiencing abusive and neglectful parenting. There are a number of potential reasons for this.

RELUCTANCE OF PRACTITIONERS TO REFER CONCERNS

The contradictions enshrined in policy and societal norms and values can help answer the question as to why practitioners can be reluctant to effectively intervene. Although practitioners generally agree regarding the threshold for referral in relation to physical and sexual abuse, there is a lack of a shared agreement in relation to neglect and emotional abuse. The absence of a consensus regarding what constitutes 'good enough' care and conversely what is not good enough, is problematic when successfully identifying children at risk of significant harm (Horwath, 2013). This is especially problematic given the extensive research that highlights these categories of abuse as having the potential to cause the most damaging long-term consequences (Daniel et al., 2011). Not having an agreed standard can lead practitioners to become accepting of poor standards of care, judging what should be serious concerns as 'normal for here'. This level of acceptance was highlighted in the SCR of the five 'W' children, two of whom experienced life-threatening neglect.

 case study 13.1

The Five 'W' Children

The SCR noted that despite the children living in appalling squalid conditions, including being left in soiled and maggot-infested underwear and a 1-year-old twin being 'within hours of death', the children had not been referred to child protection professionals. The review was critical of the low expectations practitioners held of the parenting skills in the community where the family lived (Sheffield Area Child Protection Committee, 2005).

1. Would it be possible to have an agreed definition of 'good enough' parenting?
2. What could be the benefits and challenges of such a definition?

Practitioners are also influenced by wider societal beliefs regarding attitudes to intervention. By examining the numbers of children referred to social care services, 'spikes' can be identified following a high-profile death. For example, there was a rise of over 10% in referrals between 2008/9 and 2009/10 following the death of Peter Connelly and again after the deaths of Daniel Pelka and Hamzah Khan (NSPCC, 2015).

The behavioural consequences of neglect and abuse can take time to manifest and this can make it more difficult for ECEC practitioners to identify young children who are in need of additional support. Munro's comprehensive review of child protection highlighted the complexity for practitioners in recognising abuse and neglect 'because the signs and symptoms are often ambiguous and a benign explanation is possible' (DfE, 2011: 18). Conversely, having practitioners repeatedly refer their child protection concerns to social care services, only to have their concerns ignored, inevitably leads to future decisions not to refer children as they may feel 'what's the point?' (Brandon et al., 2009).

Even when practitioners have accurately identified that a child is at risk of harm, some are still reluctant to pass their concerns onto social care services. Child protection is a difficult and emotive subject. It challenges our core belief in the sanctity of the family and quite simply it is difficult to believe that some families will harm their children – intentionally or not. Also, given the potential far-reaching consequences of referring, practitioners can be reticent to do this due to a fear of 'getting it wrong' (Horwath, 2013).

FAILURE TO ADEQUATELY PROTECT CHILDREN

Once a child has been referred to social care services, the extent of the concerns should determine what, if any, action is taken. The complexity is in determining how serious the concerns are and what response is required. The responsibility of the referring agency does not end with the referral; rather, all agencies must continue to work together to protect the child. There is a range of actions available to social care services once a referral has been received; they must though follow the statutory laws and guidance outlined earlier in the chapter, for example undertaking a section 47 investigation or calling a child protection case conference (see Chapter 17 for further discussion).

Despite being referred to social care services, children are not always protected. Although discussions regarding child protection policy and practice tend to focus on the deaths of children, there is also evidence highlighting the damage sustained by children left for far too long in abusive and neglectful situations, despite being referred to social care services. This was clearly articulated in a longitudinal study by Ward, Brown and Westlake (2012), which analysed the responses to child protection concerns in ten different LAs. The study identified marked inconsistencies; for some of the children, the practitioners had failed to adequately protect them over a protracted period of time, again raising serious concerns regarding the accepted threshold for determining if the care was 'good enough'.

By looking back over this and the previous century, the pendulum of public opinion and consequently practice has swung between supporting intervention and non-intervention in families. The tragic deaths of children have arguably had the most significant impact on child protection policy and practice. The first high-profile death of a child was Dennis O'Neil in 1945. Dennis was murdered by his foster carers, leading to a public outcry. This, along with the publication of Bowlby's work regarding attachment, influenced the belief that children should remain with their birth family. It was almost 30 years later and the death of Maria Colwell in 1973 which again ignited public opinion, this time in the opposite direction: against the belief that children should necessarily remain with their birth family. Maria was murdered by her stepfather after being returned to her mother's care following five years of being fostered by her aunt and uncle (Reder et al., 1993).

The years following Maria's death have seen changes in child protection policy and practice. The death of Dennis and Maria, alongside the more recent tragic deaths of other children, for example Victoria Climbié, Peter Connelly, Daniel Pelka and Hamzah Khan, have greatly influenced the continuing shift between the belief in the need for children to remain with their birth families and the requirement for practitioners to protect children from harm. Each high-profile death has acted as a catalyst for change and the subsequent inquiries have led to changes in policy and practice (Davies and Ward, 2012).

Financial pressure on LAs has also led to a number of problems, including raising the threshold for access to services; closure of early intervention and community services; and rising demand due to the increase in poverty. Social service practitioners can develop a 'bunker mentality' whereby the experience of feeling overwhelmed and under-resourced causes the focus to be on 'gate keeping', pushing families away, rather than providing a service to those in need (Daniel et al., 2010). A report by the All-Party Parliamentary Group for Children (APPGC) (2017) highlighted the increasing move by LAs from early intervention services to focusing on children already at risk of significant harm. It highlighted the lack of consistency between the responses of LAs and the difficulties faced in meeting their duties following increasing financial constraints. The rising demand for children's services is in direct contrast with the reduction in funding available to LAs from central government. Figures show that:

- 4,740 more children went into care in 2015–16 than in 2010–11
- 6,470 more referrals to local authority children's services in 2015–16 than in 2010–11
- 12,000 more children were classified as 'in need' under section 17 of the Children's Act in 2015–16 than in 2010–11
- 14,310 more children became subject to a child protection plan in 2015–16 than in 2010–11. (APPGC, 2017: 10)

As already highlighted, safeguarding children is the responsibility of all agencies and professionals. Doing this successfully necessitates working together at both an organisational and individual level, commonly referred to as multi-agency working. This is crucially important, especially where there are child protection concerns. Despite this, numerous studies have highlighted how problematic this can be (Ferguson, 2011). The findings of SCRs repeatedly highlight these issues: the failure of services to work together effectively and share crucial information, alongside a lack of focus on the child and of questioning the information given (Cheminais, 2009).

SUMMARY

- Safeguarding is the term used to describe the proactive policies and practice undertaken to both protect and promote the welfare of all children. Child protection is an integral component of safeguarding, however it is reactive and focuses on responding to specific concerns regarding individual children.
- ECEC practitioners have a key role in relation to the safeguarding of young children, including working together to promote the wellbeing of all children and to ensure individual children are protected from harm. The impact of abuse and neglect on children can be catastrophic, potentially causing both immediate and long-term harm.
- Legislation is central to safeguarding children. There are a broad range of statutory laws and policies aimed at promoting the positive development and safety of all children and specifically for child protection. The local authority has a statutory responsibility to investigate the welfare of any child in their area if there are concerns that the child is at risk of or suffering significant harm.
- Financial pressures, inconsistency in when practitioners refer, lack of an agreed threshold of neglect and emotional abuse, and the failure of agencies and practitioners to work together effectively, have been cited as the most significant barriers to the protection of children.

online resources

Make sure to visit https://study.sagepub.com/fitzgeraldandmaconochie for selected SAGE videos (with questions), SAGE journal articles, links to external sources and flashcards.

FURTHER READING

Lindon, J. (2012). *Safeguarding and Child Protection 0–8 Years*. London: Hodder Education.

This book discusses safeguarding and child protection, detailing policy and practice issues; for example, identifying abuse and neglect, law and guidance in the UK and supporting children and their families.

NSPCC (2017). Child Protection in the UK. [online] Available at: www.nspcc.org.uk/preventing-abuse/child-protection-system [Accessed 9 July 2017].

This details how the systems and laws of the UK and its four nations work to keep children safe from abuse and harm. It contains research reports, relevant statistics and links to current legislation.

REFERENCES

All Party Parliamentary Group for Children (APPGC) (2017). No Good Options: Report of the Inquiry into Children's Social Care in England. [online] Available at: www.ncb.org.uk/sites/default/files/field/attachment/No%20Good%20Options.pdf [Accessed 23 February 2017].

Brandon, M., Bailey, S., Belderson, P., Gardner, R., Sidebotham, P., Dodsworth, J., et al. (2009). Understanding Serious Case Reviews and their Impact: A Biennial Analysis of Serious Case Reviews 2005–7. DCSF Research Report No. DCSF-RR129. [online] Available at: www.uea.ac.uk/documents/3437903/4264977/DCSF-RR129%28R%29.pdf/245d68a9-3fa2-442e-bc56-bd74d22ab23c [Accessed 26 February 2017].

Cheminais, R. (2009). *Effective Multi-Agency Partnerships: Putting Every Child Matters into Practice*. London: Sage.

Children Act (1989). London: HMSO. [online] Available at: www.legislation.gov.uk/ukpga/1989/41/contents [Accessed 26 February 2017].

Children Act (2004). London: HMSO. [online] Available at: www.legislation.gov.uk/ukpga/2004/31/contents [Accessed 26 August 2017].

Children and Young People (Scotland) Act (2014). [online] Available at: www.legislation.gov.uk/asp/2014/8/contents/enacted [Accessed 31 October 2017].

Cleak H., Roulston, A. and Vreugdenhil, A. (2016) The Inside Story: A Survey of Social Work Students' Supervision and Learning Opportunities on Placement. *British Journal of Social Work*, *46*(7): 2033–2050.

Daniel, B., Taylor, J. and Scott, J. (2010). Recognition of Neglect and Early Response: Overview of a Systemic Review of the Literature. *Child and Family Social Work*, *15*(2): 248–57.

Daniel, B., Taylor, J. and Scott, J. (2011). *Recognising and Helping the Neglected Child: Evidence-Based Practice for Assessment and Intervention*. London: Jessica Kingsley Publishers.

Davies, C. and Ward, H. (2012). *Safeguarding Children across Services: Messages from Research*. London: Jessica Kingsley.

Department for Children Schools and Families (DCSF) (2009). The Common Assessment Framework. Available at: http://webarchive.nationalarchives.gov.uk/20090809171023/http://www.dcsf.gov.uk/everychildmatters/strategy/deliveringservices1/caf/cafframework [Accessed 20 June 2017].

Department for Children, Schools and Families (DCSF) (2010). Early Intervention: Securing Good Outcomes for all Children and Young People. Available at: http://dera.ioe.ac.uk/11385/1/DCSF-00349-2010.pdf [Accessed 26 February 2017].

Department for Education (DfE) (2011). *The Munro Review of Child Protection: Final Report – A child-centred system.* London: The Stationery Office. [online] Available at: www.gov.uk/government/publications/munro-review-of-child-protection-final-report-a-child-centred-system [Accessed 20 March 2017].

Department for Education (DfE) (2014). Early Years: Guide to the 0 to 25 SEND Code of Practice – Advice for early years providers that are funded by the local authority. [online] Available at: www.gov.uk/government/uploads/system/uploads/attachment_data/file/350685/Early_Years_Guide_to_SEND_Code_of_Practice_-_02Sept14.pdf [Accessed 16 July 2017].

Department for Education (DfE) (2018). *Working Together to Safeguard Children: A Guide to Inter-agency Working to Safeguard and Promote the Welfare of Children.* London: Department for Education 2018. [online] Available at: https://assets.publishing.service.gov.uk/government/uploads/system/uploads/attachment_data/file/729914/Working_Together_to_Safeguard_Children-2018.pdf [Accessed 23 August 2018].

Department for Work and Pensions (DWP) (2017). Households below Average Income Statistics. Gov UK. [online] Available at: www.gov.uk/government/statistics/households-below-average-income-199495-to-201516 [Accessed 26 February 2017].

Department of Health (DoH) (2011). Start Active, Stay Active: A Report on Physical Activity for Health from the Four Home Countries' Chief Medical Officers. [online] Available at: www.gov.uk/government/uploads/system/uploads/attachment_data/file/216370/dh_128210.pdf [Accessed 16 July 2017].

Ferguson, H. (2011). *Child Protection Practice.* London: Palgrave Macmillan.

GOV.UK (undated). Bullying at School. [online] Available at: www.gov.uk/bullying-at-school/the-law [Accessed 26 July 2017].

HM Treasury (2003). Every Child Matters. Available at: http://webarchive.nationalarchives.gov.uk/20130401151715/http://www.education.gov.uk/publications/eOrderingDownload/DfES10812004.pdf [Accessed 20 March 2017].

Home Office (2016). *Revised Prevent Duty Guidance for England and Wales.* [online] Available at: www.gov.uk/government/uploads/system/uploads/attachment_data/file/445977/3799_Revised_Prevent_Duty_Guidance__England_Wales_V2-Interactive.pdf [Accessed 20 July 2017].

Horwath, J. (2013). *Child Neglect: Planning and Intervention.* London: Palgrave Macmillan.

Lepper, J. (2017). School funding changes 'put children at risk of harm'. In Children and Young People Now. [online] Available at: www.cypnow.co.uk/cyp/news/2003353/school-funding-changes-put-children-at-risk-of-harm [Accessed 26 February 2017].

Mahony, S. (2017). *Understanding Childhoods: Growing Up in Hard Times.* London: The Children's Society. [online] Available at: www.childrenssociety.org.uk/sites/default/files/understanding-childhoods-report-2017.pdf [Accessed 26 March 2017].

Main, G. and Bradshaw, J. (2016). Child Poverty in the UK: Measures, Prevalence and Intra-Household Sharing. *Critical Social Policy,* 36(1): 38–46.

NSPCC (2015). Children in Need: Statistics. [online] Available at: www.nspcc.org.uk/what-we-do/news-opinion/children-in-need-statistics [Accessed 12 February 2017].

Ofsted (2016). Inspecting Safeguarding in Early Years, Education and Skills Settings. London: Ofsted. [online] Available at: www.gov.uk/government/publications/inspecting-safeguarding-in-early-years-education-and-skills-from-september-2015/inspecting-safeguarding-in-early-years-education-and-skills-settings [Accessed 20 June 2017].

Reder, P., Duncan, S. and Gray, M. (1993). *Beyond Blame: Child Abuse Tragedies Revisited*. London: Routledge.

Sheffield Area Child Protection Committee (2005). Executive Summary of the Serious Case Review in Respect of the W Children. [online] Available at: www.cscb-new.co.uk/downloads/Serious%20 Case%20Reviews%20-%20exec.%20summaries/SCR_Archive/Sheffield%20Serious%20Case%20 Review%20-%20JWW%20&%20CLW,%20SW,%20NW%20ansd%20JDW%20(2005).pdf [Accessed 26 March 2017].

Taylor, M. (2015) What Undergraduate Early Childhood Education and Care Students Find 'Troublesome' During the Early Period of Practice Placements, *The all-Ireland journal of teaching and learning in Higher Education*, *7*(2): 18410–18415.

Ward, H., Brown, R. and Westlake, D. (2012). *Safeguarding Babies and Very Young Children from Abuse and Neglect*. London: Jessica Kingsley Publishers.

Wickham, S., Anwar, E., Barr, B., Law, C. and Taylor-Robinson, D. (2016). Poverty and Child Health in the UK: Using Evidence for Action. *Archives of Disease in Childhood*, *101*(8): 759–766. London: BMJ Publishing Group and Royal College of Paediatrics and Child Health. [online] Available at: http://adc.bmj.com/content/101/8/759.info [Accessed 20 March 2017].

.

YOUNG CHILDREN'S WELLBEING: CONCEPTUALISING, ASSESSING AND SUPPORTING WELLBEING

BY SIGRID BROGAARD-CLAUSEN, SOFIA GUIMARAES, MICHELLE COTTLE AND SALLY HOWE

I am studying 'Embodied Childhoods' as a module and had forgotten about the importance of wellbeing for children and young people until reading this chapter. I don't think there is always enough confidence placed in children to entrust them with their own wellbeing; perhaps because they do not necessarily know, or understand, what wellbeing is. However, the chapter emphasises how much children already know or have the capacity to learn, as well as the importance of supporting them to achieve their best.

I particularly liked the detail on the contributing factors that make up wellbeing, from all practices. Seeing how many different views are taken on one subject is vital, as the subjects are so intrinsically involved with each other.

TONI HOWLETT
MA CHILDHOOD STUDIES
UNIVERSITY OF SUFFOLK

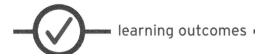

learning outcomes

By actively reading this chapter and engaging with the material, you will be able to:

- recognise that there are different factors that influence children's wellbeing
- describe different ways of supporting young children's wellbeing
- critically evaluate the complexity of children's wellbeing and the way it is assessed in early childhood
- identify barriers within early childhood education and care policy and practice that impact on children's wellbeing.

INTRODUCTION

The wellbeing of children, professionals and parents matters and relates to the individual person's life experiences, their communities and society as a whole. Wellbeing is a highly complex concept that can be understood in different ways, based on life experiences within families and communities, as well as theoretical and disciplinary viewpoints. This chapter begins with an exploration of multi-disciplinary approaches to understanding wellbeing. It then explores some of the most influential theories and concepts around wellbeing, which are largely located within positive psychology, before focusing on the importance of promoting and supporting young children's wellbeing in an early childhood education and care (ECEC) context. To exemplify some of the ways that wellbeing theories can be used to inform practice, the chapter will draw on findings from a case study focusing on teachers' assessment of young children's wellbeing and learning in transition to school in England. In so doing, the chapter explores the links between wellbeing and learning and the importance of providing environments that acknowledge and support young children's wellbeing. The chapter concludes with a discussion of the overall place of wellbeing in early years policy, research and practice.

THE COMPLEXITY IN DEFINING AND ASSESSING WELLBEING: MULTI-DISCIPLINARY APPROACHES

Wellbeing should be a central concern for those who work with young children. However, this is no simple matter as wellbeing cannot be reduced to an individual responsibility. It is complex and multi-faceted, often used interchangeably with other concepts such as happiness and life quality, and needs to be understood within the diverse context of children's experiences. Considering wellbeing theories and research from different disciplines can enable early years practitioners/professionals to recognise that different factors can promote or challenge the wellbeing of children and families. This knowledge and understanding can enable practitioners to act more reflectively and provide stronger arguments for the promotion of young children's wellbeing. A distinct attribute of the wellbeing research put forward in this chapter is that it embraces and bridges several disciplines and fields: psychology, philosophy, sociology, economics, education, health and pedagogy.

Sociology, philosophy and psychology, in particular, are often considered foundation disciplines in relation to education and early childhood research, although there are different branches within each (see Ingleby, 2013 for further discussion of disciplines). Sociology is the study of human behaviour, focusing on social structures, phenomena and interactions on a large or small scale. Wellbeing research, in the context of sociological traditions, predominantly considers contextual factors such as material status, housing and environment (see Chapter 11 for further discussion). These contextual features link to economic wellbeing on a national and global scale, which then has specific impacts on the context of education and pedagogy (for further reading on positioning wellbeing as a goal for public policy, see Layard, 2011).

The United Nations (UN) World Happiness Report (Helliwell et al., 2017) provides an example of using multi-dimensional measures such as a nation's **gross domestic product (GDP)** per capita, social support, healthy life expectancy, social freedom, generosity and absence of corruption. Sociological approaches can also include conceptions of social wellbeing which are linked to philosophical and psychological approaches. Philosophy is particularly concerned with meaning making and values, which are crucial to the way that wellbeing is conceptualised (White, 2007). Philosophical understandings of wellbeing are also an important part of psychological thinking about wellbeing as both focus on mind and behaviour. Recent wellbeing research extends this multi-disciplinary focus, combining measures relating to sociology and positive psychology, as can be observed in the United Nations International Children's Emergency Fund (Unicef) Index of Children's Wellbeing, where measures include scores on six domains: material wellbeing, educational wellbeing, health and safety, family and peer relationships, behaviour and risk, and subjective wellbeing (Unicef Office of Research, 2016).

The above discussion highlights the variety of factors that contribute to wellbeing and to understandings of wellbeing, and it is important for early childhood students and professionals to recognise these features. However, ECEC professionals may expect to have less influence over some of these domains, such as the material and societal parameters in particular. Therefore, from this point, the chapter focuses on psychological features and the more philosophical values-based principles of wellbeing that relate to children's rights and agency in order to support young children's wellbeing in practice. Specifically, the field of positive psychology is considered in more depth below because research evidence from this particular branch of psychology has considerably raised the profile of wellbeing internationally.

WELLBEING AND THE TRADITIONS OF POSITIVE PSYCHOLOGY

Traditionally, psychology has been dominated by a deficit approach, where the role of psychology has been to address the problems that arise in people's lives (Seligman, 2011). Positive psychology introduced a different approach by focusing on the importance of wellbeing, health and people's quality of life, collating evidence and developing frameworks for promoting wellbeing (see Csikszentmihalyi, 1992; Diener et al., 2010; Seligman, 2011). There is a considerable body of research in this area, which draws on philosophical discussions of subjective wellbeing and two general approaches or foci: the **hedonic** focus (the presence of positive feelings and the absence of negative ones) and the **eudaimonic** focus (the meaning and purpose of life) (Ryan and Deci, 2001). Recent developments in positive psychology have incorporated both the hedonic and eudaimonic approaches, and, in so doing, this research highlights the importance of social aspects such as relationships, trust and belonging (Diener et al., 2010; Seligman, 2011; McLellan and Steward, 2015).

Different theorists have developed different dimensions of psychological wellbeing, at times building on each other's work, which contribute to perceptions of the importance and complexity of this construct. Table 14.1 has been developed to present an overview of a number of predominant theories of wellbeing, with specific attention paid to the discipline of positive psychology. However, it is important to note that the concepts presented have been simplified and this table should be considered as a starting point for further reading.

Table 14.1   An overview of a number of predominant theories of wellbeing

Researchers	Attached Concepts	Components
Diener (2000; et al., 2010)	Subjective wellbeing	People's longer-term levels of pleasant affect: experience of positive, good, pleasant, happy, joyful, contented feelings.
		Lack of unpleasant affect: such as negative, bad and unpleasant feelings, being sad, afraid and/or angry.
		Life satisfaction: life close to ideal, life conditions excellent, satisfaction, obtained important things, not wanting to change.
Seligman (2011)	Subjective wellbeing/	Positive emotion: what we feel - pleasure, rapture, ecstasy, warmth, comfort, and the like.
	Flourishing	Engagement is about flow: the loss of self-consciousness/ awareness during an absorbing activity.
		Relationship: connections, love, intimacy and strong emotional and physical interactions with others.
		Meaning and purpose of life: belonging to and serving something that a person believes is bigger than self.
		Accomplishment: setting and putting effort into achieving realistic goals, achievement fulfils and satisfies.
Csikszentmihalyi (1992, 2002)	Flow	Flow is when a person is engaged and experiences: • an immediate response and gratification in the activity • an activity that is intrinsically motivated but without the search for a specific outcome • the right degree of challenge • concentration and exclusion of internal and external 'noise'.

(Continued)

Researchers	Attached Concepts	Components
Laevers (1993, 2000, 2011)	Involvement and wellbeing	Emotional heath: confidence, resilience and spontaneity, need for tenderness, affection, safety and clarity, social recognition, feeling competent, need for meaning and moral values in life, keep in touch with feelings.
		Motivation: intensity of mental activity and satisfaction.
		Curiosity and the explorative drive: openness for and alertness to a variety of stimuli→arousal→ most intense form of concentration and involvement intrinsic source of motivation/ flow (engrossed and persevere).
		Expression and communicative skills: Symbols and words are uesd to make and connect meaning, to better define and articulate 'felt senses' (imagination is the disposition to do this).
		Imagination and creativity: produce unique ideas.
Ryan & Deci (2000, 2001)	Self-determination theory and wellbeing	Competence, cognitive aspects: curiosity, interest and coherence in knowledge.
		Relatedness, social aspects; relationships with significant others.
		Autonomy, emotional/motivational aspects; self-regulation.
		Intrinsic motivation: energy, direction and persistence.
Ryff (2014)	Psychological wellbeing	Autonomy: seeking a sense of self-determination, regulating behaviour from within.
		Environmental mastery: managing the environment and its complexity, making effective use of surrounding opportunities.
		Personal growth: open to new experiences, a continual process of developing one's potential.
		Positive relations with others: developing trusting relationships with others; empathy and affection.
		Purpose in life: finding meaning in one's efforts and challenges; a sense of directness.
		Self-acceptance (positive self-regard): positive attitude toward the self while aware of own limitations.

 action point 14.1

With this indicative overview of wellbeing in mind, find examples of key similarities and differences in the different approaches to wellbeing.

IDENTIFYING FEATURES OF WELLBEING IN EARLY CHILDHOOD PRACTICE AND RESEARCH

The above theories present significant concepts to aid understandings of wellbeing in the field of early childhood. However, differences in the conceptualisation of psychological and/or subjective wellbeing have also led to the development of different measurement tools (McLellan and Steward, 2015). The model developed by Mayr and Ulich (1999, 2009) is an important example to discuss in more detail. They initially included 11 dimensions of wellbeing specific to the context of early childhood: (1) empathic, prosocial behaviour, (2) social initiative and vitality, (3) self-assertiveness, openness, (4) pleasure in exploring, (5) the ability to cope with stress, (6) positive self-defence, (7) pleasure in sensory experiences, (8) persistence/robustness, (9) a sense of humour, (10) a positive attitude towards warmth and closeness, (11) the ability to rest and relax. In an attempt to develop an empirical-based instrument for practitioners, Mayr and Ulich (2009) have re-conceptualised these 11 dimensions into six dimensions of social-emotional wellbeing (PERIK, translated into English as 'Positive development and resilience in kindergarten'). This raises important issues about the complexity of not only conceptualising wellbeing, but also how it can be measured.

The development of valid ways to capture and measure young children's experience of wellbeing have received significantly less attention than the development of tools for older populations (Mayr and Ulich, 1999; Unicef, 2016). The lack of attention paid to young children's perspectives has been justified by challenges in developing valid measures for young children (Ben-Arieh, 2005), but also by the misconception that young children's responses may not be reliable and are therefore less 'credible'. This belief has often led to a reliance on using parents/carers and practitioners to report on children's experiences of wellbeing, including tools that focus on observable behaviours with varying degrees of structure (Mayr and Ulich, 2009; Mashford-Scott et al., 2012; Marbina et al., 2015).

Self-report measures of subjective wellbeing have mainly been developed for children from the age of 8 years (see previous references to Unicef, 2016). One example is the Stirling Children's Wellbeing Scales that were developed for children aged 8 to 15 (Liddle and Carter, 2015). Other examples include scales developed to consider wellbeing specifically in the school context: 'How I feel about myself and school?' (McLellan and Steward, 2015). Self-report measures have, however, only sporadically been extended to younger children. One such example is the Personal Wellbeing Index: Preschool aged children (PWI:PS) developed by Cummins and Lau (2005) in Australia and now translated into different languages. This instrument is an 11-point scale where respondents 'who cannot use the 11-point scale … [use] … a simplified format … consisting of outline faces, from very sad to happy' (Cummins and Lau, 2005: 6). It was adapted from an instrument developed for people with learning difficulties, which may be problematic when considering children as a distinct sector of society (McLellan and Steward, 2015).

Developing valid measures that try to capture how young children experience their life from their perspective should therefore be a priority in early childhood practice, research and policy development (Guimaraes et al., 2016; Unicef, 2016). It requires practitioners, researchers and policy makers to first recognise young children's agency and their ability to express their experiences about their wellbeing in multiple ways. Alongside the focus on individual factors, there is a need to recognise the impact of environments on children's individual and collective wellbeing. The Leuven Involvement Scale for Young Children (Laevers, 2011) has been developed specifically for assessing and developing environments that support young children's wellbeing.

spotlight on research 14.1

The Leuven Involvement Scale for Young Children

The Leuven Involvement Scale for Young Children (Laevers, 2011) is a widely used observation-based tool to assess environments in order to support wellbeing and learning. This scale requires a close consideration of important indicators of children's wellbeing and involvement in the context of an early childhood setting. For Laevers (1993), *involvement* is a necessary condition for development. It is when we are involved and absorbed in what we are doing that we experience the deepest form of learning, allowing us to experience *flow* – a key component of wellbeing as identified by Csikszentmihalyi (1992, 2002; see Table 14.1). Laevers (2000) argues that adults should focus on helping children to feel confident and at ease, and provide continuous opportunities for spontaneity. Accordingly, adults should create environments that respond to children's need for tenderness and affection, relaxation, inner peace, enjoyment, openness, safety, clarity and social recognition. This requires professionals and parents to be in tune with children's feelings and emotions in order to recognise their agency. Some of the characteristics of deep-level learning are more directly observable, such as concentration and persistence, whilst the affective and emotional aspects are more fluid (Laevers, 1993). However, Laevers also highlights the challenges of maintaining focus on children's intrinsic motivation, exploration and curiosity in ECEC:

> An exploratory attitude, defined by openness for, and alertness to, the wide variety of stimuli that form our surroundings, makes a person accessible, lowers the threshold for getting into the state of 'arousal' that brings a person into the most intense forms of concentration and involvement. That person will never stop developing. The challenge for education is not only to keep this intrinsic source of motivation alive, but also to make it encompass all domains that belong to reality. (Laevers, 2000: 21)

Case study 14.1 reports on teachers' assessment of children's wellbeing using the Leuven scales as part of an on-entry-to-school assessment. It focuses on teachers' assessment and perspective of children's wellbeing in the context of their transition to school. From the perspective of positive psychology, Ryff (2014) has made a particular association between wellbeing and the impact of transitions on people's lives. Brooker (2008) further emphasises the impact that early educational transitions can have on wellbeing. The process of transition is demanding and involves negotiating relationships, understanding expectations, and roles in a new and challenging environment. A positive transition, where children are supported in developing relationships and managing their learning, tends to promote positive wellbeing, whereas too great a challenge can impact negatively on wellbeing (Brooker, 2008). For young children, one of the most significant transitions is when they begin school.

 case study 14.1

The Assessment of Young Children's Wellbeing on Transition to School

The research involved interviews with 12 teachers and 5 head teachers who discussed their experiences of piloting an assessment of 4- to 5-year-olds, upon entry to school in England (Guimaraes et al., 2016; Howe et al., in press). This was an observation-led baseline assessment scheme: the Early Excellence Baseline Assessment for Reception (EExBA-R; Early Excellence, 2015). The EExBA-R included two separate parts. The first was a screening of 4–5-year-old children's levels of wellbeing and involvement using the Leuven scales in order 'to ensure that children are assessed at the optimum time within these 6 weeks'. The second part assessed attainment according to the English government criteria for language, literacy and numeracy outcomes in the early years curriculum (The Early Years Foundation Stage (EYFS); DfE, 2014), as well as the **characteristics of effective learning** (**CEL)** also found in the EYFS.

Findings

The analysis of the interview data suggests that a focus on wellbeing was central to supporting children in transition. One teacher, for example, told the research team: 'I think the children's wellbeing is so important that we needed to make sure that they were happy and settled before we did any sort of lessons'. For many of the teachers involved in the research, the use of the Leuven scales and CEL to evaluate observations of children, gave them permission to focus on the importance of helping children to be happy and settled, rather than being overly focused on the curriculum at the beginning of the school year: 'I think it's definitely helped the focus, [previously] you focused too much on the curriculum, [...]. It's clearly practice you want to do, it brings the CEL and the wellbeing to the forefront, it's great practice' (Head teacher 1). The time spent on observations of children in self-initiated activities in the first few weeks of term allowed the teachers to get to know all of the children really well. One teacher commented on how the process led them to spend equal amounts of time with each child and so the quiet children became more visible due to the process.

Furthermore, evaluating observations of children engaged in self-initiated activities provided practitioners with evidence to suggest that the children's levels of wellbeing and involvement were dependent on the activity they were undertaking. These observations provided important opportunities for closer collaboration with colleagues within the school and the child's previous setting. The strengthened attention to involvement and wellbeing also offered constructive starting points for supportive dialogue with parents about their children's learning and that they had 'a shared vocabulary', focusing on the child's involvement in activities. The focus on wellbeing prompted teachers to articulate an understanding of the demands placed on the children in the transition to school and even changing their prac-tice: 'In the past I probably would have done the children that were with low wellbeing first, because I would have thought that would have been a good idea for them to come and sit with me. On reflection that's probably not the best thing to do, to pummel them with work before they've even settled into a place.' Moreover, engaging with the Leuven scales with children at the beginning of school was experienced as so valuable that it prompted one head teacher to introduce it throughout the whole school.

In the case study, children's wellbeing was taken into account when enabling children to explore what they were curious about, have space and time to become involved in activities, to be creative and spontaneous. The focus on wellbeing enabled children to settle into the environment and to develop relationships with peers and with their teachers. Such practice requires continued reflection by professionals evaluating their role in ensuring children are supported in their wellbeing, both in transitions to and throughout ECEC and school.

YOUNG CHILDREN'S VOICE AND WELLBEING

As discussed, a clear gap remains in the knowledge of younger children's wellbeing. The lack of representation of young children's voice is recognised nationally and internationally. The Unicef Office of Research (2016: 41) draws attention to the voice of the children, arguing that 'Children need to be able to shape the questions asked in surveys of their own lives and well-being'. Similarly, the Good Childhood Report (The Children's Society, 2005–16), representing the voice of 60,000 children aged 8–15, recommended that: 'Much more needs to be done to intervene early to improve children's subjective well-being' (The Children's Society, 2016: 15).

However, international research into young children's perspectives on their lives is growing. Different methods are being considered to gather younger children's perspectives, including visual methods such as drawings, photographs and mapping. These methods offer researchers and ECEC professionals valid ways of gaining children's experiences of their environment and wellbeing (Kousholdt, 2006; Clark and Moss, 2011; Estola et al., 2014; Krag-Muller and Isbell, 2017; Koch, 2018). Using children's photographs as starting points for individual and group conversations, Koch (2018) gathered 5-year-olds' subjective perspectives on wellbeing, drawing on Diener's work (described in Table 14.1). She identifies how children link their experience of wellbeing to involvement and the opportunity to feel in control of their actions. In this research study, children also acknowledge the need for social relations with both peers and adults (Koch, 2018), thereby emphasising the challenge of balancing social recognition, rules and environmental mastery – key concepts in wellbeing theories. Similarly, Nightingale (2015) worked with 40 children between the ages of 3 and 8 years, using visual and verbal means to elicit their interpretation and understanding of wellbeing. The findings from this study exem-plify young children's ability to conceptualise, categorise and report on their wellbeing, and highlight the importance of multiple relationships, sense of self and the outdoors to young children.

YOUNG CHILDREN'S WELLBEING WITHIN A POLICY CONTEXT

This chapter aims to draw attention to the crucial role of the adult in supporting young children's wellbeing. However, it is important to recognise how the ECEC policy context can create challenges in prioritising young children's wellbeing. In the context of our case study, assessment policy placed teachers in a conflict between focusing on children's wellbeing and the need to teach and assess academic skills. The impact of increasing assessment requirements on ECEC and the expectations in relation to 'school readiness' are causing pressure on young children, parents and professionals (see further discussion of this in Brogaard-Clausen et al., 2015; Guimaraes et al., 2016; Howe et al., in press). ECEC professionals need to be able to use evidence from research to counteract policy priorities that create diversions from focusing on young children's voice and wellbeing.

 reflection point 14.1

- What are the challenges and dilemmas early childhood practitioners may face in supporting young children's wellbeing and learning?

To support your reflection, you might also wish to draw on Brogaard-Clausen et al. (2015), Guimaraes et al. (2016) and Howe et al. (in press).

SUMMARY

- When supporting young children's wellbeing and learning, environmental, social and personal factors need to be considered. Sociology offers a consideration of multiple contextual factors that contribute to or hinder young children's wellbeing. Combined with psychological, health and philosophical research, these considerations need to be applied when supporting young children's wellbeing holistically.
- Supporting young children's wellbeing includes creating spaces for listening to children's views and feelings about their social and emotional wellbeing. Relationships to other children and adults are key for young children's wellbeing and it is important to observe how children engage in their environment and experience meaning, deep-level learning and flow. The case study presented in this chapter highlights the importance teachers placed on wellbeing, not just in the transition to school and in the context of assessment, but as a contributing factor for young children to thrive, flourish and learn.
- The Children's Society (2016) and Unicef (2016) advocate for children's voice and perspective to be included when assessing their wellbeing. Perspectives from the teachers in the

case study exemplified how collaboration with and between ECEC settings and parental engagement is an integral part of that process. However, it is important to acknowledge the balance between the individual child's wellbeing and the whole group of children's experience of wellbeing in ECEC settings.

- Despite increased attention being paid to young children's wellbeing, the requirement to track young children's attainments against externally set outcomes leads to pressure on teachers and consequently on young children and their families. In order to prevent barriers to children's wellbeing, development and learning, these interrelated areas should be considered holistically and contextually.

 online resources

Make sure to visit https://study.sagepub.com/fitzgeraldandmaconochie for selected SAGE videos (with questions), SAGE journal articles, links to external sources and flashcards.

FURTHER READING

Guimaraes, S., Howe, S., Brogaard Clausen, S. and Cottle, M. (2016). Assessment of What/For What? Teachers' and Head Teachers' Views on Using Wellbeing as a Screening for Conducting Baseline Assessment on School Entry in English Primary Schools. *Contemporary Issues in Early Childhood*, 17(2): 248–54.

This article offers further discussion to consider the opportunities and barriers in supporting young children's wellbeing in transition to school. Recommendations are made and current ECEC assessment policy contexts critically considered.

Howe, S., Guimaraes, S., Brogaard Clausen, S. and Cottle, M. (in press). Baseline Assessment: A Brief Re-introduction/Encounter in 2015/2016. In: M. Urban (ed.), *Assessment in Early Childhood: A Critical Examination of Approaches to Assessment of Young Children in International Contexts. Report to Educational International.*

This chapter provides a broader discussion of the baseline assessment study (case study). The full report examines approaches to the assessment of young children in international contexts.

Marbina, L., Mashford-Scott, A., Church, A. and Tayler, C. (2015). *Assessment of Wellbeing in Early Childhood Education and Care: Literature Review, Victorian Early Years Learning and Development Framework.* Melbourne: Victorian Curriculum and Assessment Authority.

This review presents an overview of existing assessments of young children's wellbeing, whilst providing recommendations for further development of assessment tools and processes.

REFERENCES

Ben-Arieh, A. (2005). Where are the Children? Children's Role in Measuring and Monitoring their Well-being. *Social Indicators Research, 74*: 573–96.

Brogaard Clausen, S., Guimaraes, S., Howe, S. and Cottle, M. (2015). Assessment of Young Children on Entry to School: Informative, Formative or Performative? *International Journal for Cross-Disciplinary Subjects in Education, 6*(1): 2120–5.

Brooker, L. (2008). *Supporting Transitions in the Early Years*. Maidenhead: Open University Press.

Children's Society, The (2016). *The Good Childhood Report 2016*. London: The Children's Society.

Clark, A. and Moss, P. (2011). *Listening to Young Children: The Mosaic Approach*, 2nd edn. London: National Children's Bureau.

Csikszentmihalyi, M. (1992). *Flow: The Psychology of Happiness*. New York: Rider & Co.

Csikszentmihalyi, M. (2002). *Flow: The Psychology of Happiness – The classic work on how to achieve happiness*. London: Rider.

Cummins, B. and Lau, A. (2005). Personal Wellbeing Index: Preschool Aged Children (Manual). [online] Available at: www.acqol.com.au/iwbg/wellbeing-index/pwi-ps-english.pdf [Accessed 2 July 2018].

Department for Education (DfE) (2014). *Statutory Framework for the Early Years Foundation Stage*. London: DfE Publications.

Diener, E. (2000). Subjective Well-being: The Science of Happiness and a Proposal for a National Index. *American Psychologist, 55*: s.34–43.

Diener, E., Wirtz, D., Tov, W., Kim-Prieto, C., Choi, D., Oishi, S. and Biswas-Diener, R. (2010). New Measures of Well-being: Flourishing and Positive and Negative Feelings. *Social Indicators Research, 39*: 247–66.

Early Excellence (2015). Reflect Good Baseline Assessment Practice: Choose EExBA. Huddersfield: Early Excellence. [online] Available at: http://earlyexcellence.com/wp-content/uploads/2015/05/reflect-good-baseline-assessment-practice-choose-eexba.pdf [Accessed 25 November 2015].

Estola, E., Farquhar, S. and Puroila, A. (2014). Well-being Narratives and Young Children. *Educational Philosophy and Theory, 46*: 929–41.

Guimaraes, S., Howe, S., Brogaard Clausen, S. and Cottle, M. (2016). Assessment of What/For What? Teachers' and Head Teachers' Views on Using Wellbeing as a Screening for Conducting Baseline Assessment on School Entry in English Primary Schools. *Contemporary Issues in Early Childhood, 17*(2): 248–54.

Helliwell, J., Layard, R., Sachs, J., De Neve, J., Huang, H. and Wang, S. (eds) (2017). World Happiness Report 2017, United Nations. [online] Available at: https://s3.amazonaws.com/sdsn-whr2017/HR17_3-20-17.pdf [Accessed 2 July 2018].

Howe, S., Guimaraes, S., Brogaard Clausen, S. and Cottle, M. (in press). *Baseline Assessment: A Brief Re-introduction/Encounter in 2015/2016*. In: M. Urban (ed.), *Assessment in Early Childhood: A Critical Examination of Approaches to Assessment of Young Children in International Contexts. Report to Educational International*.

Ingleby, E. (2013). *Early Childhood Studies: A Social Science Perspective*. London: A&C Black.

Koch, A.B. (2018). Children's Perspectives on Happiness and Subjective Wellbeing in Preschool. *Children and Society, 32*(1): 73–83.

Kousholdt, D. (2006). *Familieliv fra et boerneperspektiv* (Family Life from the Perspectives of the Children). Thesis, Roskilde University Center.

Krag-Muller, G. and Isbell, R. (2017). *Children's Perspectives on their Everyday Lives in Child Care in Two Cultures: Denmark and United States*. In: G. Krag-Muller and C. Ringmose (eds), *Nordic Social Pedagogical Approach to Early Years*. Dordrecht: Springer.

Laevers, F. (1993). Deep Level Learning: An Exemplary Application on the Area of Physical Knowledge. *European Early Childhood Educational Research Journal*, 1(1): 53–68.

Laevers, F. (2000). Forward to Basics! Deep-level Learning and the Experiential Approach. *Early Years: An International Journal of Research and Development*, 20: 20–9.

Laevers, F. (2011). Experiential Education: Making Care and Education more Effective through Well-being and Involvement. [online] Available at: www.child-encyclopedia.com/Pages/PDF/LaeversANGxp1.pdf [Accessed 17 December 2015].

Layard, R. (2011). *Happiness: Lessons from a New Science*, 2nd edn. London: Penguin Books.

Liddle, I. and Carter, G. (2015). Emotional and Psychological Well-being in Children: The Development and Validation of the Sterling Children's Well-being Scale. *Educational Psychology in Practice*, 31: 174–85.

McLellan, R. and Steward, S. (2015). Measuring Children and Young People's Wellbeing in the School Context. *Cambridge Journal of Education*, 45(3): 307–32.

Mashford-Scott, A., Church, A. and Tayler, C. (2012). Seeking Children's Perspectives on their Wellbeing in Early Childhood Settings. *International Journal of Early Childhood* 44(3): 231–247.

Marbina, L., Mashford-Scott, A., Church, A. and Tayler, C. (2015). *Assessment of Wellbeing in Early Childhood Educationand Care: Literature Review, Victorian Early Years Learning and Development Framework*. Melbourne, Victorian Curriculum and Assessment Authority.

Mayr, T. and Ulich, M. (1999). Children's Well-being in Day Care Centres: An Exploratory Study. *International Journal of Early Years Education* 7(3): 229–239.

Mayr, T. and Ulich, M. (2009) Social-Emotional Well-being and Resilience of Children in Early Childhood Settings. *Early Years*, 29(1): 45–57.

Nightingale, B. (2015). An Exploration of Young Children's Interpretation and Understanding of Well-being. Unpublished thesis, University of Essex, December.

Ryan, R. M. and Deci, E. L. (2000). Self-determination Theory and the Facilitation of Intrinsic Motivation, Social Development, and Well-being. *American Psychologist*, 55: 68–78.

Ryan, R. M. and Deci, E. L. (2001). On Happiness and Human Potentials: A Review of Research on Hedonic and Eudaimonic Well-being. *Annual Review of Psychology*, 52(1): 141–66.

Ryff, C. D. (2014). Psychological Well-being Revisited: Advances in the Science and Practice of Eudaimonia. *Psychotherapy and Psychosomatics*, 83(1): 10–28.

Seligman, M. E. P. (2011). *Flourish: A New Understanding of Happiness and Well-being – and how to achieve them*. London: Nicholas Brealey Publishing.

Unicef Office of Research (2016). *Fairness for Children: A League Table of Inequality in Child Well-being in Rich Countries*. Innocenti Report Card 13. Florence: Unicef Office of Research – Innocenti.

White, J. (2007). Wellbeing and Education: Issues of Culture and Authority. *Journal of Philosophy of Education*, 41(1): 17–28.

CHILDREN, FAMILIES AND ENGLISH AS AN ADDITIONAL LANGUAGE

BY ESTER EHIYAZARYAN-WHITE

This chapter gives an insightful account of working with children who are learning English as an additional language (EAL). Language acquisition is a vital step of early childhood development. As a student and practitioner, being able to draw on a quality resource such as this is so valuable.

The case study and action points provide useful suggestions for working with children and highlight the child's perspective when learning in an unaccustomed setting. When working with children with EAL I will use this chapter to support my plan, working in collaboration with the child's family and engaging with them in their own language as much as possible. This will help strengthen relationships and draw on their knowledge of resources that are enjoyed by the child at home.

This makes for a resource that I will turn to time and time again as the information is well written and easily absorbed.

LAURA ANNE WIGHTWICK
BA (HONS) EARLY CHILDHOOD STUDIES
UNIVERSITY OF EAST LONDON

 learning outcomes

By actively reading this chapter and engaging with the material, you will be able to:

- recognise that approaches to EAL pedagogy need to take into account the child's complex linguistic and personal identities
- evaluate the stages of early EAL language learning, relating these to learning theory
- apply participatory strategies for supporting EAL learners
- identify ways of assessing early childhood EAL learners in their home language as well as in English
- appraise different approaches to supporting EAL children's learning in family and community contexts.

INTRODUCTION

English as an Additional Language (EAL) is a term which refers to approaches to teaching and learning which aim to meet the needs of children whose first language is not English (British Council, 2016). These approaches involve the practitioner in both understanding children's linguistic experience and background, and developing strategies which make language learning accessible to them. Often, EAL pedagogy is based on classroom practice and experiences, however more attention has been given in recent years to EAL language acquisition in the early childhood context (Mistry and Sood, 2015). A key principle of EAL is to build on the language acquisition skills which the child may have already developed while learning the **home language**. Taking this approach also means that the child continues to develop as a confident bilingual learner.

This chapter outlines the processes children go through in acquiring a new language and adapting to a new culture in an early childhood context. References are made to both linguistic and cognitive learning theory in order to provide an insight into children's experiences of learning EAL, as well as to identify approaches to good practice for ECEC practitioners. The chapter primarily discusses EAL practices and principles in a UK context.

The need to see children as active in these processes and as experts in their own heritage and culture is emphasised. The role of participatory approaches in empowering children is explored. The more formal aspects of assessing preschool EAL children are also discussed with relation to the Early Years Foundation Stage (EYFS) early learning goals.

In all of these areas, a common theme is the role of parents as the child's first language educators and therefore the need for practitioners to actively engage with parents in order to understand the child's circumstances, and to be able to assess their ability fairly.

EAL CHILDREN'S LINGUISTIC IDENTITIES

There are increasing numbers of children entering early childhood settings and primary schools in the UK for whom English is not the dominant language. Recent statistics show that the share of primary school-aged children with EAL has steadily risen – from 7.8% of children in primary schools in 1997, to 18.7% in 2014 (Statista, 2016). These statistics show that there is a substantial need for teachers and early childhood practitioners to plan curricula that address children's diverse learning needs. When working with EAL children in early childhood, the key factors which need to be considered include the child's linguistic background and history of language learning, as well as the child's journey to the UK. New arrivals are those children whose parents have migrated to the country due to economic circumstances, or as **refugee** or **asylum seekers**. New arrivals are a diverse category, which could include children who have been bilingual from birth, those who are advanced in learning English, as well as those who do not speak any English (British Council, 2016). They can also vary according to their socio-economic status and their previous experiences with education. For refugee or asylum seeker children, learning may have been disrupted as they may have had to move from their home country for reasons such as civil war. These children may have had traumatic experiences and disruption in their daily routine for some time. Many will have also spent a period of time in refugee camps, where they are offered shelter and food as well as basic education. However, despite this provision, their early education will have likely been disrupted and so will their lives. As an ECEC practitioner, when welcoming these children into a setting it is important to be aware of the loss these children may have experienced (of loved ones, of a home) and to endeavour to provide a stable and welcoming environment. Working closely with parents to understand the child's needs is essential.

Thus, the task of the early childhood practitioner in accommodating the diverse needs of EAL children is complex. It is worth noting however that beyond the challenges discussed, EAL learners have some significant advantages over their monolingual peers.

CHALLENGES AND ADVANTAGES OF GROWING UP WITH EAL

One key characteristic of EAL is that children are likely to be drawing on two or more **heritage cultures** – the dominant British cultural context which they are growing up in and that of their family, including the mother tongue. While some of the policy documents and curriculum guidance around EAL emphasise the acquisition of English as a priority (Rochford, 2016), others consider the significant value of the child's home language and culture (DCSF, 2007). Numerous studies have demonstrated the advantages of children growing up bilingual (Bialystok et al., 2003; Gonzalez et al., 2005; Kenner and Ruby, 2012). Bilingual children have better cognitive and **metalinguistic abilities** – they can process language tasks faster and more successfully than their monolingual peers (Boyd and Bee, 2014).

In the longer term, there are advantages of multilingualism such as broader career opportunities in the global knowledge economy. Furthermore, speaking two or more languages has been shown to improve cognition and reduce the likelihood of developing Alzheimer's (O'Sullivan, 2015). On the other hand, some studies indicate that if the child is less fluent in the language in which they are taught at school or in an early childhood setting, they may fall behind academically, for a period of time (Boyd and Bee, 2014). This is a daunting prospect for many parents and may be the reason some families choose not to introduce the home language to their children.

Thus, the ECEC practitioner's role is to be supportive of the needs of families with a diverse language heritage. For some families, it is essential that their child learns the home language and mothers may be speaking the mother tongue to their children exclusively at home. Other families however may choose to introduce English to their child from birth. Being mindful and respectful of the parents' approach, whilst also working towards developing the child's English language and communication skills, is key. Essentially, the aim is to develop all children as confident communicators who are also empowered to draw on their heritage culture, as part of forming a positive sense of self.

LANGUAGE LEARNING AND CULTURAL LEARNING GO HAND IN HAND IN THE ECEC SETTING

ECEC settings are spaces for children to explore, play and interact alongside and with peers of different backgrounds. Within these spaces, children learn to adapt to routines and cultural norms which may be different from those in their home learning environment. Clarke (2015) identifies that when entering an ECEC setting, EAL learners face not only the challenge of language learning but also of cultural communication. Cultural communication refers to the unwritten cultural norms and assumptions which naturally evolve in settings, through interactions with others and within the shared space (Clarke, 2015).

In order to participate and begin to communicate effectively, EAL children must first build their understanding of the cultural framework. The ECEC setting will involve a number of 'shared cultural assumptions' (Clarke, 2015) which the child will come up against and which may be unfamiliar. One example is the assumption that when they walk into the setting they are free to start playing with any of the toys, areas and objects available to them. Another unfamiliar aspect may be 'free flow play', that is, the freedom to choose whether to play indoors or outdoors.

Language learning and cultural learning therefore have to go hand in hand. How the practitioner listens to and interacts with children is crucial to facilitating such understanding. The ECEC practitioner has a significant role in this context. As a **more knowledgeable other (MKO)** (Smidt, 2009), they scaffold the EAL child's learning interactions. In order to get the child in the **zone of proximal development (ZPD)** (Vygotsky, 1978), the practitioner needs to adopt the role of sensitive listener and of someone who supports, rather than guides, children's play. Clarke emphasises that to achieve this, the successful ECEC teacher needs to do all of the following:

- notice the child's interactions and non-verbal signs, however minimal these may be
- provide a running commentary on the child's actions and interactions, in this way modelling the use of language
- listen to the child's responses, build on and extend these
- use questions sparingly and in a sensitive way. (Clarke, 2004: 4)

 case study 15.1

Communication Skills

Manuk is 3 years and 6 months and is of Armenian origin. He has been attending the nursery for several weeks. He speaks in sentences in his home language, but has had limited opportunities to practise English. He is at a stage where he has realised that his home language does not 'work' in the new setting. Instead, he often communicates with staff by using gestures, crying or whimpering.

When Manuk arrives in the preschool room, the children are engaged in free play. He finds a tractor toy and starts pushing it around on the floor. As he is pushing the car, he makes a low humming noise. After a while, he goes to the LEGO table where another peer, Olivia, is building with the bricks. Manuk takes some bricks which are on the table and starts to build with them. He takes the brick which is shaped like a house roof. Olivia says, 'Mine' and takes the roof brick out of Manuk's hand. Manuk protests by whimpering and tries to take the roof brick back from Olivia. A practitioner approaches the table and says to Manuk: 'What are you building, Manuk? This is a very good structure! Is it a house?' Manuk does not respond but lets go of the roof brick. Olivia says, 'I'm doing a house with a roof'. The practitioner says: 'That's very good, Olivia. But we only have one roof brick'. The practitioner takes two other bricks and turns to Manuk: 'Manuk, let's join these two bricks to make a roof'. Manuk takes the two bricks which the practitioner gives him but promptly drops them on the floor. Olivia loses interest in the LEGO and goes to the dressing-up area. Manuk takes back the roof brick and places it on his structure; pointing to the structure, he says 'roof'.

1. Consider the different ways in which Manuk communicates, including non-verbal communication.
2. How does Manuk's language ability affect the way he interacts with peers? How does it affect his social standing within the peer group?
3. As a practitioner, what activities or situations could you use to scaffold Manuk's use of language?

Engaging with and noticing the child's actions is key here; taking them into account may create small steps into language and small steps into interactions with others. According to O'Sullivan (2015), the ECEC practitioner should be involved at the level of looking and listening first, gradually extending his knowledge, gained through looking and listening, into the child's play and interactions within this play. Based on this careful observation and interaction, the practitioner scaffolds the child's understanding of spoken language, which will eventually lead to talk. The practitioner's role is therefore reflective, one of patient observation and physical and playful interaction, prior to the act of scaffolding talk with the child.

STAGES OF EARLY EAL LEARNING

 spotlight on research 15.1

Patton Tabors' Research on Second-Language Acquisition

American researcher Patton Tabors has carried out extensive research in the area of second-language acquisition (the American equivalent of EAL) for children in their preschool years. She emphasises that children acquiring a second language are starting from a position of knowledge – they do not need to understand what language is about or how to interact through language as they already have this knowledge from starting out in their home language. Rather, they go through a process of 'discovering what *this* language is' (Tabors, 2008: 12).

Tabors further outlines a series of steps which a child would usually go through when acquiring a new language. Being aware of these steps allows the ECEC practitioner to plan for the child's needs and to respond in an encouraging way:

1. The child continues to use their home language in the ECEC setting.
2. The child discovers their home language does not work in the new situation and she enters a **non-verbal (silent) period**. She proceeds to collect information about the new language.
3. The child begins to go public, trying out individual words or phrases in the second language.
4. The child starts to speak in sentences in the second language.

Source: adapted from Tabors in Drury and Robertson (2008)

Based on Tabors' research (see Spotlight on Research 15.1), it is necessary to consider that the actions which the practitioner takes in this process are key in enabling the child to overcome the **silent period**. Within the steps identified, including the silent period, the child is active in 'collecting information' and processing the world around them. It would therefore be counterproductive to mistake the child's silence for a lack of interaction. The practitioner's role is to make the child feel accepted regardless of the level of their interactions, as these could be quite minimal and not involve talk. Clarke provides some useful strategies for ECEC practitioners supporting children while they are in the non-verbal (silent) period:

- continued talking even when children do not respond
- persistent inclusion in small groups with other children
- use of varied questions
- inclusion of other children as the focus in the conversation
- use of the first language
- acceptance of non-verbal responses
- praising of minimal effort
- expectations to respond with repeated words and/or counting
- structuring of programme to encourage child-to-child interaction
- providing activities which reinforce language practice through role play. (Clarke, 1992: 17–18)

The following section discusses in more detail how a practitioner can take a creative and participatory approach to applying some of these strategies.

CREATING OPPORTUNITIES FOR EAL CHILDREN'S PARTICIPATION

Accepting that EAL children come to English language learning from a position of strength, as little language explorers, means considering ways of introducing English which are empowering and participatory. The **Mosaic Approach**, developed by Clark and Moss (2011), is a framework for listening to children's voices and creating opportunities for children to participate actively in meaning making. The key premise of the Mosaic Approach is that children are seen as experts in their own lives (see Chapter 23 for further discussion). In the case of EAL learners, it can also be considered that children are experts in language acquisition. Chomsky's theory of the **language acquisition device (LAD)** (Smith et al., 2011) proposes that language acquisition is an innate ability which every child has. As evidence for his theory, Chomsky points out the speed with which young children acquire language – much faster than an adult trying to learn a new language with instruction. He further points out that children develop an understanding of grammar very early on, without specifically being instructed in the rules of grammar. Chomsky's theory allows us to see that EAL children have a unique advantage, in experiencing the process of acquiring two languages at once, and developing the ability to switch between the two languages with ease. It is worth noting, however, that this advantage is greatly enhanced by being in a language-rich environment, where adults as more knowledgeable others (MKOs) scaffold the child's language interactions (Smidt, 2009). As discussed earlier in the chapter, the practitioner's role in supporting children's interactions remains essential.

Thus, in the context of EAL children, who are seen as experts in language acquisition, the Mosaic Approach can have a specific purpose. As EAL children are going through a journey of cultural and second-language learning, they may have a silent or non-verbal period, as discussed by Tabors, and they may interact less actively with practitioners and other children in a setting for a period of time. In this situation, the Mosaic Approach is a tool for practitioners to empower children in the process of cultural and language learning. According to Drury and Robertson (2008), the multi-method Mosaic Approach can provide EAL children with opportunities to interact with others which are not entirely based on verbal ability. For example:

- *Multi-method approach* – practitioners need to notice non-verbal communication such as gestures, mark making, singing and play.
- *Participatory process* – practitioners need to notice instances where the child uses their home language with their parents, for example, and accept and encourage the use of the home language as well as try to understand some, even if a small, part of this.

McGilp's (2014) research with EAL children and their parents in an ECEC setting in Scotland is one example of how some of the principles of the Mosaic Approach could be applied in practice. In this project, multicultural versions of fairytale books were chosen to produce a multilingual collage (Figure 15.1). In addition, the children's parents were involved in contributing with written words, relating to the fairytales and written in the home-language script.

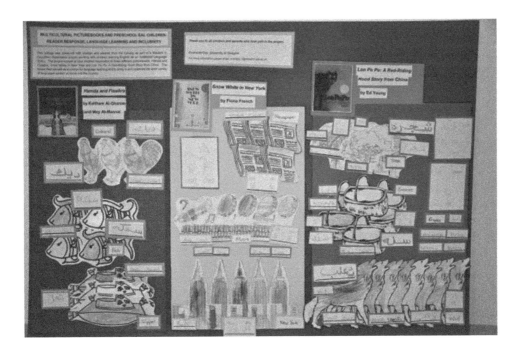

Figure 15.1 An example of a multilingual collage, created by children with the help of the practitioner and the children's parents

Source: McGilp (2014)

This approach encouraged children to respond to the cultural elements in the books, in this way engaging children with symbols, visuals and letters from a variety of cultural backgrounds. Taking an active part in such multicultural play and reading enabled the children to see that there was both place and value attributed to cultural heritage, including their own. Essentially, children were able to 'recognise themselves in the text' (McGilp, 2014: 40). Making this the topic of conversation in the ECEC setting is in itself an act of validating the child's own cultural and language heritage, and instilling the sense that their background matters and is important. Indeed, this type of activity can make a difference to the child at the micro and meso levels – in the family context and in the early childhood setting. Ada and Campoy (2004) highlight this issue in their book on transformative education by arguing that a refusal to acknowledge the child's home language can have far-reaching negative effects on the child, including on their relationships within the family and within the heritage community.

 action point 15.1

Following the multilingual collage example above, consult with a child's parent to identify a picture book or favourite story from their country of origin, which the child is familiar with and likes reading. Ask the parent to contribute a short list of written words that relate to the story. Use this book and the parent's written words to read and talk about the story in circle time. This can be followed up with drawing activities and working with the children to develop a multilingual collage - the collage would have images, select words in the home language and translations of the words in English, thus promoting engagement with both languages.

Up to now, this chapter has discussed the need to acknowledge children's cultural identities and ways to engage them in language learning through participatory approaches. It is worth considering, however, that EAL children in early childhood will also need to be assessed on their progress through the EYFS profile (Standards and Testing Agency, 2016). The following section discusses some of the challenges in this context and offers points for further consideration.

ASSESSING EAL LEARNERS IN EARLY CHILDHOOD

Assessment of EAL learners in the early years presents specific challenges. EAL children can have language proficiency in languages other than English, however when it comes to assessing EAL learners there is no available guidance from the government which requires that the assessment for bilingual children should be adapted to suit their needs (NALDIC, 2011). While the assessment in the EYFS profile against the 17 key areas – the early learning goals (ELGs) – can be carried out in any language, the assessment for communication, language and literacy has to be carried out in English (Coles, 2015; Mistry and Sood, 2015).

Thus, knowing as much as possible about the child's background and linguistic experience is very important to conducting a fair assessment. The National Assessment Agency (NAA, 2007) emphasises that EAL children should not be considered to have special needs solely on the basis that they do not currently speak the language. Furthermore, practitioners need to be mindful that EAL children can and will demonstrate competence using their home language in the prime and specific areas. A fair assessment of a bilingual child therefore involves working closely with families to gain a more holistic understanding of the child's development. This could include finding out whether the child is regularly exposed to their heritage language at home, whether their parents or grandparents speak the heritage language with the child and whether the child is learning their home language in the community, for example in a **complementary school**. Many EAL children also make annual trips to their home country which can provide a rich opportunity to be immersed in the heritage language and converse with extended family. Practitioners can be mindful of this and note this as an achievement or a significant event for the child as part of a discussion on 'holidays' or 'family'.

Practitioners also need to bear in mind that the child's English-language development may be 'emerging' at present and for the foreseeable future (Mistry and Sood, 2015; O'Sullivan, 2015). At present, baseline assessments (the Early Years Foundation Stage Profile (EYFSP)) are carried out in English only. However, O'Sullivan (2015) argues that assessment of learning can and should be carried out in the child's home language. She points out that: 'Where any item in the EYFS contains the word "talks" or "speaks" children can use their established or preferred mode of communication', which could of course be their home language (O'Sullivan, 2015: 27).

Similarly, researchers working with EAL Nexus (Coles, 2015) have developed an assessment tool for EAL children's language and communication in ECEC. The assessment is developed to work alongside the EYFSP statutory assessment, rather than to replace the assessment in English. Figure 15.2 shows an example of a Nepali girl's assessment in the Reception year, with the English assessment set out beside this in the home language. The value of this way of recording the child's progress is that a fuller picture can be developed of the child's level of communication and language development. This results in a more accurate assessment of whether the child is making progress in listening and attention, understanding and speaking. This can also aid early identification and intervention for the child if extra support is required. More than this, carrying out the assessment in this way sends a positive message to the child and her parents, that continuing to develop ability in the home language is valuable and important and a practice which is recognised in the work of the school and/or ECEC setting.

 reflection point 15.1

Explore the example of an assessment of an EAL child in Figure 15.2. What are the benefits of using this approach to assessment? What are the challenges? Refer to the Assessing Young Learners Toolkit available at: www.teachingenglish.org.uk/article/assessing-young-learners

Hampshire EMTAS

Initial observations on use of language

Pupil: Kheena	Year Group: R
First language (L1): Nepali	**English**
	Using QCA Step Descriptors where appropriate
Listening and Speaking	**Listening and Speaking**
• Uses short simple sentences and phrases to express her likes and dislikes	• Speaks using simple sentences and phrases
• Speech in clear and understandable	• Speech is clear and understandable
• Quite talkative and friendly	• Able to follow simple instructions accurately
• Understands simple instructions very well	• Very chatty and friendly
Reading	**Reading**
• Not yet able to read Nepali	• Able to recognize initial sounds in a word
	• Able to read most CVC words
	• Able to recognize and read numbers up to 10
	• Developing knowledge of shapes
Writing (Sample attached)	**Writing (sample attached) Yes**
• Not yet able to write Nepali	• Able to write her first name neatly and correctly
	• Able to write the initial of CVC words correctly
	• Letters are very well formed and has a very good pencil control
	• Produced a neat drawing of Peppa Pig's family

Figure 15.2 An example of a language, communication and literacy assessment of an EAL child, using the First Language Assessment Tool developed by the EAL Nexus project

THE HOME LEARNING ENVIRONMENT AND THE COMMUNITY CONTEXT

So far, this chapter has discussed EAL children's linguistic and cultural learning, participatory ways of working with EAL children in the early years and ways of assessing EAL children. In each section, the role of parents and the need to involve parents in the EAL child's learning journey have been a significant factor. This section focuses specifically on the home learning environment and the community context as spaces for early multilingual learning, and on parents as the child's first educators.

In relation to EAL, the concept of '**funds of knowledge**' (Conteh, 2015) is often used to discuss the value of parental and community involvement in the child's learning. This concept refers to the knowledge, skills, strategies and values which are embedded in communities and families. Where the community and family have a strong presence in the child's life, these aspects become valuable assets through which the child herself learns about the world and ways of being in the world. Conteh makes recommendations that in order to enable the child to draw on these funds of knowledge, the teacher must first of all become aware of the different ways in which EAL children learn outside the classroom, and, second, must develop ways in which such knowledge can be made part of the mainstream curriculum.

PHOTO STORY-TIME

An activity within the mainstream curriculum which invites children to share their heritage language and culture and involves the children's parents in the process can utilise the funds of knowledge principle. For example, most families who have migrated will have brought old or new photographs with them, taken in their home country. Children can be asked to bring in a 'photograph with a story'. The story can be written on a template sheet provided to the parents, with simple questions such as 'Who?' 'What?' 'Where?', to be completed both in the home language and in English. Each child can complete the story with their parent and bring this to class to be exhibited on a display board at the preschool or school. On consecutive days, during a brief session titled 'Photo story-time', each child can be given an opportunity to tell the story of their heritage photograph. Through telling these stories, children will share something important with their peers, regarding their personal history and culture, drawing on their parents' and families' funds of knowledge. Every child can be given an opportunity to participate, regardless of whether they are EAL learners.

Besides being integrated in the mainstream, the funds of knowledge principle is applied in community learning contexts, through complementary schools, where both parents and the broader community contribute.

COMMUNITY LEARNING THROUGH COMPLEMENTARY SCHOOLS

Complementary schools are often started by a few volunteer parents and gradually involve more members of the community who share a linguistic and cultural heritage. Their curricula are varied, with some being much stricter on aspects such as content and learning interactions than others. However, the overall ethos is to consistently promote children's engagement with their home language and culture. Where targeted language learning takes place, this is also taught by volunteer parents, who have an interest in their own child learning the language and developing friendships with other children from their linguistic background. Many of these complementary schools have an early childhood strand. For example, Languages Sheffield runs a number of complementary schools, including a Japanese play group, The Spanish Language Club and Les Petits Poissons, for children aged 0–12 of French-speaking heritage (Figure 15.3).

Figure 15.3 Snack time at Les Petits Poissons, the French Complementary School in Sheffield

Source: https://lespetitspoissonssheffield.wordpress.com

The parents involved are motivated by the need to maintain their cultural and linguistic identity and pass this on to their children. Teaching materials are often provided by parents themselves, or imported after a visit to the home country. These informal practices are at the heart of preserving the community feel of complementary schools, thus making them more accessible to families. It is important to notice that parents themselves use this as an opportunity to connect with other parents and share their experience of working and living in the country, thus utilising the funds of knowledge principle.

Once these cultural and language foundations have been laid, further opportunities become available for these children. The Home Languages Accreditation Project (HOLA) is funded by the Paul Hamlyn Foundation. It provides opportunities for children to gain national accreditation in their home language. The project aims to create cohesive links between mainstream schools, complementary schools and communities. This provides a valuable pathway for the child into more advanced bilingual practice.

This chapter has discussed the multiple benefits of bilingualism, and highlighted the role of the family and community contexts in setting children on a path to bilingualism. Moreover, early childhood practitioners need to be aware of the role that families and communities play in maintaining young children's links to their home culture and personal history. The examples discussed around making use of funds of knowledge in the classroom are a further acknowledgement of the EAL learner's belonging to more than one culture and are likely to help children develop a positive sense of self.

SUMMARY

- Recognising the EAL child's personal and linguistic identity will allow practitioners to develop learning and teaching strategies which enhance the child's self-esteem.
- Developing effective strategies for working with children with EAL involves consideration of the stages of early EAL learning, and of the cultural learning which the child will engage in as they enter an unfamiliar setting.
- One way of giving EAL children a voice in the learning process is to make use of participatory techniques.
- Assessments of EAL children's language, literacy and communication as part of the EYFSP can be carried out in the child's home language, alongside the assessment carried out in English.
- Parents and communities play a significant role in empowering children to continue to acquire both the home language and English. ECEC practitioners need to be aware of these advantages and work closely with parents, both to get to know the child and to successfully facilitate their learning.

 online resources

Make sure to visit https://study.sagepub.com/fitzgeraldandmaconochie for selected SAGE videos (with questions), SAGE journal articles, links to external sources and flashcards.

FURTHER READING

Mistry, M. and Sood, K. (2015). *English as an Additional Language in the Early Years: Linking Theory to Practice*. London: Routledge.

This book provides a useful account of theory and advice for practitioners working with EAL learners.

National Association for Language Development in the Curriculum (NALDIC): https://naldic. org.uk

This website provides a range of useful resources related to EAL research, practice and policy.

REFERENCES

Ada, A. F. and Campoy, I. (2004). *Authors in the Classroom: A Transformative Education Process*. Boston: Pearson.

Bialystok, E., Majumder, S. and Martin, M. (2003). Developing Phonological Awareness: Is There a Bilingual Advantage? *Applied Linguistics, 24*: 27–44.

Boyd, D. and Bee, H. (2014). The Development of Language. In: *The Developing Child*, 13th edn. Harlow: Pearson, pp. 241–66.

British Council (2016). EAL in Context. *EAL Nexus*. [online] Available at: https://eal.britishcouncil.org/eal-sector/current-context [Accessed 7 July 2017].

Clark, A. and Moss, P. (2011). *Listening to Young Children: The Mosaic Approach*, 2nd edn. London: National Children's Bureau.

Clarke, P. (1992). *English as a 2nd Language in Early Childhood*. Richmond, VIC, Australia: FKA Children's Services, Multicultural Resources Centre.

Clarke, P. (2004). *Creating Positive Environments that Promote Speaking and Listening*. NALDIC conference report. Watford: NALDIC. [online] Available at: www.naldic.org.uk/NR/rdonlyres/C320F615-0818-4DC2-A521-EF21650ACA4C/0/Creatingpositiveenvironments.pdf [Accessed 28 March 2017].

Clarke, P. (2015). *Supporting EAL Children in the Early Years*. Watford: NALDIC. [online] Available at: www.naldic.org.uk/eal-teaching-and-learning/outline-guidance/early-years [Accessed 24 February 2017].

Coles, S. (2015). First Language Assessment of Young EAL Learners. British Council, EAL Nexus Research. [online] Available at: https://eal.britishcouncil.org/eal-sector/first-language assessment-young-eal-learners [Accessed 27 March 2017].

Conteh, J. (2015). All about Language and Learning: The 'Funds of Knowledge' Concept. In: *The EAL Teaching Book*, 2nd edn. London: Sage, pp. 66–70.

Department for Children Schools and Families (DCSF) (2007). *Primary National Strategy: Supporting Children Learning English as an Additional Language: Guidance for Practitioners in the Early Years Foundation Stage*. Ref: 00683-2007BKT-EN. London: DCSF. [online] Available at: www.naldic.org.uk/Resources/NALDIC/Teaching%20and%20Learning/ealeyfsguidance.pdf [Accessed 28 March 2017].

Drury, R. and Robertson, L. (2008). Listening to Bilingual Children. NALDIC. [online] Available at: www.naldic.org.uk/Resources/NALDIC/Teaching%20and%20Learning/Documents/Listen_Bilingual_Children.pdf [Accessed 24 February 2017].

Gonzalez, N., Moll, L. and Amanti, C. (eds) (2005). *Funds of Knowledge: Theorising Practices in Households, Communities and Classrooms*. New York: Routledge.

Kenner, C. and Ruby, M. (2012). *Interconnecting Worlds: Teaching Partnerships for Bilingual Learning*. Stoke-on-Trent: Trentham.

McGilp, E. (2014). From Picturebook to Multilingual Collage: Bringing Learners' First Language and Culture into the Pre-school Classroom. *Children's Literature in English Language Education (CLELE Journal)*, 2(2): 31–49.

Mistry, M. and Sood, K. (2015). Assessment for Learners with EAL in Early Years. In: *English as an Additional Language in the Early Years: Linking Theory to Practice*. London: Routledge, pp. 62–77.

National Assessment Agency (NAA) (2007). *Guidance Notes: Assessing Children who are Learning English as an Additional Language*. London: NAA.

National Association for Language Development in the Curriculum (NALDIC) (2011). Is there a Nationally Agreed EAL Assessment System? [online] Available at: www.naldic.org.uk/eal-teaching-and-learning/faqs/assfaq [Accessed 28 March 2017].

O'Sullivan, T. (2015). Assessment for Learning in the Early Years. *National Association for Language Development in the Curriculum (NALDIC) Quarterly*, 15(4): 27–8.

Rochford, D. (2016). *Statement on the Interim Recommendations of the Rochford Review*. London: DfE. [online] Available at: www.gov.uk/government/uploads/system/uploads/attachment_data/file/484847/Interim_recommendations_of_the_Rochford_Review_-_Final_version_to_upload_111215.pdf [Accessed 28 March 2017].

Smidt, S. (2009). On Bridging the Gap: More about the ZPD. In: *Introducing Vygotsky: A Guide for Practitioners and Students in Early Years Education*. London: Routledge, pp. 121–39.

Smith, P., Cowie, H. and Blades, M. (2011). Language. In: *Understanding Children's Development*, 5th edn. Chichester: Wiley, pp. 427–30.

Standards and Testing Agency (STA) (2016). *Early Years Foundation Stage Profile: 2017 Handbook*. Ref: STA/16/7838/e. London: STA.

Statista (2016). Share of Primary Pupils with English as an Additional Language in England in January 2016, by Region. [online] Available at: www.statista.com/statistics/331675/england-region-english-additional-language-primary-pupils [Accessed 30 June 2017].

Tabors, P. (2008). *One Child, Two Languages: A Guide for Early Childhood Educators of Children Learning English as a Second Language*, 2nd edn. Baltimore, MD: Brookes Publishing Co.

Vygotsky, L. (1978). *Mind in Society: The Development of Higher Psychological Processes*. London: Harvard University Press.

PART 4

THE SOCIAL ENVIRONMENT

GO TO
https://study.sagepub.com/fitzgeraldandmaconochie *for free access to SAGE videos on topics covered in this book*

THE EDUCATIONAL ENVIRONMENT

BY ALISON GLENTWORTH

Beginning with curriculum development for young children really helped me to understand more about how legislation, policy and curricula have been shaped over the years, which can be an area that sometimes seems complex and confusing. The links between, and impact of, different legislation, policy and curricula are clear and vital areas of practice, such as play and outdoor learning, are clearly covered.

The case study about Polly made me consider an alternative perspective of education, which helped me reflect critically about what we value in education and whether this is always in the best interest of all children. I feel that by developing a greater understanding of home-schooling it will enable me to be more confident and flexible if I come across this in my future practice.

With my final placement approaching, in a mixed FS1 and FS2 class, the chapter has made me consider how I and other members of the team can work together to successfully support the younger children as they approach their transition to Reception and the older children as they approach Year 1.

JOSIE PURCELL
BA EARLY YEARS AND
PRIMARY EDUCATION WITH QTS
SHEFFIELD HALLAM UNIVERSITY

 learning outcomes

By actively reading this chapter and engaging with the material, you will be able to:

- reflect on a range of historical influences on the Foundation Stage (FS) and Key Stage 1 (KS1) curricula
- debate approaches to current curricula in early childhood education and care (ECEC) and KS1, including awareness of the devolved nature of UK governance and wider educational influences
- consider complexities of school readiness, the importance of play-based pedagogies and effective partnership working to support young children's learning needs
- identify the importance of a shared ethos and well-defined philosophy of education supporting educational transitions through high-quality learning and practice.

INTRODUCTION

How an educational environment is constructed to support young children's learning varies significantly across settings, however common features exist. This chapter identifies features of high-quality provision and practice in support of children's learning, taking account of relevant curricula, key transitions and **school readiness**. To set this in context, the chapter includes an historical overview of educational influences; and discusses the use of play-based pedagogy in ECEC and KS1 and in transitions for children between home/school and FS/KS1. Practice is presented in the context of English social policy with evolved approaches across the UK included to provide a broader perspective. The connection between a child's immediate and broader environments, reflected in Bronfenbrenner's ecological theory, is relevant as the 'social values, cultural beliefs, political ideologies, customs and laws' (Paat, 2013: 956) impact directly on when, what and how children are taught.

CURRICULUM DEVELOPMENT FOR YOUNG CHILDREN

Legislation, policy and curricula provide the context in which ECEC practitioners and primary school teachers determine provision for learning. A defining principle of Early Childhood Studies is to understand early childhood and children in an ecological context. As discussed in other chapters, children are active agents in their learning, with a focus on what they are and not what they will become. Prior to the Education Reform Act 1988 (ERA), government intervention and curriculum planning and implementation were limited in England. The introduction of the National Curriculum could be described as the starting point of increased government intervention and, consequently, the much-debated decrease in professional autonomy for ECEC practitioners (see Chapter 12 for further discussion). The 1988 Act set out a National Curriculum for England and Wales to raise standards and provide a broad and balanced curriculum. The National Curriculum subject-based approach contradicted the child-centred nature of preschool education. From a historical perspective, key events and influences on UK ECEC reflected a growing awareness of the importance of early education for young children. Examples include the establishment of the first UK nursery school in 1816 in New Lanark, Scotland, established by Robert Owen for the children of cotton mill workers. The 1870 Education Act ensured compulsory education for all children over 5 years and, in 1880, elementary education was made compulsory for all children between 5 and 13 years of age. In 1911, the McMillan sisters, inspired by their socialist ideology, created an open-air nursery at Deptford. Their priority was children's health and wellbeing, aided by free access to gardens and play areas.

Awareness of the importance of education for young children was gradually increasing, although not always in a pedagogically appropriate way. This was seen in the 1960s, for example, when reduced family sizes and post-Second World War nursery closures limited play opportunities for children. Increased awareness of the value of play resulted in the establishment of the 'playgroup movement' (Harrison, 2009). In 1972, a government White Paper presented by Margaret Thatcher, the Secretary of State for Education, 'Education: A Framework for Expansion' (DES, 1972), proposed nursery education for all. This could be seen as a step forward but, in reality, preschool provision in the 1970s and 1980s remained significantly underdeveloped. In 1990, the Rumbold Report (DES, 1990) emphasised the importance of high-quality early years education.

From the 1990s, there was a much greater focus on the early years in government policy. This included policies to promote social mobility; professionalisation of the children's workforce; changes to early years pedagogy and research to increase the evidence base for early childhood (such as **Effective Provision of Preschool Education (EPPE)**). A priority for New Labour from 1997 was welfare reform with measures to reduce social inequality. Government initiatives and interventions included a universal offering of 15 hours a week free ECEC entitlement for all 3–4-year-olds (2006) and the extension of free education for 130,000 2-year-olds in deprived areas (2010). Further enhancements with 30 hours of free ECEC provision for 3–4 year olds from September 2017 depended on family income and work arrangements. High-quality nurseries became 'Early Excellence Centres' (1998) and the piloted Sure Start Local Programme (1999) encouraged 'early participation and active parental involvement … and a child-centred, structured approach to children's learning and development' (Faulkner and Coates, 2013: 249). The Desirable Outcomes (DOs) for Children's Learning (1996) offered non-statutory guidance for ECEC. This was significant as it was one of the first publications to do so.

In 2000, a Parliamentary Select Committee inquiry was conducted focused on the 3–7 age range. Consultation with early years experts resulted in this being widened to 0–8. The resulting 'Birth to Three Matters' framework (DfES, 2002) with guidance for working with the youngest children, together with the **Curriculum Guidance for the Foundation Stage** (QCA, 2000), replaced DOs. For the first time, national education policy recognised that young children thrived best with an appropriately play-based pedagogical curriculum. Other key developments included **Every Child Matters** (ECM) (HM Treasury, 2003), leading to the introduction of Sure Start. The ECM agenda demonstrated a commitment to children's rights and supported their holistic development. Although not part of current government policy, principles underpinning ECM remain evident, demonstrated in the ethos of many educational settings. European and worldwide initiatives had some influence on the English curriculum. For example, Te Whāriki in New Zealand (Ministry of Education, 1996) highlighted the importance of effective partnerships between practitioners, families and the wider community. Malaguzzi in Reggio Emilia, Italy's focus on following children's interests (Hall, 2010; Smidt, 2013) and the Scandinavian focus on outdoor learning and Forest School are approaches to learning which continue to be developed in the UK.

The Childcare Act 2006 made the early years curriculum statutory and the updated Early Years Foundation Stage Framework (EYFS) was introduced in 2008. For the first time, this set out statutory expectations for 'learning, development and care (of) young children ... ensuring ... every child makes progress and no child gets left behind'. The new curriculum set out a play-led curriculum in school Reception classes. Further revisions occurred, with the most recently revised Statutory Framework for the EYFS published in March 2017 and effective from April 2017 (DfE, 2017). Guidance sets standards for learning, development and care of children from 0–5, with quality and consistency, a secure foundation, partnership working and equality of opportunity being key aspects of practice. The seven areas of development, three of which are described as key (prime) to children's learning and development (communication and language; physical development; personal, social and emotional education) retain a play-based pedagogy. 2017 revisions include reference to expectations about the Mathematics and English qualifications of staff and paediatric first aid training requirements (PFA) announced in July 2016. New and updated government advice and guidance includes 'Working Together to Safeguard Children' (DfE, 2015a, updated in February 2017) and the 'Prevent Duty Guidance' (DfE, 2015b, updated in March 2016), both published since the previous update of the EYFS in 2014.

The importance of practitioner understanding of progression from the EYFS Statutory Framework to the Primary National Curriculum is key to effectively supporting children's transition to Key Stage 1 (KS1). There is often a stark change from a play-based approach to a more subject-specific style of learning. The English National Curriculum Framework document (DfE, 2013) sets out the statutory curriculum for maintained schools. Understanding the progression from EYFS to KS1 curriculum subjects, including Science, Art & Design, Computing, Design & Technology, Geography, History, Languages, Music and Physical Education (PE), is crucial. The importance of English and Mathematics remains constant but opportunities for children to develop understanding across the wider curriculum are vital to prepare children for later life. Personal, social, health and economic education (PSHE) provision is prioritised and settings include other subjects or topics of their choice to meet children's learning needs.

 reflection point 16.1

How do you think the best outcomes for young children are achieved across the curriculum? What features of high-quality provision support their learning?
What key principles underpin effective educational environments in FS and KS1?
Why do you think a shared ethos and philosophy of education is important across the Foundation phase and Key Stage 1? Draft your own personal philosophy of education for children 0–7 and justify your thinking.

DEVOLVED APPROACHES: ECEC AND KS1 AND EFFECTIVE TRANSITIONS

Since 1997 devolution has brought substantial changes to how the UK is governed. Simkins (2013) explored jurisdictions, contexts and histories of the four home countries. Noteworthy points include Scotland's unique education system, governed from the Scottish Parliament since devolution in 1999. Northern Ireland historically had its own education system where, before devolved powers were restored in 2007, there was an unsettled 20-year period in which powers were removed/restored at different times. This turmoil over governance continues. Prior to 1999, Wales was governed through the Welsh Office from Westminster. This restriction continued after this date with limited devolution, resulting in the UK primary legislation remaining intact, meaning Welsh policy was 'limited to interpretation as opposed to execution' (Simkins, 2013: 990). In 2018 additional powers were devolved to Wales to enhance self-governance and the establishment of additional parliamentary powers.

The 'culture of governance' considered by Simkins (2013) supports a wider professional educational understanding. In England, key aspects of school governance reflect those for most schools following the Education Reform Act of 1988 (ERA). Delegated power to schools is a key feature, for example school budgets and personnel/staffing arrangements. In contrast, government direction on curricula has increased substantially. In addition, frequent testing of children and the inspection process reflect increasing teacher accountability to government rather than outcomes for children. A potential impact of this is for teachers to focus on the core subjects, tested at the expense of the wider curriculum. Overall, this potentially narrows educational experiences. A speech by **Ofsted** Chief Inspector Amanda Spielman (September 2017) acknowledged the importance of 'a rich and deep curriculum in subjects such as history, English and geography' (to name a few), with children emerging as 'educated adults with a broad, informed perspective on the world'. This suggests a potential shift in expectations through greater emphasis on values-rich education. Interestingly, this coincides with a broadening in the **Programme for International Student Assessment (PISA)** 2018 remit. This is a triennial international survey in which 15-year-old students from **Organisation for Economic Co-operation and Development (OECD)** countries taking the 2018 PISA tests will be required to use their knowledge and understanding to think critically about a specific intercultural issue for the first time. This is in addition to existing assessments measuring science, mathematics, reading, collaborative problem solving and financial literacy. This highlights increasingly complex demands, with teachers focusing on core subjects to achieve the best test outcomes but international measures requiring broad critical thinking. In contrast, Scotland has maintained its emphasis on offering a broad curriculum, within a local authority structure and maintained schools.

Since 2010 in England, the structure of the school system has been increasingly centrally governed, removing the majority of the functions of previous local education authorities (LEAs). State schools have been strongly encouraged to become academies. Academies are independent, state-funded schools, receiving funding directly from central government rather than a local authority, with some sponsored by businesses, universities, other schools, faith or voluntary groups. Wales and Northern Ireland have, overall, maintained more centrally orientated approaches. Beauchamp et al. (2015) summarised the Welsh government's aim to 'help everyone reach their potential, reduce inequality, and improve economic and social well-being', making the political decision, similar to Scotland, to do this with a continued focus on local authorities.

EXPLORING A PLAY-BASED APPROACH TO LEARNING IN ECEC AND KS1

Education has been influenced by many people. For example, Maria Montessori (in the late nineteenth century) emphasised the importance of active learning through experience and working co-operatively with others. John Dewey's contribution to twentieth-century educational thinking emphasised the importance of experience, thinking, reflection and interaction with the learning environment. Bruner (1990) and Rogoff's (2003) work linked to social interaction and contact with the physical environment with a focus on collaborative learning. Potential for an individual's response to be influenced by their point of view, feelings and experience is acknowledged as meaning is constructed through a play-based approach to learning.

Examples of philosophical principles underpinning ECEC highlight key influences on learning approaches. The 1967 Plowden Report was significant in emphasising the importance of play as 'vital to children's learning and therefore vital in school' (DES, 1967: 193), re-emphasising the approach of many of the early pioneers. In Wales, the Foundation Phase runs from age 3 to 7 years, suggesting that this is a key period when play-based strategies particularly support learning. It is interesting to note that some Scandinavian children are aged 7 when more formal schooling starts. Based on this, it could be argued that the divide between curricula for children from age 5 to 7 in England may be perceived as potentially problematic (Curriculum for Wales: Foundation Phase Framework; DfES/Welsh Government, 2015: 3).

Martlew et al. (2011) explored growing interest in a play-based pedagogy in Scotland, with children's engagement reflecting 'active involvement, autonomy and … opportunity for choice' (p. 71). Principles underpinning the current Scottish National Curriculum for Excellence reflect the commitment to planning 'challenging, inspirational and enjoyable learning and teaching activities' supported through statements of experience and outcomes. Approaches to learning include active, co-operative and peer learning together with effective use of technology. Children's active involvement underpinned the Welsh Assembly Government's focus on children learning best through first-hand experience. In Northern Ireland, play-based approaches reflected the importance of 'the social and cultural context for children's learning', the adult's role as 'scaffolder' and 'co-constructor' of children's knowledge being significant (Walsh et al., 2011: 108). Alasuutari (2014) emphasised taking 'account of children's views … with "the individual and competent" child being the starting point' (p. 242). Exploring how learning is interpreted through young children's active involvement in high-quality provision is vital but does not assume learning only occurs in school/nursery. A common factor across the nations over the past decade has been a move towards more play-based pedagogy for young children, reflecting the ethos of early pioneers. However, in England this is against the regular backdrop of calls for a more formalised approach to learning.

SCHOOL READINESS

A debate about school readiness is often, mistakenly, linked to play-based pedagogy. When is it appropriate for children to start school and what is meant by school readiness? The most common school starting age in Europe and the rest of the world is 6 years. In Northern Ireland, the age is 4 so some children start full-time school when aged just 4 years and 2 months. In Scotland, children start school in the August of/or following their 5th birthday. In Finland and Sweden, the school starting age is 7. When exploring school readiness, Unicef (2012) consider three perspectives – a child's readiness for school, a school's readiness for children and a family and community's readiness for school. The United Nations' World Fit for Children (WFFC) mission statement of 2002, highlights the importance of 'a good start in life … a nurturing and safe environment … enabl(ing) children to survive and be physically healthy, mentally alert, emotionally secure, socially competent and able to learn' (Unicef, 2002: 16). The importance of a caring, safe and stimulating environment for young children's holistic development is central to achieving this (Unicef, 2012: 6). When 'ready for school', children have the skills, abilities and attitudes required to succeed at school, with 'competencies required for a smooth transition'. School readiness is acknowledged here as the point at which a child has the confidence, independence and skills to actively engage in their school/learning environment.

From birth, infants bring a unique perspective to the world. As practitioners committed to inspiring and motivating young children in their learning, it is vital to acknowledge children's unique and individual nature, creating the appropriate conditions to nurture 'authentic curiosity, deep creativity and wild diversity' (Ayers cited in Lorio and Parnall, 2015: xiv). Exploring how natural abilities can be nurtured and encouraged calls on parents/educators to trust children. A rich and stimulating learning environment allows young children the freedom to follow their own interests using inspiring resources to support learning. Whether in a school or alternative ECEC setting, interesting and insightful perspectives can be explored on school readiness. These approaches are key to providing children with opportunities and experiences to support their development and being ready for school. Whilst most children in the UK follow a traditional transition from home to school, there are alternatives.

case study 16.1

Exploring School Readiness – Coming ... Ready or Not?

Immediately after her fourth birthday, Polly did not begin full-time education in school but attended on a part-time basis. The rest of the week she was **home-schooled**. Her parents explored alternatives as they did not want her to begin full-time school in Reception. This was partly due to her being born in August, which meant she would have attended school full-time from within weeks of turning 4. They considered starting Polly in school a year later, an option in Scotland but one not so easy to pursue in England. Polly initially attended a home-school nursery (nursery provision for children who may later be home-schooled). Polly's parents believe the age a child is ready to begin school is dependent on the child. When asked, Polly's mum reflected on the difficulty of making this decision. She was clear that her school was 'brilliant but the teachers were stuck between a rock and a hard place' in terms of how staff ideally wanted to teach and the pressures of achieving high KS1 results as an Ofsted 'outstanding' school.

Polly's parents also felt the classroom environment restricted her creative and physical experiences and she benefited greatly from opportunities to play. Y1 was an even greater challenge, her mum reflecting that 'she's really struggling with any formal teaching' but through 'free-play, she learns very quickly'. Her parents believed flexi home-school (attending school on a part-time basis) would help her become 'an interested and motivated life-long-learner'. Polly initially achieved a balance of creativity from school and physicality from the drama, dance and gymnastics she experienced for physical wellbeing. There were, however, challenges when in a gymnastics session Polly looked miserable. Asked why, she replied 'I just want to play'. By the end of the session, she had taught herself to forward/backward roll and make a bridge. This could be seen as a pivotal moment because soon afterwards her parents decided Polly would be full-time home-schooled to be reviewed at the age of 7.

Within home-schooling, Polly's learning includes weekly Forest School; reading including active phonics at home; and practical mathematics (e.g. weighing out flour for her sister's birthday cake). Learning opportunities are also offered by the home-school community communicated to parents/carers by email, highlighting daily options with up to four workshop choices for selection. **World School**, through which home-school families take opportunities for world travel, also provides support, an example being when Polly's family recently stayed with a family in Spain. Relaxed lunchtimes spent speaking Spanish, swimming and creating a collaborative composition of new words for a song provided time to play and chance to do it. More local opportunities include a summer sports day and camping trip coinciding with return-to-school week in September.

Socialising is an issue frequently raised about home-schooling with worries that being out of school may limit a child's social interaction. A key reason Polly's parents wanted her to be in school was friendship and the social elements. When asked about her friends, interestingly, Polly mentioned friends from Nursery two years ago and Forest School each Friday morning. Her mum reflected: 'It has to be what they're doing rather than how much they see each other that's building these relationships and lessons about friendship.' An important point Polly's mum made was about separation anxiety. This is a real issue for some children and not about them being silly or the parent/carer being over-protective. In this situation, flexi-home-schooling initially provided the solution for Polly. She is a bright, articulate, confident and engaging child, keen to share what she has been doing, including acting, singing and, recently, an animation project.

1. List reasons why a parent might home-school their child.
2. In Reception, Polly attended school three days a week initially, continuing this pattern in Y1. After six months, she began full-time home-schooling for review when she is 7 years of age. How can a child's age affect their transition to a new class/setting?
3. What other factors might have contributed to Polly's parents' decision to fully home-school?
4. Identify potential pros/cons of home-schooling a child from the perspective of:
    *   the child
    *   siblings
    *   parents/carers
    *   school
    *   friends.

TRANSITIONS: FROM HOME TO SCHOOL AND FOUNDATION STAGE TO KS1

Fisher reflected on concerns from teachers, children and parents about the 'sometimes abrupt change from a play-based curriculum to … more formal approaches prevalent in many Y1 classes' (Fisher, 2010: 1). A three-year project in Oxfordshire helped identify ways in which FS and Y1 teachers could effectively work together to create a more positive transition for children. From a teacher's perspective, high-quality relationships guide and underpin effective practice, supporting smooth transitions. Creative cross-curricular approaches to learning with enrichment opportunities are other features of good practice that support effective transitions.

 case study 16.2

Facilitating Effective Transitions: Shared ethos and effective relationships underpin high-quality provision

Alicia is a Foundation Stage teacher. The head teacher confirmed that Jack, a child new to the area, would visit with his mum before beginning Reception full time in September. Jack was unsettled at the nursery he attended during the summer term. It has been a time of change for Jack. He has a new sibling (born in May) and the family was busy preparing to move house to the new area in July. Jack attended two 'taster' sessions with his new teacher, Alicia, before the summer holiday.

The setting's transition programme to Reception is facilitated through close partnership working with parents/carers as part of supporting children to be ready for school. Staff collaboration and sharing of ideas between the setting and the home is highly valued. Transition from nursery settings to Reception is effectively supported in the Foundation Unit setting. For children who attend the school nursery (often referred to as FS1), they interact on a daily basis with children in the Reception class (often referred to as FS2) to support school readiness. A range of other strategies are used to support transition, including photographs of adults working in the different areas, meeting the teacher and an emphasis on effective communication with parents/carers. There are also a number of taster sessions in the Foundation Unit and home visits taking place in the months before entry. These are particularly important for children who do not attend the school nursery, to increase their familiarisation with the Reception classroom.

Effective provision is facilitated through all, including the management team, working together to promote learning through play. Key to successful provision is the leadership team's shared commitment to a broad, engaging curriculum using approaches which most effectively meet children's learning needs. Children's interests are followed wherever possible with opportunities to talk about topics and pose questions. This contributes to creating an environment where children are engaged in exploratory play, outdoor and indoor, and interacting with peers to benefit from the varied learning opportunities of the setting.

Valuing the team's professional expertise through effective partnership and collaborative working is highlighted through the school's teaching and learning policy. Foundation Stage planning includes continuous provision across the whole Foundation Stage with a shared ethos of high-quality, meaningful learning opportunities embedded in all areas of the setting. This is supported by close interactions with parents/carers. Partnership working secures inclusive practice and supports children's specific learning needs.

Planned 'special weeks' encourage a 'community feel' supported by an active Home School Association (HSA) including Enterprise, Arts and Active Weeks (the latter in National Sports Week including Healthy Eating) and special events planned, such as on World Book Day. Such opportunities help parents to be engaged in a meaningful way in their child's education.

Quality time for practitioners to talk with children increases confidence in their new learning environment. Learning is supported through language modelling inspired and motivated by role-play areas such as the home corner, to provide opportunities for children to explore 'real-life' scenarios. Supporting and encouraging communication is also a key part of learning in the Foundation Stage. For example, 'communication-friendly spaces' create an atmosphere conducive to talk with opportunities such as bicycles for two, an easel for two and the sharing of iPads.

1. How can Jack's transition to FS2 be supported by Alicia, his teacher? In addition to the practice outlined above, identify some strategies she will use to support his successful transition to FS2.
2. How might Jack's family become more involved in the school community from September?
3. Identify the different aspects of practice above and link them to the relevant areas of learning in the EYFS. How is effective practice to support transitions beneficial for children's learning?

Provision of developmentally appropriate practice is important, as just because a child is in a particular year group 'it does not mean … they have the same abilities or learning needs as other children in the same class' (Fisher, 2010: 20). In the education system, which is structured by age, this can present difficulties for children who are above or below the level of development associated with the year group. If a child is highly motivated and ready for learning, individually or scaffolded by adult support, then 'learning is more likely to be successful' (Fisher, 2010: 22). This emphasises the importance of looking at the child holistically, taking account of their individual situation and not being overly focused on their chronological age. This is addressed in the Oxford Transition Project referred to earlier. Key Stage 1 teachers were invited to comment on their daily first-hand teaching experiences. They acknowledged effective learning takes place, 'naturally and spontaneously … given time and space … when motivated … supported by knowledgeable adults … alongside peers … by initiating their own enquiries, rehearsing and repeating in a relaxed, supportive atmosphere' (Fisher, 2010: 28–31). This emphasises the importance of children in Key Stage 1 being active constructors in their own learning, an approach often associated more with the Foundation Stage.

 spotlight on practice 16.1

Building on Foundations of High-Quality Foundation Stage Pedagogy Supports Transition to Key Stage 1

Some Y1 and Y2 classes use play-based and topic-based approaches, drawing on key features of high-quality Foundation Stage provision. Examples include effective outdoor provision; role-play areas including talk for learning opportunities; and a range of continuous provision. An example is the planning, development and creation of a KS1 post office role-play area. Inspired by a visit to the local post office, Y1 and 2 children helped to plan and design the post office role-play area, leading to the preparation of materials including signs, parcels to be weighed and posted and cards made for sale. A 'grand opening' ceremony followed, with the official cutting of a ribbon to mark the occasion. In role, the class teachers initially modelled the use of the post office, inspiring and motivating children's engagement in the area. Cross-curricular learning opportunities include talk for learning; social skills and team working; Art and Design; Geography, English, Religious Education and Foreign Languages.

Many KS1 settings are, however, more formal than Foundation Stage with limited opportunities for free-flow/continuous provision. Moving from an active play-based FS learning environment to a more formal KS1 setting can be challenging for children. Transition from the EYFS Curriculum to the Primary National Curriculum may be problematic for some children. There are times when practitioners might face a tension between the kind of KS1 provision they want to develop, underpinned by their philosophy of education, and potential constraints through other influential factors.

To understand this transition and how it impacts on children, take opportunities to observe Foundation Stage and KS1 practice.

Research how 'school readiness' and 'transition' are supported elsewhere in the UK and wider world to develop your understanding of how key educational policy and practice impact on children aged 3-7.

Consider the support provided across devolved nations for children following a less 'traditional' educational route and how provision and transitions in this age range are managed. This emphasises the importance of each setting having a shared philosophy on the approach to transition, to guide the behaviour and attitudes of practitioners in approaches that most effectively enable each child to aspire to their potential. The everyday practice and pedagogical approach is of course central to this. However, effectively managed transitions, that provide support for children and parents, make an important contribution to children's learning, but also, just as importantly, to their social and emotional wellbeing.

SUMMARY

- Foundation Stage and KS1 curricula continually evolve yet reflect historical influences and perspectives. Common features of high-quality provision can be seen across Foundation Stage and KS1 practice but there are significant differences in provision.

- ECEC policy and provision across the UK reflect wider educational influences. Education policy is devolved and this creates differences across the four nations. However, collaborative and partnership working are seen as underpinning effective practice across all of the nations.
- Awareness of principles underpinning play-based pedagogies and complexities of school readiness is crucial. Effective relationships between key educational stakeholders are fundamental to partnership working and successful interaction supporting children's learning needs.
- Effective transitions are achieved through commitment to a shared ethos and well-defined philosophy of education. These support the planning of high-quality inclusive learning opportunities with high expectations of children to achieve their potential.

 online resources

Make sure to visit https://study.sagepub.com/fitzgeraldandmaconochie for selected SAGE videos (with questions), SAGE journal articles, links to external sources and flashcards.

FURTHER READING

Fitzgerald, D. and Kay, J. (2016). *Understanding Early Years Policy*, 4th edn. London: Sage.

This text is helpful to develop a more detailed understanding of the influence of policy and practice for young children, with a chapter focusing specifically on devolution.

Iorio, J. M. and Parnell, W. (eds) (2015). *Rethinking Readiness in Early Childhood Education*. New York: Palgrave Macmillan.

This book provides an example of a wider perspective with reference to practice in the USA. Chapter 11 focuses on the importance of childhood wonder, applicable to all children.

REFERENCES

Alasuutari, M. (2014). Voicing the Child? A Case Study in Finnish Early Childhood Education. *Childhood*, *21*(2): 242–9.

Beauchamp, G., Clarke, L., Hulmes, M. and Murray, J. (2015). Teacher Education in the United Kingdom Post Devolution: Convergences and Divergences. *Oxford Review of Education*, *41*(2): 154–70.

Bruner, J. S. (1990). *Acts of Meaning*. Cambridge, MA: Harvard University Press.

Department for Education (DfE) (2013). *The National Curriculum in England: Key Stages 1 and 2 Framework*. London: TSO.

Department for Education (DFE) (2015a). *Working Together to Safeguard Children: A Guide to Interagency Working to Safeguard and Promote the Welfare of Children*. London: TSO.

Department for Education (DfE) (2015b). *Prevent Duty Guidance*. London: TSO.

Department for Education (DfE) (2017). *Statutory Framework for the Early Years Foundation Stage (EYFS)*. London: TSO.

Department for Education and Skills (DfES) (2002). *Birth to Three Matters*. London: TSO.

Department for Education and Skills (DfES)/Welsh Government (2015). *Curriculum for Wales: Foundation Stage Framework*. London: TSO.

Department of Education and Science (DES) (1967). *The Plowden Report: Children and their Primary Schools*. London: HMSO.

Department of Education and Science (DES) (1972). *Education: A Framework for Expansion*. Government White Paper. London: HMSO.

Department of Education and Science (DES) (1990). *The Rumbold Report: The Report of the Committee of Inquiry into the Quality of the Educational Experience Offered to 3 and 4 Year Olds*. London: HMSO.

Faulkner, D. and Coates, E. A. (2013). Early Childhood Policy and Practice in England: Twenty Years of Change. *International Journal of Early Years Education*, 21 (2–3), 244–63.

Fisher, J. (2010). *Moving on to Key Stage 1: Improving Transition from the Early Years Foundation Stage*. Maidenhead: Open University Press.

Hall, K. (2010). *Loris Malaguzzi and the Reggio Emilia Approach*. London: Continuum.

Harrison, B. H. (2009). *Seeking a Role: The United Kingdom 1951–1970*. Oxford: Oxford University Press.

HM Treasury (2003). *Every Child Matters*. [online] Available at: http://webarchive.national archives.gov.uk/20130401151715/http://www.education.gov.uk/publications/eOrdering-Download/DfES10812004.pdf [Accessed 20 March 2017].

Iorio, J. M. and Parnall, W. (eds) (2015). *Rethinking Readiness in Early Childhood Education: Implications for Policy and Practice*. New York: Palgrave Macmillan.

Martlew, J., Stephen, C. and Ellis, J. (2011). Play in the Primary School Classroom? The Experience of Teachers Supporting Children's Learning through a New Pedagogy. *Early Years*, *31*(1): 71–83.

Ministry of Education (1996). *Te Whāriki Early Childhood Curriculum*. Wellington, NZ: Learning Media.

Paat, Y. F. (2013). Working with immigration children and their families: An application of Bronfenbrenner's Ecological Systems Theory. *Journal of Human Behaviour in the Social Environment*, *23*(8): 954–66.

Qualifications and Curriculum Authority (QCA) (2000). *Curriculum Guidance for the Foundation Stage*. London: QCA.

Rogoff, B. (2003). *The Cultural Nature of Human Development*. Oxford: Oxford University Press.

Simkins, T. (2013). Governance of Education in the United Kingdom: Convergence or Divergence? *Local Government Studies*, *40*(6): 986–1002.

Smidt, S. (2013). *Introducing Malaguzzi: Exploring the Life and Work of Reggio Emilia's Founding Father*. London: Routledge.

United Nations Children's Fund (Unicef) (2002). *A World Fit for Children (WFFC)*. New York: Unicef. [online] Available at: www.unicef.org/bangladesh/wffc-en_main.pdf [Accessed 8 June 2017].

United Nations Children's Fund (Unicef) (2012). *School Readiness: A Conceptual Framework*. New York: Unicef.

Walsh, G., Sproule, L., McGuinness, C., Trew, K., et al. (2011). Playful Structure: A Novel Image of Early Years Pedagogy for Primary School Classrooms. *Early Years*, *31*(2): 107–19.

WORKING WITH FAMILIES AND PROFESSIONALS FROM OTHER AGENCIES

BY HELOISE MACONOCHIE AND JILL BRANCH

I wish I had this chapter for multiple modules I have completed previously!

I really liked the continual links to policy, theory and practice and I thought all of the reflection and action points were very engaging and interactive. I like how, for one of the activities, you can work with others to complete it. This will allow you to think critically about the activity and work in partnership, which is one of the key messages within this chapter. Similarly, I thought the case study on making a joint referral was really interesting and allowed me to see how this translates into practice. The activity linked to the case study has helped me to develop my own practice and think critically if I were faced with this situation myself as a practitioner.

In other books when key terms and definitions are not clear, it can result in the rest of the chapter being confusing. However, this chapter clearly illustrates key terms and definitions which I find really helpful in understanding the different concepts.

ALICE UNWIN
BA (HONS) EARLY CHILDHOOD STUDIES
SHEFFIELD HALLAM UNIVERSITY

 learning outcomes

By actively reading this chapter and engaging with the material, you will be able to:

- explain what is meant by 'family' and 'working with others'
- give reasons for why practitioners work in partnership with parents/carers, children and other professionals, with reference to theory, policy and research evidence
- identify some of the challenges of partnership working
- critically reflect on partnership working as espoused in policy and as enacted in practice.

INTRODUCTION

Working with families and collaborating with other professionals are key components of professional practice across the early childhood sector. Practitioners from health, social care and education are all expected to develop effective **partnerships** with parents/carers, as well as work together with professionals from other disciplinary backgrounds, with the aim of improving outcomes for children and their families. This chapter explores the nature, importance and challenges of partnership working, particularly with regards to **family** involvement in education, the Family–Nurse Partnership programme, safeguarding and supporting disabled children.

WHAT IS MEANT BY 'FAMILY'?

Before early childhood students and practitioners begin their work with families, it is essential that they consider what is meant by this construct. As outlined in Chapter 8, every family and child is unique, and it is important that professionals acknowledge and respect this diversity. Knitzer (1997) stresses the need to develop '**cultural competence**' when working with families. This involves delivering services to families in a way that is respectful of their cultural values and traditions. Increasingly, practitioners are aware of the need to develop more inclusive definitions of 'family' than the traditional minority world notion of the nuclear family (often defined as 'mum, dad and 2.4 kids'). At its simplest, the family is a basic social unit typically consisting of one or more adults together with the children they care for. However, definitions of 'family' vary across time, and across cultures and social norms. Bernardes (1997) suggests that in this postmodern era family relationships are characterised by choice, freedom, diversity, ambivalence and fluidity. He suggests that we can no longer think of the family as a fixed or static structure, and instead we should talk of '**family practices**'.

reflection point 17.1

Make a list of different family groupings you are aware of, e.g. blended families, adoptive families:

- Why is it important that early childhood professionals develop cultural sensitivity to different family configurations, practices and values and bring this into their work with children and their carers?

WHAT IS MEANT BY 'WORKING WITH OTHERS'?

Another aspect of early childhood education and care (ECEC) is the ability to work with professionals from other disciplines to plan and implement appropriate interventions with young children and their families. Professionals can come from a range of **agencies** that are either external to the ECEC setting (for example, a speech and language therapist visiting a child who attends a preschool) or who are co-located within the same setting (for example, a family support worker and early years teacher working in the same children's centre). Collaboration between professionals, and between professionals and parents, is vital in supporting children's learning and development both at home and in the ECEC setting or school. This is important for all children, including disabled children, and children whose families require additional support. For example, the **Special Educational Needs and Disability (SEND) Code of Practice** (DfE/DoH, 2015) states that practitioners may need to 'liaise with professionals or agencies beyond the setting' (para 5.54) and that this should be done 'with the parents' agreement' (para 5.39). The aim of professionals working in partnership is to ensure comprehensive, holistic and consistent approaches to children's care and education (Flottman et al., 2011).

action point 17.1

Work with others to draw up a glossary explaining the roles of a range of professionals from health, social care and education who work with children aged 0–8 and their families, e.g. clinical psychologists, portage home visitors:

- How could this knowledge inform your practice with children and families?
- What were the benefits and challenges of working with others to complete this activity?

THEORETICAL RATIONALE

Bronfenbrenner's (1979) ecological theory (explained in Chapter 1) provides a rationale for working in partnership with parents and others. He suggested that the 'developmental potential' of a child's participation in two or more settings or 'microsystems' (such as home and early childhood service) is enhanced when there are shared goals and supportive interactions between these microsystems. These interactions (for example, between parent and practitioner) are what Bronfenbrenner referred to as the 'mesosystem'. Thus, a strong partnership between parents/carers and professionals, built on good communication and shared planning, can have a positive influence on a child's development. For example, professionals can draw on parents' '**funds of knowledge**' (González et al., 2005) about their child's interests, abilities, routines and health care needs and incorporate this into their planning and provision. Likewise, practitioners can work with parents/carers to develop shared learning goals for children and provide families with resources to support learning at home. Strategies such as these ensure continuity of care, and progression in learning, between home and setting.

To optimise effectiveness, partnership working needs to be reflected at all levels of the ecological system (see Table 17.1). Whereas partnership with families comes to the fore at the meso level, partnership with other professionals, and between different agencies, is more evident at the exo and macro levels. Although the child does not participate directly in these **distal** levels, according to Bronfenbrenner, what happens here also affects children's development.

Table 17.1 Applying Bronfenbrenner's ecological theory to partnership working

Level	Type of Partnership Working
Microsystem	The child as partner, developing within the context of different microsystems: within the family, in their early childhood service/school, in their local community, within their peer group
Mesosystem	ECEC practitioners working in partnership with parents for the benefit of the child and his/her family: • E.g. the connection between the child's key person or teacher and his/her family members • E.g. staff and families making story sacks for children to explore at home and at school
Exosystem	Other professionals and agencies working together to coordinate services for children and their families: • E.g. a nursery practitioner collaborating with a Reception teacher to ensure a smooth transition for a child moving from nursery to school • E.g. schools and ECEC settings developing partnerships with other agencies, businesses and the community to ensure children are healthy, safe and able to learn • E.g. multi-agency support teams working with children and families who need extra help

(Continued)

Level	Type of Partnership Working
Macrosystem	The policy context for promoting and resourcing partnership working: • E.g. *SEND, EYFS, Working Together to Safeguard Children* • E.g. the Department of Health and the Department of Education working in partnership with each other to establish integrated systems of assessment and care for children and their families
Chronosystem	Partnership working taking place across different system levels over the lifespan of a person

PARTNERSHIP WITH FAMILIES

Although working with families is often referred to as 'partnership working', a variety of other terms are also used. Phrases such as 'parental involvement', 'family engagement', 'parental participation' and 'partnership with parents' are common. These terms are sometimes used interchangeably, however they convey slightly different meanings. 'Parental involvement' and 'family engagement' often refer to the involvement of families in their children's education. This can include parents/carers participating in the life of the early childhood setting or school, for example through volunteering, accompanying children on field trips or joining the parent–teacher association. However, this is different from 'parental participation' in which families participate in decision making or 'parental partnership' that presupposes seeing families as equal partners with professionals in addressing mutual concerns. Epstein's (2011) typology of parental involvement helps to distinguish between different types of partnership working with families:

* *parenting* – professionals assisting families with parenting skills and family support; parents/carers assisting professionals in understanding their family background, their child's interests and needs, and goals for their children
* *communicating* – creating two-way communication between setting and home
* *volunteering* – involving families as volunteers and enabling volunteers to support children and the setting
* *learning at home* – providing information and ideas to families about how to support their child's learning at home
* *decision making* – including families as participants in ECEC/school decisions, governance and advocacy activities
* *collaborating with the community* – coordinating resources and services in the local community to strengthen schools/ECEC settings, families, and children's learning.

Epstein's model can be used as a tool for settings and schools to evaluate and develop their work with families. Indeed, Brunton and Thornton (2010: 3) describe true partnership as being 'positive mutually respectful relationships between parents and early years practitioners'. This requires a shift from privileging the practitioner's expert knowledge to valuing knowledge generated jointly. A useful definition of partnership working is provided by the World Health

Organization (2009: 2), which states that 'partnership is a collaborative relationship between two or more parties based on trust, equality and mutual understanding for the achievement of a specified goal. Partnerships involve risks as well as benefits, making shared accountability critical.'

This implies sharing power, experiences, knowledge and skills to enable joint decision making and collaboration. However, as this definition suggests, partnership working involves potential risks such as loss of autonomy, conflicts of interest and a drain on resources (for example, it can be time-consuming). Nevertheless, the potential benefits include enhancing children's welfare, learning and development, strengthening families and improving ECEC settings.

BENEFITS AND CHALLENGES OF WORKING WITH FAMILIES

The research literature abounds with empirical studies of partnership with families, in child and family health nursing (e.g. Fowler et al., 2012), family support programmes (e.g. Van Houte et al., 2013), social work services (e.g. Roose et al., 2013), child protection processes (e.g. Alfandari, 2017) and in children's education and early childhood services (e.g. Nutbrown et al., 2005). Many of these studies have demonstrated the benefits of practitioners supporting families to be involved in their children's health care, welfare, learning and development. Research studies also highlight the difficulties of realising partnership with families, particularly in child welfare practice, given the imbalances of power so inherent in professional interventions in the private sphere of family life (Van Houte et al., 2013).

In the area of education, the Rumbold Report (DES, 1990) was particularly influential in promoting the idea that parents are their children's first and most enduring educators. The next section outlines some of the benefits and challenges of home–school partnerships as it pertains to parental involvement in early childhood education.

FAMILY INVOLVEMENT IN EDUCATION

Research spanning the last 40 years or so suggests that high levels of family involvement in children's education are associated with improved cognitive, language, literacy, social and emotional outcomes (Ryan and Bronfenbrenner, 1974; Fan and Chen, 2001; Sylva et al., 2004; Fantuzzo et al., 2004; Loughlin-Presnal and Bierman, 2017). Longitudinal studies, notably EPPE (Sylva et al., 1999; Melhuish et al., 2001) and REPEY (Siraj-Blatchford et al., 2002), argue that when families are involved in learning activities at home (such as reading, singing nursery rhymes, playing with letters and numbers) this is strongly associated with better cognitive achievement. Indeed, the EPPE study concluded that what parents/carers do with their young children makes a real difference to their development and is more important than who their parents are (i.e. than their socio-economic status or educational level). Since family involvement is critical to children's attainment, particularly for low-income families, schools and ECEC settings are increasingly aware of the need to support families in developing the **home learning environment**. Furthermore, REPEY demonstrated that one of the marks of high-quality settings is that they encourage a continuity of learning between the setting and the home, leading to consistently better developmental outcomes for children. This is achieved through two-way partnership working, with families being encouraged to participate in children's learning, and practitioners incorporating the contributions of families into their own work with children.

Based on this and other research evidence, family involvement is heavily promoted in policy documents related to the care and education of young children. For example, partnership with parents is a key principle in the Early Years Foundation Stage (EYFS) (DfE, 2017). However, several scholars have highlighted that there is a difference between **policy as espoused** and policy as experienced. For example, Biddulph et al. (2003) caution that the approaches taken by some settings may espouse the ideals of partnership working, but in reality are more about controlling parents and promoting 'the values of staff at the expense of important local cultural values' (p. 11). Hughes and MacNaughton's (2000) analysis of family involvement studies found that a consistent problem arose 'from the constant "othering" of parental knowledge by staff' (p. 242), where parental knowledge was seen as of secondary importance, or even deficient, compared to the knowledge of staff. Critical reflection on practice can help early childhood practitioners to guard against this.

In a number of research studies, parents, including fathers, report that there are other challenges to their involvement in children's learning. These include:

- work commitments, social and economic pressures (Peters et al., 2007)
- lack of skills in knowing how to support children's learning; language barriers (for parents for whom English is not a first language); and low levels of parental literacy/numeracy (Harris and Goodall, 2007)
- parents feeling intimidated in school and preschool settings due to their own experience of education (Harris and Goodall, 2007)
- the perception that family involvement programmes are largely geared towards women (Bayley et al., 2009).

Goodall and Vorhaus (2011) argue that if settings are to overcome these barriers, practitioners need to demonstrate cultural sensitivity, work with parents to conduct a 'needs analysis', which includes understanding what parents already do with their children, establish mutual priorities and offer specific guidance and support to families, in an inclusive and non-judgemental way.

 reflection point 17.2

Look at a copy of the EYFS and the role of the Key Person (DfE, 2017):

1. How does the EYFS in general, and the Key Person in particular, support working in partnership with families and other professionals?
2. How does this compare with what you have observed in practice?
3. How could you promote working with families who appear reluctant to engage?

CHILDREN AS PARTNERS

Just as viewing parents as partners in children's care and learning is important, so too is viewing children as partners. However, in practice, the voice of the child may be lost as parents/carers, teachers, social workers and others discuss, plan and make decisions about matters that affect children. Tomlinson (2008) argues that there is a danger that the child is encompassed under the term 'family', with the emphasis being on the family as a whole, rather than seeking children's perspectives alongside those of adults. One way of involving young children as partners in their care, protection and education is by listening to their views and observing them (for example, through using methods from the Mosaic Approach, as discussed in Chapter 23) and in supporting them to participate in decision making (see Chapter 10). Maconochie's (2013) research provides examples of how practitioners from one children's centre in England worked with disabled children to ascertain their views about their care, therapy and education. Children worked with practitioners to create 'visual review books' which were used to inform their review meetings and individual education plans.

Of course, it is also vital to work in partnership with children in order to protect and safeguard them effectively. Research into child protection assessments highlights that insufficient attention has been given to listening to what children say, how they look and how they behave (Broadhurst et al., 2010). Therefore, professionals from all sectors need to develop the skills to be able to collaborate not just with parents/carers and with professionals from other agencies, but also with children themselves. This is reflected in policy documents such as *Working Together to Safeguard Children* (DfE, 2015) (explained further below and in Chapter 13).

 —— spotlight on practice 17.1 ═══════════════

Family-Nurse Partnership

The Family-Nurse Partnership (FNP) works with young, first-time mothers (aged 19 or under), partnering them with a specially trained nurse who visits them regularly, from early pregnancy until their child is 2. The FNP is a targeted early intervention programme that was introduced to the UK in 2006, having originated in the USA. Since the 1970s the US programme has been tested in several randomised controlled trials (RCTs) and has demonstrated significant short- and long-term benefits for children and their mothers (Olds, 2006). In the UK, the programme works alongside the midwifery service until after the birth of the child and replaces universal health-visiting services until the child is 2 years of age. Once the child is aged 2 years, the family is integrated into health-visiting services. The FNP consists of 64 intensive home visits structured around three core aims:

1. To improve pregnancy health and behaviours – e.g. a reduction in using cigarettes, alcohol and illegal substances; greater intervals between first and subsequent births; preparing emotionally for the arrival of the baby.

(Continued)

2. To improve child health and development outcomes - e.g. breastfeeding; providing coaching/modelling to enable parents to engage in positive parenting behaviours; home-learning activities leading to a reduction in language delays and behavioural difficulties.
3. To improve economic self-sufficiency - e.g. finishing school, finding maternal employment, increasing paternal presence in the household.

In order to work in partnership with families, the FNP is based on the following principles:

- voluntary - mothers choose to enrol in the programme
- client-centred - the nurse constantly adapts to ensure the visit and materials are relevant and valued by the parent
- relational - the relationship between the nurse and mother is the primary tool used for learning and growth
- strengths-based - nurses work from a credit, rather than deficit, view of the mother, building on her knowledge, strengths and successes.

---

 reflection point 17.3

How could an attitude of paternalism (e.g. 'professionals know best') threaten principles of partnership working, such as those advocated by the FNP?

PARTNERSHIP WITH OTHERS

When it comes to agencies and professionals from different disciplinary backgrounds working together, a number of terms are used. Sometimes terms are used interchangeably, under the general umbrella of 'partnership working'; at other times, researchers attempt to provide separate definitions. Owens (2010) distinguishes among:

- *collaboration* – agencies working together to pursue a common goal while also pursuing their own organisational goals
- *inter-agency working* – more than one agency working together in a formal way; this can be at a strategic or an operational level
- *multi-agency working* – more than one agency working with a client, not necessarily jointly, either concurrently or sequentially, with joint planning
- *joined-up working* – deliberate and coordinated planning and working across multiple agency policies and practices
- *integrated working* – agencies working together within a single, often new, organisational structure.

Sometimes these different models are depicted as a continuum: from agencies collaborating on an ad hoc basis whilst maintaining their distinct role at one end, to integrated services that no longer see separate identity as significant at the other end (Whittington, 2003). An example of integrated working was seen in the establishment of Sure Start Children's Centres (SSCCs) in England from 2006. SSCCs were created to provide integrated health, care and education for young children and their families. Professionals from different backgrounds were often co-located within children's centre hubs, enabling parents to access a range of services in the same place, and fostering greater partnership working between different professional teams. However, since 2010, with the removal of ring-fencing for children's centres, and cuts to early intervention funding, many specialist services have been removed, or centres have closed entirely. Despite these policy and funding changes, the 2014 Children and Families Act (CFA) retains a strong commitment to multi-agency working. Indeed, whichever model is employed, policy and practice over the last three decades has sought to move away from 'silo' working – where agencies and professionals work in isolation and do not share information and knowledge with each other – to that of different professionals and agencies working together. This way of working is seen as important for responding to the needs of, and supporting, the best outcomes for children and families, particularly those who are facing multiple challenges (Siraj-Blatchford and Siraj-Blatchford, 2010). The next two subsections and case study examine this in relation to safeguarding and supporting disabled children.

WORKING TOGETHER TO SAFEGUARD CHILDREN

The goal of agencies and professionals working together was reflected in the 1989 Children Act, particularly in relation to safeguarding and child protection. This was given fresh impetus in the 2004 Children Act, following the death of Victoria Climbié, which stressed the need for improved collaboration and integrated working (see Chapter 13). A failure to share information between agencies was identified as significant in the circumstances leading to Victoria's death. The **statutory guidance** for England, *Working Together to Safeguard Children* (DfE, 2015), states that inter-disciplinary collaboration is critical to ensure that children are adequately protected, since no single professional can have a full picture of a child's needs and circumstances. *Working Together* also stresses the need to identify children and families who would benefit from **early help**, including disabled children, young carers, children showing signs of engaging in anti-social or criminal behaviour, children experiencing challenging home circumstances or trauma, and children at risk of abuse and neglect. Where children would benefit from coordinated support from more than one agency (e.g. education, housing, health), there should be an early help inter-agency assessment, such as the **Common Assessment Framework**, outlining the action to be taken and services to be provided. Hence, collaboration between different professionals and agencies is essential for effective identification, assessment and service provision.

WORKING TOGETHER FOR DISABLED CHILDREN

Professional partnerships are also particularly important for disabled children. This is the case not only in terms of safeguarding, since it is known that disabled children are amongst those at greatest risk of all types of abuse (NSPCC, 2014), but also on account of their impairments. The legislative framework in the UK has promoted **interprofessional** collaboration in relation to special educational needs and disability since the Warnock Report (HMSO, 1978), which led to the Education Act 1981. Inter-service collaboration has been given further emphasis in the CFA 2014 and SEND Code of Practice (DfE/DoH, 2015). Under the CFA, disabled children have the right to coordinated assessment, planning and provision. Local authorities must ensure 'that services work together where this promotes children and young people's wellbeing or improves the quality of special educational provision' (Section 25 CFA). Local authorities and health bodies are also required to jointly plan and commission education, health and social care services for children and young people with SEN or disabilities (Section 26 CFA). Thus, collaboration between services has to occur at a strategic as well as an operational level.

Collaboration between professionals on the ground may look different depending on the type of need and provision offered. Children with complex impairments may access several services, as set out in their **Education, Health and Care (EHC) Plan** (see Chapter 10), and require the support of multiple professionals. For example, in addition to family members, a young child with mixed cerebral palsy could be supported by:

1. the Key Person in her early childhood setting/school
2. a Special Educational Needs Coordinator (SENCO)
3. an early years teacher
4. an Early Years Inclusion Advisor/Area SENCO
5. an educational psychologist
6. an occupational therapist
7. a physiotherapist
8. a speech therapist
9. a paediatrician
10. a health visitor
11. an audiologist
12. an orthopaedic surgeon.

Some of these professionals could be based in the child's ECEC setting (e.g. 1–3 in the above list), whereas others may come from other organisations based in the community, such as local authority support services (e.g. 4–5), child development centres (e.g. 6–9) or clinics and hospitals (e.g. 10–12). Liaising with this number of professionals can be exhausting for parents/carers and can make interprofessional collaboration challenging. Some professionals will work with the child directly in their home or ECEC setting, whilst others may provide specialist resources and training to the staff in the child's ECEC setting, and for other professionals it may be necessary for the family to travel to their base of operation in order to access services. The role of a '**lead professional**' (often the SENCO) is therefore key in ensuring that the input needed for the EHC Plan is coordinated, that the provision of services and support is joined up and that information is shared between the child, family, professionals and agencies. The lead professional may also convene the multi-agency review meetings with all the professionals involved and family members (which may include the child themselves).

 case study 17.1

Making a Joint Referral

In my role as a health visitor, I (Jill) recently visited a baby at home who was just under 12 months of age, to assess her health and development. Prior to the visit, her mother had been asked to complete an 'Ages and Stages ASQ-3' questionnaire on the baby's physical and social and emotional development. The baby was sitting on a blanket on the floor surrounded by toys. The completed questionnaire indicated the baby's development to be age-appropriate and did not highlight any concerns. The baby's mother stated that the baby attended a local nursery four days per week whilst she went to work.

I assessed the baby's development and noted concerns in all aspects of her development – gross motor, fine motor, communication, problem solving and personal and social. The baby's mother was not aware of any problems the baby may have and agreed for me to consult with the nursery as to their view on the baby's development. Nursery said they felt the baby's development was satisfactory but when I pointed out my concerns they agreed with the findings. A joint referral to the hospital was made in order for the baby to be assessed fully by the specialist. The baby was found to have global developmental delay and needed specialist intervention.

As a result, a care plan directed by the specialist was formulated for the nursery to work with the baby on a day-to-day basis in partnership with her family, and the baby began to make small significant improvements in her development.

1. Working in partnership with families and other professionals requires sensitivity. What were the sensitive issues Jill had to navigate in this situation to ensure the baby and her family received the appropriate services and support they needed?
2. List the steps you would need to take if you suspected a child was in need of assessment and additional/specialist support:

   (a) for a child under 5 not attending an ECEC setting
   (b) for a child under 5 attending an ECEC setting
   (c) for a child over 5 attending school.

(The SEND resources on the book's website can assist you with this.)

BENEFITS AND CHALLENGES OF WORKING WITH OTHER PROFESSIONALS

Evidence of the effectiveness of inter-agency collaboration, in terms of improving outcomes for children, is currently limited to a few examples (Barnes and Melhuish, 2017). There is considerably more evidence of the process of inter-agency working, such as perceptions from professionals about the benefits of integrated working, than there is out-come data. Abbott et al.'s (2005) study of the impact of multi-agency working on children with complex impairments noted that the health needs of the children were improved. Pettit's (2003) evaluation reported that joint working between Children and Adolescent Mental Health Services (CAMHS) and schools led to measurable improvements in children's behaviour. The EPPE research concluded that integrated centres that fully combine educa-tion and childcare were more effective than others in promoting positive cognitive and social-emotional outcomes for children, particularly disadvantaged children (Melhuish et al., 2001). Evidence from the National Evaluation of Sure Start also found that partnerships were associated with improvements in child and family outcomes (Melhuish et al., 2007).

In their review of the research literature, Barnes and Melhuish (2017) summarise the fol-lowing barriers to partnership working: geographical boundaries between agencies; power, status and pay inequalities between professionals; differences in professional knowledge, training and disciplinary cultures; resource limitations (such as time and money); lack of clarity of purpose for integration; and a failure to agree partnership outcomes. They draw on Atkinson et al.'s (2007) review to conclude that establishing effective partnerships depends on the following factors:

- clarifying roles and responsibilities
- securing commitment at all hierarchical levels (practitioners and managers)
- valuing diversity and recognition of individual expertise
- engendering trust and mutual respect
- fostering understanding, for example through joint training
- effective communication and information sharing
- developing a shared purpose with joint goals
- effective planning and organisation with clearly defined structures and shared protocols.

SUMMARY

- Notions of 'family' vary across time, cultures and social norms. Early childhood profession-als need to develop cultural competence in working with families. Another key principle of early childhood practice is the need for professionals from a range of backgrounds to work together to achieve positive outcomes for children and families.
- Ecological theory suggests that strong partnerships between families and professionals at the meso level, coupled with inter-agency collaboration at the exo and macro levels, can have a positive influence on children's development.
- The benefits of working in partnership include safeguarding children, enhancing their learning and development, strengthening families and improving ECEC services.
- Some of the challenges of partnership working include disparities in power and status, differences in knowledge, training and disciplinary background, and organisational bound-aries. This can mean that there is a difference between partnership working as espoused in policy and as enacted in practice.

 online resources

Make sure to visit https://study.sagepub.com/fitzgeraldandmaconochie for selected SAGE videos (with questions), SAGE journal articles, links to external sources and flashcards.

FURTHER READING

Walker, G. (2018). *Working Together for Children: A Critical Introduction to Multi-Agency Working*, 2nd edn. London: Bloomsbury.

This text outlines principles and frameworks for multi-agency assessment and practice, including information sharing, safeguarding children and working with parents.

Wilson, T. (2016). *Working with Parents, Carers and Families in the Early Years*. Abingdon: Routledge.

This book summarises recent legislation and provides research evidence and practical advice from practitioners and parents to support partnership work with families.

REFERENCES

Abbott, D., Watson, D. and Townsley, R. (2005). The Proof of the Pudding: What Difference Does Multi-Agency Working Make to Families with Disabled Children with Complex Health Care Needs? *Child and Family Social Work*, *10*(3): 229–38.

Alfandari, R. (2017). Partnership with Parents in Child Protection: A Systems Approach to Evaluate Reformative Developments in Israel. *British Journal of Social Work*, *47*(4): 1061–77.

Atkinson, M., Jones, M. and Lamont, E. (2007). *Multi-agency Working and its Implications for Practice: A Review of the Literature*. Reading: Centre for British Teachers.

Barnes, J. and Melhuish, E. (2017). *Inter-agency Coordination of Services for Children and their Families: Initial Literature Review*. Utrecht: ISOTIS Project.

Bayley, J., Wallace, L. M. and Choudhry, K. (2009). Fathers and Parenting Programmes: Barriers and Best Practice. *Community Practitioner*, *82*(4): 28–31.

Bernardes, J. (1997). *Family Studies: An Introduction*. London: Routledge.

Biddulph, F., Biddulph, J. and Bidddulph, C. (2003). *The Complexity of Community and Family Influences on Children's Achievement in New Zealand: Best Evidence Synthesis*. Wellington, NZ: Ministry of Education.

Broadhurst, K., White, S., Fish, S., Munro, E., Fletcher, K. and Lincoln, H. (2010). *Ten Pitfalls and How to Avoid Them: What Research Tells Us*. London: NSPCC.

Bronfenbrenner, U. (1979). *The Ecology of Human Development*. London: Harvard University Press.

Brunton, P. and Thornton, L. (2010). *The Parent Partnership Toolkit for Early Years*. London: Optimus Education.

Department of Education and Science (DES) (1990). *The Rumbold Report: The Report of the Committee of Inquiry into the Quality of the Educational Experience Offered to 3 and 4 Year Olds*. London: HMSO.

Department for Education (DfE) (2015). *Working Together to Safeguard Children: A Guide to Inter-agency Working to Safeguard and Promote the Welfare of Children*. London: The Stationery Office.

Department for Education (DfE) (2017). Statutory Framework for the Early Years Foundation Stage. [online] Available at: www.foundationyears.org.uk/files/2017/03/EYFS_STATUTORY_FRAMEWORK_2017.pdf [Accessed 8 August 2017].

Department for Education/Department of Health (DfE/DoH) (2015). Special Educational Needs and Disability Code of Practice: 0 to 25 years. [online] Available at: www.gov.uk/government/publications/send-code-of-practice-0-to-25 [Accessed 29 November 2017].

Epstein, J. L. (2011). *School, Family, and Community Partnerships: Preparing Educators and Improving Schools*, 2nd edn. Philadelphia, PA: Westview Press.

Fan, X. and Chen, M. (2001). Parental Involvement and Students' Academic Achievement: A Meta-Analysis. *Psychology Review*, *13*(1): 1–22.

Fantuzzo, J., McWayne, C., Perry, M. and Childs, S. (2004). Multiple Dimensions of Family Involvement and their Relations to Behavioral and Learning Competencies for Urban, Low-income Children. *School Psychology Review*, *33*(4): 467–80.

Flottman, R., McKernan, A. and Tayler, C. (2011). *Victoria Early Years and Development Evidence Paper: Partnerships with Professionals*. Melbourne: Department of Education and Early Childhood Development.

Fowler, C., Rossiter, C., Bigsby, M., Hopwood, N., Lee, A. and Dunston, R. (2012). Working in Partnership with Parents: The Experience and Challenge of Practice Innovation in Child and Family Health Nursing. *Journal of Clinical Nursing*, *21*(21–22): 3306–14.

González, N., Moll, L. and Amanti, C. (2005). *Funds of Knowledge: Theorizing Practices in Households, Communities and Classrooms*. Mahway, NJ: Erlbaum.

Goodall, J. and Vorhaus, J. (2011). *Review of Best Practice in Parental Engagement*. London: DfE.

Harris, A. and Goodall, J. (2007). *Engaging Parents in Raising Achievement: Do Parents Know they Matter?* London: Specialist Schools and Academies Trust.

Her Majesty's Stationery Office (HMSO) (1978). The Warnock Report: Report of the Committee of Enquiry into the Education of Handicapped Children and Young People. [online] Available at: www.educationengland.org.uk/documents/warnock/warnock1978.html [Accessed 4 November 2017].

Hughes, P. and MacNaughton, G. (2000). Consensus, Dissensus or Community: The Politics of Parent Involvement in Early Childhood Education. *Contemporary Issues in Early Childhood*, *1*(3): 241–58.

Knitzer, J. (1997). Service Integration for Children and Families: Lessons and Questions. In: R. J. Illback, C. T. Cobb and H. M. Joseph (eds), *Integrated Services for Children and Families: Opportunities for Psychological Practice*. Washington, DC: American Psychological Association, pp. 3–21.

Loughlin-Presnal, J. E. and Bierman, K. L. (2017). Promoting Parent Academic Expectations Predicts Improved School Outcomes for Low-Income Children Entering Kindergarten. *Journal of School Psychology*, *62*: 67–80.

Maconochie, H. (2013). Young Children's Participation in a Sure Start Children's Centre, Sheffield Hallam University. [online] Available at: http://shura.shu.ac.uk/7437 [Accessed 2 July 2018].

Melhuish, E., Sylva, C., Sammons, P., Siraj-Blatchford, I. and Taggart, B. (2001). *Social, Behavioural and Cognitive Development at 3–4 years in Relation to Family Background: The Effective Provision of Pre-school Education (EPPE)*. London: DfEE.

Melhuish, E., Belsky, J., Anning, A., et al. (2007). Variation in Community Intervention Programmes and Consequences for Children and Families: The Example of Sure Start Local Programmes. *Journal of Child Psychology and Psychiatry*, *48*(6): 543–51.

National Society for the Prevention of Cruelty to Children (NSPCC) (2014). We Have the Right to be Safe. In: *Protecting Disabled Children from Abuse*. London: NSPCC.

Nutbrown, C., Hannon, P. and Morgan, A. (2005). *Early Literacy Work with Parents: Policy, Practice and Research*. London: Sage.

Olds, D. (2006). The Nurse Family Partnership: An Evidence-Based Preventative Intervention. *Infant Mental Health Journal*, 27(1): 5–25.

Owens, S. (2010). *An Introductory Guide to the Key Terms and Interagency Initiatives in Use in the Children's Services Committees in Ireland*. Dublin: Centre for Effective Services.

Peters, M. K., Seeds, K., Goldstein, A. and Coleman, N. (2007). *Parental Involvement in Children's Education*. London: DCSF.

Pettit, B. (2003). *Effective Joint Working between CAMHS and Schools*. RR412. London: DES.

Roose, R., Roets, G., Van Houte, S., Vandenhole, W. and Reynaert, D. (2013). From Parental Engagement to the Engagement of Social Work Services: Discussing Reductionist and Democratic Forms of Partnership with Families. *Child and Family Social Work*, 18(4): 449–57.

Ryan, S. and Bronfenbrenner, U. (1974). *A Report on Longitudinal Evaluations of Preschool Programs Vols 1 and 2: Is Early Intervention Effective?* Washington, DC: DHEW.

Siraj-Blatchford, I. and Siraj-Blatchford, J. (2010). *Improving Development Outcomes for Children through Effective Practice in Integrating Early Years Services*. London: C4EO.

Siraj-Blatchford, I., Sylva, K., Muttock, S., Gilden, R. and Bell, S. (2002). *Researching Effective Pedagogy in the Early Years (REPEY)*. London: DES.

Sylva, K., Melhuish, E., Sammons, P., Siraj-Blatchford, I. and Taggart, B. (1999). *The Effective Provision of Pre-School Education (EPPE): Technical Paper 1 – An Introduction to the EPPE Project*. London: Institute of Education, University of London.

Sylva, K., Melhuish, E., Sammons, P., Siraj-Blatchford, I. and Taggart, B. (2004). *Effective Provision of Pre-School Education (EPPE) Project: Final Report*. London: DfES.

Tomlinson, P. (2008). Assessing the Needs of Traumatized Children to Improve Outcomes. *Journal of Social Work Practice*, *22*(3): 359–74.

Van Houte, S., Bradt, L. and Vandenbroeck, M. (2013). Professionals' Understanding of Partnership with Parents in the Context of Family Support Programmes. *Child and Family Social Work*, *20*(1): 116–24.

Whittington, C. (2003). Collaboration and Partnership in Context. In: J. Weinstein, C. Whittington and T. Leiba (eds), *Collaboration in Social Work Practice*. London: Jessica Kingsley, pp. 13–38.

World Health Organization (WHO). (2009). Building a Working Definition of Partnership: African Partnerships for Patient Safety. [online] Available at: www.who.int/patientsafety/implementation/apps/resources/defining_partnerships-apps.pdf [Accessed 29 November 2017].

CHILDHOOD IN A GLOBAL CONTEXT

BY MONICA EDWARDS

This chapter has given me an understanding of how children and the childhoods they experience are affected by globalisation, international organisations, migration and communication in a global context. The knowledge I have gained through reading about the topics in this chapter will support me in my studies of children and childhood.

The chapter case study looks at conditional cash transfer schemes used in low- and middle-income countries as an incentive for low-income families to send their children to school.

In practice, I have seen that some children frequently do not attend school. It made me think about how high-income countries incentivise families to make sure their children attend school regularly, and the kinds of schemes that are run.

I found this chapter very informative and engaging.

SARAH DELISSEN
BA (HONS) EARLY YEARS AND CHILDHOOD STUDIES
MANCHESTER METROPOLITAN UNIVERSITY

learning outcomes

By actively reading this chapter and engaging with the material, you will be able to:

- recognise some of the ways globalisation affects the lives of young children in the majority and minority worlds
- explain how international organisations (IOs) and non-governmental organisations (NGOs) influence the lives of children in the majority world
- examine the role of young children in the international migration process
- debate how global communication shapes young children's lives.

INTRODUCTION

Globalisation refers to the way systems such as trade, travel and communication interconnect the world. As a result, events happening in one nation can affect events in distant nations; globalisation is visible at all levels of Bronfenbrenner's ecological system (see Chapter 1 for an explanation) and shapes children's experiences. It is not new, natural or inevitable; it relies on political and technological ideas and is sustained by economic processes and organisations far beyond most people's lives. Yet the global population, particularly children, feel the cultural and environmental impacts of globalisation every day. This is true both for children living in **majority world** nations and those in the Western **minority world**.

The scholarly study of early childhood is characterised by the recognition that just as young children are different from one another, so are the childhoods they experience. This chapter considers how different elements of globalisation influence contemporary childhoods. Studying childhoods in a global context is important because it helps reveal how apparently distant macro systems such as **international organisations (IOs)** can affect the local micro-level experiences of young children, their families and communities. In addition, the study of globalisation helps demonstrate the ways inequalities across different countries create pluralities of childhood experiences.

It is important for early years professionals to be aware of and knowledgeable about childhood in a global context because it influences the early childhood education and care policies that governments put into place at home and when working with other nations or international organisations. However, being aware of what is happening globally is also important for the practice of early childhood and education professionals within nations, as they work with children who may have experienced the impact of globalisation on their lives. This chapter takes three aspects of globalisation to frame an analysis of the way global experiences represent, problematise and empower children and their childhoods:

1. The impact that international organisations and international non-governmental organisations have on children's lives in the majority world.
2. The role of young children in the international migration process.
3. Children engaging with global mass visual media.

THE IMPACT THAT INTERNATIONAL IOs AND NGOs HAVE ON CHILDREN'S LIVES IN THE MAJORITY WORLD

Some of the most powerful global institutes that operate in the macro system aim to tackle one of the greatest challenges connected to globalisation – how to reduce global inequality. Following the Second World War, two major international organisations (IOs) were founded with a view to promote and secure international economic development and prosperity between nations – the World Bank, founded in 1944, and the **United Nations** (UN), founded in 1945. Together, they play a major role in shaping global economic development to this day. These organisations have become highly influential not only in economic development but also on the actions of national governments. These large and distant organisations impact the micro-level experiences of children, particularly children in low-income majority world nations. For example, the UN leads in creating international agreements such as the Universal Declaration of Human Rights, 1948 (UN, 2017a) and the United Nations Convention on the Rights of the Child, 1989 (UN, 1989). These clarify not only a person's rights but also a government's responsibility to uphold and protect these rights, for example the rights of children with any disability to receive appropriate care and support, leading to legislation and policies that support children with special educational needs in mainstream education in the UK (HM Government, 2015).

In addition, the funding and resources that IOs provide to reduce the causes and effects of poverty and inequality influence numerous activities that national governments engage in. Babb and Chorev (2016) identify how the approaches IOs take to tackling inequality change over time and, therefore, so do the actions of governments. During the 1950s and 1960s, IOs encouraged governments in low- and middle-income countries to borrow money for large infrastructure projects such as dams and roads. In recent decades, IOs have focused money on health, and disease prevention such as AIDS and malaria prevention programmes. Yet, IOs do more than distribute money – they also research and use their expertise to create norms and values about what **international development** should look like. This has led to one of the biggest shifts in the global approach to tackling inequality. The contemporary view IOs promote is for a more coordinated, inclusive approach to international development. The result is changes to the way high-income minority world nations provide aid to lower-income majority world nations. This is most clearly seen in the 17 United Nations Sustainable Development Goals (SDGs) launched in 2015 (UN, 2017b), and prior to this the Millennium Development Goals (MDGs).

INCLUSIVE DEVELOPMENT

The 17 SDGs which have been adopted by all the world's nations are specific, statistically measurable goals aimed at promoting inclusion as part of sustained global growth. **Inclusive development** utilises human rights to challenge inequalities in wealth and opportunities that occur through globalisation, and to reduce the environmental damage resulting from global economic growth. Thus, for example, the goals include ending poverty and hunger, improving health and education and combating climate change. Through redistributing resources and power, SDGs aim to promote people's wellbeing, including the poorest and most marginalised people. They have led governments of wealthy minority world nations to donate financial aid to majority world nations, only if their governments agree to policies set out in the SDGs. These include policies that directly influence children, such as education reform promoting and protecting the education of children, particularly girls, as well as policies related to early childhood, such as seeking to increase the proportion of children accessing and completing pre-primary education. The result is that children in majority world nations experience education and health policies that directly result from the influence IOs have on their own country's government, and on the governments of wealthy nations who donate money to support these policies.

Investing in the **human capital** of individuals, particularly children, that balances global growth with supporting inclusive development is not easy (Gupta and Veglin, 2016). Economic growth that leads to increased pressure on environmental resources and risks increasing inequality is very different to economic growth that brings equitable opportunities to all communities and does not risk wasting limited environmental resources. Gupta and Veglin (2016) apply five principles of social inclusion to identify inclusive development:

1. Equitable sharing of opportunities and development
2. Recognising experiences of marginalisation in development processes
3. Ensuring minimum levels of protection for marginalised individuals and communities
4. Ensuring all benefit from development opportunities
5. Engaging marginalised communities in decision making.

These principles help measure how effective macro-level approaches such as the SDGs are in making a meaningful difference to the micro-level lives of communities and individuals, for example how policies adapt to support the health and nutrition of the increasing numbers of young children living in cities and towns across the world. One way SDGs make a difference in the micro-level is through the actions of non-governmental organisations (NGOs).

NON-GOVERNMENTAL ORGANISATIONS

Non-governmental organisations (NGOs) have become increasingly important, working with IOs such as the United Nations to challenge global inequalities. NGOs cover a mix of organisations who generally propose a service to meet the needs of a targeted community or population group in areas such as education or health, and operate under strict not-for-profit international legislation (Young and Merschrod, 2010). NGOs frequently use global communications to raise awareness and fundraise for campaigns aimed at addressing specific social problems and contributing positively to the global or national community, often becoming bridges between governments and people, even taking roles that might otherwise be the responsibility of governments. The United Nations International Children's Fund (Unicef) collaborates with numerous NGOs in countries, utilising their specific knowledge of communities and families. The NGO Committee on Unicef encourages collaboration and communication with and between these NGOs and acts as a forum for NGOs to discuss Unicef programmes and policies.

 spotlight on organisations 18.1

Unicef

In 1946 the United Nations General Assembly formed Unicef to work with children living in the aftermath of the Second World War. Today, Unicef works in 190 countries with a remit to protect the rights of children and provide children and mothers with assistance through different programmes in education, protection and emergency provision. One programme Unicef is involved in is early childhood development (Unicef, 2017). This programme combines support to parents, carers and communities on young children's nutrition, protection and stimulation. Unicef (2015) estimates that, globally, 200 million young children in majority world nations fail to reach their developmental potential by 5 years of age. This is in part due to poverty, inadequate health and nutrition services, and understanding young children's psychological and social development. Unicef engages health professionals working with women and families during pregnancy to promote early child development.

Working in partnership with NGOs on community levels, Unicef employs strategies and resources such as 'The Care for Child Development' package (Unicef, 2015) that health workers working with families can deliver. These focus on parenting programmes that teach parents about building relationships, communication, and play with young children. The package includes materials for classroom activities with parents, such as toy making and resources such as cards and posters, with advice counselling for families about coping with problems in child development.

Britto et al. (2017) note that this Unicef programme, when combined with improved maternal nutrition and health, has had positive effects on young children's cognitive and language development as well as their psychosocial and physical development. They do note, however, that programmes promoting the role of fathers need further development. When children experience harsh or neglectful parenting or when the family suffers extreme distress, they can have problems parenting when they grow up. Britto et al. (2017) identify that intensive programmes such as 'Care for Child Development', when specifically aimed at parents who experienced these conditions as children, can help reduce the likelihood of harsh or abusive parenting continuing the cycle.

 action point 18.1

Choose a majority world country of interest to you. Make a list of some of the NGOs working with young children in this country and provide a brief description of what they do. Write a short reflection of how you think these actions might affect not only the children involved, but also the rest of the nation and other nations.

THE ROLE OF YOUNG CHILDREN IN THE INTERNATIONAL MIGRATION PROCESS

The second part of this chapter considers the relationship between children and international migration. It is important to understand the terms used when examining international migration. The United Nations Educational, Scientific and Cultural Organisation (UNESCO, 2016) defines a **refugee** as a person forced to flee their own country as a result of war, persecution or violence, and who has been granted protection. They define an **asylum seeker** as a person seeking sanctuary in another country, who is applying for asylum and the right to recognition as a refugee and thus to receive legal protection and assistance. UNESCO defines a **migrant** as a person living temporarily or permanently in a country s/he was not born in but has significant social ties to. These terms demonstrate the complexity of any discussion about children and the international movement of people. Indeed, international migration has become a focus of much debate in recent years, in the context of security concerns and in the face of global economic challenges and inequalities. Within this debate, O'Connell Davidson (2011) argues that the image frequently presented of the 'migrant child' is weak, passive, dependent and innocent, whilst the image of the 'migrant adult' is more often associated with danger, risk, cunning and threat.

RESPONSIBILITIES FOR CHILDREN WHO ARE PART OF INTERNATIONAL IMMIGRATION

Children and adults are often merged into the generic use and misuse of terms such as 'refugees', '**immigrants**' and 'asylum seekers'. The risk is that this not only ignores complex differences between adults and children's experiences of migration, it effectively removes words such as 'people', 'family' and 'community' from the lexicon of international migration, rendering invisible the identity and the experiences of the children and adults behind these terms. For children involved in international migration, 'family' often involves extended families, or families dispersed across different countries. Therefore, the 'migrant child' occupies what Huijsmans (2011) refers to as a contradictory space, caught between stereotypes and hidden behind the use of language. The 'migrant child' challenges Western views of an ideal stable childhood and a child innocent and reliant; the 'migrant child' lives in families that challenge Western normative views of family and often experiences a childhood not stable in the way a Western perspective recognises.

The United Nations Convention on the Rights of the Child (UNCRC) (UN, 1989) sets out 54 universal principles aimed at preventing discrimination and providing for the best interests of all children. These principles have been widely taken up by countries, with nation states taking the main responsibilities for guaranteeing these rights to children. However, as O'Connell Davidson (2011) points out, international migration and the movement of people across borders disrupts how these principles are acted on, as national governments balance their responsibilities for protecting children with their obligation to manage and enforce immigration legislation. There is a risk that in the process, governments see children as migrants first and children second (McLeigh, 2013). Taking responsibility for the care and protection of children who are international migrants can mean that national policies on immigration affect the lives of children, particularly those who migrate through irregular channels in ways counter to their rights.

International migration and responsibilities for people who are refugees and asylum seekers have become important and contentious topics, not least in the UK. The debate before and since the Brexit Referendum brought international migration to the fore of the minds of politicians and the public. The immigration policies of President Trump in the USA and the rise of right-wing political parties across Europe frequently reflect a view of the migrant as an 'outsider' and therefore problematic. It is worth examining international migration more closely. Statistical data on children and international migration is difficult to attain as figures frequently merge adults and children. In addition, adults are often suspicious and unwilling to provide data that might question their legal position. However, data does show that most international migration occurs across countries of the **global south** and is between developing, majority world countries (Goldstein and Venturini, 2016). The Organisation for Economic Co-operation and Development (OECD) (2016) reports that the overall percentage of the world's population who live outside the country they were born in rose from 2.7% in 1995 to 3.3% in 2015, and the percentage of that migrant population from developing countries has risen from 79% to 80% in the last 20 years. In that time, the percentage of that migrant population who have moved from low- and middle-income to high-income countries has risen from 36% to 51%. As gaps in income and wellbeing factors (such as education and health) between richer countries and poor and middle-income countries grow, so incentives to move increase. Yet migration is not easy; there is a high monetary, social and emotional cost to moving for individuals and families. Children often play an important part in a family's decision to move, whether for economic, safety or education reasons. Family poverty, lack of education and conflict are frequent triggers that make families and children move. National governments play a role, both intended and unintended, in this decision-making process.

HOW NATIONAL GOVERNMENTS SHAPE CHILDREN'S EXPERIENCE OF INTERNATIONAL MIGRATION

National governments must balance their duty to protect their territories and citizens with the need to ensure economic stability and their international human rights obligations. Governments combine laws and policies to gain as much benefit as possible from migration, whilst meeting their responsibilities for international human rights and addressing concerns about security. These include numbers of people, their composition (for example, age and level of education) and the requirements placed on people who enter or leave (such as a requirement to attend language classes). Whilst legislation generally aims to directly control international migration (such as the Immigration Act 2016), other policies may aim to encourage immigration to fulfil skill shortages. For families who have migrated through irregular channels, legislation can have a very direct impact on the lives of young children. In 2017, for example, the UK government proposed changes resulting from the Immigration Act 2016 to alter mechanisms for providing accommodation and subsistence support to migrant families with children who are not entitled to mainstream welfare support (if, for example, their asylum claim and appeals have been rejected). Therefore, how governments use legislation and policies to balance and manage international migration can directly impact children's lives.

Government policies not specifically aimed at migration can also have an effect. Policies in areas such as employment, education and health may well influence people's decision to move.

case study 18.1

Conditional Cash Transfer Schemes

Governments in a number of low- and middle-income countries use conditional cash transfer schemes (CCTS) as anti-poverty policies aimed at improving the health and education of children, particularly young girls. CCTS pay low-income families to send their children to school. CCTS aim to improve family income and children's education. Whilst not aimed at influencing migration, CCTS can affect migration in interesting and complex ways. Families receiving CCTS have better access to loans due to a rise in family income. These loans can be used to fund the cost of migration.

Imagine a family with young children that receives a CCTS for ensuring the children attend school. The family discuss the possibility that some of the adults move abroad to find work.

1. Why might an increase in family income mean an adult member of the family wants to emigrate?
2. Why might CCTS decrease the short-term chances of the family emigrating?
3. Why might CCTS increase the long-term chances of members of the family emigrating?

The United Nations High Commissioner for Refugees (UNHCR) is assigned to work with countries and the United Nations to protect and support refugees. The 1951 UN Convention Relating to the Status of Refugees identified the rights of refugees (UNHCR, 1951). Whilst children make up a small percentage of international migration through regular international migration routes, the UNHCR reports that over half of the world's refugees are children and, within that population, only 50% of young child refugees have access to primary education (UNHCR, 2016).

THE ROLE YOUNG CHILDREN PLAY IN MIGRATION

International migration brings social change and young children often play an important role in this. Yeoh et al. (2005) point out that while parents and families often migrate in order to secure better education or economic futures for their children, the expense of migration may require that children work to contribute to the cost. Young children may also be sent abroad to live with extended family to access better educational opportunities. Yeoh et al. (2005) identify that across Asia, increasingly, mothers migrate abroad to secure domestic work and send remittances home to support young children. This leads to transnational families who use global communication systems to maintain contact between children and parents. Castles et al. (2014) note that when families do migrate together, children play an important part in settling into and adjusting to the new country. Children starting in the education system learn the language and social expectations of the new country and often act as go-betweens, interpreting and translating for parents. Indeed, as children settle and adjust to life in the new country, they may question it when parents want to return to a home country the children do not remember or wish to live in.

1. As the manager of an early years setting, how would you find out about the best ways to support young children and their families who have recently immigrated into the area?
2. How would you use this to help staff plan and offer this support?

DEBATES ABOUT THE BENEFITS AND CHALLENGES OF GLOBAL COMMUNICATION TO THE LIVES OF YOUNG CHILDREN

The third section of this chapter examines the relationship between children and the global growth of mass visual media. Holland (2004) considers how the image of a child in popular mass media is often aimed as much, if not more, at adults than children. In today's global communication systems, an image of a child can be a powerful tool, transmitted around the world instantly. Children often become the subject of images not directed at them, however that does not mean these images do not affect them. Images can shape social views about children and childhood that influence the way children are treated. For example, International NGOs may use images of children to raise awareness or funds for campaigns, whilst newspapers frequently use images of children in stories about threats to society. Advertisers use children's images to sell products to adults as much as to children.

So images, still or moving, are potent devices, able to communicate powerful and complex ideas. They are also open to multiple interpretations and readings. Unlike text, images require no previous literacy training to decode and access, and so are open to adults and children from an early age and across nations. In many ways, this accessibility reflects both their value and risk in today's global communication systems. It is useful to place the relationship between children and the media in some historical context.

CHILDREN'S RELATIONSHIPS AND ADULTS' CONCERNS WITH VISUAL MEDIA

Visual media such as films, television, computer games and the Internet reflect ongoing and complex relationships between children's engagement with these media and the concerns adults have. The relationship between children and the media began early in the twentieth century with the introduction and popularity of film. As Critcher (2008) notes, children quickly became major consumers of these images that, with the introduction of sound, required no literacy skills to enjoy. Films aimed at children, such as those made by Disney, became and remain popular international cultural symbols of childhood. At the same time, adults' concern to control and protect children's engagement with this media led to countries introducing the forms of censorship that we see today.

So began the moral concerns of adults for children's consumption of visual media that continues today. Television brought a new dimension to this worry. Television saw mass visual media leave the public arena of cinema and enter the private space of home. Managing children's engagement with visual media became more complicated. Government could control the public space of the cinema; they could not easily do the same in the private space of the family. Therefore, parents became controllers of children's access and use of visual media. This continued with video games, the Internet and today in the range of electronic devices, through which children can instantly access mass visual media from around the world.

Through each development, visual media has provoked concerns in adults that, Critcher (2008) argues, consistently follow a similar pattern. The mass marketing of new media is taken up by children, and provokes concerns in adults that the content may be unsuitable, that children cannot differentiate fact from fiction, or risk exploitation, obsession and isolation from social norms. So, mass visual media has joined with the social institutions of family and school to play a part in socialising children into society. The arrival of global mass media in this remains an area of much public debate as access to and engagement with technology continues to change, and children become not only consumers of mass visual media, but also contributors, through global social media platforms such as Facebook, YouTube, Instagram, Snapchat and Flickr.

Children commonly engage with mass visual media outside school, in their own time. Critcher (2008: 103) argues that much of the discussion about the role of mass media centres on 'moral panic, class-based cultural preferences and mythical images of childhood, which have dogged past attempts to understand children and the media'. Critcher (2008) is not arguing against the regulation of mass media; he recognises that engaging with these media inevitably carries risks. Rather, he raises the point of how concerns based solely on the moral values adults attribute to children and childhood translate into 'moral panics' about what play children 'should' and 'should not' be engaging in during their 'leisure time'. This, Critcher (2008) suggests, does not move legitimate concerns forward.

 reflection point 18.2

1. What do you see as the benefits and risks to children from accessing global mass media such as YouTube and video blogs?
2. What do you see as the role of adults in mediating children's engagement with the different forms of mass visual media?
3. What is your opinion of Critcher's argument?

GLOBAL SOCIAL MEDIA AND CHILDREN

Taking an historical perspective reveals how parents, family and government have traditionally attempted to mediate the relationship children have with mass media. However, it is worth examining how changes in technology and the use of technology continue to influence this. Strauss and Howe's (1991) generational theory is usually credited with suggesting an idea of recurring generation cycles that have led today to terms such as 'Generation X', 'Generation Y' and 'Millennials'.

'Generation Y' and 'Millennials' are generally distinguished as those adults who were born between the mid-1980s and 1990s, and are familiar consumers of global mass media and digital technology, and who are now increasingly becoming parents. They differ slightly from the next generation, born between 1995 and 2009, and who are often referred to as 'Generation Z' or 'Post-Millennials' and who are the 'digital natives', born into a world where global mass media and the Internet already existed. There is an ongoing debate about what to call those children born from 2010 to today, possibly 'Generation Alpha'. This generation comprises today's young children.

These labels help reveal the changing ways digital technology and global mass communication media shape the lives of different generations. Changes in technology, combined with increased Internet access in homes and public spaces, mean adults and children are no longer passive consumers of visual media; they now actively engage in creating these media at a time when global communication technology and social media have created spaces where the lives of children are increasingly lived and displayed.

Carrington (2008) refers to this shift in technology as part of the 'post-traditional risk society' (Carrington, 2008: 161), in which children's engagement with global online technologies forms part of the current re-shaping of childhood. The point where adults' views of childhood and children's views of childhood interact, is evident in the discussion of how children engage with these new global mass media. Carrington (2008) highlights how adults frequently reflect concerns about the risk to children and their childhoods from engaging with a global, unknown and therefore potentially dangerous community reminiscent of the same fears historically shown for other mass visual media. Yet children's mastery of this technology opens up a space where they can directly connect to, and contribute their thoughts to, a global community shared with other children as well as adults. In doing so, children are redefining understandings of childhood as a space separate to and protected from adulthood. Carrington (2008) cites blogs created by children around the world such as 'Baghdad girl' that have entered and contributed to both adults' and children's understanding of broader social issues. Today, Generation Z children increasingly share their lives and interests on global mass media sites, for example 'Ethan Gamer', 'Nikki Lilly', 'Full-time Kid' and 'Jake's Bones'. Generation Y children who become parents increasingly take their confidence in using global mass media to express their self-identity and communicate about their lives into their parenting. Lomborg (2012: 431) refers to this as a sociability that 'allows some room for "being oneself" without disclosing one's entire personality'. Young Generation Alpha children now appear on global communication platforms such as YouTube, as parents use these platforms to create representations of their family life (for example, 'Baby Yebin' and 'ItsJudyslife').

SUMMARY

- Globalisation affects the lives of young children in the majority and minority worlds in various ways. This includes how distant economic processes, organisations, media and technology, as well as international laws and policies, influence the ways governments work with young children and their families.
- International organisations and international non-governmental organisations can promote the welfare of children in the majority world through international development that funds and resources activities, and through raising awareness of global, national or local issues that affect children.

- Children often play an important role in international migration processes, for example in a family's decision to emigrate, whether for economic, safety or education reasons. Children can also be involved in acting as interpreters for parents in a new country and influencing decisions about returning to a home country.
- Global communication can affect the lives of young children, as children have become both objects and agents of visual media, and through children directly contributing their thoughts to a global community.

 online resources

Make sure to visit https://study.sagepub.com/fitzgeraldandmaconochie for selected SAGE videos (with questions), SAGE journal articles, links to external sources and flashcards.

FURTHER READING

Bell, D., Raynice, J. and Yangshee, A. (2015). Going Global in Early Childhood Education. *Childhood Education, 91*(2): 90–100.

This article discusses how learning about being global citizens can be woven into early years programmes.

Organisation for Economic Co-operation and Development (OECD) Programme for International Student Assessment – www.oecd.org/pisa

This international assessment tool provides comparisons of education attainment globally that influence UK and other governments' decision making on children's education.

United Nations International Children's Emergency Fund (Unicef) – www.unicef.org.uk

This website provides information on the activities of Unicef UK, including activities and campaigns people can get involved in.

REFERENCES

Babb, S. and Chorev, N. (2016). International Organizations: Loose and Tight Coupling in the Development Regime. *Studies in Comparative International Development, 51*(1): 81–102.

Britto, P., Lye, S., Proulx, K., Yousafzai, A., Matthews, S., Vaivada, T., et al., and the Early Childhood Development Interventions Review Group, for the Lancet Early Childhood Development Series Steering Committee (2017). Advancing Early Child Development: From Science to Scale 2 – Nurturing care: promoting early child development. *The Lancet, 389*(10064): 91–102.

Carrington, V. (2008). 'I'm Dylan and I'm Not Going to Say My Last Name': Some Thoughts on Childhood, Text and New Technologies. *British Education Research Journal, 43*(2): 151–66.

Castles, S., Haas, H. and Miller, M. (2014). *The Age of Migration: International Population Movement in the Modern World*, 5th edn. Basingstoke: Palgrave Macmillan.

Critcher, C. (2008). Making Waves: Historical Aspects of Public Debates about Children and Mass Media. In: K. Drotner and S. Livingstone (eds), *The International Handbook of Children, Media and Culture*. London: Sage.

Goldstein, A. and Venturini, A. (2016). International Migration Policies: Should they be a New G20 Topic? *China & World Economy*, 24(4): 93–110.

Gupta, J. and Veglin, C. (2016). Sustainable Development Goals and Inclusive Development. *International Environmental Agreements: Politics, Law and Economics*, 16(3): 433–48.

HM Government (2015). *The UK's Compliance with the UN Convention on the Rights of the Child*. London: The Stationery Office.

Holland, P. (2004). *Picturing Childhood: The Myth of the Child in Popular Imagery*. London: I. B. Tauris.

Huijsmans, R. (2011). Child Migration and Questions of Agency. *Development and Change*, 42(5): 1307–21.

Lomborg, S. (2012). Negotiating Privacy through Phatic Communication: A Case Study of the Blogging Self. *Philosophy and Technology*, 25(3): 415–34.

McLeigh, J. (2013) Protecting Children in the Context of International Migration. *Child Abuse and Neglect*. 37(12): 1056 – 68.

O'Connell Davidson, J. (2011). Moving Children? Children Trafficking, Child Migration and Child Rights. *Critical Social Policy*, 31(3): 454–77.

OECD. (2016). *Perspectives on Global Development: International Migration in a Shifting World*. Paris: OECD Publishing.

Strauss, W. and Howe, N. (1991). *Generations: The History of America's Future 1584 to 2069*. New York: William Morrow and Co.

UNESCO (2016). Learning to Live Together: Glossary of Migration Related Terms. [online] Available at: www.unesco.org/new/en/social-and-human-sciences/themes/international-migration/glossary [Accessed 2 February 2017].

UNHCR (1951). Convention and Protocol Relating to the Status of Refugees. Geneva: UNHCR. [online] Available at: www.unhcr.org/protect/PROTECTION/3b66c2aa10.pdf [Accessed 3 February 2017].

UNHCR (2016). Missing Out: Refugee Education in Crisis. Geneva: UNHCR. [online] Available at: www.unhcr.org/57d9d01d0 [Accessed 2 February 2017].

Unicef (2015). Care for Child Development Package. [online] Available at: www.unicef.org/earlychildhood [Accessed 20 February 2017].

Unicef (2017). Early Childhood Development. [online] Available at: www.unicef.org/earlychildhood [Accessed 20 February 2017].

United Nations (UN) (1989). The United Nations Convention on the Rights of the Child (UNCRC). London: Unicef UK. [online] Available at: https://353ld710iigr2n4po7k4kgvv-wpengine.netdna-ssl.com/wp-content/uploads/2010/05/UNCRC_PRESS200910web.pdf [Accessed 2 February 2017].

United Nations (UN) (2017a). Universal Declaration of Human Rights. [online] Available at: www.un.org/en/universal-declaration-human-rights [Accessed 20 February 2017].

United Nations (UN) (2017b). Sustainable Development Goals. [online] Available at: www.un.org/sustainabledevelopment [Accessed 20 February 2017].

Yeoh, B., Huang, S. and Lam, T. (2005). Transnationalizing the 'Asian' Family: Imaginaries, Intimacies and Strategic Intents. *Global Networks: a Journal of Transnational Affairs*, 5(4): 307–15.

Young, F. and Merschrod, K. (2010) Child Health and NGOs in Peruvian Provinces. *Social Indicators Research*, 98(2): 291–99.

CONTEMPORARY ISSUES

BY JENNY ROBSON

Prior to reading this chapter, I had some knowledge of social policy. Yet once engaging with the text, I was confident in establishing discussions with peers about ideas and concepts discussed in the chapter.

The chapter outcomes make clear what you will gain by engaging with this text. The dual focus on those working in early childhood education and care (ECEC) and how policies relating to ECEC are affected by a socio-cultural context provides a clear structure for this chapter. The chapter is inclusive, whatever your level of study, and the use of recent academic literature and policy will help you to use it as a point of reference when studying the impact of social policy.

REBECCA SAMUEL
MA EARLY CHILDHOOD STUDIES
UNIVERSITY OF EAST LONDON

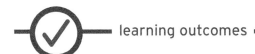

learning outcomes

By actively reading this chapter and engaging with the material, you will be able to:

*   recognise how social policy responds to socio-cultural contexts
*   apply Bronfenbrenner's theory of the ecology of human development to explore how social policy affects young children in ECEC settings
*   analyse and question ideas and concepts embedded in social policy (e.g 'fundamental British values') and explore how societal fears may permeate and influence ECEC policy in the UK
*   appraise the strategies ECEC practitioners adopt to mediate and implement social policy in ECEC settings.

INTRODUCTION

This chapter explores how UK societal fears of the threat of terrorism and extremism have permeated and influenced ECEC policy. Fear is not a new phenomenon in the study of childhood in society, as illustrated by Guldberg's (2009: 25) critique that 'the culture of the fear that dominates today's society' leads adults to projecting 'fears and uncertainties' (2009: 180) onto children, with the possible effect of limiting children's opportunities to resolve conflicts and challenges in their lives. Global and national events such as the terrorist attacks in London and Manchester and on the offices of Charlie Hebdo in Paris initiated debates in the UK centred on the fear of terrorism. The representation of terrorism and terrorists in the media, government publications and training materials for professionals has been critiqued because it promotes and reinforces a stereotypical view that terrorism is located in Muslim communities (Hickman et al., 2011, cited in Coppock, 2014) and that Muslims are a 'suspect community' (Farrell, 2016: 283). Government policy took a turn from a reactive approach to acts of terrorism to prevention. The idea of prevention emphasised the importance of working with communities (Panjwani, 2016) including children and their families. The shift in focus to preventative work brought a wide range of practitioners working with communities within the scope of government counter-terrorism policy. The fear of terrorism within the socio-cultural context and the focus on working with communities is mirrored in an extensive policy framework emerging from the Counter-Terrorism and Security Act 2015 (The Act). The Prevent Duty (Section 26 of The Act) requires named public authorities, including schools and registered ECEC settings, to have 'due regard to the need to prevent people from being drawn into terrorism' and to promote 'fundamental British values'. Lander (2016) argues that this imposes a political agenda of securitisation on practitioners, including those working directly with children. The implications of this new statutory duty for practitioners in ECEC settings are critically examined in this chapter, together with an exploration of the ways in which ECEC practitioners creatively mediate in their practice with young children the requirements of the Prevent Duty and the alignment of their roles to the national security agenda.

CONTEMPORARY SOCIETAL ISSUES AND SOCIAL POLICY

 reflection point 19.1

What questions might ECEC practitioners raise about the requirement to have 'due regard to the need to prevent people from being drawn into terrorism'?
What might this duty mean in practice in ECEC settings?

Academics within the field of Early Childhood Studies continually examine societal issues and the ways they may affect children and those working in **early childhood education and care (ECEC) settings**. This process is central to understanding how ECEC policies and practices may be shaped by, and integral to, the socio-cultural context. In this way, policy and the debates surrounding policy can be viewed as a 'sociocultural mirror' (New, 2009: 309). Within this socio-cultural context in the United Kingdom (UK), children have come increasingly within the 'public world of policy makers' (Leonard, 2016: 48) as a result of the changing relationship between the parents, children and the state. In this dynamic relationship, the state has an evolving role in the lives of young children and their families through an expanding policy portfolio across ECEC since 1997, influenced by the political agendas of each government (Fitzgerald and Kay, 2016).

 action point 19.1

List all the social policies that affect your life and the life of your family.
Choose one policy from your list and describe its intention or its aim; does it aim to improve human welfare and meet human needs?
Examine whether and how any policies on your list could be considered instruments of social control (limiting the actions of an individual or group within society).

The term 'policy' can be applied in many different contexts, including at a local level, in an ECEC setting, or by national government. It is a statement of intention or action to be taken by those with responsibility and it may indicate the formal status of a course of action (Levin, 1997, as cited by Fitzgerald and Kay, 2016: 2). Social policy is concerned with social phenomena (Alcock et al., 2008), such as poverty, crime, migration, domestic abuse, destitution and, more recently, national security. In this way, social policy is broad and reaches into multiple aspects of the lives of children and families. Blakemore (2003) argues that social policies aim to improve human welfare and meet human needs; this implies they have a positive intent. Social policies set the parameters for interventions by the state into families' lives and this raises the question of whether policies become instruments of social control (Lavalette and Pratt, 2006).

spotlight on policy 19.1

The Counter-Terrorism and Security Act 2015

The Counter-Terrorism and Security Act 2015 (The Act) is the legislative framework for the government's counter-terrorism strategy. The Prevent Duty (Section 26 of The Act) as it applies to England and Wales came into effect on 1 July 2015 and a wide range of public authorities (e.g. schools and local authorities) are subject to this duty. Guidance has also been developed to support the implementation of the Prevent Duty in Scotland. For ECEC settings, the requirements from the Prevent Duty are to have 'due regard to the need to prevent people from being drawn into terrorism' (HM Government, 2015).

So what expectations does the Prevent Duty place on ECEC settings and practitioners? Preventing young children from being drawn into terrorism is linked by government to the policy framework for safeguarding and child protection. ECEC practitioners in England, Wales and Scotland already have a statutory duty to safeguard children. This includes being alert to any safeguarding and child protection concerns in a child's life at home or elsewhere. Local Safeguarding Children's Boards in England and Wales and Child Protection Committees in Scotland co-ordinate training and provide local advice on a broad range of safeguarding issues for children, including the responsibilities of practitioners to have 'due regard to the need to prevent people from being drawn into terrorism' (HM Government, 2015). The Terrorism Act 2000 defines terrorism as 'an action that endangers or causes serious violence to a person/people; causes serious damage to property; or seriously interferes or disrupts an electronic system. The use or threat must be designed to influence the government or to intimidate the public and is made for the purpose of advancing a political, religious or ideological cause'.

As part of the Prevent Duty, the government requires public bodies, including registered ECEC settings, to promote the fundamental British values of 'democracy; the rule of law; individual liberty and mutual respect and tolerance of different faiths and beliefs' as a strategy to prevent children being drawn into terrorism. ECEC settings are already required to focus on children's personal, social and emotional development through the *Statutory Framework for the Early Years Foundation Stage* (DfE, 2017) in England, the *Curriculum for Wales: Foundation Phase Framework* (DfES, 2015) in Wales, and the *Early Years Framework* (Scottish Government, 2009) in Scotland.

FUNDAMENTAL BRITISH VALUES: A CRITICAL VIEW

'Fundamental British values' are defined in the Prevent Strategy (HM Government, 2015) as 'democracy; the rule of law; individual liberty and mutual respect and tolerance of different faiths and beliefs'. For government, they are a mechanism to build 'resilience to radicalisation' (DfE, 2015) in young children and to equip them to challenge extremist views. In promoting fundamental British values, ECEC practitioners have become instruments of state counter-terrorism policy and for many this may seem far removed from the ECEC setting (Robson, 2015). ECEC practitioners are expected to engage in values education with young children. This is not a new requirement as the Early Years Foundation Stage (EYFS) (DfE, 2017) already provides a structure for children to engage with values through the Early Learning Goal 'Understanding the World'. Values education can be understood as a set of practices where children learn values as well as the norms and skills reflected in those values (Halstead and Taylor, 2000). Values can serve as criteria or standards for what is good or bad (Schwartz, 2012) and if fundamental British values are perceived as 'good' then there is a risk that values held by other nations or cultural groups have lower status. A persistent challenge for ECEC practitioners operating within governments' 'top-down' approach to policy making (Osgood, 2006) is interpreting these 'top-down' values with children in ways that are relevant to their lives. The government's approach of prescribing national values has been subject to critique, particularly the claim that they are uniquely British may not be shared by all citizens (Lander, 2016); furthermore, there is a risk that in advocating British values there is a suggestion that only British values are acceptable (Maylor, 2016). This may limit dialogues that recognise democracy or liberty as values shared across diverse national and cultural groups.

 action point 19.2

Collaborating with another person, identify opportunities for children to engage with values through your local early years curriculum.

List the values that might be observed in the relationships between children, between children and practitioners, and between practitioners during a day at an ECEC setting.

What might be the challenges for ECEC practitioners through the emphasis on 'British' values in the legislation?

APPRAISING SOCIAL POLICY: APPLYING BRONFENBRENNER'S THEORY OF THE ECOLOGY OF HUMAN DEVELOPMENT

The theory of the ecology of human development can be applied to support an understanding of the operation of social policy. Bronfenbrenner suggests that events in the environment influence a child's development. This theory conceptualises the structure of ecological environment as a series of concentric circles, ranging from the child at the centre to the broader structures of society in the outer circles. Each circle is a system and the systems are linked and influence each other; Bronfenbrenner refers to this as 'interconnectedness' (Bronfenbrenner, 1979: 7). This means that changes in the **macrosystem** (the beliefs, ideologies and public policies that influence all the systems) may impact on children at the centre of the **microsystem** (the relationships and activities experienced by the child in their immediate setting, including parents/carers, wider family, faith centre, ECEC setting). The **mesosystem** is the pattern of relationships and activities experienced by two or more of the settings (e.g. home, school or neighbourhood). Other changes, referred to as an **exosystem**, can have an influence. This is where in one or more settings (that do not directly involve the child) change may happen that would impact on the child (e.g. media reports, local government, housing association, police).

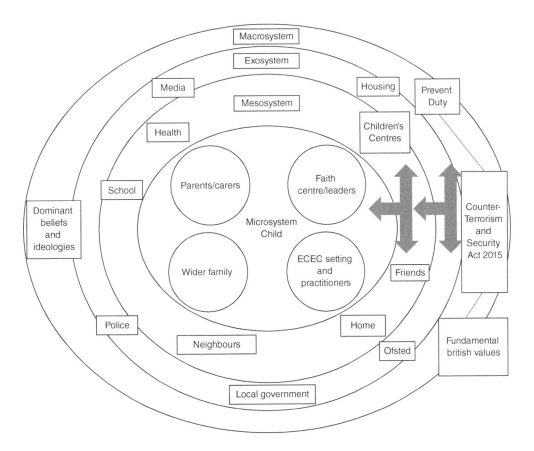

Figure 19.1 Applying Bronfenbrenner's theory to appraise the operation of policy across the ecological environment

Source: Based on Bronfenbrenner (1979)

Bronfenbrenner states that government policy is a part of the macrosystem and it determines the events and relationships in the exo-, meso- and micro-systems. Applying this framework to support the analysis of social policy reveals how policy developments in the macrosystem may impact the child. Similarly, we can understand how social attitudes and political ideology influence policy development in the macrosystem. Bronfenbrenner argues that it is essential to understand the 'ideological preferences' of policy makers. A visual appraisal of the operation of the Prevent Duty across the ecological environment is presented in Figure 19.1. Government policy to address terrorism is in the macrosystem and this permeates all other systems; for example, Ofsted (located in the exosystem) is required to inspect the way ECEC settings promote fundamental British values.

action point 19.3

Consider the way the Counter-Terrorism and Security Act operates in the ecological environment by considering the following questions:

- How might the requirement to promote fundamental British values impact on ECEC settings in the microsystem?
- What questions might practitioners ask about the implications of the Counter-Terrorism and Security Act 2015 for their role in the ECEC setting?
- What questions might parents/carers/faith leaders ask of ECEC settings about how they promote fundamental British values?

YOUNG CHILDREN AND SOCIAL POLICY: THE COUNTER-TERRORISM AND SECURITY ACT 2015

As young children are within the scope of the Counter-Terrorism and Security Act 2015, any analysis should include a consideration of the status of children as subjects of this policy. As early childhood academics, we are supported in this process by both the sociology of childhood and theoretical positions arising from the study of children's rights. In their paradigm for the sociology of childhood, Prout and James (1997: 8) argue that:

> Children are and must be seen as active and constructive in the determination of their own social lives, the lives of those around them and of the societies in which they live. Children are not just passive subjects of social structures and processes.

Viewing the operation of policy in the child's microsystem through this theory suggests that children are not passive recipients of British values that are pre-determined by a government at some distance from their lives. ECEC practitioners working within this paradigm view children as powerful actors capable and competent of critiquing, mediating and re-imagining 'values' relevant to their microsystem. Such a view of childhood would have implications for ECEC practitioners' pedagogical practice, where values are negotiated and mutually understood in the setting. Analysis of the implementation of child rights in early childhood further enhances this view of the active child. The United Nations Committee on the Rights of the Child (UNComRC, 2005: 3) argued that 'young children should be recognized as active members of families, communities and societies, with their own concerns, interests and points of view'. MacNaughton et al. (2007) develop this idea further, suggesting that children are social actors making valid meanings about the world and their place in it. Viewed in this way, children become citizens with an active role in enacting legislation and policy in their own context. By recognising children as social actors and citizens, ECEC practitioners establish collaborative and equitable child–adult relationships in their pedagogical practice. Dialogue in ECEC settings between practitioners and young children about British values advances children's citizenship as they actively reimagine values in their lives.

 reflection point 19.2

Reflect on your own beliefs about the status of children in relation to the implementation of policy. Use the questions below to stimulate your ideas:

- How do you, or will you, view children in your practice? Are they 'active' participants in decisions that affect their own lives?
- How do, or would, children determine their own lives?
- How do you, or would you, recognise children's concerns, interests and points of view?
- Reflect on Prout and James's (1997) view of children set out above; what are the implications for ECEC settings in the way they work with children to promote British values?

ECEC PRACTITIONERS' CRITICAL ENGAGEMENT WITH POLICY

ECEC practitioners are governed by national policy. For example, the Early Years Foundation Stage (DfE, 2017) sets out the statutory framework for ECEC practice in England and there are comparable policies in Wales, Scotland and Northern Ireland as part of the arrangements for devolved government in the UK. The mediation of national policy within the child's microsystem is central to practitioners, if we imagine leadership of the implementation of policy as an everyday practice (Sachs, 2000). Lea (2014) argues that hidden-value preferences in policies present challenges for practitioners as they attempt to comprehend what policies are trying to achieve. By questioning assumptions, practitioners may identify alternative possibilities for the implementation of policy (Moss and Petrie, 2005) relevant to ECEC settings, and in doing so they become the 'policy entrepreneur' (Lea, 2014). As 'policy entrepreneurs', ECEC practitioners focus on generating innovative ideas and exploring alternative strategies (Cohen, 2016) for implementation of policy within the microstructure. Developing a critical approach to national policy becomes a deliberate process for ECEC practitioners. Simpson and Connor's (2011: 2) notion of 'policy literacy' as a continuous process of becoming discriminating readers and performers of policies may be supportive for ECEC practitioners as they engage with policy.

 action point 19.4

The three phases of the development of policy literacy are reimagined below in the context of ECEC practice:

Phase 1: ECEC practitioners need to understand and become aware of the breadth of the impact of policy on young children's lives and on ECEC practice.

How might this policy impact on children's lives? How might this policy impact on ECEC practice?

Does the policy allow for options or flexibility in the way it might be interpreted and implemented?

Phase 2: ECEC practitioners need to develop skills in analysing how policies have been constructed. In this way, practitioners begin the process of analysis of policy and exploration of the implications for ECEC practice.

What issues does the policy seek to address? How does the policy justify the focus on these issues?

What solutions or actions does the policy propose or recommend?

How are children, families and practitioners presented in the policy? Are their views visible?

What is the role of the ECEC practitioner in implementing the policy? What questions might arise in the implementation of the policy?

Phase 3: ECEC practitioners explore the hidden meaning of policy, revealing the purpose of policies and the aims of policy makers. This requires a deeper level of analysis by asking questions such as:

Why does this policy exist (or not exist)? How does the policy relate to the experiences of children and families, or is the policy written from the perspective of the policy maker?

How does the policy persuade the reader that the aim, intentions and actions in the policy are needed and important? Are alternative actions considered or is only one option presented?

Whose views are missing from the policy text?

(Adapted from Simpson and Connor, 2011: 2)

Apply the three phases of policy literacy to analyse the requirement to promote fundamental British values in ECEC settings.

Now select a current ECEC national policy and apply the three phases of policy literacy to support your analysis. Work with a group in this task and develop a critique of the policy. Your group might contribute a short piece to a blog or discussion forum hosted by an ECEC organisation.

Applying the phases of policy literacy is a useful strategy to gain a fuller understanding of policy aims and objectives. There is also a clear link between policy and practice. For example, with the Counter-Terrorism and Security Act (2015) it is important to consider the ways in which ECEC practitioners have interpreted fundamental British values in their practice.

 case study 19.1

Lower Castle Community Nursery

Lower Castle Community Nursery provides ECEC to children aged from 2 to 5 years on a term-time only basis. The majority of children access 15–30 hours a week early education and childcare entitlement through the government scheme over 38 weeks. Situated in the centre of social housing, the nursery welcomes children and their families from a wide range of language and cultural backgrounds. The diversity of children's backgrounds is reflected in the visual environment of the nursery, including the lobby where children's names, drawings and photographs are positioned above their individual pegs for coats, shoes and bags. Words of welcome in the languages spoken in the nursery greet families on arrival. The nursery is part of a social enterprise that manages over 30 nurseries in a large urban area; organisational values of 'inspiring', 'brave', 'fun' and 'nurturing' are at the centre of both its curriculum and pedagogy. Rosa, the deputy manager, leads the planning of pedagogy and curriculum in the nursery and reflects that 'Although promoting fundamental British values is a new requirement of government at this nursery our practice was already shaped by values. We have considered how our values, pedagogy and curriculum link to fundamental British values'. In a walking tour of the nursery, Rosa stops at points where visual displays communicate values in action. There are photographs of a recent visit by the whole nursery to a local care home for people with learning disabilities or people living with dementia. Images reflect the communication between children and people living in the care home as drawings are exchanged and dialogues emerge, based on mutual curiosity. The social enterprise is committed to connecting nurseries with the local community; the visit to the care home is part of a regular scheme of visits in the local community. The nurseries practise a pedagogical approach which is centred on harmonious relationships and connecting with the community through multi-generational work. Rosa reflects that children are inspired, they are nurturing to others and they are brave in experiencing new and different circumstances. She suggests that providing children with these opportunities does promote the fundamental British values of 'mutual respect and tolerance' by engaging children with diversity and difference. Our next stop was at a display of the outcome of 'children's planning meetings'. Rosa explains that children and practitioners meet regularly in order that children share their interests and ideas for the curriculum for the next week. Practitioners take these ideas forward, matching the curriculum to children's interests. Children make a visual record of the meeting and then discuss this with the practitioner; they form a display of shared-planning documents between children and practitioners. Rosa reflected that children freely shared their knowledge and ideas; this is a democratic practice.

- How does the nursery approach the statutory requirement to promote fundamental British values?

There are different pedagogical approaches that will provide opportunities for children to both share their values and learn about others. When selecting pedagogical approaches, it is important to consider how this reflects the needs of children, families and the community where settings are situated.

case study 19.2

Middle House Day Nursery

Middle House Day Nursery provides ECEC to children aged 2 to 5 years; it is open from 7am to 6pm each day and offers a flexible range of sessional and full-day care. This private nursery is an independent business on a single site and was established by a recent graduate in Early Childhood Studies. Children access the 15-30-hour early education and childcare entitlement and many families use this flexibly across the week, depending on their employment patterns. Situated in a small parade of shops on the edge of a large city, the nursery reaches into a community where there are many families new to the UK. The nursery welcomes children and families from a wide range of language and cultural backgrounds. Middle House Day Nursery's organisational values focus on nurturing learning; encouraging openness; working together and stimulating energy (fun and inspiration); they are central to their pedagogy. Farah, the nursery owner, has a display in the lobby for parents illustrating the way the pedagogy in the nursery links to fundamental British values. This emphasises the nursery's commitment to children and practitioners making decisions together and providing 'opportunities to develop enquiring minds in an atmosphere where questions are valued'. Farah explains that this practice supports the statutory requirement to promote 'democracy' as a fundamental British value; however, this approach is integral to the pedagogy. Similarly, the fundamental British value of 'liberty' is interpreted as the pedagogical practice of promoting independence in learning and supporting children in making informed choices. Farah and Rebecca, the deputy manager, discuss the links between values and pedagogical practices in the setting. Together we review a 'children's voice' book where child-initiated activities are documented; they describe the practice of child-initiated meetings where children are involved in the governance of the nursery. As Middle House Day Nursery does not have an outdoor space, the children go out for walks and activities in the local community several times a day. Rebecca says that these have a purpose and structure; for example, children observe the weather and changes in the environment. Children are involved in the planning of the outdoor activities including the risk assessments; they develop rules to ensure safety for all.

A visual record of the risk assessment meeting (5 Golden Rules) is included in the 'children's voice' book (see Figure 19.2). This is a shared resource for children and practitioners when planning new outdoor activities. Their pedagogy is centred on the values associated with working together, including co-operation and openness to new ideas. Rebecca suggests that this might be an example of the way the nursery promotes the fundamental British value of the 'rule of law', but their practice begins with children's interests and their role in the governance of the nursery.

- How does the nursery approach the statutory requirement to promote fundamental British values?

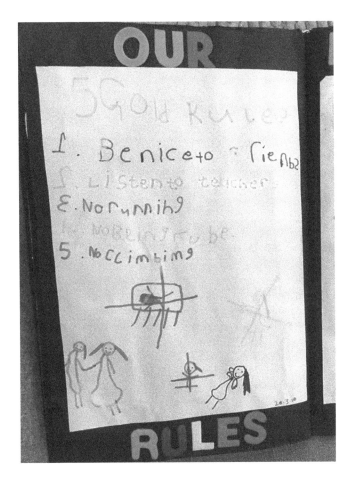

Figure 19.2 Children's voice

 reflection point 19.3

After reading the two case studies in this chapter, reflect on the ways in which the two nurseries place values at the centre of their pedagogy and practice. What interests you the most about their approach?

How might the nurseries extend their connections within the community? How would this support values education?

How do the nurseries strengthen the microstructure for the child?

How do the nurseries have a broad view of values – beyond those defined as fundamental British values?

SUMMARY

- Social policies are concerned with social phenomena such as poverty, migration, human welfare and security; they may be expressed as a statement of action or intention on the part of government. They set out the parameters for the intervention of the state into the lives of children and their families. Social policies are shaped by and integral to the socio-cultural context and they respond to emerging issues in society.
- Bronfenbrenner's theory of the ecology of human development supports an understanding of how social policy affects young children in ECEC settings. National policies are developed in the macrosystem and they reflect the belief and ideology preferences of government and society. Implementation of policy is within the exosystem, the mesosystem and the microsystem. Policy developed in the macrosystem may strengthen or disrupt the child's microsystem.
- Fundamental British values are embedded in ECEC practice through the Prevent Duty (s. 26) of the Counter-Terrorism and Security Act 2015. ECEC practitioners have become instruments of state counter-terrorism policy through a top-down approach that requires them to promote a pre-determined set of fundamental British values. By recognising children as social actors and citizens, practitioners participate in dialogues about values. Through this process, children reimagine values in the microsystem.
- ECEC practitioners can be 'policy entrepreneurs' where they focus on generating innovative ideas and exploring alternative strategies for implementation of policy within the micro-structure. They can develop skills in 'policy literacy' where they become discriminating readers and performers of policies; so they can critically question the aim, intentions and actions in policies and their relevance to children's lives.

 online resources

Make sure to visit https://study.sagepub.com/fitzgeraldandmaconochie for selected SAGE videos (with questions), SAGE journal articles, links to external sources and flashcards.

FURTHER READING

Fitzgerald, D. and Kay, J. (2016). *Understanding Early Years Policy,* 4th edn. London: Sage.

This book analyses the complexity of ECEC policy developments over time and the way policy has impacted on ECEC practice.

Kingdon, Z. and Gourd, J. (eds) (2014). *Early Years Policy: The Impact on Practice.* London: Routledge.

This book explores ECEC policy developments and how they have affected children, ECEC settings, parents and the ECEC workforce.

REFERENCES

Alcock, P., Daly, G. and Griggs, E. (2008). *Introducing Social Policy*, 2nd edn. Harlow: Pearson Education.

Blakemore, K. (2003). *Social Policy: An Introduction*. Buckingham: Open University Press.

Bronfenbrenner, U. (1979). *The Ecology of Human Development*. London: Harvard University Press.

Cohen, N. (2016). Policy Entrepreneurs and Agenda Setting. In: N. Zahariadis (ed.), *Handbook of Public Policy Agenda Setting*. Cheltenham: Edward Elgar, pp. 180–200.

Coppock, V. (2014). Can You Spot a Terrorist in Your Classroom? Problematising the Recruitment of Schools to the 'War on Terror' in the UK. *Global Studies of Childhood*, 4(2): 114–25.

Department for Education (DfE) (2015). *The Prevent Duty: Departmental Advice for Schools and Childcare Providers*. London: DfE. [online] Available at: www.gov.uk/government/publications/protecting-children-from-radicalisation-the-prevent-duty [Accessed 11 March 2017].

Department for Education (DfE) (2017). *Statutory Framework for the Early Years Foundation Stage*. London: DfE. [online] Available at: www.gov.uk/government/publications/early-years-foundation-stage-framework--2 [Accessed 11 March 2017].

Department for Education and Skills (DfES) (2015). *Curriculum for Wales: Foundation Phase Framework*. Cardiff: DfES. [online] Available at: http://learning.gov.wales/docs/learningwales/publications/150803-fp-framework-en.pdf [Accessed 11 March 2017].

Farrell, F. (2016). Why all of a Sudden do We Need to Teach Fundamental British Values? A Critical Investigation of Religious Education Student Teacher Positioning within a Policy Discourse of Discipline and Control. *Journal of Education for Teaching, International Research and Pedagogy*, 42(3): 280–97.

Fitzgerald, D. and Kay, J. (2016). *Understanding Early Years Policy*, 4th edn. London: Sage.

Guldberg, H. (2009). *Reclaiming Childhood*. London: Routledge.

Halstead, J. M. and Taylor, M. J. (2000). Learning and Teaching about Values: A Review of Recent Research. *Cambridge Journal of Education*, 30(2): 169–202.

HM Government (2015). *Revised Prevent Duty Guidance: for England and Wales*. London: HM Government. [online] Available at: www.gov.uk/government/uploads/system/uploads/attachment_data/file/445977/3799_Revised_Prevent_Duty_Guidance__England_Wales_V2-Interactive.pdf [Accessed 11 March 2017].

Hickman, M. J., Thomas, L., Silvestri, S. and Nickels, H. (2011). *Suspect Communities? Counter-terrorism Policy, the Press and the Impact on Irish and Muslim Communities in Britain*. London: London Metropolitan University.

Lander, V. (2016) Introduction to Fundamental British Values. *Journal of Education for Teaching*, 42(3): 274–9.

Lavalette, M. and Pratt, A. (eds) (2006). *Social Policy: Theories, Concepts and Issues*, 3rd edn. London: Sage.

Lea, S. (2014). Early Years Work, Professionalism and the Translation of Policy into Practice. In: Z. Kingdon and J. Gourd (eds), *Early Years Policy: The Impact on Practice*. London: Routledge, pp. 13–32.

Leonard, M. (2016). *The Sociology of Children, Childhood and Generation*. London: Sage.

MacNaughton, G., Hughes, P. and Smith, K. (2007). Young Children's Rights and Public Policy: Practices and Possibilities for Citizenship in the Early Years. *Children & Society*, 21(6): 458–69.

Maylor, U. (2016). 'I'd Worry about How to Teach It': British Values in English Classrooms. *Journal of Education for Teaching*, 42(3): 314–28.

Moss, P. and Petrie, P. (2005). *From Children's Services to Children's Spaces: Public Policy, Children and Childhood*. London: Routledge.

New, R. S. (2009). ECE Policies (and Policy Debates) as a Sociocultural Mirror. *Contemporary Issues in Early Childhood, 10*(3): 309–11.

Osgood, J. (2006). Professionalism and Performativity: The Feminist Challenge Facing Early Years Practitioners. *Early Years, 26*(2): 187–99.

Panjwani, F. (2016). Towards an Overlapping Consensus: Muslim Teachers' Views on Fundamental British Values. *Journal of Education for Teaching, 42*(3): 329–40.

Prout, A. and James, A. (eds) (1997). *Constructing and Reconstructing Childhood: Contemporary Issues in the Sociological Study of Childhood*. London: RoutledgeFalmer.

Robson, J. (2015). Fundamental British Values in the Early Years. [online] Available at: www. consider-ed.org.uk/fundamental-british-values-in-the-early-years-a-dilemma-for-the-sector [Accessed 23 August 1918].

Sachs, J. (2000). The Activist Professional. *Journal of Educational Change, 1*(1): 77–95.

Simpson, G. and Connor, S. (2011). *Social Policy for Social Welfare Professionals: Tools for Understanding, Analysis and Engagement*. Bristol: Policy Press.

Schwartz, S. H. (2012). An Overview of the Schwartz Theory of Basic Values. *Online Readings in Psychology and Culture, 2*(1): 11.

Scottish Government (2009). *The Early Years Framework*. Edinburgh: Scottish Government. Available at: www.gov.scot/Publications/2009/01/13095148/0 [Accessed 11 March 2017].

United Nations Committee on the Rights of the Child (UNComRC). (2005). *General Comment No. 7: Implementing Child Rights in Early Childhood*. Geneva: UN. [online] Available at: www2. ohchr.org/english/bodies/crc/docs/AdvanceVersions/GeneralComment7Rev1.pdf [Accessed 11 March 2017].

YOUNG CHILDREN, CHILDHOOD AND GENDER

BY DAMIEN FITZGERALD

The definitions of sex and gender were easy to understand and helped me to distinguish between the two terms throughout the rest of the chapter. The section on gender identity development gave a broad overview of the theories, allowing a basic understanding which could be developed through further reading. The case study and activities throughout the reading made me reflect on my own experiences of sex and gender and how I and others gender stereotype to such an extent. For example, whilst I was on placement in a pre-school they had two groups of children creating a large picture. There was a group of girls who had been given flowers and fairies and a group of boys who had been given dinosaurs and monsters. At the time I hadn't thought too much about this but after reading the chapter I would challenge this and hope to create more gender inclusive practice.

I think the examples really aided my understanding by showing how gender is stereotyped in society and how practice and environments can be amended to be more gender inclusive.

SOPHIE DIXON
BA HONS EARLY CHILDHOOD STUDIES
SHEFFIELD HALLAM UNIVERSITY

learning outcomes

By actively reading this chapter and engaging with the material, you will be able to:

- discuss different approaches to account for sex and gender development
- examine how gender is positioned in society and the potential challenges this creates for young children, families and practitioners
- question how approaches to practice can promote gender equality and diversity
- appraise the role of research in providing an insight into gender constructions within early childhood education and care (ECEC) and for young children.

INTRODUCTION

Differentiation between male and female has been emphasised at different times, in different ways and in different cultural situations throughout time. In the UK, the industrial revolution, in the eighteenth century, exacerbated differences between men and women. Prior to this, many people worked on the land and gender differentiation was less stark, with many land jobs completed by all. Industrialisation, which brought factories, shops and offices, led to the dominant idea of men as 'bread winners' and women as 'home makers'. There have been changes but these ideas often still dominate. Throughout the lifespan, gender can impact on many areas of life, from clothes, friendships, toy/play choices and activities to school subjects and career choices. Kilvington and Wood (2016) refer to this as the 'gender dance' which starts at birth and continues throughout life. This chapter outlines how gender is positioned and how the impact of the gender dance can be explored to challenge ideas and practices to recognise diverse gender identities and strive for equality for all.

HOW IS GENDER POSITIONED?

Gender pervades so many aspects of everyday life. In fact, it is unlikely that a day will ever pass where gender does not have significance to you. This may seem an exaggeration but thinking about this for one day is likely to confirm the impact.

reflection point 20.1

For one day keep a record of all the occasions that you see or hear a reference to gender that could impact on individuals. The impact may be direct (e.g. stopping or encouraging an action because of the gender of the individual) or indirect (e.g. contributing to perceptions of gender that create gendered expectations in society). For example, it is just before 10am and I have already heard the phrases 'provides jobs for men' and 'an industry where sons follow their

(Continued)

fathers'; seen an advert for a film on the side of a bus where the female superhero is wearing revealing clothing and has an hour-glass figure; and heard a young child say, 'why the man has long hair? This is for girls.'

At the end of the day, reflect on your list. Are gender references more prevalent than you had thought?

Are the references to gender you noted more likely to have a positive or negative impact on young children?

SEX AND GENDER IDENTITIES

The terms *sex* and *gender* are often used interchangeably. Both have relevance to gender but it is important to distinguish them. Sex refers to biological and physical differences between individuals and is usually considered as a binary – either male or female. This can be problematic and is discussed later in the chapter. One pair of chromosomes determine sex, an XX pairing female and XY male. The sex of a child is determined by the father. If a **zygote** receives an X sex **chromosome** from the father, the child will be female; if a Y chromosome, male. The sex of a child determines biological identity and is associated with other factors, such as physical characteristics and hormonal influences (Shaffer and Kipp, 2014; Smith et al., 2015). The concept of gender is broader than biological sex (Money and Ehrhardt, 1972; Yelland and Grieshaber, 1998). The terms masculinity and femininity are often used when referring to gender. Gender is often seen as a role and there are dominant expectations – social constructions – that are seen as gender appropriate. These vary according to time, place and culture, and construct what is often referred to as gender identity. Again, in many cultures gender is seen as a binary with males expected to be masculine and females feminine. The awareness an individual has of their gender is often referred to as **gender typing** and the roles a child adopts can be thought of as their public expression of gender (Shaffer, 2009; Kilvington and Wood, 2016).

GENDER IDENTITY DEVELOPMENT

A number of theories explain gender development covering varied disciplines, including psychology, sociology and anthropology. In this chapter, it is not possible to discuss a broad range of theories in depth, so this section draws mainly on psychological theories. In the 1960s Kohlberg developed a theory of cognitive development, which included a focus on gender. The theory has three broad stages: basic gender identity (gender labelling) from around the age of 3; gender stability from 4 to 5 years old; and gender constancy from the age of 6–7. The first stage is when a child has a sense of their male or female self, but does not understand this is a constant state. Young children see their gender as dependent on variables (e.g. hair length, clothing). The second stage is when a child understands that their gender is stable over time. At the final stage, gender constancy, children develop a sense of their gender as consistent and not reliant on their appearance, the activities they choose or any other variables (Kohlberg, 1969; Smith et al., 2015). Although this theory has been critiqued for its lack of focus on biological and cultural factors, it did focus on gender as separate to sex and also sees children as active agents (albeit in response to environmental factors) in the process of developing a gendered identity. This focus on children as active agents in forming a gendered identity is now prevalent.

Bem (1981) built on this with gender schema theory, stating that gender characteristics are processed and maintained through **schema**. Gender typing is impacted by the environment in different ways. For example, at a micro level family influence concepts and ideas around gender; at a macro level government influences individuals (e.g. through policy direction). Children develop a gender schema by assimilating information that they perceive as gender congruent and this forms and maintains gendered stereotypes. If a child is in an environment with strongly reinforced gender boundaries, they may develop a stronger gender schema, which leads to the individual being more sex-typed (categorising information that is seen as appropriate to their gender more strongly). Bem (1981) also identified three other types of children in terms of gender: cross-sex (integrate traits opposite to their biological sex); androgynous (integrate traits from both genders); and undifferentiated (low integration on both masculine and feminine traits). Children who process information in a sex-typed way are more likely to invoke a hetero-sexuality sub-schema and this can lead to more gender stereotyping. This has been referred to as the 'sponge model of identity development', where children develop their sense of concepts from environmental experiences. To counter this, Bem (1981) argues that those who parent/care for young children should reduce the amount of sex-typing that children are exposed to. However, this approach has been critiqued, as it presents identity as a relatively simple process, as something that can be easily encouraged and then reinforced (MacNaughton, 2000).

Martin and Halverson (1981) present an alternative view to stereotyping. They suggest that stereotyping is an efficient cognitive process for children to handle large amounts of information, and prevents cognitive overload as children constantly revisit and amend stereotypes by assimilating new information. To do this they suggest children have two key types of schema: in-group–out-group; and own-sex schema. The first is where children make broad categorisations of information as relevant to either boys or girls. The latter allows children to process more complex information, such as behaviours, traits and appearance, as they see it linked to their in-group. This is often visible during children's play (Garner and Bergen, 2006). This approach sees children as more active and as having the ability to self-regulate, and is not just about being regulated by others.

 action point 20.1

Identify a space that children use. This could be a classroom, nursery, children's play space or an outside area. Look at any toys/resources in the space and how children play and interact with them. Record your response to each question separately for boys and girls:

1. How interested are children in the toys/resources?
2. What level of proximity do children have to the toys/resources?
3. What level of verbal interaction do children have when engaging in play?
4. What level of physical interaction do children have when engaging in play?

Martin and Ruble (2004) draw caution about using theoretical accounts of gender development as they can have two potential consequences: evaluative and motivational/informational. Evaluative consequences occur when a child identifies with a group and evaluates it positively. Martin and Ruble (2004) hypothesise that lower levels of understanding, such as a child recognising their own sex, may increase in-group bias. This is readily visible when looking at groups of children around the age of 3–4 playing – often they will segregate into single-sex play groups. In terms of motivating behaviour, children frequently use the sex of a peer to make judgements about what they will like and dislike. For example, boys will often gravitate towards boys as they assume similarities. When observing children, this can be seen as exacerbating segregation. However, this is part of expected development, and, as children increase in age, this relatively rigid behaviour will start to gradually reduce (Maccoby, 1990; Halim et al., 2017) as understanding of gender increases (e.g. a child recognises the consistency and stability of their gender).

So what benefit do gender development theories have? They provide a basis to understand behaviour. For example, children playing in single-sex groups should not be seen as surprising or problematic. They show that gendered stereotyped behaviour and responses generally rise substantially from the age of 3 but will most likely start to reduce from the age of 5–6. Having an understanding of gender development theories can be useful in many ways. For example, for a student studying early childhood it can help them appreciate how gender impacts on development; and identify ways to support anti-oppressive gender practices and to support parents who want to avoid gendered stereotypes. Therefore, a theoretical understanding is positive, when used appropriately, to gain an insight into children's behaviour, and not as stringent rules and expectations to make inappropriate judgements about aspects of development.

GENDER AS A SOCIAL CONSTRUCTION

Whilst theoretical perspectives can give an insight into gender within a child, it is important to consider the wider environment and the impact of this, as emphasised in ecological theory (Bronfenbrenner and Ceci, 1994). Many theories construct gender identity as fixed, which is problematic. For example, Bem never intended for her theory to explain gender identity or how children 'do' gender – rather, it is about how a child integrates gender into their identity (Starr and Zurbriggen, 2017). Gender is a lived experience, constructed by children through interactions and **discursive practices**. Cultural ideals of gender from society become embodied and from these, expectations for men and women develop. This has been prevalent throughout history. Examples include foot binding and expectations of a slim body shape for women; physical strength and provider for men. Children are socialised into gender in this environment and start to develop fixed notions of what is and is not acceptable. The child receives multiple messages about identity and has to negotiate and make choices between dominant and alternative gender **discourses** to form their gender identity (MacNaughton, 2000).

 case study 20.1

Forming a Gender Identity

Sophie is 5 years old. After visiting some friends with her mum and dad, she raised the following. The friends are two men, who are married. She has known them since birth and sees them regularly. Prior to this she had not raised any questions about the relationship between them. Her mum and dad were talking in the car about their wedding day. Sophie heard the conversation and asked:

Sophie: Adrian and Damien are married?
Mum: Yes.
Sophie: But they can't be. They're two boys and boys can't marry boys?
Mum: They can if they love each other. And girls can get married too if they love each other.

There was silence for a couple of minutes.

Sophie: Oh, OK.

1.   What does this tell you about the gender stereotypes held by Sophie?
2.   How may it support and refute the different models of gender development discussed in this chapter?

A POST-STRUCTURALIST VIEW OF GENDER

Maleness and femaleness are based on **essentialist** notions of biology. This constructs these qualities as being innate and having a 'natural' essence determined by biological factors. This positions male/female; masculine/feminine as dualisms (two options) and when an individual is labelled as male or female, it creates an expectation that they meet the discourses associated with this. So a boy is expected to be physically strong and engage in rough and tumble play. By contrast, post-structuralist approaches position a person as having multiple identities (e.g. gender, sexual, peers) and these are constantly amended (Turner and Reynolds, 2010). Issues of gender and sexuality are not separate from individual identity and society but integral to each (MacNaughton, 2000). This emphasises the interactional nature of identity as it is formed through contact and interactions with others, and this positions identity as a power-laden concept which constructs **hegemonic** ideals (Foucault, 1982; Donaldson, 1993).

A post-structuralist approach argues that gender is not determined by biology and other essentialist factors but is formed from the relationship between individuals, their environment and the social world. These continuously interact and construct and reconstruct gendered identities. This view of gender looks beyond the dualism of male–female, allowing for less rigid notions of gender identity and providing an opportunity to challenge gendered stereotypes (Davies, 2003; Arribas-Ayllon and Walkerdine, 2007). Not all scholars accept this theoretical position and you can also choose to challenge it. However, it does offer an alternative to the traditional essentialist positions and considers gender in a way that sees it as situated and influenced by the individual, their environment and broader societal expectations. Post-structuralism also offers a methodological approach for research related to gender in which the notion of 'discourse' is used as an analytic technique (Baxter, 2003).

Traditional essentialist positions place expectations on individuals to occupy legitimate gender positions. However, post-structuralists, such as French social theorist Foucault, argue that what are seen as legitimate positions are constructed from the rules, divisions, practices, objects and concepts through which bodies of knowledge are formed. This produces positions for subjects (e.g. motherhood, fatherhood) – in other words, the discourses. Foucault (1982) argues that discourses (e.g. masculinity, femininity) make meaning and are relevant as they legitimise accepted/prescribed actions and ways of behaving. To fit in requires a child to learn and accept dominant discourses of masculinity and femininity (MacNaughton, 2000). If a child resists dominant gender discourses and occupies a non-traditional gender position (e.g. boys playing with dolls), they may become accountable to peers, family and society for violating dominant gender expectations.

GENDER CHALLENGES: HEGEMONIC MASCULINTY, FEMININITY AND HETERONORMATIVITY

Although gender identity starts to form around the age of 2, the meaning of gender to children forms more slowly, as it requires them to negotiate gender discourse and practices (Jordan, 1995). If a child's practices are contradictory to expected gender practices (e.g. their actions do not align with their biological self), this can be seen as problematic by other children, parents or practitioners. There is a complex interaction of sex, gender and sexuality in constructing identities. The default sexuality is heterosexuality and assumptions of this are present in language and remain unquestioned. **Heteronormative** thinking assumes heterosexuality is 'natural, coherent, fixed and universal' (Yep, 2002: 163). Heterosexuality is seen as the benchmark in most societies for what is considered appropriate masculinity and femininity. Heteronormativity assumes that all people, including children and parents, will or do identify as heterosexual (Kilvington and Wood, 2016). This constructs heterosexual identity as privileged and sustains heterosexual privilege (Kitzinger, 2000). These social forces (sometimes referred to as institutions or traditions) hold power and create expectations – as a set of unwritten 'rules'. This creates discourses that sustain dominant expected positions (Foucault, 1982; Clarke et al., 2010). These discourses make individuals accountable for acting in ways contradictory to their biological identity.

For young children, hegemonic masculinity can (and often does) create expectations, that expect, stop or problematise behaviours (West and Zimmerman, 1987). Think about the label 'Tomboy', which is generally accepted as a 'phase' girls may go through. Why does it even exist? It is because of hegemonic masculinity. When girls do not behave in 'girl' ways, they are labelled as boys. When boys play with dolls or in the 'home corner', there is concern about this behaviour. What it often equates to is concern that the boys have a problem with gender, and this is likely to lead to them not identifying as heterosexual – the natural coherent sexuality (Kane, 2013). This is further evidenced by the fact that there is no equivalent accepted term of 'Tomboy' for boys. Being aware of this in ECEC is vital as it allows practices to be questioned to avoid dominant expectations impacting negatively on children, staff and more broadly in the community.

GENDER AND RESEARCH: THE ROLE OF RESEARCH IN EXPLORING GENDER

There are different approaches to gender research (often referred to as paradigms). Positivist approaches could measure levels of sex hormones (e.g. testosterone) and hypothesise how these impact on behaviour. Cognitive approaches could use questionnaires to explore thinking patterns in completing tasks and how these may vary between male and female children. An interpretivist approach to gender research focuses on how humans interpret themselves and the environment. An example of this could be a case study of how a new curriculum document takes account of gender in practice. Alternatively, a post-structuralist approach, as shown by the discussion above, explores how individuals are positioned by relationships and discursive practices. This views gender as constructed by social relationships (e.g. peers, practitioners) and institutions (e.g. families, the education system, government) and as not being under the control of the individual.

USING RESEARCH TO INFORM PRACTICE

Research from different paradigms can inform practice, as well as developing knowledge and understanding of subjects and concepts related to children. Abstracts present a summary of a research project. Reading an abstract offers a summarised insight into the aims of the research, the methodological approach and associated methods, the findings and the relevance of these.

 —— spotlight on research 20.1 ——————

Using Research Abstracts

This is the abstract from Martin and Ruble's (2004) study on cognitive cues to gender understanding:

> Young children search for cues about gender – who should or should not do a particular activity, who can play with whom, and why girls and boys are different. From a vast array of gendered cues in their social worlds, children quickly form an impressive constellation of gender cognitions, including gender self-conceptions (gender identity) and gender stereotypes. Cognitive perspectives on gender development (i.e., cognitive developmental theory and gender-schema theory) assume that children actively search for ways to make sense of the social world that surrounds them. Gender identity develops as children realise that they belong to one gender group, and the consequences include increased motivation to be similar to other members of their group, preferences

(Continued)

for members of their own group, selective attention to and memory for information relevant to their own sex, and increased interest in activities relevant to their own sex.

Martin and Ruble (2004) found that cognitive processes contribute to the formation and application of gender stereotypes and that the rigidity of these stereotypes increases from around the age of 3, becoming most rigid at around 5-6 years and then the level of rigidity reduces rapidly over the next two years. The reduction in the rigidity of information related to gender stereotypes continues to decrease in middle childhood (the full version of this short article is available as part of the online resources).

1. Thinking about what you have read in this chapter, how can a broad knowledge of different theories contribute to an understanding of how gender identity develops in young children?
2. This abstract focuses on cognitive approaches. A critique of cognitive theories is that they lack focus on how gender identity is positioned in society. How does a post-structuralist approach address this?
3. Cognitive research is generally situated in a positivist paradigm (e.g. quantitative data; broad generalisations; aims to identify 'the' truth). Post-structuralist research is situated in a critical paradigm (e.g. qualitative data; and accepts there are 'multiple' truths). What are the advantages and disadvantages of each paradigm?

There are two broad approaches to undertaking research: literature-based and empirical. Literature-based projects involve a systematic review of the literature around a specific topic. They are suited to areas where it may not be possible to gain ethical approval for a research study (e.g. approaches to support transgender children). A desk-based study (also known as literature-based) draws on a range of documents, for example an exploration of the notion of sexual agency in policy over time. Another example of a desk-based study would be to conduct a discourse analysis of the ECEC workforce in government policy. On the other hand, empirical research involves the collection of data from participants. Choosing a focus for any project can be difficult. A good starting point is to identify a broad subject area, such as gender, and think about how each of these approaches may be used.

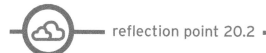 reflection point 20.2

For a short time, observe how adults interact with children. This could be within your own family or observations of a practitioner engaged with children.

Do they behave differently towards boys and towards girls?

If so how?

What do you think may explain this?

This approach can be valuable in allowing you to 'see' things that may not be 'visible' without careful observation. By reflecting on your observations, it can help you to identify potential areas of research. Looking at different media (e.g. reading books, research reports, policy documents) can also inform possible areas for research. Whilst writing this chapter, I spent less than an hour looking through some of the resources I used. From this I was able to list eight possible research areas:

- How gender is represented in children's television programmes, books or film
- Play choices of girls, boys and mixed groups
- Response to children's literature focused on gender
- How children represent discursive gender practices in their play
- How do discursive practices in a setting/classroom construct and challenge gendered identities?
- Styles of play interactions with boys and girls
- A discourse analysis of gender in children's media
- The construction of heroes in Disney films.

This shows the variety of potential topics exploring gender and how academic sources and insights from work with children can inform a research focus.

GENDER-INCLUSIVE ENVIRONMENTS, CHILDREN'S PLAY AND PRACTICE

Gender is often seen as a binary, with gender identity based on biological sex (male or female). However, binaries create hierarchical structures and regulate individuals by limiting their freedom to choose. A post-structuralist approach is critical of broad theories that claim to explain concepts such as identity. Identities are not about the individual but are based on ideologies, discursive practices and relationship within society (Coyle, 2016). Individuals do not need to be constrained or regulated by fixed notions of identity. This has implications for practice, as acknowledging the potential fluidity of identities can challenge hierarchical structures and create more inclusive environments. Those who work with children have an important role in helping to mitigate gender stereotypes that form in childhood (Starr and Zurbriggen, 2017), as these ultimately create unrealistic gendered expectations that serve to disempower all and maintain gender inequalities in society.

 action point 20.2

Clough, Nutbrown and Atherton (2013) emphasise the importance of inclusive environments. Inclusion can be promoted at a macro level (e.g. socio-political decisions within a society), exo level (e.g. within a community) and micro level (e.g. the interactions a child has with others). Considering this, review a setting where you have worked with children for images, activities, resources, areas or practice that potentially stereotype gender:

(Continued)

1. Make a note of any potential stereotypes you identify.
2. What is it about each of these that has the potential to stereotype gender?
3. What actions could you take to avoid acting in ways that may be stereotypical and to promote an inclusive approach?
4. What are the potential benefits of this for children, their families and practitioners?

Children are generally subject to gender expectations from prior to birth. For example, gender expectations are inherent in the style of their nursery/bedroom; clothing choices; toy choices; the way people interact with young children; and the influence of parents (Ayres and Leve, 2006). Gender play differences, in terms of toy and activity choices, are generally evident by the age of 3 and this is a worldwide phenomenon. These differences should not be seen as problematic but part of development.

Kilvington and Wood (2016) categorise different ways that adults respond to gender:

*   gender ignorant – no thought about gender
*   gender neutral – differences are socially constructed and an inclusive environment will address this
*   gender controlled – adults set out to prevent perceived gender-stereotyped play
*   gender appreciative – accept there are differences in how boys and girls play. Address this by creating a gender-neutral environment and allowing children choice over how they play.

A gender-appreciative approach has similarities to post-structuralism. Both focus on the environment and empowering individuals to carve out their own gender role. A liberal humanist approach, which focuses on the individual and challenges dominant discursive practices that disempower individuals, has the potential to challenge inequalities and create opportunities for all. Davies (2003: 167) summarises this by arguing:

> Children need to be given access to a discourse that frees them from the burden of liberal humanist obligations of coming to know a fixed reality in which they have a unified and rationally coherent identity separate and distinct from the social world.

Ayres and Leve (2006) outline a sequence of play: functional (e.g. movement of objects such as shaking); constructive (e.g. making artefacts); dramatic (e.g. role play, make believe, pretend play) and games with rules (e.g. accepting and conforming to pre-established rules). The types of play become sequentially visible as children develop, and gender is usually evident in all but functional play. Awareness of this is important as it can provide practitioners with a way to look at play environments and try approaches to avoid gendered stereotypes. This is relevant as gender still creates power differentials in society. In most societies, men continue to dominate key social, political and economic roles; despite many legislative reforms patriarchal privilege continues.

For boys, power is often evident in their play, (e.g. rough and tumble, super-hero dramatic play or how space is used). Girls are often tentative about getting involved and boys are often reluctant to let them join in (Ramsey, 2006). One response could be to remove toys or activities that create segregation. Alternatively, creating inclusive opportunities offers more choice for the engagement of all children. For example, one setting built a race track in the outside area and added a café and booking desk. Initially, the car races were dominated by boys. However, over a few days the space evolved to become predominantly gender inclusive, showing how changes to the environment can impact positively.

Within any setting, language (discourse) features heavily, particularly in literature. Books can introduce children to new storylines. MacNaughton (2000) explains that including diversity through stories has great potential to show different ways it is possible 'to be, act, feel and experience as boys and girls' (p. 123). The range of children's literature suited to this has expanded and is readily available. Books by Negley (2015), Pessin-Whedbee (2017) and Walton (2016) (see chapter references) are examples that empower children to make choices for themselves, irrespective of dominant gender discourses. This is important for two reasons: to provide options for children who feel alienated by dominant gender discourses; and, equally, to present alternatives to all children to help to develop their awareness of non-binary gender identities as part of a plurality of genders. Concern may exist about exposing children to difference and the impact this may have. However, there is a clear and reassuring response to this. Children develop their awareness of gender from multiple sources. Raising awareness of alternatives will not make them question their identity. It does though contribute to creating a world that values every person, irrespective of how they 'do' gender.

 reflection point 20.3

Based on your reading of this chapter, are there any aspects of practice with children you may now approach differently?

SUMMARY

- Gender can be understood in multiple ways. Sex is traditionally biologically determined and gender is constructed by cultural/social influences. A post-structuralist approach sees gender as constructed by ongoing interactions between the individual, the environment and the broader social world.
- Established ideas of gender produce discursive practices and these hold power that maintain dominant expectations throughout life. Hegemonic masculinity creates dominant expectations that have the potential to disempower all children, irrespective of gender identity.
- Traditional approaches that only see gender as binary (male–female) can be challenged to include opportunities to promote gender equality and value diversity in practice.
- Utilising evidence and undertaking research can play an important role in understanding gender in different contexts and can lead to anti-oppressive practice in ECEC.

 online reosurces

Make sure to visit https://study.sagepub.com/fitzgeraldandmaconochie for selected SAGE videos (with questions), SAGE journal articles, links to external sources and flashcards.

FURTHER READING

Kids' Guide to Gender – https://kidsguidetogender.com

This website provides suggestions on a range of resources for use by practitioners and families to explore the plurality of gender identities and valuing all in society.

MacNaughton, G. (2000). *Rethinking Gender in Early Childhood Education*. London: Paul Chapman Publishing.

This text provides an excellent exploration of how a post-structuralist approach, rather than a focus on individual development, offers the potential to move towards gender equality.

REFERENCES

Arribas-Ayllon, M. and Walkerdine, V. (2007). Foucauldian Discourse Analysis. In: C. Willig and W. Stainton-Rogers (eds), *The Sage Handbook of Qualitative Research in Psychology*. London: Sage, pp. 91–108.

Ayres, M. and Leve, L. D. (2006). Gender Identity and Play. In: D. P. Fromberg and D. Bergen (eds), *Play from Birth to Twelve*, 2nd edn. London: Routledge, pp. 3–12.

Baxter, J. (2003). *Positioning Gender in Discourse: A Feminist Research Methodology*. London: Palgrave Macmillan.

Bem, S. L. (1981). Gender Schema Theory: A Cognitive Account of Sex Typing. *Psychological Review*, 88: 354–64.

Bronfenbrenner, U. and Ceci, S. J. (1994). Nature–Nurture Reconceptualised in Developmental Perspective: A Bioecological Model. *Psychological Review*, 10(4): 568–86.

Clarke, V., Ellis, S., Peel, E. and Riggs, D. (2010). *Lesbian, Gay, Bisexual, Trans and Queer Psychology: An Introduction*. Cambridge: Cambridge University Press.

Clough, P., Nutbrown, K. and Atherton, F. (2013). *Inclusion in the Early Years*, 2nd edn. London: Sage.

Coyle, A. (2016). Discourse Analysis. In: E. Lyons and A. Coyle (ed.), *Analysing Qualitative Data in Psychology*, 2nd edn. London: Sage, pp. 160–81.

Davies, B. (2003). *Frogs and Snails and Feminist Tails* (revised edition). Cresskill, NJ: Hampton Press.

Donaldson, M. (1993). What is Hegemonic Masculinity? *Masculinities*, 22(5): 643–57.

Foucault, M. (1982). The Subject and Power. In: H. Dreyfus and P. Rainbow (eds), *Michel Foucault: Beyond Structuralism and Hermeneutics*. Brighton: Harvester, pp. 208–26.

Garner, B. P. and Bergen, D. (2006). Play Development from Birth to Age 12. In: D. P. Fromberg and D. Bergen (eds), *Play from Birth to Twelve*, 2nd edn. London: Routledge, pp. 3–12.

Halim, M. L. D., Ruble, D. N., Tamis-LeMonda, C. S., Shrout, P. E. and Amodio, D. M. (2017). Gender Attitudes in Early Childhood: Behavioral Consequences and Cognitive Antecedents. *Child Development*, 88(3): 882–99.

Jordan, E. (1995). Fighting Boys and Fantasy Play: The Construction of Masculinity in the Early Years of School. *Gender and Education*, 7(1): 69–86.

Kane, E. W. (2013). *Rethinking Gender and Sexuality in Childhood*. London: Bloomsbury.

Kilvington, J. and Wood, A. (2016). *Gender, Sex and Children's Play*. London: Bloomsbury.

Kitzinger, C. (2000). Doing Feminist Conversation Analysis. *Feminism and Psychology*, *10*(2): 163–93.

Kohlberg, L. (1969). Stage and Sequence: The Cognitive Developmental Approach to Socialization. In: D. Goslin (ed.), *Handbook of Socialization Theory and Research*. Chicago: Rand McNally, pp. 347–480.

Maccoby, E. E. (1990). Gender and Relationships: A Developmental Account. *American Psychologist*, *45*(4): 513–20.

MacNaughton, G. (2000). *Rethinking Gender in Early Childhood Education*. London: Paul Chapman Publishing.

Martin, C. L. and Halverson, C. F. (1981). A Schematic Processing Model of Sex Typing and Stereotyping in Children. *Child Development*, *52*(4): 1119–34.

Martin, C. L. and Ruble, D. (2004). Children's Search for Gender Cures: Cognitive Perspectives on Gender Development. *Current Directions in Psychological Science*, *13*(2): 67–70.

Money, J. and Ehrhardt, A. (1972). *Man and Woman, Boy and Girl*. Baltimore, MD: Johns Hopkins University Press.

Negley, K. (2015). *Tough Guys (Have Feelings Too)*. London: Flying Eye Books.

Pessin-Whedbee, B. (2017). *Who Are You? The Kids' Guide to Gender Identity*. London: Jessica Kingsley Publishers.

Ramsey, P. G. (2006). Influences of Race, Culture, Social Class and Gender: Diversity and Play. In: D. P. Fromberg and D. Bergen (eds), *Play from Birth to Twelve*, 2nd edn. London: Routledge, pp. 3–12.

Shaffer, D. R. (2009). *Social and Personality Development*, 6th edn. Boston, MA: Wadsworth Cengage Learning.

Shaffer, D. R. and Kipp, K. (2014). *Developmental Psychology: Childhood and Adolescence*, 9th edn. Boston, MA: Wadsworth Cengage Learning.

Smith, P. K., Cowie, H. and Blades, M. (2015). *Understanding Children's Development*, 6th edn. Chichester: Wiley and Sons.

Starr, C. R. and Zurbriggen, E. L. (2017). Sandra Bem's Gender Schema Theory after 34 Years: A Review of its Reach and Impact. *Sex Roles*, *76*(9–10): 566–78.

Turner, J. C. and Reynolds, K. J. (2010). The Story of Social Identitiy. In T. Postmes and N. Branscombe (eds.), *Rediscovering Social Identity: Core Studies*. New York: Psychology Press, pp. 13-32.

Walton, J. (2016). *Introducing Teddy: A Story about Being Yourself*. London: Bloomsbury.

West, C. and Zimmerman, D. (1987). Doing Gender. *Gender and Society*, *1*: 125–51.

Yelland, N. and Grieshaber, S. (1998). Blurring the Edges. In: N. Yelland (ed.), *Gender in Early Childhood*. London: Routledge, pp. 1–14.

Yep, G. A. (2002). From Homophobia and Heterosexism to Heteronormativity: Toward the Development of a Model of Queer Interventions in the University Classroom. In: E. P. Cramer (ed.), *Addressing Homophobia and Heterosexism on College Campuses*. New York: Haworth Press, pp. 163–76.

CHAPTER 21

TECHNOLOGY AND EARLY DIGITAL CULTURE

BY ADAM HOLDEN

I would have loved to have read this chapter earlier in my studies. Having this information is vital when thinking about how and when to use digital devices in the classroom safely. In my previous placements and current job, I have seen how important digital culture has become in education with many activities in lessons done on iPads, laptops and tablets. However, with the challenges of technology and young children, practitioners can often find it difficult to use the right amount of electronic devices in lessons and ensure safety, as I gathered from my placements and personal experience.

The chapter offers a balanced view, presenting different arguments as well as the concerns and worries around implementing ICT in young children's education. The questions in the section on guiding principles (p.330) are useful to consider when reflecting on what practice is suitable to use with young children.

SAIQA KHAN
BA (HONS) EDUCATION STUDIES
SHEFFIELD HALLAM UNIVERSITY

learning outcomes

By actively reading this chapter and engaging with the material, you will be able to:

- analyse the importance of digital literacy in early childhood education and care
- critically appraise the arguments for and against technology use with young children
- evaluate the role of the practitioner in the use of technology in early childhood
- identify and assess the implications of technology use in early childhood settings for early childhood professionals
- consider effective strategies for technology use in early childhood settings.

INTRODUCTION

This chapter will assess the role that **information and communication technologies (ICT)** play in the education of young children, and specifically in early childhood education and care (ECEC) settings. It is difficult to imagine a world without technology. In fact, there are few aspects of modern society that have expanded faster or had more impact on our daily lives than ICT. Young children now enter a world with **interactive technology** and **media** at its very heart, and have come to develop a greater level of comfort in using **digital devices** than the generations that have gone before them (Kalas, 2012). These devices have revolutionised the way we acquire knowledge, communicate with each other, and, in many ways, understand the world. Few would argue that **digital technology** is not here to stay; it now plays an integral part in our lives, especially in the lives of our youngest generation. Questions remain, however, as to how technology interacts with the brain as it develops, especially at an early age. This chapter will define the technologies included under the umbrella of ICT, discuss the significance of ICT and **digital literacy** for young children, highlight the importance of **online safety**, and outline what current research indicates about effective options for ICT use in early childhood classrooms and the implication for early childhood teachers.

DEFINING ICT

While our world is infused with technologies of all types, there remains a surprising lack of consensus regarding what ICT specifically consists of. This can be attributed to the fact that knowledge of, and comfort with, specific technologies tend to change generationally, and in the case of hardware and software even more frequently.

ICT is a term encompassing all forms of technology. In recent years, this has predominantly included smartphones, computers, tablets and a multitude of hardware, software and applications. Previous generations, however, witnessed the introduction of the Internet, satellite technology, basic mobile phones, intercom systems, digital printers and scanners, compact disks (CDs), digital versatile disks (DVDs), and even television, radio, tape recorders, photocopiers, vinyl records and landline phones before that. Each of these technologies has impacted society, some more than others, but many with lasting effect. Naturally, each of these technologies has also impacted children's play and other cultural practices, as well as their education. Over the past decade, there has been a sharp increase in young children's access to online technology of all types, though most specifically in the use of tablets, where an increased use from 11% in 2012 to more than 65% in 2015 has been reported in UK children between the ages of 5 and 7 (Ofcom, 2016). More than 21% of UK children under the age of 8 regularly use smartphones or tablets to go online (Ofcom, 2016).

action point 21.1

Make two lists of ICT technologies: (1) technologies created during your lifetime, and (2) technologies that were created prior to your birth. Select two technologies from each list and discuss how each has impacted education.

THE IMPORTANCE OF DIGITAL LITERACY

The importance of literacy has long-since been accepted as one of the foremost elements of a young child's cognitive development. Learning to read, write, speak, listen and interact with others has a positive impact on health, wellbeing and family structure (Levy, 2016). It is not simply the ability to develop these skills that is important, but also a child's capacity to understand how and when to use each skill to communicate effectively. Indeed, these are substantial skills in creating productive and successful citizens – the primary purpose of any system of education (Reaburn, 2016).

As early as 2001, Prensky (2001) suggested that children entering school were no longer the people that our education system was designed to teach. Claiming them as **digital natives**, Prensky argued that the new generation of school children had comfort levels living with technology previously unseen (Prensky, 2001). Given the increased saturation of all forms of media and technology into our daily lives since this time, I would argue that even the youngest children are now exposed to a technology-rich culture from birth. As such, they enter classrooms possessing a sophisticated understanding of various forms of technology and media that matches or surpasses many of their teachers (Zevenbergen, 2007).

As society has become increasingly digital in nature, it is difficult to imagine successful social integration without the ability to communicate using emails, texts or social media. As a result, there is an increasing need for children to be educated about online safety, **digital identity**, **digital citizenship** and the ability to critically assess the quality of material obtained from the Internet (Tamayo, 2016). Technology has the potential to provide rich and worthwhile opportunities to expand and personalise the learning environment of children of all ages, consistent with the life that they experience outside the classroom (Plowman and Stephen, 2005). While sceptics remain resistant to the widespread integration of technology, citing research that indicates potentially negative consequences, many studies have now determined that technology has the potential to be a significantly positive influence on the development of children, both cognitively and sensually (Zaranis and Oikonomidis, 2013).

 reflection point 21.1

Find a peer and discuss the following two questions: (1) In what ways are you digitally literate – what technology do you use to communicate or interact with the world around you? (2) How would your life be different if you were digitally illiterate (imagine that you could not use any of this technology in your daily life)?

TECHNOLOGY AND EARLY BRAIN DEVELOPMENT

In Chapter 2, you will have read about the ways in which the brain develops in early childhood. This is a highly complex process that is heavily influenced by a child's genes and the environment experienced. This brain development is particularly acute in the first seven years of life, where cognitive development, through repeated experiences of seeing, touching, hearing, smelling and tasting, constructs neurological connections that serve as a foundation or scaffold for all that children subsequently learn (David et al., 2003). It is unsurprising, therefore, that the use of technology at this young age has the potential to have dramatic effects well into later life.

For years, research has indicated the importance of a stimulating environment for healthy brain development, coupled with a nurturing and safe environment in which children can interact actively (Nagel, 2012). Children rapidly learn to connect with other humans using eye contact, touch, gestures and sounds, all the time refining, categorising and sorting these experiences for future reference (Institute of Medicine and National Research Council, 2015). This human interaction is critical to healthy child development, and so while a tablet or smartphone might be used as an entertaining distraction, it is unable to be responsive or pick up on cues from the child in the same way that an adult would. As a result, the child does not gain from a positive and interactive exchange.

In the first years of life, the brain is at its most adaptable and is therefore heavily influenced by the quality of interaction that it encounters (Malekpour, 2007). It is also susceptible to potentially negative stimulants, including over-stimulation and stress. Loud music, flashing lights, aggressive movements or even violence can all cause hyperarousal of the systems in the brain that trigger aggression rather than affection (Singer, 2017). It is important, therefore, that the types and amount of technology that a young child is exposed to be monitored closely by an adult, and that these technology interactions are constructed as part of a positive and balanced interactive environment (NAEYC, 2009).

 case study 21.1

Generational Gap and Digital Culture

Cassie is an intelligent, social and media-savvy 7-year-old girl. She is visiting her 80-year-old great-grandmother, Alice, who does not have an email account and does not use a smart-phone. Cassie wants to use her tablet to watch Dora and play her online games while she is visiting, but her great-grandmother doesn't have the Internet set up in her house. Alice is nervous, she has heard stories of people stealing online information, and doesn't feel comfort-able having a stranger come into her house to set up an Internet connection that she doesn't understand and does not want. While Cassie doesn't understand how the tablet is any differ-ent from the TV in the front room, Alice still marvels at the fact that her new 'Freeview' allows her to watch dozens of channels rather than the three or four she was used to. The technologi-cal divide between Cassie and Alice is vast and, thus, the ability for the two to communicate effectively is genuinely problematic.

1. What would the benefits be for Alice if she were to have access to the Internet in her home?
2. What does Cassie need to understand about using the Internet? Is there a difference between watching Dora and playing her online games?
3. If you were in Alice's position, what might you say to Cassie to help her understand that being so digitally connected might not be a good thing?

THE DEBATE SURROUNDING ICT IN ECEC

Despite the undeniable promise that technology holds in ECEC settings, there has been consider-able debate and controversy regarding its use over many years. Opinion remains sharply divided as to whether the benefits to the learning process outweigh the potentially negative outcomes often associated with too much screen time for young children (Plowman and McPake, 2013).

CONCERNS

In the case of very young children (0–2 years), there is a consensus that technology and media are not recommended at all and that screen time be limited to no more than 30 minutes a day up to the age of 5 (Council on Communications and Media, 2013). The research to date, however, is far from definitive, and therefore the discussion surrounding what technology and media, and how much, are appropriate for young children remains open to individual interpretation. What is agreed on is the fact that not all technology and media should be viewed in the same way, as there is a significant difference in early technologies where a child might be a passive recipient, and more advanced technology where a child can physically interact (Daugherty et al., 2014).

Opponents of technology integration point to a variety of potentially negative outcomes that have been linked to children using technology, including 'technology distracting children (Sheppard, 2011) and even negatively impacting the quality of work produced (Culén & Gasparini, 2012)' (Haßler et al., 2015: 144). Research points to the critical importance of technology being used only when developmentally appropriate and only by teachers who are qualified and experienced in teaching using digital tools (Falloon, 2013). Without careful planning and supervision, it is easy for children to spend more time interacting with technology than is optimal.

There is a growing concern regarding the addictive characteristics of ICT use, and the impact that prolonged technology use might have on young children (MacMullin et al., 2015). Research has shown a strong correlation between problematic technology use and increased feelings of loneliness, depression, anti-social behaviour and a diminished ability to manage time (MacMullin et al., 2015). These challenges suggest the potential for overuse of ICT to be unhealthy for young children. Similarly, research indicates that there is a strong link between use of electronic media and a lack of and disrupted sleep (Séguin and Klimek, 2015). Given the importance of sleep in early childhood and the fact that the preschool years are a highly sensitive period of development, this is of particular concern. Additionally, research has shown significant links between digital media use and the dimensions of hostile-aggressive, anxious-fearful and hyperactive-distractible behaviours (Séguin and Klimek, 2015).

Some professionals feel that the use of digital devices often stifles children's creativity in an environment where children's learning is closely linked to play (Cordes and Miller, 2000). They raise concerns that technology should not be a substitute for play experiences, and that children run the risk of losing good opportunities to learn through constructive play activities due to the increased presence of technology in their lives (Plowman and McPake, 2013). This has the potential to negatively impact children's health as they move their play experiences indoors and online – play that does not include actual physical activity (Slutsky and DeShetler, 2016). In contrast, however, scholars have also suggested that:

> contemporary play draws on both the digital and non-digital properties of things ... and as such provide[s] a counterpoint to those who seek to dichotomise digital and non-digital play, suggesting that play with digital technologies is not 'real play'. (Marsh et al., 2016: 250)

Children being exposed to inappropriate media is also an area of concern. This can happen intentionally, where children deliberately access the sites on the Internet that they may have witnessed previously (often in the presence of older siblings), or unintentionally, when children inadvertently find unsuitable material while actively involved in an investigative learning process. Either way, every time a 'connected' technology is placed in the hands of a young child there is the possibility that they can access material that is developmentally inappropriate for them (Marsh et al., 2017). It should be noted that this material may not be immediately apparent as unsuitable.

Issues of equality of access should also be considered. Not all children enjoy the same access to personal technologies, nor to the Internet. For example, children raised in low socio-economic circumstances may not enjoy the same access to technology, nor to the Internet, as their peers in more affluent circumstances. As such, these children do not have the opportunity to develop digital literacy at the same rate, and cannot benefit from the same resources, whether they are at home, school, or in the community generally (Rideout, 2011).

BENEFITS

Perhaps the greatest potential for the use of technology in education is the ability for it to personalise learning to meet the specific needs of individual children. The ability to differentiate the curriculum, resources and assessment for each child to ensure that everyone enjoys a personalised experience is often beyond the scope of ECEC practitioners who are increasingly expected to manage large and diverse classrooms. Technology, while not a complete solution, does provide a resource that can assist professionals in a variety of ways as they attempt to personalise instruction (Majumdar, 2015). Recent years have witnessed the emergence of educational applications, instructional videos, online textbooks and learning management software, where technology has played a significant role in allowing practitioners to present learning with a level of personalisation that had not previously been possible (West, 2011). This approach is not only recognised as more engaging for children, but can also result in improved achievement.

In the same way that ICT has the potential to help meet the individual needs of children, it also can address differences in learning style. Educators have come to understand that children learn in very different ways, and that this learning is optimised when the brain is engaged using multiple **modalities**. Technology can play a significant role in helping practitioners present information using a full range of intelligences:

> Indeed, the process of using technology to mobilize the multiple intelligences of children has already begun. Technologies and technologically based exhibitions in museums invite children to use several intelligences: moreover, even when one is simply typing on one's keyboard one can 'think' in spatial, musical, linguistic, or bodily intelligences. (Gordon, 2001: 33)

ICT also has 'a transformative and equalizing potential for efforts to achieve integration and inclusion of children with "special educational needs" in mainstream classrooms' (Istenic Starcic and Bagon, 2013). Given the flexibility of adaptive technology, children who experience any type of barriers to learning can personalise the way in which they study. In this capacity, 'the use of information technology is often the vital link that enables disabled children to participate fully in learning' (Wisdom et al., 2007: 222). This is especially true with young children given the cognitive development that takes place in the early years. The emergence of developmentally appropriate learning applications can provide children with learning opportunities and a learning environment that otherwise would not be available to them (Istenic Starcic and Bagon, 2013). In addition, assistive technology can offer children with Autism Spectrum Disorders and other impairments digital media that can help them learn the meaning of emotions and understand more about the way they communicate (Bishop, 2003).

Technology also has a significant role to play in improving the practices of early childhood professionals by helping practitioners maximise their capability in the non-teaching elements of the profession (Copple and Bredekamp, 2012). Technological tools can transform a variety of job essential skills from planning and record keeping, to sharing best practice with colleagues and communication with parents. Many of the ways that technology can benefit ECEC may not even take place in the classroom at all.

 spotlight on policy 21.1

Statutory Framework for the Early Years Foundation Stage

Notwithstanding this increased understanding of the importance of ICT integration into the early childhood curriculum, the Statutory Framework for the Early Years Foundation Stage (DfE, 2017a) makes no explicit reference to digital technology. However, the 'Understanding the World' area of learning requires that 'Children recognise that a range of technology is used in places such as homes and schools. They select and use technology for particular purposes' (p. 12). In order to meet this requirement adequately, it is incumbent upon ECEC practitioners to provide children with opportunities to experience a range of digital technologies as well as analogue. For example, young children can be given digital cameras, audio recorders, phones, tablets and simple robots to explore on their own and with others, as well as opportunities to use older technologies such as pen and paper, scissors, magnifying glasses, and so on. Given the role that digital technology can play in supporting early communication, it is perhaps surprising that the early learning goals related to communication, language and literacy in the EYFS make no mention of digital literacy. In spite of this, a number of organisations, such as the National Literacy Trust, provide training and resources for parents and practitioners to develop children's digital literacy skills at home and in ECEC settings.

For school-aged children, the government uses the Primary National Strategy Network for Literacy (DfES, 2006) as the basis for literacy. This requires teachers to develop the use of **digital texts** in the classroom, but it is far from comprehensive and 'the assessment criteria still reflect the skills and knowledge associated with print-based alphabetic literacy' (Burnett, 2010: 250). Education policy regarding the use of technology in school is addressed in the National Curriculum in England 'computing programmes of study', where schools are required to teach children to 'become digitally literate – able to use, and express themselves and develop their ideas through information and communication technology – at a level suitable for the future workplace and as active participants in a digital world' (DfE, 2017b: 1). As part of this, the Key Stage 1 attainment targets for 5–7-year-olds specifically address the need for children to be able to 'create, organize, store, manipulate, and retrieve digital content ... recognize common uses of information technology beyond school, and use technology safely and respectfully' (DfE, 2017b: 5).

ECEC TEACHERS AND ICT

Over the past decade, evidence has emerged that once children get to school, no single factor is as critical as the quality of teachers (Luque and Bruns, 2014). The confidence and competence of teachers to deliver the required curriculum has enormous impact on children's achievement at all levels of education. This is especially the case when it comes to the use of ICT where there tends to be a lack of self-efficacy, especially for those professionals who are not 'digital natives' (Albion, 1999). Learning how to effectively integrate technology has become an increasingly important skill for early childhood teachers.

There has been an emergence of a more digitally adept early childhood workforce in recent years, and this has heralded a shift in the approach to technology integration in early childhood settings (Simon and Nemeth, 2012). These younger, and more technologically comfortable, professionals have slowly changed the underlying attitude toward the use of technology from scepticism and fear to one of potential and comfort. Over time, teachers have come to understand that appropriately utilising technology in the classroom allows them to benefit from the children's positive disposition towards digital devices, while denying their use merely increases frustration and distances children from seeing the relevance of the learning process (Simon and Nemeth, 2012).

If teacher quality holds the key to digital literacy, then it stands to reason that those who prepare teachers for the classroom must also become digitally literate. The knowledge and preparation of the teaching force is one of the most important factors in children's academic performance (Alvarez and Majmudar, 2001), and this poses a challenge that the system is yet to fully embrace digital fluency. Most preservice teachers have very high levels of comfort with the personal use of various communication technologies, specifically when communicating through social media and using the Internet, but these same educators readily admit to knowing very little when it comes to using those same technologies in a professional setting (Daggett, 2010). Early childhood professionals and teachers need to develop their own **digital competence** in order to enable the children they work with to do the same (Hatlevik, 2016). Furthermore, there is a need for definition of precisely what professional digital competence means, and how this can best be implemented in both teacher education programmes and the field more generally (Instefjord and Munthe, 2017).

GUIDING PRINCIPLES FOR ICT USE IN ECEC SETTINGS

Even though guidelines surrounding the use of ICT in ECEC are in their infancy, there are several principles that make sense when it comes to using technology with young children. Early childhood practitioners would be wise to consider the following ten questions when reflecting on whether any resource is suitable for use with young children:

1. **Is it safe?** The most important consideration must be to ensure that any technology used promotes the social, emotional and physical wellbeing of all children. No digital resource should be introduced into the classroom that might be socially or emotionally damaging or physically dangerous in any way.
2. **Does it really support learning?** Any use of technology should be thoughtfully introduced to the classroom, only if it is intentionally and purposefully used in the learning process. Any tendency to use digital tools simply because they are available should be avoided. Technology is only successfully integrated if it genuinely plays a role in delivering the curriculum or develops required skills.
3. **Are the children actively learning?** Digital tools should be used only when they promote active learning. Young children should not be passive in their use of technology, and should be encouraged to use digital tools interactively and collaboratively whenever possible.

4. **Do we have the right balance?** Early childhood professionals should always trust their own professional judgement when it comes to using technology in the classroom. Finding the right balance of educational activity is key, and so using digital technology as only one part of this balance is advisable.

5. **Are we using the technology correctly?** Young children develop at different rates and therefore need to interact with digital sounds, images and content in different ways. In the case of very young children, their initial introduction to digital media is best experienced alongside an adult who can guide the process.

6. **Do I let them play?** Children must be given time to play, explore and experiment with digital tools before being expected to use them in a meaningful learning experience. Children must be allowed to be freely creative when they are first introduced to technology, learning through interactive experimentation in the same way that they do with other resources.

7. **Do I know the content?** Practitioners should always be aware of the details of all content used in classroom learning. Even if the source of digital media is a trusted one, staff must always take the time to fully understand what they are introducing to the children. Aligning the content with relevant curriculum goals is of key importance.

8. **Do I have the appropriate support?** In the same way that teachers should be aware of the content, they must also be aware of all devices that are used. Understanding how technology works, and the features and access that are available in each device, is important. Having the necessary technical support to effectively manage technology in the classroom is critical.

9. **Do I have the right training?** The rate of change in educational technology can be a source of real frustration for many professionals, and keeping abreast of new technologies can be overwhelming. Taking the time to benefit from regular professional development opportunities can help early childhood professionals remain current with their understanding of new digital devices and new software.

10. **How much technology do families have?** Not all technology is readily available to all families. Practitioners should find out what types and amounts of technology young children and their families have regular access to, and make decisions about the use of technology in and out of the setting with this information at hand.

SUMMARY

- Young children now enter a world with interactive technology and media at its very heart, and have come to develop a greater level of familiarity using digital devices than the generations that have gone before them.
- There is an increasing need for children to be educated about online safety, digital identity, digital citizenship, and the ability to critically assess the quality of material obtained from the Internet.
- Despite the importance of ICT integration into the early childhood curriculum, there remains a lack of national guidelines relating to digital literacy in early years education.
- It is important that the types and amount of technology that a young child is exposed to be monitored closely by an adult, and that these technology interactions are constructed as part of a positive and balanced interactive environment.

- Early childhood professionals should always trust their own professional judgement when it comes to using technology in the classroom. This entails finding a good balance of educational activity with and without digital technology.

 online resources

Make sure to visit https://study.sagepub.com/fitzgeraldandmaconochie for selected SAGE videos (with questions), SAGE journal articles, links to external sources and flashcards.

FURTHER READING

Marsh, J., Mascheroni, G., Carrington, V., Árnadóttir, H., Brito, R., Dias, P., et al. (2017). The Online and Offline Digital Literacy Practices of Young Children: A Review of the Literature. [online] Available at: http://digilitey.eu/wp-content/uploads/2017/01/WG4-LR-jan-2017.pdf [Accessed 2 July 2018].

A comprehensive review of the literature of the digital literacy practices of 0–8-year-olds.

RAND Corporation (2014). Moving beyond Screen Time. Policy brief. [online] Available at: www.rand.org/pubs/research_reports/RR673z2.html [Accessed 2 July 2018].

A research-based outline of the developmentally appropriate use of ICTs in ECEC.

UNESCO (2012). ICTs in Early Childhood Care and Education. Policy brief. [Online] Available at: http://iite.unesco.org/pics/publications/en/files/3214720.pdf [Accessed 2 July 2018].

An international set of guidelines produced by the United Nations establishing safety protocols and recommendations for practice.

REFERENCES

Albion, P. (1999). *Self-Efficacy Beliefs as an Indicator of Teachers' Preparedness for Teaching with Technology*. Chesapeake, VA: Association for the Advancement of Computing in Education, pp. 1602–8.

Alvarez, B. and Majmudar, J. (2001). *Teachers in Latin America: Who is Preparing Our Children for the Knowledge Century?* LCSHD Paper Series. Washington, DC: World Bank.

Bishop, J. (2003). The Internet for Educating Individuals with Social Impairments. *Journal of Computer Assisted Learning, 19*(4): 546–56.

Burnett, C. (2010). Technology and Literacy in Early Childhood Educational Settings: A Review of Research. *Journal of Early Childhood Literacy, 10*(3): 247–70.

Copple, C. and Bredekamp, S. (2012). *Developmentally Appropriate Practice in Early Childhood Programs Serving Children from Birth through Age 8*. Washington, DC: National Association for the Education of Young Children.

Cordes, C. and Miller, E. (2000). *Fool's Gold: A Critical Look at Computers in Childhood*. College Park, MD: Alliance for Childhood.

Council on Communications and Media (2013). Children, Adolescents, and the Media. *Pediatrics*, *132*(5): 958–61.

Daggett, W. (2010). *Preparing Students for their Technological Future*. Rexford, NY: International Center for Leadership in Education, pp. 1–14.

Daugherty, L., Dossani, R., Johnson, E. and Wright, C. (2014). *Families, Powered On: Improving Family Engagement in Early Childhood Education through Technology*. Santa Monica, CA: RAND Corporation.

David, T., Goouch, K., Powell, S. and Abbott, L. (2003). *Birth to Three Matters: A Review of the Literature*. London: Department for Education and Skills.

Department for Education (DfE) (2017a). Statutory Framework for the Early Years Foundation Stage: Setting the Standards for Learning, Development and Care for Children from Birth to Five. Available at: www.foundationyears.org.uk/files/2017/03/EYFS_STATUTORY_FRAMEWORK_2017.pdf [Accessed 10 October 2017].

Department for Education (DfE) (2017b). National Curriculum in England: Primary Curriculum. [online] Available at: www.gov.uk/government/publications/national-curriculum-in-england-primary-curriculum [Accessed 16 October 2017].

Department of Education and Skills (DfES) (2006). *Primary Framework for Literacy and Mathematics*. Norwich: DfES Publications.

Falloon, G. (2013). What's Going on behind the Screens? *Journal of Computer Assisted Learning*, *30*(4): 318–36.

Gordon, D. (2001). *The Digital Classroom: How Technology is Changing the Way we Teach and Learn*. Cambridge, MA: Harvard Education Letter.

Haßler, B., Major, L. and Hennessy, S. (2015). Tablet Use in Schools: A Critical Review of the Evidence for Learning Outcomes. *Journal of Computer Assisted Learning*, *32*(2): 139–56.

Hatlevik, O. (2016). Examining the Relationship between Teachers' Self-Efficacy, their Digital Competence, Strategies to Evaluate Information, and Use of ICT at School. *Scandinavian Journal of Educational Research*, *61*(5): 555–67.

Instefjord, E. and Munthe, E. (2017). Educating Digitally Competent Teachers: A Study of Integration of Professional Digital Competence in Teacher Education. *Teaching and Teacher Education*, *67*: 37–45.

Institute of Medicine and National Research Council (2015). *Transforming the Workforce for Children Birth through Age 8: A Unifying Foundation*. Washington, DC: The National Academies Press.

Istenic Starcic, A. and Bagon, S. (2013). ICT-supported Learning for Inclusion of People with Special Needs: Review of Seven Educational Technology Journals, 1970–2011. *British Journal of Educational Technology*, *45*(2): 202–30.

Kalas, I. (2012). *ICTs in Early Childhood Care and Education*. Russian Federation: UNESCO Institute for Information Technologies in Education.

Levy, R. (2016). A Historical Reflection on Literacy, Gender and Opportunity: Implications for the Teaching of Literacy in Early Childhood Education. *International Journal of Early Years Education*, *24*(3): 279–93.

Luque, J. and Bruns, B. (2014). *Great Teachers: How to Raise Student Learning in Latin America and the Caribbean*. Washington, DC: World Bank.

MacMullin, J., Lunsky, Y. and Weiss, J. (2015). Plugged in: Electronics Use in Youth and Young Adults with Autism Spectrum Disorder. *Autism*, *20*(1): 45–54.

Majumdar, S. (2015). Emerging Trends in ICT for Education and Training. [online] Available at: https://unevoc.unesco.org/fileadmin/up/emergingtrendsinictforeducationandtraining.pdf [Accessed 10 June 2018].

Malekpour, M. (2007). Effects of Attachment on Early and Later Development. *British Journal of Development Disabilities*, *53*(105): 81–95.

Marsh, J., Mascheroni, G., Carrington, V., Árnadóttir, H., Brito, R., Dias, P., et al. (2017). The Online and Offline Digital Literacy Practices of Young Children. Available at: http://digilitey.eu/wp-content/uploads/2017/01/WG4-LR-jan-2017.pdf [Accessed 10 October 2017].

Marsh, J., Plowman, L., Yamada-Rice, D., Bishop, J. and Scott, F. (2016). Digital Play: A New Classification. *Early Years*, *36*(3): 242–53.

Nagel, M. (2012). *In the Beginning: The Brain, Early Development and Learning*. Camberwell: Acer Press.

National Association for the Education of Young Children (NAEYC) (2009). *Developmentally Appropriate Practice in Early Childhood Programs Serving Children from Birth through Age 8*. Washington, DC: NAEYC.

Ofcom (2016). Children and Parents: Media Use and Attitudes Report. [online] Available at: www.ofcom.org.uk/__data/assets/pdf_file/0034/93976/Children-Parents-Media-Use-Attitudes-Report-2016.pdf [Accessed 10 October 2017].

Plowman, L. and McPake, J. (2013). Seven Myths about Young Children and Technology. *Childhood Education*, *89*(1): 27–33.

Plowman, L. and Stephen, C. (2005). Children, Play, and Computers in Pre-school Education. *British Journal of Educational Technology*, *36*(2): 145–57.

Prensky, M. (2001). Digital Natives, Digital Immigrants Part 1. *On the Horizon*, *9*(5): 1–6.

Reaburn, R. (2016). What is the Purpose of Education? In: S. Fan and J. Fielding-Wells (eds), *What is Next in Educational Research?* Rotterdam: Sense Publishers.

Rideout, V. (2011). *Zero to Eight*. San Francisco, CA: Common Sense Media.

Séguin, D. and Klimek, V. (2015). Just Five More Minutes Please: Electronic Media Use, Sleep and Behaviour in Young Children. *Early Child Development and Care*, *186*(6): 981–1000.

Simon, F. and Nemeth, K. (2012). *Digital Decisions: Choosing the Right Technology Tools for Early Childhood Education*. Lewisville, NC: Gryphon House.

Singer, E. (2017). The Neurological Roots of Aggression. *MIT Technology Review*. [online] Available at: www.technologyreview.com/s/409013/the-neurological-roots-of-aggression [Accessed 31 March 2017].

Slutsky, R. and DeShetler, L. (2016). How Technology is Transforming the Ways in which Children Play. *Early Child Development and Care*, *187*(7): 1138–46.

Tamayo, P. (2016). *Digital Citizenship Recommendations*. Olympia, WA: Report to the Legislature.

West, D. (2011). Using Technology to Personalize Learning and Assess Students in Real Time. [online] Available at: www.brookings.edu/wp-content/uploads/2016/06/1006_personalize_learning_west.pdf [Accessed 9 October 2017].

Wisdom, J. P., White, N., Goldsmith, K., Bielavitz, S., Rees, A. and Davis, C. (2007). Systems Limitations Hamper Integration of Accessible Information Technology in Northwest US K-12 Schools. *Educational Technology & Society*, *10*(3): 222–32.

Zaranis, N. and Oikonomidis, V. (2013). Profiling the Attitudes of Greek Kindergarten Teachers towards Computers. *Education and Information Technologies*, *20*(1): 201–15.

Zevenbergen, R. (2007). Digital Natives Come to Preschool: Implications for Early Childhood Practice. *Contemporary Issues in Early Childhood*, *8*(1): 19–29.

PART 5

YOUR JOURNEY

GO TO
https://study.sagepub.com/fitzgeraldandmaconochie *for free access to SAGE videos on topics covered in this book*

OBSERVING AND ASSESSING CHILDREN

BY JANE MURRAY

This chapter has helped me with my studies by giving me a good understanding of the different types of child observations. This is vital when studying early childhood as it is required for so much of the course content. Being able to undertake good quality child observations and have the ability to form useful, meaningful data, which can be acted upon, is crucial for any student. This is particularly true for the research project in the third year.

I liked the way the chapter leads into the subject of observations, discussing types of professionals who make observations, explaining why observations are important when matched with data and how this data needs to be correctly used to make the observation worthwhile. I also found the action points useful for being able to test my understanding of the information that I had just read and for developing critical thinking skills. The further reading provides invaluable additional content to read to widen your horizons.

CHERYL KENNEDY
BA (HONS) CHILDHOOD AND
SPECIAL EDUCATIONAL NEEDS
UNIVERSITY OF EAST LONDON

learning outcomes

By actively reading this chapter and engaging with the material, you will be able to:

- distinguish who observes children
- explain why and how observation and assessment underpin early childhood provision
- choose and justify how to observe, report and store observation and assessment data from young children
- know how to respond to young children's voices as part of observation and assessment processes in an ethical way.

INTRODUCTION

This chapter focuses on a highly valuable tool that early childhood practitioners use: observation and **assessment** for supporting and enhancing young children's development and learning. The chapter, which focuses on practice in England, is written from the perspective that early childhood practitioners can advocate for young children by ensuring that processes of observation and assessment they adopt prioritise the needs of each young child they work with.

The chapter focuses on who might observe young children, why observation is used, its historical roots and how observations of young children's behaviours can be conducted in early childhood settings. The chapter considers how **data** from child observations might be recorded, reported and stored safely and securely, and it addresses ethical considerations that early childhood practitioners may need to consider concerning their observations and assessments of young children's behaviours, development and learning in early childhood settings.

WHO OBSERVES CHILDREN AND WHY?

'Observation educates the senses' (Daston and Lunbeck, 2011: 1) and, in the professional context of an early childhood setting, is defined as 'the systematic watching and noting of people and phenomena' (Podmore and Luff, 2012: 8). This chapter is concerned with early childhood practitioners' observations of young children's behaviour, development and learning. Observation is defined here as 'early childhood practitioners' systematic uses of their senses to capture data and **evidence** about young children's behaviours and related events'. 'Data' and 'evidence' are defined later in the chapter.

Although the chapter focuses predominantly on early childhood practitioners observing and assessing in settings, other practitioners also observe young children. This section also briefly acknowledges child observations undertaken by others as part of making holistic provision for young children. Wragg (2012: vii) suggests that 'Observing the behaviour of our fellow humans is something we all start in babyhood and never finish.' The intense parental observation that occurs during eye contact between parents and infants is key for securing successful early attachment (Underdown et al., 2013; Magagna and Pasquini, 2014). Additionally, different professionals conduct observations which feed into assessments of different aspects of young children's development and learning.

RADIOGRAPHERS AND OBSTETRIC PRACTITIONERS

Radiographers conduct scans to observe and establish the stage of the foetus and its development, according to specified norms (Nicolson and Fleming, 2013). Following birth, obstetrics staff observe new born babies' capacity for independent life using the **Apgar score**, followed by 'careful physical examination and careful observation over the first few hours of life' (Hughes et al., 2002: 642).

SOCIAL WORKERS

Social workers observe some children who may require special protection by capturing body language, for example the nature of children's gestures and posture, and for children who have learned to speak, qualities of their verbal communication. Social workers evaluate their child observation data in conjunction with other data to interpret the significance of the observation data as a sound basis for deciding what actions may need to be taken to protect children (Trevithick, 2012: 168–9).

HEALTH VISITORS, EARLY CHILDHOOD PRACTITIONERS AND PARENTS

An important element of health visitors' work in England is child health surveillance and screening. They observe every child aged 24–30 months to identify delays in young children being 'ready to learn at two and ready for school at five' (Public Health England, 2016: 4). Health visitors conduct observations for the 2-year-old health and development review in partnership with parents using *The Ages & Stages Questionnaires*® (Squires and Bricker, 2009), so it is often parents who conduct observations of their children, for report to health visitors. For children aged 2–3 years attending early childhood settings, the health visitors' review is combined with 'The EYFS Progress Check at Age Two', completed by early childhood practitioners in settings. This integrated review captures data gathered over time through parents', health visitors' and practitioners' observations concerning learning and cognitive development, including children's speech, language and communication, personal, social and emotional development, physical development and health. The data are used to assess individual children's 'progress, strengths and needs' at 2–3 years to secure outcomes identified by government, including school readiness, to inform planning for children's services and to initiate early intervention if needed (Public Health England, 2016: 4). Using these data, practitioners must provide parents/carers with a written summary of their child's communication, language, personal, social, emotional and physical development, including 'areas where the child's progress is less than expected' (Dorset County Council, 2015).

OBSERVING DEVELOPMENTAL NORMS

The 'progress' referred to in the integrated review for 2-year-olds in England is framed by developmental norms: the stages a child is expected to reach by each age (e.g. Sharma and Cockerill, 2014). Whilst using such measures may be well intended, there is potential for misjudgement caused by early labelling of children's progress as 'less than expected', so practitioners should exercise sensitivity in conveying messages to parents/carers. Informed practitioners avoid assuming all developmental norms apply to all children; they constantly review and respect individual children's development and learning, taking into consideration children's cultures, ethnicities and other experiences. These variations are why *Development Matters* (Early Education, 2012) features overlapping ages for stages of development and learning within the Early Years Foundation Stage (DfE, 2017a).

OBSERVING CHILDREN FOR ACCOUNTABILITY

When thinking about accountability, data and to some degree evidence are usually considered. Therefore, it is important to consider what these mean. Data can be defined as 'plain facts', 'distinct pieces of information, usually formatted in a special way' (Boston University Libraries, 2017). Data that inform the educational improvement agenda have tended to focus on narrow measures, particularly standardised test scores (Pella, 2012), yet 'Data that include observations of students as they are learning, as well as artefacts from a variety of learning activities, contribute to the development of an informed and responsive pedagogy' (Pella, 2012: 73). Thinking about this in terms of young children, data is defined as 'information about young children's behaviours and related events, captured by early childhood practitioners' systematic observations and notes that record those observations'.

Although data is an important component of child observation, it can only help early childhood practitioners to address young children's development and learning needs if practitioners interpret the data so that it becomes evidence to inform their practice with young children. Evidence means different things in different contexts but is often regarded as the organisation and explanation of 'observable data' (Oancea and Pring, 2009: 20). Effective early childhood practitioners build full pictures of children's development and learning, not only by capturing their own observation data in settings but also by considering it in context with other trustworthy data concerning young children's behaviours, development and learning provided by others, including parents, other agencies, colleagues, researchers and the children themselves. For this chapter, then, evidence is defined as: data about young children's behaviours that have been captured, organised and explained by early childhood practitioners to inform decisions about provision for young children's development and learning. Evidence can then be used to assess children's development and learning.

Practitioners in England must observe young children in settings to provide data that comply with government requirements because they are accountable for young children's progress. In respect of the Early Years Foundation Stage in England (DfE, 2017a), this accountability is characterised by practitioners' conversion of rich information they capture in their real-world observations of children's daily lives, into numerical data linked to Early Learning Goals, a set of developmental norms that children are expected to attain, or exceed, in England before entry to school, aged 5. However, many practitioners in England seem unenthusiastic about generating such data and about the ways they are used – and misused – for accountability (Bradbury, 2014). Practitioners' lack of enthusiasm may reflect their concerns that 'performance data' detract from their primary use of observation as a tool to diagnose how best to support individual young children's development and learning (Roberts-Holmes and Bradbury, 2016: 119).

OBSERVING YOUNG CHILDREN ON A GLOBAL SCALE

On the largest scale, global monitoring is another way young children are observed. For example, the Organisation for Economic Co-operation and Development (OECD) is a group of 35 countries including the UK which has developed the *International Early Learning and Well-Being Study* (IELS) (OECD, 2017) to observe and assess children's performance aged 4½ to 5½ years across domains 'predictive of positive life outcomes', likely to include social skills, language and emergent literacy, mathematics and numeracy, self-regulation, locus of control and executive function. A key purpose of the IELS is to capture 'in-depth insights on children's learning development at a critical age', to 'provide countries with a common language and framework' for early childhood'. The IELS will provide a large data set and is also another tool concerned with developmental norms, but it contains an assumption that all young children everywhere develop and learn similarly at the same age. This assumption runs contrary to an appreciation that every child has distinctive capacities and individual needs, which practitioners who work with children each day understand very well and, for these reasons, the IELS is strongly contested (Moss et al., 2016).

 reflection point 22.1

How can practitioners share news about their children's progress being 'less than expected' in sensitive ways that are supportive of the child and the parent?

THE TRADITION OF OBSERVING YOUNG CHILDREN

Notwithstanding the accountability demands made of practitioners, there is a rich tradition in the field of ECEC of using child observation data as a rich seam of evidence for understanding young children's actions and for taking that understanding forward to make appropriate provision for each child's development and learning. Pioneers including Froebel (1826), Pestalozzi (1894), Montessori (1912), Isaacs (1930, 1933) and Piaget (1962) all based judgements about the young children they worked with on first-hand evidence they derived from their child observations. The earlier pioneers practised observation from a philosophical perspective, but more recent pioneers – Piaget, Montessori and Isaacs – had scientific training which they used to develop further the tradition of observation as a key tool for enabling practitioners to make every child's experience of early childhood provision meaningful to each child's life and authentic interests.

 spotlight on people 22.1

Susan Isaacs

Susan Isaacs pioneered progressive teaching methods with young children. Born in 1885 in Lancashire, England to middle-class parents, she studied infant teacher training, philosophy, psychology and psychoanalysis. In 1924, Isaacs was appointed head of the progressive Malting House School in Cambridge. She regarded children as researchers whose 'epistemic interest and inquiry' is no different from those of adult researchers (Isaacs, 1944: 322). Isaacs did not approve of child observations conducted in laboratory environments, as practised by Piaget (1936). The role of teachers at the Malting House School was to observe children's behaviours naturalistically in play and to apply their knowledge of child psychology to understand behaviours observed in children and inform appropriate provision for their development and learning: 'Any judgement as to the educational value of the method followed must in the end rest upon the soundness or otherwise of the psychological basis' (Isaacs, 1930: 1). Isaacs became the inaugural Head of Child Development at the University of London's Institute of Education in 1933 where she was highly influential in training teachers of young children to use observation and psychology as a basis for their teaching. That legacy has prevailed, in the UK and internationally (Gardner, 1969; Isaacs, 1929, 1930, 1933).

Take some time to explore how the other pioneers used observation in their work with young children.

Consider how this is similar and different to how observation is seen and used today.

HOW TO CHOOSE, CONDUCT AND RECORD CHILD OBSERVATIONS IN A SETTING

Child observations can be carried out in many formats (Sharman et al., 2007); different observation methods help practitioners to gather different types of data for different reasons. To choose the type of observation that you carry out, ask yourself:

'What do I want to find out?'

'What can I manage practically?'

In this section, four observation techniques that are commonly used in early childhood settings are explained: narrative observation, checklist observation, sampling observation and tracking observation.

Whichever technique the early childhood practitioner opts to use in a situation, it is important that they report factually what they observe the child doing. After the observation, the practitioner will evaluate the observation notes they have made. To do this, they will spend time reflecting critically on what was observed, drawing on knowledge of child psychology theory and research, as well as knowledge of the child. This enables the practitioner to assess what the observation data mean in terms of (a) what and how the child has developed and learned and their interests, and (b) what the practitioner can do to support the child's development and learning, going forward.

This section of the chapter focuses purely on capturing data during the observation. Examples of observation case studies are provided in the form of observations undertaken (see Figures 22.2–22.6). It is usually advisable to plan for observation, though it is not always feasible to do so.

When making observation notes, note the observation type, the objective of the observation, the date, the time the observation was undertaken, the child's name and age, and the practitioner's name (Figure 22.1).

Observation Type:

Objective:

Date:

Time:

Child / Age:

Practitioner:

Figure 22.1   Observation information

It may also be useful to include contextual information about the setting. At the end of each observation, a space should also be made for 'Evaluation', which is conducted after the observation to assess how the observation can inform understanding about the child's development and learning, and what it may mean for practice in the setting.

NARRATIVE OBSERVATION

There are different forms of narrative observation, including child study, structured narrative, unstructured narrative and anecdotal narrative (diary).

Child study

The practitioner observes a child and makes detailed notes at intervals over many weeks, months or even years. The purpose of conducting a child study might be to capture data to inform an assessment of a child's overall progress.

Structured narrative

The practitioner observes a child and makes notes according to a pre-determined set of criteria. The purpose of conducting a structured narrative would usually be to capture data for a specific reason, for example how a child plays with other children.

Unstructured narrative

The practitioner observes the child to capture data about the child's naturalistic behaviour and writes down everything the child does. An unstructured narrative provides rich detailed data about everything a child does over a period of medium length, perhaps 30 minutes or an hour. An unstructured narrative might be used to help a practitioner to get to know a new child in the setting, or to enable the practitioner to assess how a child engages in activities during free-flow play sessions, for example.

Anecdotal narrative (diary)

The practitioner observes the child over one day, several days or several weeks and makes unstructured notes about what the child does on each occasion. The purpose of conducting an anecdotal narrative is to build a picture of a child's behaviour over time, which may enable the practitioner to spot patterns in the behaviour. An anecdotal narrative may also enable a practitioner to understand the antecedents for a child's behaviour.

CHECKLIST OBSERVATION

The practitioner observes the child to see if they present with a specific behaviour, usually over an identified period, for example one week. The practitioner makes a note with a tick or another symbol when the behaviour presents. The note might be a tick and/or other symbols and the practitioner may also add brief notes. The purpose of conducting a checklist observation may be to identify if a specific behaviour presents, or to see if a pattern of behaviour emerges over an identified period. Examples might include a phonics checklist, a Portage checklist which breaks down the norms into smaller steps which are used to develop a plan for the parents and carers, or an activity list that the practitioner might use to ensure all children have had access to an activity. A checklist observation is quick and objective but lacks detail. In Figure 22.2 are Sukina's checklist observations of children in her key group who can jump, hop and kick a ball in the autumn term.

Observation Type: *Time Sampling*
Objective: *To identify if key group children can jump, hop or kick a ball*
Date: 1.11.17 – 30.11.17 *(Autumn Term)*
Time: *Varied*
Child: *Alfie (age 3.1), Betty (age 3.5), Charles (age 3.2), Didier (age 3.0)*
Practitioner: *Sukina*

Autumn 2017	Alfie	Betty	Charles	Didier
Jumps	✓ 3.11.17	✓ 6.11.17	✓ 1.11.17	
Hops	✓ 3.11.17		✓ 3.11.17	
Kicks a ball	✓16.11.17	✓ 16.11.17	✓ 7.11.17	✓ 30.11.17
Evaluation:				

Figure 22.2   Sukina's checklist observations

SAMPLING OBSERVATION

Practitioners use sampling observations to capture data about children's specific behaviours; for example, a practitioner might observe a child who struggles to interact with other children. Different types of sampling observations include:

- time sampling observation
- event sampling observation
- snapshot observation.

Time sampling observation

The practitioner plans a number of observations at intervals, for example the practitioner notes briefly what the child is doing every two minutes over a 10-minute period (Figure 22.3). Time sampling observation may be useful for knowing what a child is doing when, for identifying antecedent behaviours and for observing children's involvement in activities.

Event sampling observation

The practitioner plans to observe, then observes a child's behaviour related to an event (Figure 22.4). Event sampling observations may help practitioners to understand individual children's behaviour and setting management issues, for example how children cope with transition into lunchtime.

Observation Type: *Time Sampling*
Objective: *To identify how Amelia plays co-operatively*
Date: *3.10.17*
Time: *9.30am – 9.35am, 1 minute intervals*
Child: *Amelia (age 3.4)*
Practitioner: *Fergus*

Time	- Observation -	Practitioner
9.30am	*Moves outside to play with big boxes*	*FM*
9.31am	*Lifts flap of box and laughs at Billy in the box*	*FM*
9.32am	*Sitting in box with Billy*	*FM*
9.33am	*Sitting on floor outside box shouting 'Get out, Get out!' at Billy*	*FM*
9.34am	*Sitting on floor outside box shouting at Billy: 'It's my box'*	*FM*
9.35am	*Sitting in box with Billy*	*FM*

Evaluation:

Figure 22.3   Fergus' time sampling observation

Observation Type: *Event sampling*   **Practitioner**
Objective: *To identify factors that help and hinder Betty from settling at nursery*
Date: *3.12.17-7.12.17 (1 week)*
Time: *Settling in each morning*
Child: *Betty (age 3.6)*
Practitioner: *Jemima*
Underlined sections: *main observation.*
(Bracketed sections: *contextual notes)*

Monday	*(Betty was at Mum's house overnight.) Betty is very tearful – she says 'No I'm not going' (into the setting). Betty's Mum brings her in to the setting (9.10am). Betty's Mum leaves (9.11am). Betty is Screaming + crying. Betty, crying, sits by Annie (practitioner), watching children play in the setting. Betty watches children sitting on the floor for story-time. Betty joins with story group. 10.05am. Betty stops crying. Betty listens to the story. (Betty continues to listen to the story. Observation stops at 10.15am)*	*JM*
Tuesday	*(Betty was at Mum's house overnight.) Betty comes in – clinging to mum [9.05]. Sees Dolly Dewdrop dolls – Annie [practitioner] takes one to her. Betty holds it. Mum leaves. Betty runs after her. Annie brings Betty back. Betty is crying. 9.35am: Betty picks up a Dolly Dewdrop. Betty stops crying. Betty picks up another Dolly Dewdrop. (Betty continues playing Dolly Dewdrops with Annie. 10am: Observation stops)*	*JM*

(Continued)

Wednesday	(Betty was at Dad's house overnight.) Betty comes into the setting holding Dad's hand [8.45am]. Betty clings to Dad. Annie shows Betty Dana (her favourite Dolly Dewdrop doll). Dad, Annie and Betty play Dolly Dewdrops. Betty absorbed in Dolly Dewdrop play. 9.20am: Dad tells Betty he will go. Betty looks up. Betty picks up a Dolly Dewdrop. (Betty continues playing Dolly Dewdrops with Annie. 9.30am: Observation stops)	JM
Thursday	Betty is absent	JM
Friday	Betty is absent	JM
Evaluation:		

Figure 22.4 Jemima's event sampling observation

Snapshot observation

The practitioner briefly observes a child's behaviour, usually spontaneously, often on Post-it notes or labels. The practitioner might include photographs and would usually transfer the short notes to an assessment record to build a picture of a child's behaviour over time (Figure 22.5).

7.11.17 - 8.45 am	10.1.18 - 8.52am
Betty (age 3.5) comes into the setting with Dad. She is screaming. Annie speaks to Betty, Betty screams very loudly. Dad goes. Betty is with Annie, crying JM	Betty (age 3.7) comes into the setting with Mum - she is smiling. Betty shows Annie her Dolly Dewdrop doll. Annie says: `Dora  - she's my Dora` JM
Evaluation:	

Figure 22.5 Jemima's snapshot observations

TRACKING OBSERVATION

The practitioner observes and charts a child's movements on a setting map over a specified period (Figure 22.6). A tracking observation might help to identify if a child goes outside during free-flow play, or avoids messy play, for example.

This section has illustrated the central role of observation to ECEC practice. However, as Isaacs demonstrated (1929, 1930, 1933), observation can be as valuable for research as it is for practice in the ECEC field. ECEC researchers decide to use observation techniques if they believe they can capture data that provide answers to their research questions. Ethical protocols must be used when observing for research purposes in the UK (e.g. EECERA, 2014), yet aside from the Data

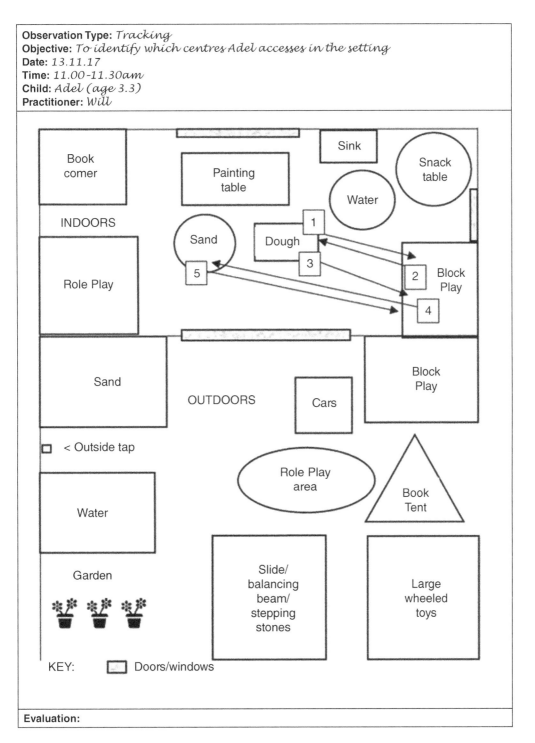

Observation Type: *Tracking*
Objective: *To identify which centres Adel accesses in the setting*
Date: *13.11.17*
Time: *11.00-11.30am*
Child: *Adel (age 3.3)*
Practitioner: *Will*

Figure 22.6   Will's tracking observation

Protection Act 1998 and General Data Protection Regulations 2018, similar protocols are rarely used when child observation is for practice purposes.

action point 22.1

Select and use one of the observation techniques indicated above to observe a child, then use these points to structure your evaluation and assessment of the observation:

- Keep the evaluation short, succinct and critically analytical.
- Referring to the observation objective, consider critically what the observation data tell you about the child's interests, behaviours, development and learning.
- Include other evidence (e.g. information from parents, other agencies, other observations), as well as data from this observation.
- Map your evidence to statutory requirements (e.g. DfE, 2017a) as a minimum, plus relevant additional achievements.
- Consider what the evidence tells you the child is ready to learn next. What provision might help them?

EVALUATION OF CHILD OBSERVATIONS AS A TOOL FOR ASSESSMENT

Assessment has different purposes. It can be used for 'teaching and learning, management and accountability [and] research' (Nutbrown, 1999: 127), it might be to ensure children have attained basic knowledge and skills required of them by policymakers, or it might be used diagnostically to know how to enhance young children's learning (Carr, 2001). Observation is valued as the basis for assessment in early childhood settings (Podmore and Luff, 2012) and it emerges from the explanatory element of evidence that practitioners produce from child observation data. For this chapter, assessment is defined as: early childhood practitioners' explanations of data that they have captured about young children's behaviours, used to enhance the young children's development and learning.

Evaluations of child observations should be conducted after the practitioner has observed the child. Practitioners evaluate observations of children's behaviour to understand what the observation data mean. Evaluating child observation data enables practitioners to:

- turn data into evidence they can use to assess children's development and learning
- understand children's behaviours, motivations and interests
- identify if a child is not developing or learning and why
- identify provision children may need next to continue to develop and learn
- reflect on the quality of their own practice.

Evaluation is the highest order learning skill (Bloom et al., 1956). It is also a high order teaching skill: to identify what children are ready to learn next, we must identify, appraise and assess what children have already learned. Evaluation is the practitioner's critical interpretation of the objective observation data. Together, the data and critical interpretation provide evidence on which to base:

1. assessment of what observation data reveal about the child's development and learning, related to the observation objective, and
2. new, informed decisions about what the child may be ready to learn next and the provision likely to help.

To make secure assessment judgements, practitioners support their critical interpretations of observation data by drawing on their professional experiences, their knowledge of the child, policy documents such as the Statutory Framework for the Early Years Foundation Stage (DfE, 2017a) and relevant literature and research.

 action point 22.2

Using the guidance in this section, evaluate the examples of different observation techniques in the section 'How to choose, conduct and record child observations in a setting'. What is helpful for making each evaluation? Does anything make your task difficult? How will you apply this experience in future?

RECORDING, STORING AND REPORTING OBSERVATION AND ASSESSMENT DATA ETHICALLY

Practitioners record, store and report child observations for different reasons. These might include:

- capturing and celebrating a child's development and learning progress over time
- identifying a child's interests and achievements to inform their next steps in learning and what provision can best support those steps
- monitoring concerns about children's behaviour, development and learning
- reporting data on children's performance to feed into big data sets
- practitioners' own performance management and accountability
- reporting children's progress to parents/carers
- practitioner research (see Chapter 23).

Practitioners are increasingly obliged to report children's progress to large-scale agencies to inform local, regional and national data sets and to satisfy performance and accountability demands (DfE, 2017b; OECD, 2017). These requirements raise significant questions about:

- who owns the child observation data that practitioners capture
- what ethical protocols are adopted to identify appropriate uses of those data (Lindgren, 2012)
- what protects children from abuse and misuse of data about them
- how children can be empowered in the collection, storage and reporting of data about themselves (Bath, 2012).

When practitioners conduct observations of children purely for professional use, they are not required to invite parents to give their informed consent for those observations to be under-taken. As indicated above, this approach differs from stringent requirements made in the UK of researchers who conduct child observations (e.g. EECERA, 2014). Yet, even for research purposes, under English law the most children can be invited to do when they are observed is to give their assent: 'affirmative agreement' (Rossi et al., 2003: 132), because consent brings greater legal compulsion (Coyne, 2010).

Child observation data are now commonly stored digitally and such storage can be secure. Data protection laws and practices requiring anonymity and encryption of data collected in practitioners' observations mean children's individual identities should be protected. However, increasingly sophisticated computer hacking incidents mean that such protection is difficult to guarantee. Moreover, we must consider not only how data are used, stored and reported today, but also how they might be mined and used in future with tools that have yet to be invented. How might data collected about a child aged 3 today affect that child when new uses are found for the data in 20, 30, 50 or more years?

Respect for children in the process of observation and assessment means that we do not treat children as data sources (Fielding, 2001), rather we engage with them as individuals who are our partners in their learning and our own. This may mean:

- finding legitimate ways to resist demands made by powerful agencies for data about children that inform their performativity agenda
- giving children ownership of their own data, by enabling them and their parents to share in collecting, evaluating, assessing, reporting and using child observation data
- using child observations to create experiences the children value
- co-constructing learning with children at a pace suited to each child (Murray, 2017)
- adopting appropriate research ethics for all child observations (EECERA, 2014).

SUMMARY

- The chapter has distinguished between those who observe children by exploring how parents, practitioners and other professionals undertake child observations as part of making holistic provision for young children.

- The chapter has explained why and how observation and assessment underpin early childhood provision, critiqued reasons for observing young children and how to respond meaningfully to the voice of the child.
- The chapter has provided an approach to choose and justify techniques to observe young children and adopt appropriate ways to record, report and store observation and assessment data.
- Children should have a voice in observations. Practitioners need to respond to young children's voices and apply ethical protocols appropriately when observing and assessing young children as partners in their learning and how early childhood practitioners can advocate for young children.

 online resources

Make sure to visit https://study.sagepub.com/fitzgeraldandmaconochie for selected SAGE videos (with questions), SAGE journal articles, links to external sources and flashcards.

FURTHER READING

McDowall Clark, R. (2016). *Exploring the Contexts of Early Learning: Challenging the School Readiness Agenda*. Abingdon: Routledge.

This book shows how evidence can be used to justify provision that supports the development of self-regulation and autonomy that young children need to flourish cognitively and emotionally.

Murray, J. (2017). *Building Knowledge in Early Childhood Education: Young Children are Researchers*. Abingdon: Routledge.

This book is based on a series of real observations that demonstrate the ways young children build knowledge in their early childhood settings and at home, and how adults can support them.

Palaiologou, I. (2016). *Child Observation: A Guide for Students of Early Childhood*, 3rd edn. London: Sage/Learning Matters.

This book provides further practical guidance for using observation to understand young children's actions and use them to plan and provide for new learning.

REFERENCES

Bath, C. (2012). 'I Can't Read it; I Don't Know': Young Children's Participation in the Pedagogical Documentation of English Early Childhood Education and Care Settings. *International Journal of Early Years Education*, 20(2): 190–201.

Bloom, B. S., Engelhart, M. D., Furst, E. J., Hill, W. H. and Krathwohl, D. R. (1956). *Taxonomy of Educational Objectives: The Classification of Educational Goals – Handbook 1: Cognitive domain*. New York: Longmans, Green and Co.

Boston University Libraries (2017). *What is 'Research Data'?* [online] Available at: www.bu.edu/datamanagement/background/whatisdata [Accessed 9 April 2017].

Bradbury, A. (2014). Early Childhood Assessment: Observation, Teacher 'Knowledge' and the Production of Attainment Data in Early Years Settings. *Comparative Education, 50*(3): 322–39.

Carr, M. (2001). *Assessment in Early Childhood Settings: Learning Stories.* London: Sage.

Coyne, I. (2010). Research with Children and Young People: The Issue of Parental (Proxy) Consent. *Children and Society, 24*(3): 227–37.

Daston, L. and Lunbeck, E. (eds) (2011). *Histories of Scientific Observation.* Chicago: University of Chicago Press.

Department for Education (DfE) (2017a). Statutory Framework for the Early Years Foundation Stage. [online] Available at: www.foundationyears.org.uk/files/2017/03/EYFS_STATUTORY_FRAMEWORK_2017.pdf [Accessed 14 April 2017].

Department for Education (DfE) (2017b). Statistics at DfE. [online] Available at: www.gov.uk/government/organisations/department-for-education/about/statistics [Accessed 14 April 2017].

Dorset County Council (2015). *The Integrated Review for Two-Year-Olds: Pan Dorset Practitioner Guidance 2015.* [online] Available at: www.dorsetforyou.gov.uk/working-in-childcare/practitioner-support/integrated-review [Accessed 11 April 2017].

Early Education (2012). *Development Matters in the Early Years Foundation Stage.* London: British Association for Early Childhood Education.

EECERA (2014). Ethical Code for Early Childhood Researchers. [online] Available at: www.eecera.org/custom/uploads/2016/07/EECERA-Ethical-Code.pdf [Accessed 14 April 2017].

Fielding, M. (2001). Students as Radical Agents of Change. *Journal of Educational Change, 2*(2): 123–41.

Froebel, F. (1826). *On the Education of Man.* Keilhau/Leipzig: Wienbrach.

Gardner, D. E. M. (1969). *Susan Isaacs: The First Biography.* London: Methuen Educational.

Hughes, S. C., Levinson, G., Rosen, M. A. and Shnider, S. M. (eds) (2002). *Shnider and Levinson's Anesthesia for Obstetrics.* Philadelphia: Lippinott, Williams and Wilkins.

Isaacs, N. (1944). Children's 'Why' Questions. In: S. Isaacs, *Intellectual Growth in Young Children.* London: Routledge, pp. 291–354.

Isaacs, S. (1929). *The Nursery Years.* London: Routledge.

Isaacs, S. (1930). *Intellectual Growth in Young Children.* London: Routledge.

Isaacs, S. (1933). *Social Development in Young Children.* London: Routledge.

Lindgren, A.-L. (2012). Ethical Issues in Pedagogical Documentation: Representations of Children through Digital Technology. *International Journal of Early Years Education, 20*(2): 190–201.

Magagna, J. and Pasquini, P. (eds) (2014). *Being Present for Your Nursery Age Child: Observing, Understanding, and Helping Children.* London: Karnac.

Montessori, M. (1912). *The Montessori Method.* New York: Frederick A. Stokes.

Moss, P., Dahlberg, G., Grieshaber, S., Mantovani, S., May, H., Pence, A., et al. (2016). The Organisation for Economic Co-operation and Development's International Early Learning Study: Opening for Debate and Contestation. *Contemporary Issues in Early Childhood, 17*(3): 343–51.

Murray, J. (2017). *Building Knowledge in Early Childhood Education: Young Children are Researchers.* Abingdon: Routledge.

Nicolson, M. and Fleming, J. E. E. (2013). *Imaging and Imagining the Fetus: The Development of Obstetric Ultrasound.* Baltimore, MD: Johns Hopkins University Press.

Nutbrown, C. (1999). *Threads of Thinking.* London: Sage.

Oancea, A. and Pring, R. (2009). The Importance of Being Thorough: On Systematic Accumulations of 'What Works' in Education Research. In: D. Bridges, P. Smeyers and R. Smith (eds), *Evidence-Based Education Policy: What Evidence? What Basis? Whose Policy?* Oxford: Wiley-Blackwell, pp. 11–35.

Organisation for Economic Co-operation and Development (OECD) (2017). International Early Learning and Well-Being Study (IELS). [online] Available at: www.oecd.org/edu/school/international-early-learning-and-child-well-being-study.htm [Accessed 14 April 2017].

Pella, S. (2012). What Should Count as Data for Data-Driven Instruction? Toward Contextualized Data-Inquiry Models for Teacher Education and Professional Development. *Middle Grades Research Journal*, 7(1): 57–75.

Pestalozzi, J. H. (1894). *How Gertrude Teaches her Children* (trans. L. E. Holland and F. C. Turner; edited with an introduction by E. Cooke). London: Swan Sonnenschein.

Piaget, J. (1936). *Origins of Intelligence in the Child*. London: Routledge & Kegan Paul.

Piaget, J. (1962). *Play, Dreams and Imitation in Childhood*. New York: W. W. Norton.

Podmore, V. and Luff, P. (2012). *Observation: Origins and Approaches in Early Childhood*. Maidenhead: Open University Press/McGraw Hill Education.

Public Health England (2016). *Early Years High Impact Area 6: Health, Wellbeing and Development of the Child Aged Two: Two Year Old Review (Integrated Review)*. [online] Available at: www.gov.uk/government/uploads/system/uploads/attachment_data/file/563926/Early_years_high_impact_area6_health_and_wellbeing_at_2.pdf [Accessed 11 April 2017].

Roberts-Holmes, G. and Bradbury, A. (2016). The Datafication of Early Years Education and its Impact upon Pedagogy. *Improving Schools*, 19(2): 119–28.

Rossi, W. C., Reynolds, W. and Nelson, R. M. (2003). Child Assent and Parental Permission in Pediatric Research. *Theoretical Medicine and Bioethics*, 24(2): 131–48.

Sharma, A. and Cockerill, H. (2014). *Mary Sheridan's From Birth to Five Years: Children's Developmental Progress*. Abingdon: Routledge.

Sharman, C., Cross, W. and Vennis, D. (2007). *Observing Children and Young People*, 4th edn. London: Continuum.

Squires, J. and Bricker, D. (2009). *The Ages & Stages Questionnaires®, Third Edition* (ASQ-3™): *A Parent-Completed Child Monitoring System*. Baltimore, MD: Brookes Publishing Co.

Trevithick, P. (2012). *Social Work Skills and Knowledge: A Practice Handbook*, 3rd edn. Maidenhead: Open University Press/McGraw Hill Education.

Underdown, A., Norwood, R. and Barlow, J. (2013). A Realist Evaluation of the Processes and Outcomes of Infant Massage Programs. *Infant Mental Health Journal*, 34(6): 483–95.

Wragg, E. C. (2012). *An Introduction to Classroom Observation*. Abingdon: Routledge.

CHAPTER

23

RESEARCHING WITH CHILDREN

BY AMANDA HATTON

Despite the fact that I have read widely and conducted research with children and young people in the past, the author created a chapter which left me scribbling notes for further consideration and further reading to explore. I found the definition of participatory research and discussion surrounding how to distinguish between consultation and participation particularly useful (p 361).

Discussion of theoretical perspectives was incredibly detailed and led to many options for wider reading. I will certainly be reading further around the 'space' of childhood using the references to other literature and other chapters in this book. Ethical considerations were extremely thorough and it was good to be reminded that confidentiality will be maintained unless there is a safeguarding concern. While this point is perhaps an obvious one, it is something that I may have forgotten to present in a proposal or consent letter which could later create further ethical concerns if there was any form of disclosure during research.

I am currently writing a proposal for my master's in Education – Early Childhood. I had not intended to conduct participatory research with children ... as a result of reading this chapter, I now need to change my plans!

CLAIRE LEWIS
BA (HONS) CHILDHOOD STUDIES
SHEFFIELD HALLAM UNIVERSITY

learning outcomes

By actively reading this chapter and engaging with the material, you will be able to:

- explain the context of conducting research with children
- identify ethical issues that relate to researching with children
- critically evaluate a range of participatory approaches and methods that can be used when researching with children.

INTRODUCTION

In recent years, there has been much interest in children's **participation** (see Chapter 10) on an international and national level, based on the United Nations Convention on the Rights of the Child (UNCRC) and children's rights expressed ethically, morally and legally. This culture of listening to and viewing how children participate in our changing world has been the focus of research, theoretical and political discourses, and debates. There is much interest shown in researching the lives of children from a diverse range of disciplines, for example **participatory research**, education, health and social care.

This chapter will consider participatory research with young children, with a particular focus on respecting children's **agency** and competency in the research process. Legal, political and social frameworks that underpin research with children will be outlined.

The research process as a whole will be discussed in relation to how we ensure this is meaningful for children and not tokenistic. This will be applied in consideration of **qualitative** methods used with children, particularly visual, creative and arts-based approaches, and how creative methods facilitate collaboration and a more experiential process. The collaborative nature and importance of relationships will also be explored along with the impact that this has on individuals but also on production and meaning making. Ethical issues will be discussed, drawing attention to being aware of power with regards to access and participation and inequalities in age and status. Power relations enacted during the research process will be discussed, and how these contribute to production and meaning making (Procter and Hatton, 2015). This will include the impact of relationships both on the researcher and on peers, and the impact group dynamics may have on the data produced and how points of view, exchange and dialogue will influence this. The chapter will provide an overview of aspects such as ethical issues, methods and participation, to consider throughout the research process.

WHY RESEARCH WITH CHILDREN?

Various legal, political and theoretical frameworks underpin **consultation**, participation and **children's voice**. It is helpful to distinguish between the two terms of consultation and participation, with consultation as 'finding out views to inform decisions' (Hill, 2006: 72) and participation, for children, as 'involving them in taking decisions about matters that affect their lives' (Bragg, 2007: 8). There is a growing interest in and motivation to find out about children's views and their perspectives on their everyday lives and issues that impact on them.

The main legal model which supports this notion is the United Nations Convention on the Rights of the Child (UNCRC; UN, 1989), which promotes the rights of children to express their views on matters that affect them, and covers concerns about the welfare of children, child protection, giving voice and citizenship. Internationally, this human rights treaty recognises children as the subjects of rights, and Article 12 (see Chapter 10 for further discussion) provides a basis for advocating children's rights and needs, covering civil, cultural, economic, political and social rights (Lansdown, 2001). Discourses around this legal and political regulation are apparent at different stages of transition in children's lives, linked to **developmental phases**, with the assumption that children need protection, care and control. This political perspective is based around adult value bases and the **social constructions** of whether children need protection and are vulnerable, or do not have the capacity or competence to make certain decisions themselves. To understand the complexities of the issues of researching the lives of children and young people, it is important to identify the different concepts of childhood. It is argued that the way we see children and our image of childhood is socially constructed (James and James, 2004), for example through chronological age, physical and cognitive development. These constructions of childhood may vary within different cultures and generations.

However, through being encouraged to make a positive contribution to the community and society, children are enabled to express their views as young citizens in a range of contexts; including within their families, early childhood settings, local neighbourhoods and beyond. Indeed, over the last 15 years or so, a number of UK policies have made provision for children to participate in decisions about the services they are involved in, such as education, health and social care.

Uprichard (2008) contrasts two constructions of childhood: children as 'becomings' and children as 'beings'. She argues that children are constructed as 'becomings' when they are considered to be adults-in-waiting. On the other hand, children as 'beings' are seen as 'social actors' with views about their lived experiences. Christensen and Prout (2005) focus on children as 'social actors' with the ability to influence their social circumstances and lives. This challenges the assumption that children are not competent in making decisions. It also contests the belief that children are passive subjects in social structures and processes. Rather, this view of childhood sees children as active in negotiating boundaries imposed by adults and active in their own space, time, interactions and experiences. Through understanding children's lives as they engage with the social world, we can recognise that they will adopt different responses and develop different identities according to the different environments and experiences that they have (James and Prout, 1990). These debates about how we view children show how social constructions of childhood may create opposed identities.

Another theoretical perspective that these issues of power and control reflect is the idea of the 'space' of childhood. Children have their own 'space' in society, not only through the social and political construction of childhood but also through their own development of sub-cultures through cultural and leisure interests. In consideration of social and cultural geography with spatiality and identity, there are defined spaces that are associated with children, which include leisure spaces, virtual spaces and, within these, there are also gendered spaces. These distinctions are also reinforced through educational institutions, which are usually defined and segregated through chronological age. This could also be seen to have a parallel with other groups who are differentiated by class, gender, ethnicity or disability. This can help us understand the position of children as citizens within a system of relationships between generations, the state and the family, and between individuals.

Researching with children is important in order to understand children's lives and their views about aspects that affect them, including their environments. Marsh (2005) highlights children's popular cultural worlds, where children use a range of media, which may be more inclusive than traditional methods, and enables them to link global practices to their own contexts and their everyday lives (see Chapter 18). In this sense, children and young people create their own identities, and their own dominant practices, which can be communicated through a range of multimodal methods (Marsh, 2005) (see Chapter 4 for further discussion).

Participatory research recognises that for children to be meaningfully involved they need to have an interest in the topic; there needs to be some relevance to their everyday lives and they should have some ownership in the process. It should also be recognised that because research involves children, it is not necessarily representative of the views of all children as we need to be aware of the diversity of their views and recognise factors such as age, gender, class and ethnicity as important to their views and experiences. Participatory research is the collaboration between researchers and participants in all aspects of the research process, including planning and design, implementation and dissemination. For children, this means that the research can be conducted with children or by children themselves. Often, there are certain children selected for consultation or participation, and this can exclude some of the hard-to-reach groups of children who may hence become more marginalised (Procter and Hatton, 2015). We therefore need to be honest about whose voices we are representing, and clear about whose voices we have not heard and why.

Punch (2002) highlights that in researching the diversity of multiple childhoods and in acknowledging the different life experiences and competencies, one way is to use a range of different methods and techniques. Our ways of seeing, as adults, are different from the perspectives of children and it is difficult for an adult to fully understand the child's point of view or experience. By involving children in research and providing an opportunity for them to communicate their responses and share these with adults in a dialogue, it enables us to adjust our perspectives and consider how children experience and view their worlds.

 reflection point 23.1

What are the key debates around why we should research with children and hear their views?

ETHICAL ISSUES AROUND RESEARCHING WITH CHILDREN

In the choice of methods, we also need to recognise that power usually resides with the adult and therefore it is necessary to use methods that relate to the children's interests, daily lives and competencies.

Inevitably, researching with children is a sensitive topic with many complexities and it is always important to consider the researcher's **positionality** and differences when conducting research with any participants, whether they are children or adults. Particularly with children, the researcher needs to be aware of how these differences impact on the interaction between them and the asymmetries of power and the subordinate position of children, especially younger ones. The main differences when researching with children are about ability, power and the developmental differences between the ages of children. The ability to understand these differences needs to be taken into account. Research with children needs to be inclusive, recognising the diversity of multiple childhoods and acknowledging the different life experiences and competencies of children, particularly if it is offering a generalised view of children's views and responses. In choosing respondents, the participation in fun activities or rewards may encourage children to take part, but ethical issues of fairness and equality need to be considered – for example, the impact on those children who are not able to take part.

Consent is required from parents and institutional gatekeepers for children to take part in research, and with regard to this they make decisions for children in their care. It is worth noting that in these environments children are often in a subordinate relationship to adults and therefore researchers need to be aware of assumed consent, passive acceptance, or non-refusal, where a child may find it difficult to not take part, dissent or disagree (Greene and Hill, 2005).

Especially in the case of children, it is essential that they understand their involvement in the research and how the data will be used. Steps should be taken for them to have 'informed consent', which means that they understand they can withdraw at any point or have the opportunity to not take part. It also means that if they agree to take part it is based on adequate knowledge of the implications. Consent should be negotiated as an ongoing concern throughout the research process, described as 'process consent' (Heath et al., 2009: 25), recognising that children may change their mind once involved. It is also worth noting that there can be misunderstanding and children, particularly younger ones, often seem to be listening when perhaps they may not be so, or they may seem to understand when they do not and wish to be compliant with adult requests. Therefore, it is important that researchers check children's understanding throughout the process and ensure this process is reflexive (Gallagher et al., 2009). In the case of very young children and those with impairments, who may not be able to give verbal or written consent, researchers should seek the ongoing **assent** of participants, in addition to the consent of parents/carers. Cocks (2006) argues that the process of seeking children's provisional assent is only possible when the adult researcher operates reflexively throughout the research process.

Reflexivity entails the researcher being cognisant of their personal assumptions about children. This should also be reflected in how the researcher presents the opinions of the participants, and there needs to be awareness that when presenting a text, it is the voice of both the researcher and the participant.

It is important to remember that the researcher has responsibilities towards the respondents. It is therefore crucial that the researcher is aware of the impact of any generalisations that might be made from the presentation of the data. Another major ethical consideration is that of anonymity and confidentiality. There must be the guarantee that taking part in the research will not harm participants and that confidentiality and anonymity will ensure that an individual could not be traced through the reporting of data. With regard to confidentiality, there may be times when this has to be suspended if information around safeguarding and child protection issues is disclosed and is required to be passed on for child protection procedures. Anonymity may be more difficult for the researcher to ensure a child or individual cannot be identified, especially when using visual data. Visual methods have their own set of ethical issues, particularly around the use of images of children, putting children at particular risk (Flewitt, 2006). This can also create difficulties around the issue of consent, as children's attitudes may change over time and they may become more conscious of how they appear or are presented.

action point 23.1

List the ethical considerations you would need to have in place when researching with children.

METHODS OF RESEARCHING WITH CHILDREN

Much of the research into children's views is designed, undertaken, interpreted and disseminated by adult researchers. However, the use of different methods now attempts to engage children in the process in a more meaningful way. In this next section, a range of research methods and how they can be used with children will be considered. Factors which affect the choice of method can include the cognitive ability of children, their understanding of vocabulary and their interpretation of meaning. There is a range of age-related developmental differences to consider for younger children. It is also important to recognise that within any age group there will be a wide range of interests, ability and diversity. The main traditional methods of research, including **quantitative** and qualitative methods, are still useful tools to use when consulting with children. However, there are also more innovative approaches that can be used alongside these traditional methods to address the ways in which children communicate.

case study 23.1

How Children Respond and Occupy Spaces

Engaging with children's views is particularly important when we consider that educational settings and spaces are designed and constructed by adults, and are places where adults hold the power. An example of participatory research which focused on pupil participation and enabled the views of primary-aged children to be expressed in the design of learning environments, was conducted by Burke (2007). Exploratory activities took place in schools over a 12-month period, with children using cameras, map-making equipment, drawings, paintings and models to document the 'visual culture' of their school. This entailed children working with members of the research team to document the visual, spatial and

(Continued)

material arrangements of the classroom, the associated culture and pedagogy. This approach recognised children as experts on their school environment, focusing on how they experienced the spaces, for example from the scale and perspective of their position of height. Through the research, many significant features were revealed, for example the significance of coat hooks, wall displays, secret gardens, meeting places, relationships, and how people moved around the spaces within the classroom. Without the children's perspectives, these features would have been unknown to the adults, which Burke refers to as 'hidden narratives' (2007: 368). Children's stories and explanations are often needed to highlight the multiple layers of meaning that people attach to material things.

1. Explain how these different methods provide an understanding of how children respond to and occupy spaces constructed by adults.
2. Identify possible aspects of the environment that adults may not have been aware of without the children's perspectives.
3. Critically evaluate how the multi-sensory methods highlighted aspects of the environment that were important to the children.

Questionnaires are a good method of data collection, particularly when the views of a large number of people are sought. As each respondent will receive an identical set of questions, this allows for consistency. However, the questions should be extensively tested beforehand to ensure children understand the questions. Considerations for younger children would be ensuring the accessibility of the questionnaire; appropriate wording of the questions; and that children are able to read and understand the language used. It is also important to be aware that children may respond differently depending on the context, for example at home or at school. Another consideration for younger children would be their interest, engagement and concentration span to complete the questionnaire. There might also be issues of children copying one another or feeling they need to provide a correct answer.

The method of interviewing tends to be used to collect more detailed information from a smaller number of people, providing a more in-depth insight into the research topic. The data collected through interviews is also likely to be based on the experiences and feelings of the informants that cover more sensitive or personal issues, which needs additional consideration for younger children. The method of the interview allows the researcher to explore these issues in more depth. Children might try to guess what answer they are supposed to give or try to please the adult researcher, as they would a teacher. It is also important to remember that a face-to-face interview is more intrusive than the use of a questionnaire and the researcher should consider the impact this may have on children. One way to address this would be to consider the choice of location, perhaps using more informal spaces in the setting where children may feel more at ease. Clark (2010) highlights that with very young children these 'conversations' are often conducted on the move.

Focus groups can be used as a form of group interviewing with the emphasis on the interaction between the group participants and the processes and dynamics of that interaction, the 'synergy' (Wellington, 2000). On a practical level, focus groups are usually facilitated by the researcher, where a theme is introduced to allow the participants' agenda to predominate and the focus of the discussion to reflect their own experiences and views. For example, in

Maconochie's (2013) research, practitioners used a persona doll in their focus groups with 4-year-olds to ascertain their views of their children's centre. However, there should be attention paid to children's relationships in group activities, where some children may dominate and others may withdraw, which could facilitate inclusion but also reinforce aspects of exclusion (Procter and Hatton, 2015).

Observations seem to be particularly useful methods to use with young children and to capture the everyday experiences of children's lives and observe the individual within their own context. Observational methods generally describe content but can also be used to gain insight into the meaning of activities and how they interact with each other and the environment or setting (Tudge and Hogan, 2005).

Engaging with children in the research process needs careful consideration. Another important point about the listening process, that Christensen (2004) makes, is that, often, adults will stop listening to a child if an adult speaks to them and they allow the interruption. It is important to be aware that if you engage with children from the position of an adult you could be seen as an outsider. Instead, Christensen (2004) suggests we should try to engage with children in a way that relates to their own practices, interactions and forms of communication. However, it is important to recognise that 'adults are unable to be full participants in children's social worlds because they can never truly be children again' (Punch, 2002: 322).

In choosing these methods, the researcher needs to consider that there are many different ways to record the data, for example audiotape, video, photographs, writing or drawing, and some of the data will be recorded and gathered by the children.

Another method that can be used with children is the use of drawings. This can be a useful warm-up activity to get to know the researcher and as data which provide direct visual representations of how children see their world. Punch (2002) highlights that this method can be creative and fun, enabling young children to be more actively engaged in the research. The creative process of drawing also provides an opportunity of space and time for children to think about what they want to portray and this gives them control. However, it should be noted that not all children will enjoy this method as they may not perceive themselves to be good at drawing or may have anxiety about what they need to produce. There is also the difficulty of analysis and the possibility of misinterpreting the children's drawings and imposing adult interpretations. It may therefore be helpful to have the children explain the detail of their work and what it represents.

Another visual method of research that can be used with children, to actively engage them in the research process, is the use of photographs. By giving children a camera, it puts them in control of what they consider important to record and represent. Cook and Hess (2007) highlight that this can be more accessible for children, as the method uses pictures rather than words. However, children may behave unusually in front of the camera. Pink (2001) suggests that we need to consider the context in which the image was made; the contexts in which it is viewed; and the content of the image. What becomes important is how the content of an image represents and gives meaning to the individual. This demands contextual knowledge and understanding. Prosser (1998) outlines that the interpretation of the data gathered through these methods would need discussion with the child about what is in the photograph or why they chose to take the photograph to gain meaning.

In using any of these methods with children, the interpretation of the data is an important factor for consideration. The accounts of children, in whatever media form, should be related to how they conceptualise and understand the social and cultural environments in which they exist. Researchers should also recognise that children of a similar age have variable perspectives and diverse views (Burke, 2007). Cook and Hess (2007) highlight that adults may not recognise the significance of interactions, spaces, places and images, and in interpreting meaning adults may not always be clear about what they are looking at or what it means.

 spotlight on research 23.1

The Mosaic Approach

The Mosaic Approach was developed as a framework for listening to children by Alison Clark and Peter Moss (2001), who were inspired by the work developed in the preschools of Reggio Emilia in Northern Italy. They developed this reflexive approach with the key elements of 'Listening, observing, gathering documentation and interpretation' (Clark and Moss, 2001: 7). The Mosaic Approach is 'a way of listening which acknowledges children and adults as co-constructors of meaning'. It is an integrated approach that combines visual data with verbal data. Clark and Moss describe the approach as 'multi-method; participatory; reflexive; adaptable; focused on children's lived experiences and embedded into practice' (2001: 5).

In developing the Mosaic Approach, Alison Clark used a range of participatory tools with young children to ascertain their views of their early childhood settings. For example, young children were given cameras to document what was important to them; they made maps and took adults on child-led tours of their environment. This enabled the children to take charge and direct the activity and to provide the researchers with their own perspectives and experiences of what it was like to be there. These tools, combined together, made up a 'mosaic of perspectives' (Clark and Moss, 2001). Clark and Moss (2001) describe the use of participatory techniques as providing a lens that enables adults to view the world through the eyes of children.

There are three key stages to this approach. Stage one is where children and adults gather documentation together. During stage two, the adults and children are involved in meaning making together by piecing together information through 'dialogue, reflection and interpretation' (Clark and Moss, 2001: 11). In the third stage, the children and adults decide on 'areas of continuity and change' (Clark et al., 2005: 33).

Using creative arts and multi-media approaches provides children with the opportunity to express themselves through codes and conventions they understand. This may include animations, music videos or sound bites, or other media platforms from their cultural worlds. However, the adult researcher may not be familiar enough with the technology to use these methods, or able to access the cultural significance of these representations as texts. With such a wide range of media that children use to communicate, it may be desirable to involve children in the analysis of data, as the adult may not be in a position to interpret the child's views and meanings. Indeed, children's explanations of drawings, artefacts or why photographs or images were taken may be needed for their relevance and significance to be understood.

In participatory research with children, there should also be consideration of involving children in the dissemination of the research findings. This could include dissemination to both peers and adults. However, this should be planned carefully so as not to put children in any situation in which they may not feel comfortable.

Having considered a range of approaches and methods of participatory research, it is important to consider the level of participation and involvement of children throughout the research process: from research design to data generation, analysis and dissemination. It is also necessary to ensure that the research process is ethical by being meaningful for the children and not tokenistic. Ongoing dialogue between adults and children, based on collaboration and listening, is vital. Hatton's (2014) model of participative practice highlights the centrality of reciprocal dialogue with a focus on respecting children's agency and competency, and is a practical model that can be applied to the research process. The model draws from the view of participation being a dialogue as part of social learning (Percy-Smith, 2006). Hatton's model highlights three key stages as part of a reciprocal and ongoing dialogue that recognises children and adults being involved in varying degrees, at different stages of the process, where these relationships are negotiated. The three stages highlighted are to communicate, listen and respond (Hatton, 2014). Communication, particularly through participatory methods, can facilitate a more collaborative process. Using creative arts and media alongside children's physical engagement with an activity, encourages a more experiential process that can be more meaningful for children. Listening, as part of a genuine dialogue, is key to ensuring that researchers hear children's views and represent them in a way that enables their voices and does not further constrain them. Responding, through feedback and the sharing of information, is essential, to inform children what will happen with the data they have generated or how their views will be responded to, either through action, dialogue or both.

SUMMARY

- Researching with children enables us to understand children's lives, experiences and views about matters that affect them. It also helps us to recognise the diversity of children's childhoods and the plurality of their views.
- Research with children is a sensitive issue, with many ethical complexities. Ethical consideration should be given throughout the research process to children's level of understanding, developmental differences and relationships of power between children and adults.
- The use of creative and participatory methods enables children to participate in research in a meaningful way that has the potential to engage their interest and provide valuable insight into children's worlds. However, researchers should adopt a reflexive and critical approach to the use of such methods, acknowledging their strengths and working to overcome their limitations.

 online resources

Make sure to visit https://study.sagepub.com/fitzgeraldandmaconochie for selected SAGE videos (with questions), SAGE journal articles, links to external sources and flashcards.

FURTHER READING

Clark, A. and Moss, P. (2001). *Listening to Young Children: The Mosaic Approach.* London: National Children's Bureau.

The Mosaic Approach offers a creative framework for listening to young children's views and experiences. It outlines a number of research methods to use with children.

Farrell, A., Kagan, S. L. and Tisdall, E. K. M. (eds) (2016). *The Sage Handbook of Early Childhood Research.* London: Sage.

This book provides an overview of the field of early childhood research in different contexts, as well as outlining different methodological approaches to research with and about children.

Westwood, J., Larkins, C., Moxon, D., Perry, Y. and Thomas, N. (eds) (2014). *Participation, Citizenship and Intergenerational Relations in Children and Young People's Lives.* Basingstoke: Palgrave Macmillan.

This book is based on research about the burgeoning area of children's and young people's participation in research.

REFERENCES

Bragg, S. (2007). *Consulting Young People: A Review of the Literature.* London: Arts Council England, Creative Partnerships team.

Burke, C. (2007). The View of the Child: Releasing 'Visual Voices' in the Design of Learning Environments. *Discourse: Studies in the Cultural Politics of Education*, 28(3): 359–72.

Christensen, P. (2004). Children's' Participation in Ethnographic Research: Issues of Power and Representation. *Children and Society*, 18: 165–76.

Christensen, P. and Prout, A. (2005). Anthropological and Sociological Perspectives on the Study of Children. In: S. Greene and D. Hogan (eds), *Researching Children's Experience, Approaches and Methods.* London: Sage, pp. 42–60.

Clark, A. (2010). *Transforming Children's Spaces: Children's and Adults' Participation in Designing Learning Environments.* Abingdon: Routledge.

Clark, A. and Moss, P. (2001). *Listening to Young Children: The Mosaic Approach.* London: National Children's Bureau.

Clark, A., Kjorholt, A. T. and Moss, P. (2005). *Beyond Listening: Children's Perspectives on Early Childhood Services.* Bristol: The Policy Press.

Cocks, A. (2006). The Ethical Maze: Finding an Inclusive Path towards Gaining Children's Agreement to Research Participation. *Childhood*, 13(2): 247–66.

Cook, T. and Hess, E. (2007). What the Camera Sees and from whose Perspective: Fun Methodologies for Engaging Children in Enlightening Adults. *Childhood*, 14(1): 29–45.

Flewitt, R. (2006). Using Video to Investigate Preschool Classroom Interaction: Education Research Assumptions and Methodological Practices. *Visual Communication*, 5(1): 25–50.

Gallagher, M., Haywood, S. L., Jones, M. W. and Milne, S. (2009). Negotiating Informed Consent with Children in School-Based Research: A Critical Review. *Children and Society*, 24(6): 471–82.

Greene, S. and Hill, M. (2005). Researching Children's Experience: Methods and Methodological Issues. In: S. Greene and D. Hogan (eds), *Researching Children's Experience, Approaches and Methods*. London: Sage, pp. 1–21.

Hatton, A. J. (2014). Shallow Democracy: In Other People's Shoes – Listening to the Voices of Children and Young People. In: J. Westwood, C. Larkins, D. Moxon, Y. Perry and N. Thomas (eds), *Participation, Citizenship and Intergenerational Relations in Children and Young People's Lives*. Basingstoke: Palgrave Macmillan, pp. 43–53.

Heath, S., Brooks, R., Cleaver, E. and Ireland, E. (2009). *Researching Young People's Lives*. London: Sage.

Hill, M. (2006). Children's Voices on Ways of Having a Voice: Children and Young People's Perspectives on Methods Used in Research and Consultation. *Childhood*, 13(1): 69–89.

James, A. and James, A. (2004). *Constructing Childhood: Theory, Policy and Social Practice*. Basingstoke: Palgrave MacMillan.

James, A. and Prout, A. (1990). *Constructing and Reconstructing Childhood: Contemporary Issues in the Sociological Study of Childhood*. London: Falmer Press.

Lansdown, G. (2001). Children's Welfare and Children's Rights. In: P. Foley, J. Roche and S. Tucker (eds), *Children in Society: Contemporary Theory, Policy and Practice*. Basingstoke: Palgrave/Open University Press.

Maconochie, H. (2013). Young Children's Participation in a Sure Start Children's Centre, Sheffield Hallam University. [online] Available at: http://shura.shu.ac.uk/7437 [Accessed 28 August 2018].

Marsh, J. (2005). Ritual, Performance and Identity Construction: Young Children's Engagement with Popular Cultural and Media Texts. In: J. Marsh (ed.), *Popular Culture, New Media and Digital Literacy in Early Childhood*. Abingdon: RoutledgeFalmer, pp. 28–50.

Percy-Smith, B. (2006). From Consultation to Social Learning in Community Participation with Young People. *Children, Youth and Environments*, 16(2): 153–79.

Pink, S. (2001). *Doing Visual Ethnography*. London: Sage.

Procter, L. and Hatton, A. (2015). Producing Visual Research with Children: Exploring Power and Meaning Making. In: E. Stirling and D. Yamada Rice (eds), *Visual Methods with Children and Young People: Academics and Visual Industries in Dialogue*. Basingstoke: Palgrave Macmillan, pp. 50–72.

Prosser, J. (1998). The Status of Image-based Research. In: J. Prosser (ed.), *Image Based Research: A Sourcebook for Qualitative Researchers*. London: Falmer Press, pp. 97–113.

Punch, S. (2002). Research with Children: The Same or Different from Research with Adults? *Childhood*, 9(3): 321–41.

Tudge, J. and Hogan, D. (2005). An Ecological Approach to Observations of Children's Everyday Lives. In: S. Greene and D. Hogan (eds), *Researching Children's Experience, Approaches and Methods*. London: Sage, pp. 102–22.

United Nations (1989). The United Nations Convention on the Rights of the Child (UNCRC). [online] Available at: https://downloads.unicef.org.uk/wp-content/uploads/2010/05/UNCRC_united_nations_convention_on_the_rights_of_the_child.pdf?_ga=2.256348812.601248384.1510181207-2058859752.1510181207 [Accessed 8 November 2017].

Uprichard, E. (2008). Children as 'Beings and Becomings': Children, Childhood and Temporality. *Children and Society*, 22(4): 303–13.

Wellington, J. (2000). *Educational Research: Contemporary Issues and Practical Approaches*. London: Continuum.

BECOMING A PROFESSIONAL: ENTANGLEMENTS WITH IDENTITY AND PRACTICE

BY KAREN BARR

The chapter draws on the idea that, like children, professionals do not form a homogeneous group. It was able to assist my studies by highlighting the paradoxical world in which we live and reminding me that for both professionals and children, no two worlds are constructed in the same manner. Combined with this is the notion that whilst we have our own worlds, these worlds can be deeply embedded with ideological discourse which can frame and constrain us. Reading this chapter will therefore help you to consider your own world view and how you construct knowledge.

The chapter included a number of transcripts from focus groups which help you see how different people are able to construct different meanings from childhood objects. The tasks at the end of each section will also help you to cement your knowledge and apply what you have just read about, making the literature more tangible whilst providing a level of reflexive thought.

CAROLYN LEADER
BA (HONS) EARLY CHILDHOOD STUDIES
UNIVERSITY OF SUFFOLK

learning outcomes

By reading this chapter and actively engaging with the material, you will be able to:

- explore systems that influence experiences of early childhood students
- reflect on processes relating to becoming an early childhood professional
- identify ideological issues that affect emerging futures in early childhood education and care (ECEC)
- create opportunities to engage with learning experiences in Early Childhood Studies (ECS).

There are numerous ways to conceptualise the learning and interactive experiences that shape who people become and how they develop. Some theories of learning draw on the notion that the world is there to be discovered, but this suggests that the world is static and can close off opportunities to embrace new possibilities in an ever-changing world (Lenz Taguchi, 2010). This chapter considers early childhood students, not as students who study to discover a static world already there, but as people interacting with and being shaped by, as well as shaping, the world. It draws on data from a focus group carried out with Early Childhood Studies students, in which their experiences illuminate elements of becoming within the field of ECEC. In this chapter, students are conceptualised as 'becoming'; they are entangled with the world and through co-dependent relationships with environments they co-construct their study of early childhood and what early childhood professionals might become.

This chapter also considers the concept of professionalism in ECEC as 'becoming', as it evolves through time and across spaces of early childhood practice. Research with those working in this field suggests that, for many, their experiences in everyday practice are often emotionally rewarding and, at the same time, characterised by ambiguity, plurality, contradictions and inconsistencies, as they navigate standardised policy requirements and government **discourse** (Brock, 2013; Osgood, 2012; Simpson, 2010). The concept of professionalism is highly contested and, as such, offers rich potential for negotiation and the creation of meanings.

BECOMING WITHIN SYSTEMS

Lenz Taguchi (2010: 49) contends that 'our meaning-making and the learning we do is dependent on the material world around us'. As asserted in Chapter 2, sensory interaction with the world has a profound effect on the development of a baby's brain and body and this continues throughout life. We are active participants in learning that happens and neurological research indicates that brain plasticity continues across a person's lifespan. Learning is never finished, but, rather, through endless interaction with our environments, we are continually learning, always becoming something new. Each encounter has the capacity to affect and change us. We can see ourselves as *becoming* in the sense that part of *being* is becoming changed through interaction with the world.

Bronfenbrenner's (1979) ecological theory, as discussed in previous chapters, suggests that a series of systems interact with and affect each other. One view of how this relates to ECS students would be to consider a student's home, university, work and social environments as a student's microsystems. These operate within an exosystem that impacts on students' experiences; for example, government policies affect children's services where students might work; student loan policies affect financial situations, which impact on the time available for study and leisure. At macrosystemic levels, political **ideology** and societal values impact on government policy. It is useful to reflect on how these influences are productive of what we do and how interactions within the systems alter our understanding and strategies.

 reflection point 24.1

- Make a list of things in your life that matter to you in your personal, academic and professional life.
- How do these relate to different systems?
- How do the systems influence each other and, in turn, affect your own experiences and responses?

We could think of these systems as '**assemblages**'. Deleuze and Guattari (1987) use this term to describe a collection of affective materials within a given situation – in other words, interconnected elements in particular circumstances that interact with and affect other elements. Assemblages are constantly in flux, or in a state of becoming, and are therefore continually renewing in response to how different elements affect one another. Assemblages and all the elements within them can be said to be *emerging*, as all parts of the assemblage, including the people within it, are constantly changing or becoming through interactions within the assemblage.

You might have thought, in the first instance, of things to do with more immediate environments. Perhaps you thought of family, friends old and new, belongings that you brought to university, transport systems such as buses to work, university library lending systems, shopping for clothes, the students' union, government policies that you are reading, a place where you study or meet friends, a job application, and so on. You might have considered how you travel to different places, how your finances affect this, how much mobile phone credit you have to contact friends or renew books online, how you access emotional support and how relationships and systems in your life affect this. Any of these things and anything else in your life can be thought of as part of an assemblage with converging factors that affect you and that are affected by your relationships with them. Dynamic relations between these factors form a network of flowing entanglements that connect us within our environments. Interactions within these entanglements generate continuous renewal of the assemblage and create unique experiences, simultaneously affirming and changing things that matter to us.

MATTERS OF TRANSITIONING

Changes in our circumstances are sometimes described as **transitions** that we need to respond and adapt to in order to manage them. Often, transitions tend to be conceptualised as one-point events, such as starting school or university, or a new job. However, Taylor and Harris-Evans

(2016) think of becoming as endless differentiation and transitions, which are not necessarily events with a clear start and finish but are ongoing processes. They challenge the idea of transitions as defined trajectories or sequenced stages and, instead, see the concept of transitioning as a dynamic, continual process of unfolding. Taylor and Harris-Evans (2016) explored the experiences of students on a BA Hons Education Studies course who were transitioning into higher education. They found that things that matter to students experiencing transition vary widely and include aspects of their lives within and beyond university. In each student's assemblage, numerous active elements played a part in their experiences, including daily processes, physical materials, surprises, people and responsibilities. Although these happen to be common factors, each student's becoming through transitioning was part of a unique web of relationships with these elements. The research findings highlighted the **heterogeneity** of students' experiences – in other words, no two students' experiences were the same.

This diversity has implications for how we think of students' experiences at university. Whilst there are written curricula specifying course content and learning outcomes, each student's experience will be unique. Continually unfolding processes of transitioning in response to connections and evolving relationships generate opportunities to further explore transitioning, becoming and things that matter.

Bennett (2010) describes such matters – material, human and non-human – as catalysts or things that can produce effects. She sees 'distinctive capacities or efficacious powers of particular material configurations' as catalytic because of the vibrancy of matter (2010: ix). Matter is vibrant in that the characteristics of these things resonate to the point that they compel engagement with them as they provoke responses. We are and feel affected in some way by matters that resonate with us. If we are attentive to the effects that are produced, this can illuminate the potential of environments to affect experiences. Mayer-Hoffer (2015) suggests that if we identify reference points or things that matter to us, we can recognise affective relationships and how interactions bring about particular effects. If we are part of a group, our very being or becoming, our beliefs, convictions and experiences, are all constructed as part of our belonging to the group. An awareness of capacities and feelings can enable us to understand how our responses to our environments are shaped.

 spotlight on practice 24.1

Focus Groups

In order to explore things that matter to Early Childhood students, after gaining ethical approval from the university I invited students to participate in a focus group. There were four students in the group of volunteers. This created opportunities for the group to listen and respond to one another's experiences and thoughts, thus building our understanding in collaborative ways that one-to-one interviews would not have afforded. I asked them in advance to bring three things – objects or ideas – that they associated with being an Early Childhood Studies student, and asked them to talk about what they had brought. The conversation was rich and only fragments of stories are told here. They tell of connections between material

(Continued)

objects and lives within and outside of university, of things that matter, that affect relation-ships between experiences past, present and future, all assembled into continual processes of becoming.

Childhood toys

A teddy bear … I thought about it and thought that when kids bring … toys into school and they are told to put them in their drawer and they get upset, … they all mean something to the kids. Like, when I broke my elbow when I was 11, it came into hospital with me, hence why it has a hospital tag on, … the nurse was really good at trying to make me feel comfortable and I had to wear the wrist band so she said 'Oh, shall we give one to your teddy bear too?' … thinking about that reminded me … why you've got to get down to children's level all the time rather than just thinking like a grown-up where like wearing a silly little wrist band wouldn't have been scary.

I had a massive box of Barbies … I used to play with them for… days, even secretly when I was in year 7 … I had lots of teddies but I preferred to have them sitting there. I didn't like to play with them and my sister was the opposite. She had a toy cat; mine was like, pristine and nice, but my sister's was like, it's been through mud, it's been everywhere and is all mangled and weird. And I think that's really interesting, the differences, like I was, 'oh that has to look nice'. I didn't touch it because it would get ruined and her attitude was, no it's coming everywhere with me, like in the bath with me … it makes me reflective, like what has that made me think about practice?

Books gifted by family members

'We're going on a bar hunt'… a parody … and the 'The very hungover caterpillar' … reading them just sort of reminded me … you can appreciate the things a child likes but still have fun at the same time … the teachers at my school are like, 'oh … you have to do paperwork', and it's just to remind me that there are the good funny sides to working with kids, so try to see them all the time, and try to have a fun time with becoming an early childhood graduate.

I chose my youth bible because the youth bible goes with other things that I did … I'm still a Christian, so that's also influenced … my attitudes towards things, how I view certain situations. Again, going back into practice, there are going to be some kids from religious backgrounds and some that aren't, so I think that being a Christian I can understand what it's like to be in a family or background where religion is important … not necessarily that's mine, but because there'll be some things that influence a way that a child is brought up and con-versations about their religious experience.

Photographs

My family was a massive part of me growing up … we were around each other a lot and we went on holiday together at least once a year … my family has influenced me and like, coming to university and my attitudes here and attitudes when I work are to do with how I've been brought up and what my family has viewed as important … I chose this one because we were on holiday together … From a very early age we went out on trips and things … when I go into settings there's gonna be some kids who always go on holiday with their family, and that's something that I'll be able to relate to, whereas there'll be some kids that maybe don't ever go on holiday, and maybe that will be something that I won't relate to but it will be something that I can maybe encourage in practice, like going out and doing stuff.

I've got a picture of my mum and my brother ... When I was five I always wanted to have a sibling so I always said 'mummy I want to have a brother'. And then she got pregnant and then my brother came ... Our personalities are really different ... I'm the one that was like, really open, and like 'Would you like to give me a hug?' and he was 'mmm, eeeww, no!'. This is, I think a month before I came to university, because I got my hair cut, I shaved my head last year in March and it's like, a woman's hair doesn't determine who you are. My brother secretly wrote a script to tell the class about introducing an important person, and he wrote about me. My mum, when she was cleaning things, she found it. I never realised that he loves me because he never says that and he always runs away when I say 'Oh I love you and I want to hug you'. And so, deep inside my heart I knew that he loved me but when you really see the letter and the script that he wrote, I burst into tears ... he introduced me because he thinks that I'm really creative and because I really want to help people. So I shaved my head ... I find this quite cool, to watch our hair grow and so our hair is like a similar length. We look really similar now but he is 5 years younger than me.

This is my little brother ... I was 13 when he was born so when I grew up I kind of matured a lot quicker because I wanted to help my mum out with my brother ... I used to teach him how to add and write letters and that sort of stuff ... I suppose that's what's kind of made me want to become a teacher, because I kind of realised I was actually alright at it ... they all look up to me for the fact that I've moved away because nobody in my family has moved away yet.

My photo album ... My mum was the most influential person because, although she didn't want me to go, she was like, 'You're gonna do great', and every time I tell her ... when I'm having problems at uni she's like, 'You're gonna be fine, you can do this, you can stay at uni, you can get through it'. ... My best friend ... she moved away because she works in the RAF but she influenced me because she was like, 'No you can do it, I've done it, you can do it, you've got to do it'. ... When I went to Butlin's for a weekend I saw all these wonderful people talking about their lives ... and I was thinking my life seems pretty dull to be fair, I don't like my job, I don't like where I live, and like, I realised then that I needed to do something about it ... so this is a picture of me at Butlin's ... after I came back, I applied for uni straight away ... I have got the experience of being in a childhood setting before and I did volunteering but ... I always thought I probably won't get in ... I'm not gonna be as far forward as everyone else, and all that sort of stuff. But my mum was like, 'Don't be silly you'll get through, you'll be fine ... you've got to work hard to get where you want to get', and that kind of inspires me.

Leaflets from placement

Because I was confused about schema when I was in uni, I asked the manager of the setting, and she gave me this and ... told me that ... you have to find the interest of that child, what they like to do. So I find this quite important and to let the parents know as well ... they put them where the parents pick up and drop off children, so parents can access this as well ... it's quite important to have that.

Paintings made with children

They use ... a squeegee sponge ... with different colours ... I'm always experimenting with things when I play with them. And the other one was a toy, like this ... a bobbin ... so then they would just like, roll it or ... stamp with it.

(Continued)

The vibrant matter in these unique assemblages includes treasured materials that invoke emotion and thought; people; places; holidays; fun; paperwork; love; anxiety; reassurance; inspiration; a nurse's kindness that now provokes new understanding of children's experiences and concern where practice jars with this understanding; reflection on similarities and uniqueness between family members; a hairstyle being cut and growing out; surprise and delight at the extent of sibling affection in a found script; spaces and materials for sharing practice and knowledge; playful experimentation; and many more things besides.

These things highlight relational entanglements between things that matter. Stories from childhood shape thinking about practice in ECEC settings. Past, present and future encounters connect notions of becoming, continual unfolding and potential. Stories provoked responses in the group, particularly where experiences resonated due to differences and similarities. This sparked off new ideas and conversations about memories of objects not brought along, which generated reflection that might not otherwise have been shared. Each story was unique and told in response to unique assemblages of things that matter. Sharing stories can open up spaces for collaborative, creative reflection:

- What things might you have brought to the focus group?
- What stories would you tell of them?
- How are they entangled with your experiences of becoming in ECS?

ENTANGLEMENTS WITH IDEOLOGY AND EMERGING FUTURES

This continual unfolding process affords rich opportunities. Semetsky (2011: 140) speaks of the 'dynamic *process* of becoming, comprising multiple evaluations and revaluations of experience. Experience is rendered meaningful … by experimentation on our very *being* for the purpose of *becoming'*. Exploring how our views and understandings are shaped, things that matter, how they influence our meaning making and open up potential adventures, can help us to make sense of how we relate to the world as part of a continuous process.

Moss (2014) urges us to see the possibilities of practice and professionalism as emerging potentiality. In this way, what we do and how we think can shape future practice as much as it shapes us, but we must be aware of ideological forces within systems of practice. As we have seen in other chapters, there are many ways in which political ideologies and government policies impact on practice throughout ever-changing systems in which ECEC settings are positioned. Therefore, ECEC professionals can face dilemmas where political ideologies and expectations are incongruent with personal values and ethics. What happens if something seems unfair – for example, if practices appear to disadvantage particular people but legislation or local policy makes this difficult to address? It is useful to reflect on how entanglements within these systems shape practice, as well as how problematic influences can be navigated and challenged.

Moss (2014) describes the story of **neoliberalism**, which in the UK and similar economic systems is the prevalent, market-driven ideology that is underpinned by assumptions that people are free to make choices about which services they access. This means that competition is a key driving force for enhancing quality in ECEC as services compete for funding and service users and are thus positioned as competitors. This can be problematic for numerous reasons, including questions of whether people are really free to choose services, whether it is ethical to force competition rather than collaboration between services, how this affects the quality of practice, how quality is conceptualised and what happens in ECEC if quality suffers. Pressures and affordances created within such systems influence what ECEC becomes.

Within neoliberal ideology, ECEC professionals are often positioned as needing to achieve quality that is measured by predetermined, quantifiable outcomes such as reading scores, school attendance, health statistics, league tables, and so forth. Quantifiable measurements of quality make it easy to compare outcomes with competitors, but we might ask how quality can be measured in other ways. We might consider the bits in between easy-to-measure outcomes, which could offer alternative evaluations that explore the intricacies of things that matter in early childhood services. The driver of competition is inequality as people compete to have needs met by limited resources, but if we want to address inequalities rather than using them for market purposes, other ways to measure and evaluate practice are needed. Quantifiable measurements are sometimes favoured because of the supposed certainty that they imply, but if we think of assemblages as ever-unfolding and becoming, there is a great deal of uncertainty involved. Quantifiable measurements play a part in producing understandings of quality in practice, but they do not tell the whole story. Ethical practices that address inequality require listening to experiences of how those involved are affected. Massumi (2015: 11) believes that ethical action involves assessing the potential of the action and 'what it brings out in the situation'. Moreover, he asserts that ethics are 'about how we inhabit uncertainty, together'. This implies a need to tune into each other's experiences to understand the bits in between quantifiable measurements and find practical, ethical responses in order to navigate uncertainty collaboratively.

Moss opens up new ways of seeing the world and opportunities to experiment with ideas of emerging futures and practices, by deliberately choosing to phrase his telling of neoliberalism as a *story* as opposed to a *truth* that must be accepted. He suggests that we can choose to see the story of neoliberalism as a frame of reference and understand that this is one view of the world, without believing that it is the only way. Furthermore, he advocates listening to alternative stories of early childhood education that are based on democratic participation in what quality might be, and explore what stories of early childhood might become through curiosity and imagination of alternative responses to the effects of political systems.

EMERGING PROFESSIONALISM

Moss contrasts neoliberal views of the ECEC professional 'as a transmitter and producer of predetermined knowledge and values' with that of 'a professional with an overriding responsibility towards her or his' role in working with people (2014: 45). Rather than being locked into preconceived ideas and discourses, he asserts that a professional can be '"rich" and competent with enormous potential, an active learner co-constructing knowledge in relationship with others … a reflective practitioner, a theorist and a critical thinker' (2014: 89).

There are numerous models and theories of professionalism in ECEC and there is a lack of consensus on what this complex concept means. Policy systems continually emerge, thus meanings of professionalism entangled with these systems are continually emerging. From neoliberal perspectives, a key aim of ECEC is to invest in children and families as an investment in the future economy, but what about the ethics of investing in ECEC as a social principle of equality? Harwood et al. (2013: 10) highlight a notion of 'oscillating identities' in relation to their findings in a multinational study with early childhood educators. Participants spoke of the complexities of their roles, which encompass both care and educational responsibilities. The researchers advocate listening to the experiences of such professionals in order to empower them to advocate for care as a social principle in their multifaceted roles as part of navigating what professionalism means.

In order to counter discourses of professionalism imposed externally by standardised, outcomes-driven measurements of quality, Brock (2013) investigated the perspectives of 12 early years educators. She emphasises a need for practitioners' voices to be part of debates around professionalism. Listening to practitioners' experiences in her study provoked the creation of a **typology** of early childhood professionalism, which took account of 'the interplay between personal voices and professional ideologies' (p. 27). This typology highlights the significance of autonomy in making appropriate judgements in changing situations, which are based on expertise, collaboration and ethical values, and not merely the application of technical competence to produce prescribed outcomes. The typology comprises seven dimensions of professionalism:

1. *Knowledge*: study of theory; experience; practical understanding of policy frameworks.
2. *Qualifications, training and professional development*: further and higher education, apprenticeships; self-directed continual professional development and training.
3. *Skills*: planning curricula and teaching through play-based pedagogies, observing and assessing children's learning; monitoring, evaluating and reflecting on practice and provision; multidisciplinary and teamwork skills; making appropriate judgements; effective communication with a range of stakeholders.
4. *Autonomy*: recognised knowledge and expertise in relation to pedagogy; making appropriate provision for groups of children based on own judgements; autonomy in professional responsibilities; using discretion; shaping policy and practice; recognition of professionalism, status and value; recognition and endorsement of vocational aspects of working with children.
5. *Values*: sharing similar ideologies and values, such as belief in play-based pedagogies and principles for appropriate provision; commitment built on moral and social purposes; accountability to children and families; creating a trusting, mutually respectful environment.
6. *Ethics*: engagement with ethical principles and values; high level of commitment to professional role and to children and families; collaboration with colleagues within and beyond the setting; inclusiveness and valuing diversity in working relationships in the setting and community.
7. *Rewards*: personal satisfaction, interest and enjoyment in work; strong, supportive relationships with children and families; strong commitment to the professional role and to personal professionalism; being valued for professional expertise; appropriate salary. (abridged from Brock, 2013: 35–6)

Brock presents her typology not as a fixed model, but instead as a mechanism to enable reflection and engage practitioners and students in debate about early childhood professionalism. The typology emerged as a response to engaging directly with practitioners who are navigating professionalism in ECEC. Views and stories of professionalism are characterised by both heterogeneity *and* commonality in experiences, so different learning communities can find different ways to 'inhabit uncertainty, together' (Massumi, 2015: 11) and produce new theories in response to unfolding assemblages. It is useful to consider how studies such as Brock's create and shape understandings of professionalism. Payler and Davis (2017) provide a useful summary and discussion of further early childhood research and policies that contribute to current conceptualisations. This can be accessed on the book's website to support reflection on issues of professionalism that Early Childhood students encounter in their learning.

Early Childhood students have a complex network of entanglements to navigate. Campbell-Barr (2016) explored ECS students' development of attitudes and dispositions in relation to professionalism and found that students value and call for support in understanding relationships between professional identities and practical experience of engaging in reflective practice. If we see the world as unfolding and emerging, an answer that we might have today will shift as it is evaluated and re-evaluated continuously.

spotlight on practice 24.1

Ideas of Professionalism

Participants in the focus group for this chapter suggested that continuous and varied experiences shape their ideas of professionalism:

> I think ... it's based on other people that you've seen ... like who you want to be like, who you see ... I think that's kind of where my idea of professionalism [comes from]. I think sometimes there's a grey area ... I can understand that some professionals don't see eye to eye ... I think professionalism means something to different people ... I'm learning what I do want to be like in a professional setting but also definitely what I don't.

> A professional challenge ... would be being in the same setting, there being a different opinion of teaching that can influence the children ... maybe in the morning a child asks to help a teacher ... and in the afternoon is there another teacher that asks children to sit back down ... but then that child's saying, 'I want to help', so then it's really difficult for the children to accept two different teaching staff.

> I think I'm shaped by my past job. I used to work for a swimming school ... which was like a family swimming school and all of the ladies I worked with were just like a big family ... when I look back we were ... almost like siblings so in a way ... you don't have to keep a professional life separate to your personal life, I think you can connect them.

> When you're working with kids it's different to working with their parents sometimes so you've got to have multiple identities while you're being professional ... If you look at other teachers it helps with your own identity and professionalism because it shows how you can actually balance all of those things, how to talk to people differently.

> With placement, some of those days where I went in and didn't have to go in I learned more than when ... I had to go in, because ... I'd be going in on different days of the week

(Continued)

and they do different activities in class ... with different teachers ... I learned a lot more about different types of teaching ... you can go and work with a different teacher or... the head teacher or... the dinner staff.

When I was volunteering ... they would kind of treat me like I was one of the teachers ... I'm on placement at a SEN school, now. I've never thought of going into that environment before ... Now I'm actually intrigued to go a bit further into research because it's very interesting.

Make the most of being at uni ... things like sports coaching courses ... first aid ... not everyone knows what they want to do so it's good to try out a few different things.

Evidently, participants found it important to be receptive and responsive to opportunities and investigate different experiences. This can create new understandings of professionalism and open up new possibilities as part of studying early childhood.

 action point 24.1

- Make a note of ways in which your experiences have shaped your ideas about professionalism.
- Think about the kind of impact you want to make in the world of ECEC.
- Imagine the opportunities that you could find, create and become entangled with to explore new possibilities within and beyond your course of study.
- Generate a plan of how you will engage with opportunities in your adventure of continually becoming professional.

Reflecting on dynamic forces within unfolding assemblages can inform our understanding of entanglements within systems. MacNaughton (2005) asserts that reflection and dialogue in collaborative learning communities enable practitioners to manage or challenge dominant ideologies that have ethical implications for practice. By sharing experiences we can explore alternative pathways and ideas can grow or change direction.

As Moss (2014: 8) puts it, 'The future is immanent and present, which has itself emerged from the potentiality of the past'. Past encounters that affect us now and in the future are entangled with continually becoming. The snippets of becoming through relational entanglements included in this chapter have offered glimpses into events and potential adventures in an emerging world, and, as Semetsky (2011: 140) explains, 'Event is always an element of becoming, and the becoming is unlimited'. Sharing reflections and responding to resonances in the stories of others create unpredictable connections that spark off new learning. If we tune into the world around us, we can begin to understand how vibrant matters provoke our responses and shape how we take part in unfolding adventures.

SUMMARY

- Continually unfolding systems, such as ECEC assemblages in which we are entangled, influence our experiences.
- Reflection on processes of transitioning and becoming affords opportunities to understand our entanglement with the world in general, and with early childhood in particular.
- Identifying ideological issues, such as the current prevalence of neoliberalism, can illuminate understandings of how ECEC professionalism is conceptualised. Considering alternatives to dominant ideology can open up the potential to challenge current influences on practice.
- Sharing stories and engaging with new learning experiences affords new opportunities as part of studying early childhood.

 online resources

Make sure to visit https://study.sagepub.com/fitzgeraldandmaconochie for selected SAGE videos (with questions), SAGE journal articles, links to external sources and flashcards.

FURTHER READING

Giugni, M. (2011). 'Becoming Worldly With': An Encounter with the Early Years Learning Framework. *Contemporary Issues in Early Childhood*, 12(1): 11–27. [online] Available at: http://journals.sagepub.com/doi/pdf/10.2304/ciec.2011.12.1.11 [Accessed 2 July 2018].

Giugni reflects on her experiences of implementing an early years curriculum policy. She challenges limited definitions of children's learning that are articulated in the curriculum document and discusses pedagogical choices that create opportunities for ethical practice.

Lenz Taguchi, H. (2011). Investigating Learning, Participation and Becoming in Early Childhood Practices with a Relational Materialist Approach. *Global Studies of Childhood* 1(1): 36–50. [online] Available at: http://journals.sagepub.com/doi/pdf/10.2304/gsch.2011.1.1.36 [Accessed 2 July 2018].

This article takes a deeper look at the concept of 'becoming' in relation to the material world. It considers alternative ways of thinking about pedagogy and opens up opportunities to challenge dominant forces in education.

REFERENCES

Bennett, J. (2010). *Vibrant Matter: A Political Ecology of Things*. Durham, NC: Duke University Press.

Brock, A. (2013). Building a Model of Early Years Professionalism from Practitioners' Perspectives. *Journal of Early Childhood Research*, 11(1): 27–44.

Bronfenbrenner, U. (1979). *The Ecology of Human Development: Experiments by Nature and Design*. Cambridge, MA: Harvard University Press.

Campbell-Barr, V. (2016). Quality Early Childhood Education and Care: The Role of Attitudes and Dispositions in Professional Development. *Journal of Early Child Development and Care*, 187(1): 45–58.

Deleuze, G. and Guattari, F. (1987). *A Thousand Plateaus*. London: Bloomsbury.

Harwood, D., Klopper, A., Osanyin, A. and Vanderlee, M. (2013). 'It's More Than Care': Early Childhood Educators' Concepts of Professionalism. *Early Years*, 33(1): 4–17.

Lenz Taguchi, H. (2010). *Going Beyond the Theory/Practice Divide in Early Childhood Education: Introducing an Intra-active Pedagogy*. London: Routledge.

MacNaughton, G. (2005). *Doing Foucault in Early Childhood Studies: Applying Post-structural Ideas*. London: Routledge.

Massumi, B. (2015). *Politics of Affect*. Cambridge: Polity Press.

Mayer-Hoffer, C. (2015). Attitude and Passion: Becoming a Teacher in Early Childhood Education and Care. *Early Years*, 35(4): 366–80.

Moss, P. (2014). *Transformative Change and Real Utopias: The Story of Democracy, Experimentation and Potentiality*. London: Routledge.

Osgood, J. (2012). *Narratives from the Nursery: Negotiating Professional Identities in Early Childhood*. Abingdon: Routledge.

Payler, J. and Davis, G. (2017). Professionalism: Early Years as a Career. *BERA-TACTYC Early Childhood Research Review*, 9–29.

Semetsky, I. (2011). Becoming Other: Developing the Ethics of Integration. *Policy Futures in Education*, 9(1): 138–44.

Simpson, D. (2010). Being Professional? Conceptualising Early Years Professionalism in England. *European Early Childhood Education Research Journal*, 18(1): 5–14.

Taylor, C. A. and Harris-Evans, J. (2016). Reconceptualising Transition to Higher Education with Deleuze and Guattari. *Studies in Higher Education*, 43(7): 1254–67.

LEARNING THROUGH PLACEMENTS

BY CAROLINE LEESON

Over the 20 years of my career I have been on several placements and more recently as manager of an ECEC setting, I have supported several students through theirs. But I have to admit that I have not given much thought to placements before. I have not given the emotional aspect of what students learn on their placements much consideration nor explored their impact on personal and professional values in such detail as I have done since reading this chapter.

This chapter is useful not only to those students about to embark on a placement but also for those hosting placements. The information contained in the chapter highlights in a clear and precise way, how the relationship between the student and their supporters can be strengthened – leading to greater growth for both partners. The chapter helped me to highlight and examine what I would be looking for in future personal placements and how to make placements in my setting a more useful experience.

Reading this chapter has altered my mind-set regarding what to expect of my placement students and also how I can better support them.

MICHELLE YEOMAN
MA EDUCATION: EARLY CHILDHOOD
YORK ST JOHN UNIVERSITY

 learning outcomes

By actively reading this chapter and engaging with the material, you will be able to:

- discuss the importance and relevance of placements when learning about working with young children and their families
- use a range of reflective practice techniques to explore professional practice
- critically debate the benefits and risks for placements being used as vehicles for proving standards or performance outcomes.

INTRODUCTION

Placements are transformative in that they enable a deeper understanding of the significant impact professionals have on the lives of the children and families that they work with (Leeson and Bamsey, 2015), and their personal **dispositions** towards the diverse communities they may work with will be critical factors in defining their relationships with, and any subsequent outcomes for, children and their families. Working with diverse communities and being introduced to many social issues, professional skills and techniques whilst learning theoretical concepts, are key opportunities for personal development and perspective change. This chapter will explore the importance and relevance of placements in the learning journeys of Early Childhood Education and Care (ECEC) students and professionals; both those undertaken formally through courses and those taken as additional learning opportunities. It should be noted that employment more related to income generation than professional experience also has its place as a great opportunity for learning about self and developing key skills and strategies for working with others, about leadership, communication and self-reliance.

RELATIONSHIP BETWEEN PLACEMENTS, LEARNING AND TRAINING

Increasingly, placements have been positioned as a crucial and central aspect of professional training and education for a wide number of people working with children and families in a range of environments as they enable practice learning as well as achieving recognised access to a professional community (Johnston, 2016). Schön (1991) stated that education *should* be regarded as the creation of opportunities to link theory to practice, to develop understanding about actions, assessing the impact of those actions towards developing enhanced knowledge and skills that can be taken forward to bear on new situations. Indeed, Schön argued that education is not merely a process of filling someone with knowledge that simply spills over into practice. Schön's perspective on the value of placements underpins a great deal of current education/training practice with various mechanisms provided which facilitate those important connections for students. Examples include placements running alongside classroom learning; modules focusing exclusively on work-based learning; and assignments requiring close examination of actions taken in practice.

Becoming a professional is more than learning the technical and rational aspects of the role; it is learning to exercise professional judgement, and being creative and appropriate in response (Sheppard, 1995). According to Sheppard, placements are ideally situated to this critical developmental process. Osgood (2012: 152) discusses the process of becoming; the importance of promoting professional authenticity through 'doing professionalism' that goes beyond technical ability; and offers an opportunity to enhance the emotional commitment to those families and children in the setting.

However, situated in a context of rapid professionalisation of the ECEC workforce through the increased construction of professional practice standards, placements have become established as the focal point of assessment for entry into many professions, creating a tension for the novice professional. Standards are helpful as they provide guidance for expected practice and operate as gauges of competence in particular skills, but there are considerable concerns that they are reductionist, placing value on certain aspects of technical, measurable practice and ignoring others, often the more relational and emotional, which are less easy to measure and assess (Oberhuemer, 2015; Barron, 2016). There are two further arguments put forward for the inclusion of placement opportunities in ECEC programmes. One which has emerged most recently, and swiftly taken hold, is the employability argument; that placement experience gives the opportunity to enhance a CV and prove to prospective employers an applicant's experience and expertise. The employability argument also claims that placements support the development of personal confidence and vigour, enabling the student to not only achieve a higher grade in their studies, but also be seen as a valuable addition to the workforce as a consequence of their superior grade and wealth of experience (Clark and Zukas, 2016). The more established argument is that placements provide great opportunities for putting theory into practice, for allowing experimentation and exploration of various scenarios, which equip the novice with the skills and knowledge for their future working life. Pollard (2005: 75) considers that the 'dialectical relationship between society and individuals' with a 'constant interplay of social forces and individual actions' is central to any consideration of professional practice and should be regarded as an important theoretical framework for reflective teachers – a view that can be extended to the entire ECEC workforce.

Both of these arguments have contributed to the current scenario where placements are seen as an integral and increasingly important aspect of professional learning. Indeed, placements are often used as a gatekeeping mechanism for entry into the profession with a requirement that they are 'passed' in order to achieve the requisite qualification (Cleak et al., 2016). The problem is that, increasingly, ECEC students are finding their placements becoming ever more formalised within their programme of education – narrowly defined by national professional standards and set within a top-down regulatory framework managed by the government through bodies such as Ofsted (Barron, 2016). Thus, their learning risks becoming codified, reduced to a mechanistic technical skills acquisition process with little attention being paid to any underlying discourses of equality, to professionalism and to a value base. What should be evident is that placements are significant opportunities to explore the emotional aspects of professional practice and should not be reduced to a rational, cognitive exercise with a narrow focus on practitioner standards and assessment regimes consisting of simplistic checklists and tick boxes. Indeed, Eden (2014) argues that the emotional challenge offered by placements should *always* be regarded as more important than any skills that might be learnt, and that we should move towards implementing a method of integrative learning where the process is viewed as more important than the skills learnt – a process of becoming.

WHAT DO PLACEMENTS OFFER?

It is clear that placements should be situated as excellent mechanisms for establishing a student's acquisition of sufficient knowledge and practical skills to meet a specified professional standard (Barron, 2016), and this aspect should not be ignored or minimised. But they are much more; they are the venue for not only putting theory into practice, but also for noticing the difference between the rhetoric and the reality to enable challenge and the possibility of perspective change.

 case study 25.1

Journal Entry

The entry is from the reflective journal of an ECEC student on placement in the criminal justice system.

Talking to the women in the queue while they were waiting to visit their men in the prison, I realised how hard their lives were and how the punishment their men are serving is also theirs. One woman told me how she is not spoken to by others in her street because of what he has done; nothing to do with her. She told me that she felt very isolated and that she was struggling with lots of things and the only help she had was anti-depressants from her GP. I had not thought about this before, but it really made me think about the unfairness of their situation, and question the level of support they receive – often nothing. Also, many of the support services available are run by charities so not always well funded or the funding is time limited. This is really not fair and I can feel my blood boil. I had not thought about any of this before; I had assumed that our criminal justice system was fair and right. I need to think more about how I might make a difference for women like those I met today.

1. How has this placement experience made the student aware of the key concepts of complexity and diversity?
2. How might this awareness help them in their future career?

Indeed, the opportunity to identify the social inequalities that exist for many families that students encounter alongside a crucial debate as to the various cultural perspectives and political ideologies that perpetuate or challenge the *zeitgeist*, is an essential part of being a responsible and accountable professional (Pollard, 2005). Placements are critical opportunities for students to develop their own theory of how their professional practice might be best articulated, offering a strong sense of ethical self that gives confidence and resilience; both qualities will be required in the future when the need to challenge unhelpful directives or outmoded practices becomes apparent (Rose and Rogers, 2012; Rouse et al., 2012).

case study 25.2

Challenging Self

A student with significant fears about illness and the sight of blood sought a placement in the play centre attached to a children's ward at her local hospital. Having recently had her own child, she wanted to scrutinise her anxieties and found through her placement that she enjoyed the challenge of working with very sick children; finding activities that engaged and amused them. This could be quite a challenge for children who were bed bound, limited in movement or in considerable pain or discomfort, as well as for those who were facing further surgery or dealing with a terminal diagnosis.

Her subsequent reflections led her to explore theoretical models of illness and disability and her enhanced awareness of concepts of hierarchy, expert power and organisational rules that underpin hospitalisation and medical care.

1. How has the student developed her own theory of illness and hospital care?
2. How might this development help her in her future career?

Such experiences are powerful and often life-changing in terms of attitudinal shift and future career decisions, nevertheless stepping out of a comfort zone, like in the example above, has to be managed carefully by both the student and their supervisors as the consequent dissonance might be too much to bear. If the student cited above had fainted at her first sight of blood or had found the situation unbearable or profoundly shocking, then her story might have been one of trauma rather than achievement, with potentially disastrous results for her world view, future confidence and subsequent career plans.

I have explored elsewhere the usefulness of the concept of 'building blocks' when considering professional practice (Campbell-Barr and Leeson, 2016) and placements can be important developmental tools to be used in a variety of ways – as some of the vital blocks needed to build a professional identity or as the mortar between individual blocks of theoretical and practical learning contributing to a robust structure that is strong and meaningful. There is, of course, the risk that any structure being built might also serve as a barrier to any experiences or thinking that threaten a particular world view, so avoiding a closed structure requires a number of strategies:

- tools that encourage and promote active reflective learning
- good, strong supervision from both tutors and placement supervisors that encourages the student to question what they are experiencing and learning, and helps to ameliorate any dissonance that might be felt
- robust opportunities to challenge and debate the learning undertaken, and explore the implications of any dispositional change.

Lefevre (2008) developed a useful model for social work practice consisting of the domains of 'knowing', 'being' and 'doing'. I suggest that her model is equally applicable to all professionals working with families as its central concern is about the quality of the relationship between worker and family/child. According to Lefevre, 'knowing' is the knowledge and understanding of the complexities of family lives and 'being' is the personal attributes of the individual worker, including their emotional capacity and value base. Only the 'doing' domain involves the techniques and skills needed to do the job and all three interrelate to develop the professional capacity of the student. Engaging in reflective practice supports the integration of the three domains, helping students and practitioners to bring forth their knowing and being to blend with their skills and techniques. As Mills (2013: 42) expresses it so eloquently, 'extensive field experiences alongside structured opportunities for reflection, self-analysis and discourse on equity issues are crucial in moving prospective teachers [*and other ECEC professionals*] towards the confrontation and modification of prior beliefs through a provocation of **cognitive dissonance**'. [*Comments inserted by author*]

A FRAMEWORK FOR THINKING ABOUT PLACEMENTS

Wenger's communities of practice (1998) are used a great deal when thinking about sharing learning from experience and developing a professional identity. The opportunity to come together, share experiences and tease out the learning and development is valuable and has been an important addition to the landscape of professional learning. Johnston (2016) argues that there are limitations to Wenger's model in terms of insufficient emphasis on the complexity of the emotional, psychological and behavioural dimensions of identity building and sense of belonging that are so very relevant in the experiences of students on placement. Using a framework based on Bronfenbrenner's (1979) ecological model, it is possible to highlight the importance of these variables, allowing for the creation of more integrated placements that are transformative in nature and offer maximum professional development.

To use Bronfenbrenner's own terminology, Figure 25.1 shows:

> the activities, social roles and interpersonal relations experienced by the developing person in a given face-to-face setting with particular physical, social and symbolic features that invite, permit or inhibit engagement in sustained, progressively more complex interaction with, and activity in, the immediate environment. (Bronfenbrenner, 1994: 1645)

The students feature as the middle ring in the model because how they regard those they are working with and their capacity for perspective shift have an important impact on the community, just as the community has a similar powerful impact on them. Using Bourdieu's thinking tools (advocated by Clarke and Zukas, 2016) helps to express the important work that the student brings to the setting, as well as that which they need to do within their placement. A disposition to think relationally (field) and to see social practices as dynamic and shifting (habitus) will offer opportunities for challenge. This will lead to what Mezirow (1991) calls disorienting dilemmas, which require reflection in order to achieve a holistic engagement with the emotional, psychological and behavioural dimensions of building their personal and professional identity.

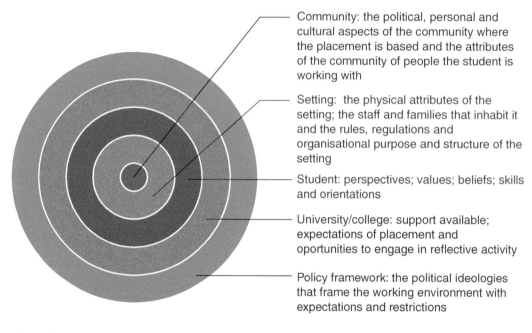

Community: the political, personal and cultural aspects of the community where the placement is based and the attributes of the community of people the student is working with

Setting: the physical attributes of the setting; the staff and families that inhabit it and the rules, regulations and organisational purpose and structure of the setting

Student: perspectives; values; beliefs; skills and orientations

University/college: support available; expectations of placement and oportunities to engage in reflective activity

Policy framework: the political ideologies that frame the working environment with expectations and restrictions

Figure 25.1 The activities, social roles and interpersonal relations experienced by the developing person

Source: Based on Bronfenbrenner (1979)

SO HOW CAN PLACEMENTS BE MAXIMISED?

Just like children, students require enabling learning environments – and the list below gives suggestions for an effective environment to be established that allows ECEC students to flourish. If possible, a student attending placement should be encouraged to find/choose or have input into where placement takes place, to reduce the risk that the placement 'fit' will not be great, and to feel accepted as 'legitimate participants' (Clarke and Zukas, 2016: 1291). Problems can ensue when students experience unsatisfactory placements or those where they are regarded as outsiders. Students can become very anxious, even traumatised by being in a placement that is too alien to them, that is unwelcoming or lacking in plans for personal development and/or structured activities for participation. Most worrying is the likelihood of damage to the development of a sense of professional self, with good students/prospective professionals rejecting their chosen career path or seeking to avoid certain aspects of their work in the future (Clark and Zukas, 2016).

Second, simply having a work-based experience and meeting any requisite standards will not be enough; it is essential for students to analyse their experiences in order to support the development of a strong sense of self; to embody their learning and acquire a detailed awareness of the situations met and experienced (Eden, 2014). Developing an awareness of what inequality looks like, of the structural and systematic inequalities that exist and of how a more just society might work to ensure that those who are vulnerable are protected and taken care of (Rawls, 1999), is an important journey for those working in ECEC. An ideal mechanism for the process of developing awareness is through reflective practice – using a learning journal or other instrument to not only record the central issues thought about or experienced, but to examine closely the associations, learning and future implications of the situation under review. There are a substantial number of models that students might use to help them make visible their understanding so that they might begin to make sense of what they are experiencing and how that fits with their world view (Leeson and Bamsey, 2015). For example, Kolb (1984) and Gibbs (1988) both developed cyclical models of reflective learning with a series of stages (for example, Kolb identifies stages of concrete experience, reflective observation, abstract conceptualisation and active experimentation) that ultimately lead to another round of the same questions to continually draw forth connections and learning in a never-ending process. Thus, the cyclical nature is deliberate, underlining that professional reflection is ongoing as we perpetually strive to understand what is going on and continue to look for any deeper meanings and/or connections with other experiences. However, cyclical ways of reflecting can imply a deficit model that induces anxiety, an assumption that there is always some improvement to make or that there is a 'right' way to reflect that requires each step to be completed, in sequence, before moving on to the next (Farrelly, 2010). Seeking to address this criticism, alternative ways of reflection were developed, such as De Bono's 'six thinking hats' to represent different ways of looking at a situation (Lindon, 2012) and Brookfield's (1995) 'critical lenses' which explore the viewpoints of others. Ghaye (2011) defines reflective practice as practice with principle and offers a spiral model which encourages each stage to be revisited, many times and in any sequence, throughout the reflective process to further develop thoughts, ideas and connections.

 action point 25.1

Try at least one of the models by choosing an event that happened recently that you wish to explore further. Do not choose an unusual event - the richest learning frequently lies in the mundane and routine. Examples of reflective models can be found at https://study.sagepub.com/fitzgeraldandmaconochie

Ghaye (2011) emphasises both the individual and the organisational context of reflection, identifying how the workplace or society in which a practitioner operates affects their actions and values and has the potential to exert power and influence over them. All practice is inevitably value-laden, so making clear links between personal values and practice, and those of the organisation, is important for future professional development. It also gives an understanding of the current placement situation and may offer helpful coping strategies to deal with the process of understanding the organisational rules of a new placement setting at the same time as practising new skills and trying to find a voice and/or sense of personal agency (Taylor, 2015). Reflective practice therefore helps with the complex process of 'fitting in' and foregrounds the emotional and physical aspects of learning (Clarke and Zukas, 2016).

REFLECTING ON PRACTICE

ECEC work is relational (Papatheodorou, 2009) and recognising, analysing and thinking about that emotional engagement promises a rich understanding of self that can only be achieved through reflective practice. Models of reflection, such as those developed by Schön, Gibbs and Ghaye, can all help to develop confidence in the initial stages of learning to reflect. Experienced reflectors are then able to find their own styles and develop the models that work for them, allowing them to access their deepest thoughts and emotions. Many advocate the use of a journal or online reflecting tool as a repository that facilitates retrospection and revisiting of previous experiences and records. Keeping a journal is common professional practice – noting the activities, thoughts and feelings of the day helps practitioners and students to remain mindful of the work being done; the personal and professional values held and how they are manifest in practice. Themes and questions arise that might otherwise go unnoticed in the 'busy-ness' of everyday working life.

 — action point 25.2

It is really important that your journal will be enjoyed when using it so time should be taken when choosing one. A big ledger might feel important, whereas a small notebook might feel more practical as it can be carried at all times. Inspiring pictures; touchy-feely coverings; vellum pages – the choice is wide and varied! Select a notebook that is suitable for you.

These journals can be unpicked and debated, internally and with peers, to help the development of greater awareness, the increase in abilities and skills, and can begin to form the basis of your own theoretical development. There is no right or wrong way to keep a journal; it should be entirely in control of the writer. Thus, for any writing to be effective and meaningful, it should be private with a right of autonomy for the writer to decide what they wish to share with others. Some institutions ask for reflective accounts to be submitted for assessment. However, these are often on an aspect of practice or focusing on a particular incident. Journal entries are a great place to draw on materials for this type of assignment. However, a distinction should therefore be made between personal reflexivity (as in a journal) and writing reflective accounts as evidence of practice, such as those required on academic courses. A reflective account for evidence purposes will be more descriptive, perhaps structured, drawing on a reflective model and links to relevant aspects of theory; whereas a reflection for personal development, is intended to be more thoughtful and exploratory, raising questions and allowing for tentative debate – it is a way to think in-depth to inform the development of personal attributes and professional skills.

Of course, writing it down is only one mechanism for reflection; discussion groups or action learning sets could be used in the classroom for sharing ideas, experiences and thoughts. Action learning sets are committed group meetings over an extended period where students come together to discuss any challenges they have faced in their practice and, through the questioning of their colleagues, develop a deeper understanding of underlying issues, complexities and points to consider. Action plans might be drawn up that can be put into effect with the opportunity to report back at later meetings, develop further understanding and identify different possible strategies. Cyclical models of reflection, such as those discussed earlier, are often utilised in action learning sets as they provide a useful framework for discussion and encourage that perpetual search for meaning.

There are many other ways in which thoughts and feelings might be accessed without necessarily writing them down. For example, identifying music which symbolises/evokes an experience offers an opportunity to engage in a more nuanced exploration of the feelings induced. Many creative mechanisms can stand as a map or a metaphor for both the experience and the subsequent thinking that have taken place. Indeed, as humans, we use metaphor all the time when explaining concepts and ideas, or expressing our emotions and thoughts, whether we know it or not. We talk about our minds as being some sort of container; we liken people to animals; we see significance in certain objects for key aspects of our lives, such as 'life is like a box of chocolates' or using a heart to symbolise love.

 spotlight on practice 25.1

Learning Journey towards Professionalism

A student chose to use the metaphor of a tree to articulate her learning journey towards professionalism. The roots of the tree were those experiences that informed her personal values, such as her upbringing, the influences of her community, her parents and peers. The trunk of the tree represented the theories that she had learnt which helped to inform her value base, change her perspective and facilitate her practice. The branches were the skills and techniques she had learnt and the risks she had taken to develop further. The leaves and blossoms were examples of practice - memories of children and families she had worked with and the potential she recognised for the future. On the ground surrounding her tree were fruits and discarded leaves; the fruit represented the future influences she might have and opportunities that might present themselves. The discarded leaves were things she had left behind, no longer needed or redundant. She hung her tree in her room and used it as a dynamic piece of work, adding to it over time, recognising her continued development and learning as well as beginning to explore what nourished her tree and how her tree nourished others in an ecological narrative.

1. What other aspects of a tree might the student have explored in her symbolism?
2. How might this awareness help the student in their future career?

According to Gibbs (1994), such metaphors are useful in any conversation, verbal or written, as a crucial aid to the thinking process. Barnden (2005) argues that using metaphors is an essential aspect of reflective practice as they can make the messy seem more tangible whilst recognising the subtleties and complexities therein. McClintock et al. (2003: 726) explore the use of metaphors in the research context, concluding that they 'have a valuable role in making understandings explicit, transparent and structured'. However, McKenzie (2010) suggests that it is not that straightforward and that metaphors should be chosen carefully to avoid further confusion and the risk of making any meaning too obscure. Therefore, good guidance as well as plenty of time to think about what is being sought through the metaphor in order to make visible and tangible that internal sense-making process, are both important aspects of the task.

 action point 25.3

Select three photos that mean a lot to you and arrange them on a piece of paper:

1. Write about each photo and why it is important to you; explore why you chose it.
2. Look closely at each photo – what is going on in the photo; might there be something there you had not fully seen before?
3. Look for any possible connections between your photos – is there a theme?
4. With another person explore what the photos say about you and what you consider to be important.
5. What other images might you wish to take to tell the story of you more clearly/more fully?
6. Select a creative method you might use to capture your learning of self. What might be the mechanism/structure for your design? How might you develop a sense of self through the photos?
7. Storyboard/plan a possible structure of self.

Finally, students can make the most of their placement experience by actively engaging with their reflections to work towards a place of 'embodied learning' (Reimer Kirkham et al., 2005: 11) where confidence grows alongside the capacity to be an agent of change. Argyris and Schön (1978) introduced the concept of double-loop learning – a further interrogation of the learning taking place with questions asked about any assumptions that underpin it; testing hypotheses and possibilities to develop an enhanced, critical and more nuanced understanding of what is happening or has occurred. Such closer inspection allows the development of embodied learning through a process of listening to the listening (Maturana, 2004), asking questions about how the original reflection fits or contradicts previous work, the perceptions and illusions that are present and where that journey takes them.

SUMMARY

- Placements are incredible vehicles for challenging assumptions and prejudices and have the capacity to create an enhanced awareness of inequality and commitment to social justice. As professionals working within ECEC in a fast-paced, ever-changing world where many inequalities are permitted to exist, frequently unchallenged, there is a clear responsibility to notice and take action, and hold to account on behalf of others.
- Reflection, supported by a range of techniques, as discussed in the chapter, offers individuals the opportunity to develop their professional practice within ECEC to support children, families and fellow practitioners.
- Placements can be useful for proving standards or performance outcomes; but they should be regarded as so much more in terms of attitude change and professional confidence, otherwise they risk being a sterile, technical exercise rather than life-enhancing and creative.

online resources

Make sure to visit https://study.sagepub.com/fitzgeraldandmaconochie for selected SAGE videos (with questions), SAGE journal articles, links to external sources and flashcards.

FURTHER READING

Hayes, C., Daly, J., Duncan, M., Gill, R. and Whitehouse, A. (2014). *Developing as a Reflective Early Years Professional: A Thematic Approach*. Northwich: Critical Publishing.

This book is a series of themed chapters that help the reader apply the theory of reflective practice to gain confidence in their own reflective capacity.

Mason, J. (2002). *Researching Your Own Practice: The Discipline of Noticing*. London: RoutledgeFalmer.

This was published some years ago, but it is still an inspiring read which urges the reader to use their taken-for-granted skill of simple observation. All too often, we think of reflective engagement as a focus on the unusual – Mason emphasises the richness of the mundane and routine and the powerful learning therein.

REFERENCES

Argyris, C. and Schön, D. (1978). *Organizational Learning: A Theory of Action Perspective*. Reading, MA: Addison Wesley.

Barnden, J. A. (2005). Metaphor, Self-Reflection and the Nature of Mind. In: D. N. Davis (ed.), *Visions of Mind: Architectures for Cognition and Affect*. Hershey, PA: Information Science Publishing, Idea Group Inc., pp. 45–65.

Barron, I. C. (2016). Flight Turbulence: The Stormy Professional Trajectory of Trainee Early Years Teachers in England. *International Journal of Early Years Education*, *24*(3), pp. 325–341.

Bronfenbrenner, U. (1979). *The Ecology of Human Development: Experiments by Nature and Design*. Cambridge, MA: Harvard University Press.

Bronfenbrenner, U. (1994). Ecological Models of Human Development. In T. Husen and T. N. Postletwaite (eds), *International Encyclopedia of the Social and Behavioral Sciences*. Oxford: Elsevier.

Brookfield, S. (1995). *Becoming a Critically Reflective Teacher*. San Francisco, CA: Jossey-Bass.

Campbell-Barr, V. and Leeson, C. (2016). *Quality and Leadership in the Early Years: Research, Theory and Practice*. London: Sage.

Clark, M. and Zukas, M. (2016). Understanding Successful Sandwich Placements: A Bourdieusian Approach. *Studies in Higher Education*, *41*(7): 1281–95.

Cleak, H., Roulston, A. and Vreugdenhil, A. (2016) The Inside Story: A Survey of Social Work Students' Supervision and Learning Opportunities on Placement, *British Journal of Social Work*, *46*(7): 2033–50.

Eden, S. (2014) Out of the Comfort Zone: Enhancing Work-based Learning about Employability through Student Reflection on Work Placements, *Journal of Geography in Higher Education*, *38*(2): pp. 266–76.

Farrelly, P. (2010). Early Years Study. In: P. Farrelly (ed.), *Early Years Work Based Learning*. Exeter: Learning Matters, pp. 23–42.

Ghaye, A. (2011). *Teaching and Learning through Reflective Practice: A Practical Guide for Positive Action*, 2nd edn. Abingdon: Routledge/David Fulton.

Gibbs, G. (1988). *Learning by Doing: A Guide to Teaching and Learning Methods*. Oxford: Oxford Polytechnic Further Education Unit.

Johnston, D. (2016). 'Sitting Alone in the Staffroom Contemplating My Future': Communities of Practice, Legitimate Peripheral Participation and Student Teachers' Experiences of Problematic School Placements as Guests. *Cambridge Journal of Education*, 46(4): 533–51.

Kolb, D. (1984). *Experiential Learning: Experience as the Source of Learning and Development*. Upper Saddle River, NJ: Prentice Hall.

Leeson, C. and Bamsey, V. (2015). In Praise of Reflective Practice. In: R. Parker-Rees and C. Leeson (eds), *Early Childhood Studies: An Introduction to the Study of Children's Worlds and Children's Lives*, 4th edn. London: Sage, pp. 251–63.

Lefevre, M. (2008). Knowing, Being and Doing: Core Qualities and Skills for Working with Children and Young People in Care. In: B. Luckock and M. Lefevre (eds), *Direct Work: Social Work with Children and Young People in Care*. London: BAAF.

Lindon, J. (2012). *Reflective Practice and Early Years Professionalism*, 2nd edn. London: Hodder Education.

McClintock, D., Ison, R. and Armson, R. (2003). Metaphors for Reflecting on Research Practice: Researching with People. *Journal of Environmental Planning and Management*, 46(5): 715–31.

McKenzie, L. (2010). Challenging the Metaphor: Reflection – Mirror or Kaleidoscope? BERA presentation, Warwick University, 4 September.

Maturana, H. (2004). *From Being to Doing: The Origins of the Biology of Cognition*. Heidelberg: Carl-Auer.

Mezirow, J. (1991). *Transformative Dimensions of Adult Learning*. San Francisco, CA: Jossey-Bass.

Mills, C. (2013). A Bourdieuian Analysis of Teachers' Changing Dispositions towards Social Justice: The Limitations of Practicum Placements in Pre-service Teacher Education. *Asia-Pacific Journal of Teacher Education*, 41(1): 41–54.

Oberhuemer, P. (2015). Seeking New Cultures of Cooperation: A Cross-National Analysis of Workplace-based Learning and Mentoring Practices in Early Years Professional Education/ Training. *Early Years*, 35(2), pp. 115-23.

Osgood, J. (2012). *Narratives from the Nursery*. London: Routledge.

Papatheodorou, T. (2009). Exploring Relational Pedagogy. In: J. Moyles and T. Papatheodorou (eds), *Learning Together in the Early Years: Exploring Relational Pedagogy*. Abingdon: Routledge, pp. 3–18.

Pollard, A. (2005). *Reflective Teaching*, 2nd edn. London: Continuum.

Rawls, J. (1999) *A Theory of Justice*. Cambridge, MA: Harvard University Press.

Reimer Kirkham, S., Van Hofwegen, L. and Harwood, C. (2005). Narratives of Social Justice: Learning in Innovative Clinical Settings. *International Journal of Nursing Education Scholarship*, 2(1): 1–15.

Rose, J. and Rogers, S. (2012) Principles under Pressure: Student Teachers' Perspectives on Final Teaching Practice in Early Childhood Classrooms. *International Journal of Early Years Education*, 20(1): 43–58.

Rouse, L., Morrissey A. and Rahimi, M. (2012) Problematic Placement: Pathways Pre-service Teachers' Perspectives on Their Infant/Toddler Placement, *Early Years*, 32(1): 87–98.

Schön, D. A. (1991). *The Reflective Practitioner*. Aldershot: Avebury.

Sheppard, M. (1995). *Social Work and Social Exclusion: The Idea of Practice*. London: Routledge.

Taylor, M. (2015) What Undergraduate Early Childhood Education and Care Students Find 'Troublesome' During the Early Period of Practice Placements. *All-Ireland Journal of Teaching and Learning in Higher Education*, 7(2):18410–15.

Wenger, E. (1998). *Communities of Practice: Learning, Meaning and Identity*. Cambridge: Cambridge University Press.

LEADING QUALITY PRACTICE

BY MARY E. WHALLEY

This chapter showed me how management and leadership are not standalone disciplines but are interchangeable and inherently linked. The chapter offered a comprehensive account of the underpinning theory for different types of leadership, helping me to distinguish between each and understand how, ultimately, the effectiveness of each leadership strategy depends on its ability to enable change in a setting. I found the strategies for overcoming challenges particularly useful, including active listening and offering ongoing support and training, and understood how these present a direct link to the skills required for effective leadership to take hold.

I enjoyed exploring the different global perspectives on leadership, as throughout my teacher training I try to distinguish how aspects of pedagogy in the UK are applied elsewhere. For example, Forest School and why it is implemented more effectively in Scandinavian countries. The paradigm between effective leadership and policy constraints was also very interesting as this resonated well with my placement experiences.

CHELSEA FREEMAN
EARLY CHILDHOOD EDUCATION WITH QTS
LEEDS BECKETT UNIVERSITY

learning outcomes

By actively reading this chapter and engaging with the material, you will be able to:

- explain the key differences between leadership and management in early childhood settings
- identify relevant leadership theory, particularly the characteristics of pedagogical leadership
- explore the concept of contextual literacy and how this can be applied to leadership
- apply a range of skills and strategies to support the leadership of quality practice
- critically evaluate leadership and its relationship to effective practice in early childhood and the policy implications raised.

INTRODUCTION

This chapter promotes leadership in early childhood settings as a key issue in enabling quality practice. 'Good leaders' are generally considered to be people who are able to think and act creatively in routine and non-routine situations and who set out to influence the actions, beliefs and feelings of others (Doyle and Smith, 1999). As such, this can be applied to leadership in early childhood settings. However, this does not equate exclusively to those holding formal 'leader' roles and, in this chapter, it is defined as applying to all early childhood professionals who have the opportunity to demonstrate leadership skills in their work. Arguably, this should encompass all, though some of the challenges in leadership are also identified, together with strategies that can be applied to lead more effectively. Differences between 'management' and 'leadership' are explored and the importance of contextual literacy (Siraj-Blatchford and Manni, 2007) highlighted to illustrate some of the distinctive skills and approaches needed to lead in different settings.

LEADERSHIP OR MANAGEMENT?

Over recent years, there has been growing global emphasis on the professionalisation (see Chapter 23) of those who work, lead and manage in early childhood settings and many argue that the way leadership is developing is a key driver for this new professionalism (Dalli, 2008; Rodd, 2013). The terms 'leadership' and 'management' are often used interchangeably – particularly in the context of early childhood practice. This can be both unhelpful and confusing. Law and Glover (2000) offer helpful definitions of the differences between the two roles. Managers organise, clarify staff responsibilities, coordinate systems and monitor an organisation's effectiveness. Leaders give direction, offer inspiration, build teamwork and set an example. More succinctly, managers are responsible for maintenance and oversight and leaders for enhancement and development. Of course, in many early childhood settings, the one 'in charge' will combine both roles and have both managerial and leadership responsibilities.

Indeed, Rodd (2013: 19) argues that leadership and management are 'inherently linked and interwoven'. There are challenges in disentangling the two but, in this chapter, the focus is on leadership and direction-setting, with no assumption that one is 'in charge'.

 reflection point 26.1

What do you understand as the difference between a 'leader' and a 'manager'? How might the notion of the leader as one who gives direction be applied to all early childhood professionals?

UNDERSTANDING LEADERSHIP

Although there is no 'one size fits all' prescription for early childhood leadership, insights can be gained from a brief foray into the development of leadership theory. The trait model of leadership suggested leaders exhibited particular characteristics – such as knowing what they want, why they want it and how to communicate this to others in order to gain co-operation (Bennis, 1998). The behavioural model was based on the belief that leaders behave in a specific way – most notably either prioritising the needs of the staff or the goals of an organisation (Blake and Mouton, 1964). Although Rodd (2013) asserts that the personal qualities and actions of the leader can have a significant influence on levels of staff motivation and engagement, effective early childhood leadership is far more than adherence to a set of traits or behaviours.

Situational or contingency leadership theories emerged as a response to the growing limitations of 'fixed' understandings of leaders' characteristics and behaviours. The basic premise here is that there is no single way to lead; rather, such factors as the environment, the time and the readiness of the 'followers' determine how leaders function (Hersey et al., 2001). Siraj-Blatchford and Manni (2007: 11) assert that early childhood leaders require contextual literacy which takes account of the 'dynamic nature of the organisation within which one operates'. Contextual literacy considers all the stakeholders – the children themselves, their families, early childhood professionals and those who drive policy. Given the diverse range of settings in early childhood practice, situational theory – particularly the concept of contextual literacy – has strong resonance for the leadership role.

Transformational leadership pointed to leaders who create the appropriate climate within their team for effecting change (Bass and Avolio, 1993) and is based on the belief that the leader can support others to understand and value changes to practice. This includes visionary leadership, defined as a leader's ideological statement about desired future outcomes or the capacity to set a direction within a setting (Leithwood and Levin, 2005). Alongside vision, the leader needs to be able to manage change within a culture of reflective review so that everyone is engaged within it. This might be viewed as lofty rhetoric, with the reality for early childhood leaders far more complex. Aspects of this 'reality' are explored a little later in the chapter but, undoubtedly, the ability to articulate a vision and develop the strategic skills required to effect change remain core to effective leadership.

Organic leadership heralded a paradigm shift in leadership thinking and placed the focus on the whole team, sharing responsibility for leadership (Avery, 2004). Spillane (2006) developed this into a concept of distributed leadership, primarily within the field of education/schools.

Leadership, then, is no longer positioned in a single person but, rather, viewed as the sum of the interaction between the leader, the team and their particular situation. Nominated 'heads' intentionally resist positioning themselves as 'in authority' but, rather, recognise the leadership skills and qualities of all, sharing these relationally and through interaction. Within early childhood settings, this allows for organic leadership to grow and develop.

LEADERSHIP IN EARLY CHILDHOOD SETTINGS

Global developments within early childhood policy and practice illustrate the evolving nature and understanding of leadership. Where there are differences between countries, these are usually reflective of the cultural and policy context of a given country (Siraj-Blatchford and Hallet, 2014). Whatever the differences, there is renewed interest internationally in the early childhood phase of learning and development and the role of leadership in the quality of this. Historically, leadership has been taken up without specific training and, globally, qualifications for the role vary hugely. Currently, in some countries – notably New Zealand, Australia and the Scandinavian nations – a high proportion are educated to graduate level and hold qualified teacher status (Dalli, 2008). In England, the majority of early childhood leaders and managers are qualified to diploma level (vocational level 3), although a graduate status for early childhood has been in place since 2006 (Children's Workforce Development Council (CWDC), 2006).

Most of the literature on early childhood leadership positions the leader as 'in charge' of a setting and usually called the 'manager'. In England, the introduction of a new graduate pathway for early childhood leadership – early years professional (EYP) – heralded a paradigm shift in thinking as the EYP was viewed as a leader of *practice*, not of a setting (CWDC, 2006). EYP status was superseded from 2013 by early years teacher (EYT) status (National College for Teaching and Leadership (NCTL), 2013) and, whilst there are significant differences between the two, EYT is not specifically positioned as a role for leader/manager of a setting either.

PEDAGOGICAL LEADERSHIP

Siraj-Blatchford and Hallet (2014) identify four aspects of early childhood leadership: directional, which includes sharing a vision and direction-setting (Leithwood and Levin, 2005); collaborative leadership, which draws on the model of distributed leadership promoted by Spillane (2006) and promotes a team culture and shared decision making; empowering leadership, which enables change to take place and encourages agency in others, drawing on principles of transformational leadership (Bass and Avolio, 1993); and pedagogical leadership, which includes directly leading the children's learning. Pedagogical leadership signifies work directly with the children or modelling to staff practice which enhances children's learning and development.

McDowall Clark and Murray (2012) took this further and, from their dialogue with graduate leaders of practice in England, refuted the view that pedagogical leadership in early childhood settings can be found in a single person. They conceptualised a new framework – leadership within – which implies an inner knowledge and confidence in the early childhood practitioner's capacity to lead, whether or not in a nominated leadership position. Leadership within is non-hierarchical and locates leadership as a process of three interconnected strands. Catalytic agency involves leaders in intentionally effecting changes to practice by their involvement within it. This embraces reflective integrity where leaders can challenge themselves and others in order to bring about improvements to practice. In this, everyone is capable of contributing to leadership in early childhood settings, thus making relational interdependence a core component.

 case study 26.1

Leadership Within

Clare, an early childhood professional, has been employed in a full day care setting for two years, in the team working with the 2-3-year-olds. She recently attended a three-day training course on enhancing outdoor provision which has made her very enthusiastic and leads her to wanting to suggest some changes to the way practice is organised, particularly in setting up mud kitchen provision. She makes sure she has re-read the notes and handouts from the training and asks to meet initially with the room leader to discuss further. In consultation with the setting manager, the room leader invites her to introduce her ideas at the next full team meeting. Clare prepares for this by strategically thinking through all that this change might involve and signify.

1. Where is Clare demonstrating:

    a. Catalytic agency?
    b. Reflective integrity?
    c. Relational interdependence?

2. How might the team respond at the meeting? What else might Clare need to think about in order to see through her ideas?

LEADERSHIP SKILLS AND STRATEGIES

Having established that early childhood leadership is something that all early childhood professionals can be involved in, we turn to focus on some of the specific skills that can be used in leadership. As with leadership in a range of contexts and not specific to early childhood, the capacity to build and maintain effective relationships is pivotal. Chapters 6, 8 and 17 focused on the relationships early childhood professionals build with the children, their families, the immediate and wider staff teams and – for many – with professionals from other disciplines. Rodd (2013: 35) reminds us that 'the (early childhood) leader seeks to act *with* others rather than assert power *over* others' which stresses the importance of relational leadership. Effective distributed leadership – with collective responsibility shared by everyone in the team – can have a major impact on the quality of early childhood provision and practice (Rodd, 2012). The capacity to play an active part in building and maintaining good team relationships is a positive factor in quality, and responsibility does not lie only with the nominated leader or manager.

Whether in formal positions of leadership or not, interpersonal and communication skills are also crucial within a team. It is vital that early childhood leaders can articulate their own reflective thinking to colleagues and, in turn, listen carefully to their ideas. Effective communication, then, is about conveying a message clearly and unambiguously and then receiving, without distortion, the information others wish to convey. Communication includes not only the verbal – either spoken or in writing – but also non-verbal indicators: gesture, posture, facial expression, eye contact and tone of voice, which are as important as the actual words used. Grover (2005) offers a helpful summary of basic communication skills required for effective team work: listening – actively, maintaining eye contact; asking open-ended questions – where there are a wide range of possible responses; asking closed questions – to gain and establish facts; clarifying meaning – probing for a little more information; paraphrasing – interpreting and providing feedback on what has been heard; assessing non-verbal cues – helpful in evaluating emotions; and silence – not rushing the other speaker but allowing them space to say what they may be struggling to express.

In leading – or sharing in leadership of – quality early childhood practice, organisational and administrative skills are also important. However, one of the main strategies required is that of change management. In many ways, leading the process of change is inseparable from building strong relationships within a team and communicating effectively. The end product of strong teamwork is an improvement in the quality of learning and development for the children (Rodd, 2012) and the ability to operate as a member of a team is usually an employment criterion in early childhood job descriptions. Linking back to the notion of visionary leadership, leading change to practice is rooted in the vision of quality practice held by the leader and shared by everyone in the setting. To be a visionary leader requires a strong knowledge base about early childhood pedagogy and a commitment to ongoing professional development in order to build a learning community within a team (Siraj-Blatchford and Manni, 2007).

It is a truism that 'change' is the only constant in early childhood services. Globally, there has been a raft of reforms that have swept through early childhood policy, the workforce and practice. In England, the graduate role early years professional was heralded as an 'agent of change' (CWDC, 2006) and whilst EYP status has been replaced by Early Years Teacher status, the capacity and skills to enable change remain core to the leader's role. As human beings, we have an ambivalent attitude to change: we tend to be both resistant to and, at the same time, strangely impelled by it. Change and adaptation have been essential for human survival and within early childhood settings, too, informed change can be essential for success. But change should never be approached without critical thinking and careful planning.

There are countless books and any number of websites which focus on different strategies for change management. Hersey and Blanchard (1988) helpfully describe the three stages, which can be applied to leadership in early childhood settings. First, the stage of diagnosis: leaders consider and reflect on current provision and practice, think critically and use sound judgement to make informed decisions about what needs to be changed, based on their vision for practice. This can include the important task of prioritising. The second stage is adaptation: where an action plan is drawn up and introduced which specifies clearly how the change will be managed. The final stage is communication: as we have already identified, all involved are consulted and listened to, kept informed and included in the change process and in ongoing reviews. This can make change management sound rather simple and formulaic and we shall see in a later section of the chapter that there are many potential pitfalls.

action point 26.1

Think about the leadership strategies outlined above: maintaining relationships; building a team; effective communication; and skills in leading and supporting change. Carry out a self-appraisal of your leadership experiences in early childhood so far in these four areas. What are your strengths? How do you know? Can you identify any areas for further development? Do you have a colleague with whom you can discuss this activity?

CHALLENGES IN LEADERSHIP

In many ways, this section of the chapter will be but a mirror image of the previous section. All the strategies outlined above have a 'shadow side'. There can be difficulties in establishing or maintaining relationships in the team. Rodd (2013) identified two types of early childhood leader: the *friend* – focused on relationships, characterised by warmth, flexibility and adaptability; the *motivator* – focused on both goals and relationships. Arguably, following this logically, there is the type of leader who focuses principally on tasks and goals – sometimes at the expense of relationships. The motivator model is one to aspire to, where the leader holds in tension the goals of practice with the need to maintain secure and dynamic teamwork.

Arguably, when relationships are strong and communication channels effective, then conflict is much less likely to arise but misunderstandings can and do develop even in the best teams. These can create challenges in relationships and breakdowns in communication and can result in conflict situations which require the leadership skill of conflict management. However, the process of conflict resolution has the potential to result in a stronger team (Noone, 1996). The leader's task is to be sensitive – drawing on emotional intelligence and empathy to 'perceive and understand another person's emotions accurately' (Arnold and Boggs, 1999: 110) and identify issues of conflict at the earliest possible opportunity.

Ury's (1991: 147) model of conflict management and negotiation offers a helpful framework for early childhood leaders. Ury conceptualised the leader's role in conflict situations as 'going on to the balcony', taking time to reflect on the situation, using a framework of: What is going on here? Am I being heard correctly? Am I hearing others accurately? What behaviours are giving cause for concern? Avoiding aggressive or stonewall tactics, the leader then employs skills in active listening, clarifying, paraphrasing and exploring all options to negotiate a positive outcome – ideally, a 'win – win' situation. Open communication is the fundamental component of successful negotiation.

Conflict situations – whilst relatively rare – are possibly the most challenging for early childhood leaders and can often arise when there is resistance to proposed changes to practice. In his 1976 poem *A March Calf*, Ted Hughes described the early experience of a newborn calf: 'A little at a time of each new thing is best. Too much and too sudden is too frightening' (Hughes, 2005). Indeed, the pace and timing of change can be crucial to its success. Where colleagues are fearful or anxious about changes, active listening, empathy for the other's position and perspective, negotiation of the actual extent and timing of the change and offering ongoing support, guidance and training to facilitate colleagues in the change are critical factors for the leader. Utilising these strategies ensures the focus remains on the quality of the children's experiences.

Whilst conflict, including resistance to change, can pose major difficulties for early childhood leaders, day-to-day responsibilities of leadership should not be underestimated either. For the nominated leader, accountability includes ensuring staff:child ratios are maintained; dealing with the planned and unexpected issues raised by parents and/or staff; balancing budgets; ensuring the health, safety and wellbeing of all – children and staff; and carrying out all these tasks whilst always giving priority to the highest quality of provision and practice. Fleet et al.'s (2015) research study is spotlighted below and highlights some of the specific challenges of those in formal early childhood leadership roles. A further challenge can be experienced by those not in positions as nominated leaders who can feel frustrated in limited opportunities to use leadership skills. Yet, all staff have responsibilities for children's wellbeing and carrying out their roles to the highest professional standards – so, again, leadership can be described as shared and distributed (Spillane, 2006).

 spotlight on research 26.1

Fleet and Colleagues (2015)

Fleet et al. (2015) conducted a survey of around 206 early childhood leaders in two regions of Australia. The paper-based survey was followed up with workshops in which leaders engaged in a process of seeking to understand their leadership roles within the context of rapid pedagogical and early childhood policy changes. The findings of this research highlighted concerns that leaders did not have clear job descriptions, were facing significant budget challenges, and – between them – defined up to 27 different aspects of their roles, ranging from developing a learning culture to conducting staff appraisals. When asked to define the 'critical issues' facing them, they identified five key challenges: the complex infrastructure of early childhood provision with its diversity (maintained, private and so on); the struggle to be viewed as professionals; their staff teams' limited understanding of the early childhood curriculum and how to implement it; budgetary constraints; and gaps in their understanding and awareness of cultural issues and inclusion (in their culture, this related mostly to Aboriginal colleagues and families). However, the greatest challenge was identified as 'the sheer volume … of what has to be done' (2015: 35) to implement the new early childhood learning framework. In conclusion, the researchers called for more training and support for early childhood leaders and a clarification of roles and responsibilities – though these would need to take full account of local contexts.

LEADING QUALITY PRACTICE CONTEXTUALLY

Fleet et al.'s study concluded with an emphasis on the context of leadership. Theories of situational leadership were outlined earlier in the chapter and the notion of 'contextual literacy'

(Siraj-Blatchford and Manni, 2007) applied specifically to early childhood where, as we noted earlier, there is no 'one size fits all' approach. Leaders need to recognise that early childhood contexts differ at every level: between individual children – and it is particularly important to take account of the individual needs and circumstances of the children; the type of setting and the provision it offers; the make-up of the staff team; families – including socio-economic status and ethnicity; and the wider community in which a setting is positioned. Leaders, therefore, need to demonstrate the capacity to 'speak fluently' about their own context and to acknowledge 'the past and present when considering the future' (Siraj-Blatchford and Manni, 2007: 11). This is best illustrated by reflection on three different stories of leadership where the leaders aim to take full account of the context and situation in which they are working.

 case study 26.2

How Professionals Respond to their Surroundings

Katie – baby room leader, full day-care provision

For the first few weeks of my new role in this setting, I prioritised building relationships – with the babies, their families and the staff – and ensuring good teamwork. This included listening to the other staff about how they viewed provision. I quickly picked up that they wanted to develop a sensory room and so I actively encouraged them to draw up an action plan, including costings, and delegated different responsibilities to each in order to see the plan to fruition. Everything was great! However, a great concern that I had was the lack of opportunity for the babies to use the outdoor area. The baby room was on the first floor of the nursery and so there were logistical difficulties in taking them out but I had this vision of this being an everyday experience for our babies – as it was for the toddlers and preschoolers. Staff were a little resistant at first and even more resistant when I shared my plans for a mud-digging area. However, I worked with them, seeking to understand and alleviate their concerns and we took the plan very slowly. Now, a year on, the team can't imagine NOT having this wonderful resource.

Abi – manager, under-3s' provision, children's centre

Our centre is in an area of significant social disadvantage and we have 24 2-year-olds who meet the criteria for funded places. At the start, many of these children have little understanding of how to play and have under-developed language and social skills. These families want the best for their children and we recognise their need for that little bit of extra support. Because they are not working parents, they are usually very responsive to our invitation to join in our sessions and are very enthusiastic about story and singing time. I sensed a measure of anxiety when the holidays were looming so, together with our outreach worker, I organised some day visits. These were nothing expensive; just using local buses to go to a local site, taking some picnic food and bats and balls and so on. Many of the families did not know these sites existed and it was a privilege to see their confidence grow in their own parenting capacity.

Leo – teacher, nursery class for 3–4-year-old children, maintained school setting

We cater sessionally (either mornings or afternoons) for 25 children and I lead a small team of three other staff, under the line management of the school's Foundation Stage Coordinator. We have strongly supportive and engaged parents and excellent attendance at our half-termly 'Stay and Play' sessions. As we now use 'in the moment planning', it emerged at our weekly meeting that one of our children is fascinated by anything French and when his key person shared this with the parents, they confirmed that this was equally so at home, especially after they had visited Paris in the summer. I know one of our team is fluent in French so I asked her to take a lead in developing resources and activities around this theme. One of the other staff was unsure about this as it was based on the interests of just one child but we talked this through and, in fact, most of the children responded really well – and particularly loved singing in French.

Think how each of these three early childhood leaders responded and led according to the context of their setting:

1.   How did the leader focus on the needs of the children in each case?
2.   How did the type of setting/provision inform the actions of the leader?
3.   Can you identify aspects here of strong leadership? What skills did the leaders use?

LEADERSHIP AND EARLY CHILDHOOD POLICY

Within the twenty-first century, early childhood leadership has undergone significant policy reform internationally. This has been, in part, to address inequalities in educational attainment and tackle issues around child poverty (Baldock et al., 2013). Strategic and effective early childhood leadership can play a 'pivotal role in creating changed circumstances and opportunities for children and families' (Hard et al., 2013: 324). This requires leaders who can rise to the challenge with resilience and who are strong advocates for social justice.

In England, early childhood leadership has been practised for many years by heads, deputy heads and teachers in nursery schools, classes and units. However, there was little acknowledgement of this in private, voluntary and independent (PVI) early childhood settings (Siraj-Blatchford and Hallet, 2014). This is indicative of the historical divide between early 'education' and 'care', with PVI settings being viewed primarily as offering childcare and, consequently, of lower status than educational settings (Oberhuemer, 2008). The sector is currently on a trajectory from this unhelpful dualist history, moving slowly towards professionalistion from its earlier position as 'caring, maternal and gendered' (McGillivray, 2008: 245). The graduate roles of EYP and EYT are providing a key challenge here as they embrace leadership of quality practice with children from birth to school age in a range of settings.

Early childhood policy globally has focused on reforming and professionalising the workforce, particularly its leadership (Miller and Cable, 2011). Whilst this is generally welcomed, it is important to reflect on this through a critical lens and consider some of the underlying drivers here. Dahlberg, Moss and Pence (2013) suggest that one key factor is the labour market requiring mothers of young children to work; many would do so only if the quality of the provision for their young children matched their expectations. The emphasis on higher qualifications, professionalisation in early childhood leadership and enhanced quality of practice indicate an important conceptual shift. However, there is also the reality that these are underpinned by the 'regulatory gaze' of government policy (Osgood, 2006: 3). This can limit leaders' capacity to lead from their own pedagogical vision – rather than one externally prescribed. Early childhood leaders should have or develop the ability to determine their own actions and make independent decisions, based on the best interests of the children and other stakeholders in their settings. Whalley's (2007) helpful concept of 'constructive discontent' urges early childhood professionals to critically question and even challenge policy in order to maintain the focus on the highest quality provision and practice. Effective leadership is critical.

SUMMARY

- Leadership and management have two distinct definitions and emphases but are also inherently linked. Many nominated leaders carry both elements in their role but *all* early childhood professionals can exercise leadership in their roles.
- Leadership development in early childhood has been informed by classic leadership theories – trait, behavioural, visionary, transformational, situational and distributed. However, none of these alone accurately describes what it means to be a leader. Pedagogical leadership – leadership for learning and development – is most effective when it is shared by all in the team and each one enabled to contribute from their own skills base.
- Situational leadership is translated as contextual literacy within early childhood, where leaders take full account of the variables in their settings.
- Leadership can be challenging and requires leaders to draw on a range of specific skills and strategies to maximise their effectiveness.
- Top-down policy and regulation can often limit and frustrate leaders, but they are encouraged to engage in 'constructive discontent' and demonstrate resilience in order to prioritise the children's best interests and advocate for social justice.

 online resources

Make sure to visit https://study.sagepub.com/fitzgeraldandmaconochie for selected SAGE videos (with questions), SAGE journal articles, links to external sources and flashcards.

FURTHER READING

Davis, G. and Ryder, G. (2016). *Leading in Early Childhood*. London: Sage.

This book provides helpful information and guidance about every early childhood professional's capacity to lead, using their knowledge, skills, personality and experience.

Kivunja, C. (2015). Leadership in Early Childhood Education Contexts: Looks, Roles, and Functions. *Creative Education, 6*: 1710–17.

This article helpfully addresses key questions about early childhood leadership, focusing on how it is defined and how it can function effectively and efficiently.

REFERENCES

Arnold, E. and Boggs, K. (1999). *Interpersonal Relationships: Professional Communication Skills for Nurses*. Philadelphia, PA: W. B. Saunders Co.

Avery, G. (2004). *Understanding Leadership: Paradigms and Cases*. London: Sage.

Baldock, P., Fitzgerald, D. and Kay, J. (2013). *Understanding Early Years Policy*, 3rd edn. London: Sage.

Bass, B. M. and Avolio, B. J. (eds) (1993). *Improving Organisational Effectiveness through Transformational Leadership*. Thousand Oaks, CA: Sage.

Bennis, W. (1998). *On Becoming a Leader*. London: Arrow.

Blake, R. and Mouton, J. (1964). *The Managerial Grid: The Key to Leadership Excellence*. Houston, TX: Gulf Publishing Company.

Children's Workforce Development Council (CWDC) (2006). *Guidance to the Standards for the Award of Early Years Professional Status*. Leeds: CWDC.

Dahlberg, G., Moss, P. and Pence, A. (2013). *Beyond Quality in Early Childhood Education and Care: Languages of Evaluation*, 3rd edn. Abingdon: Routledge.

Dalli, C. (2008). Pedagogy, Knowledge and Collaboration: Towards a Ground-up Perspective on Professionalism. *European Early Childhood Research Journal, Special Issue: Professionalism in Early Childhood Education and Care, 16*(2): 171–85.

Doyle, M. E. and Smith, M. K. (1999). *Born and Bred? Leadership, Heart and Informal Education*. London: YMCA George Williams College/The Rank Foundation.

Fleet, A., Soper, R., Semann, A. and Madden, L. (2015). The Role of the Educational Leader: Perceptions and Expectations in a Period of Change. *Australian Journal of Early Childhood, 401*(3): 29–37.

Grover, S. (2005). Shaping Effective Communication Skills and Therapeutic Relationships at Work. *American Association of Occupational Health Nurses Journal, 53*(4): 177–82.

Hard, L., Press, F. and Gibson, M. (2013). 'Doing' Social Justice in Early Childhood: The Potential of Leadership. *Contemporary Issues in Early Childhood, 14*(4): 324–34.

Hersey, P. and Blanchard, K.H. (1988). *Management of Organizational Behaviour*, 5th edn. Englewood Cliffs, NJ: Prentice Hall.

Hersey, P., Blanchard, K., and Johnson, D.E. (2001). *Management of Organizational Behavior: Utilizing Human Resources*, (8th ed.) Englewood Cliffs, New Jersey: Prentice Hall.

Hughes, E. (2005). *Collected Poems for Children*. London: Faber and Faber.

Law, S. and Glover, D. (2000). *Educational Leadership and Learning Practice, Policy and Research*. Buckingham: Open University Press.

Leithwood, K. and Levin, B. (2005). *Assessing School Leader and Leadership Programme Effects on Pupil Learning: Conceptual and Methodological Problems*. Research Report RR662. Nottingham: Department for Education and Skills.

McDowall Clark, R. and Murray, J. (2012). *Reconceptualising Leadership in the Early Years*. Maidenhead: Open University Press.

McGillivray, G. (2008). Nannies, Nursery Nurses and Early Years Professionals: Constructions of Professional Identity in the Early Years Workforce in England. *European Early Childhood Education Research Journal, 162*(2): 242–54.

Miller, L. and Cable, C. (eds) (2011). *Professionalization, Leadership and Management in the Early Years*. London: Sage.

National College of Teaching and Leadership (NCTL) (2013). *Teachers' Standards (Early Years)*. [online] Available at: www.gov.uk/government/uploads/system/uploads/attachment_data/file/211646/Early_Years_Teachers__Standards.pdf [Accessed 12 November 2016].

Noone, M. (1996). *Mediation*. London: Cavendish.

Oberhuemer, P. (2008). Who is an Early Years Professional? Reflections on Policy Diversity in Europe. In: L. Miller and C. Cable (eds), *Professionalism in the Early Years*. London: Hodder and Stoughton.

Osgood, J. (2006). Professionalism and Performativity: The Feminist Challenge Facing Early Years Practitioners. *Early Years*, *26*(2): 187–99.

Rodd, J. (2012). Building and Leading a Team. In: L. Miller, R. Drury and C. Cable (eds), *Extending Professional Practice in the Early Years*. London: Sage.

Rodd, J. (2013). *Leadership in Early Childhood: The Pathway to Professionalism*, 4th edn. Maidenhead: Open University Press.

Siraj-Blatchford, I. and Hallet, E. (2014). *Effective and Caring Leadership in the Early Years*. London: Sage.

Siraj-Blatchford, I. and Manni, L. (2007). *Effective Leadership in the Early Years Sector: The ELEYS Study*. London: Institute of Education, University of London.

Spillane, J. P. (2006). *Distributed Leadership*. San Francisco, CA: Jossey – Bass.

Ury, W. (1991). *Getting Past No: Negotiating with Difficult People*. New York: Bantam Books.

Whalley, M. with the Pen Green Team (2007). *Involving Parents in their Children's Learning*, 2nd edn. London: Paul Chapman.

INDEX

Note: Tables and Figures are indicated by page numbers in bold print. The letter *b* after a page number indicates biographical information in Further Reading sections.